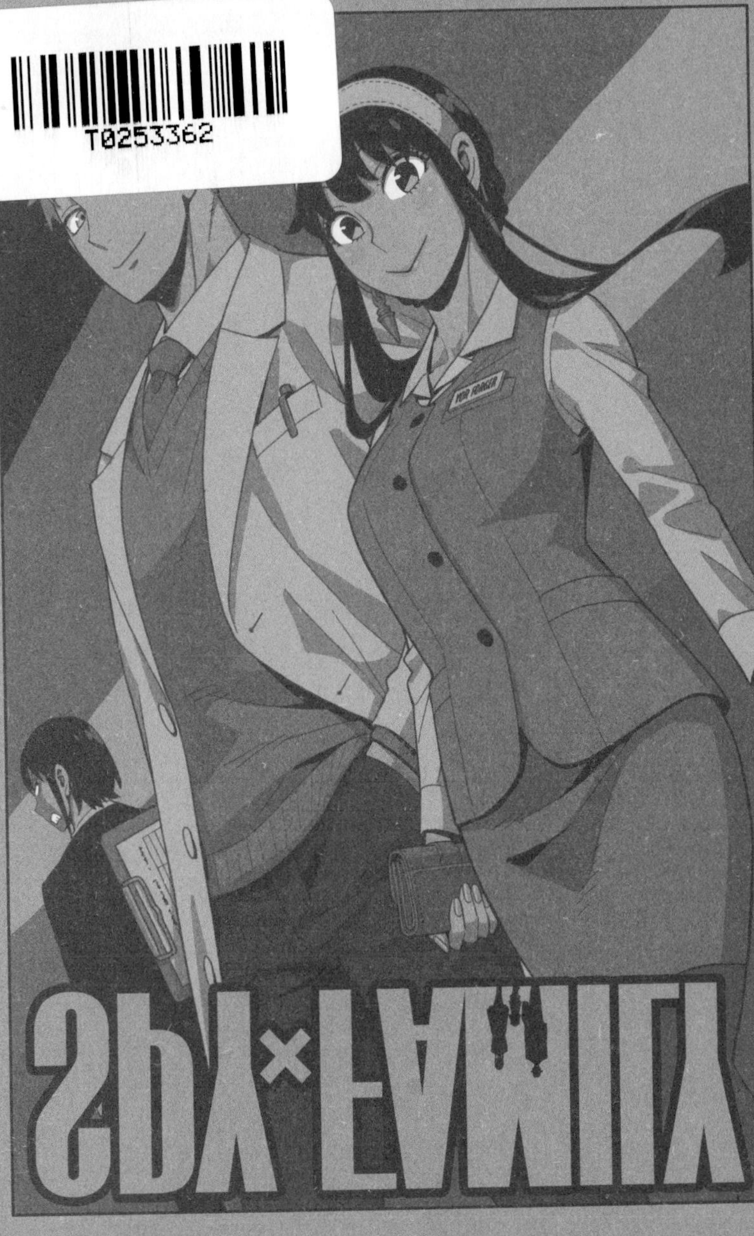
SPY×FAMILY

THANK YOU SO MUCH FOR BUYING VOLUME 11!

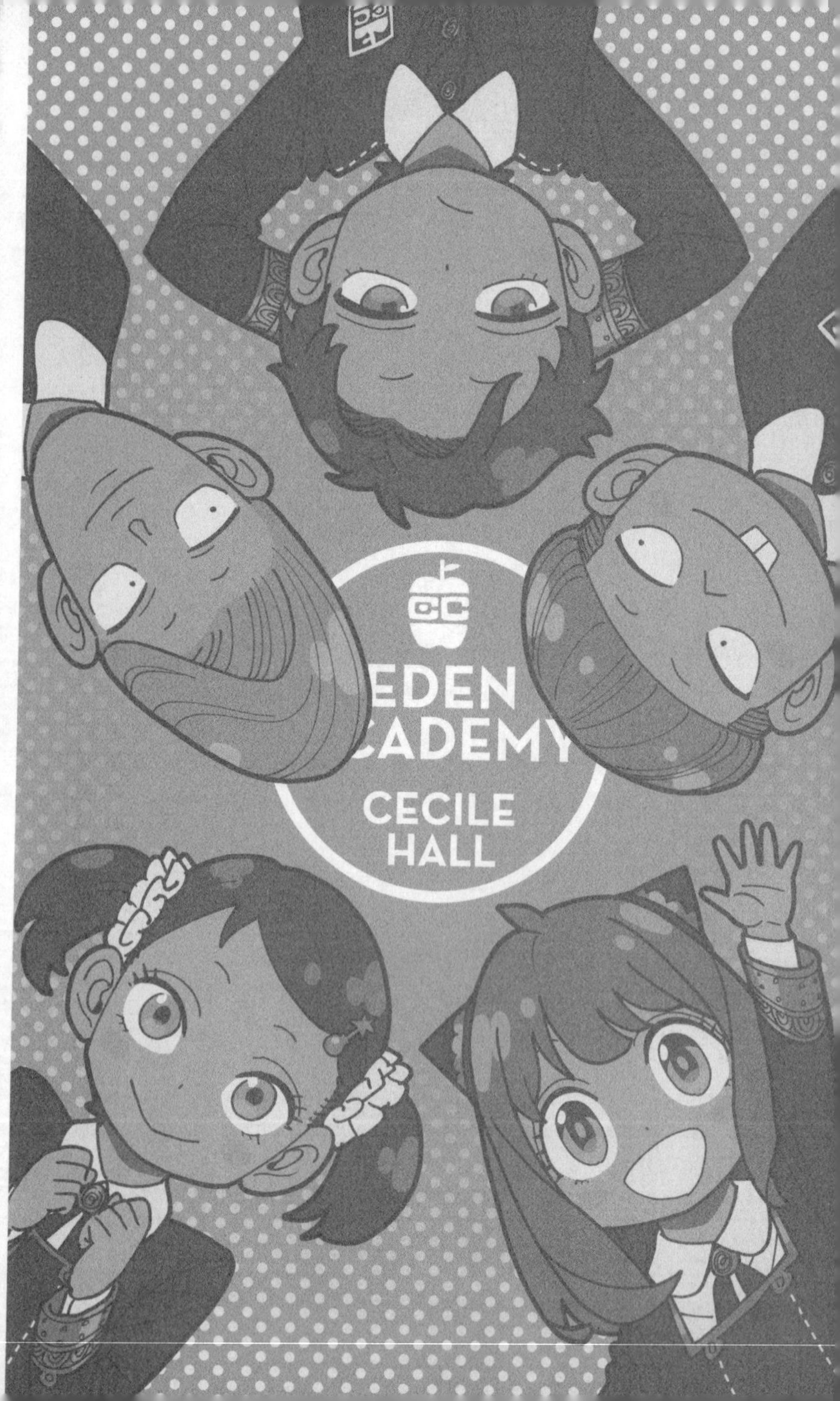
EDEN
CADEMY
CECILE
HALL

SPY×FAMILY

VOLUME

11

STORY AND ART BY
TATSUYA ENDO

SHONEN JUMP

CHARACTERS
CONTENTS

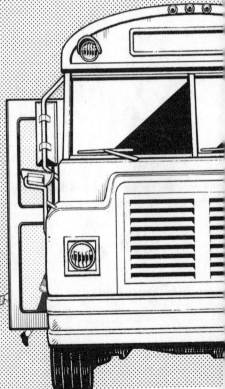

SPY×FAMILY CHARACTERS

LOID FORGER

ROLE: Husband

Known as a skilled psychiatrist, Loid is actually "Twilight," a spy and master of disguise serving the nation of Westalis.

YOR FORGER

ROLE: Wife

A city hall clerk who also lives a secret life as a talented contract killer. Her code name is "Thorn Princess."

ANYA FORGER

ROLE: Daughter

Anya is a first grader at the prestigious Eden Academy. A telepath whose abilities were created in an experiment conducted by a certain organization. She can read minds.

BOND FORGER

ROLE: Dog

Anya's playmate and the family guard dog. As a former military test subject, he can see the future.

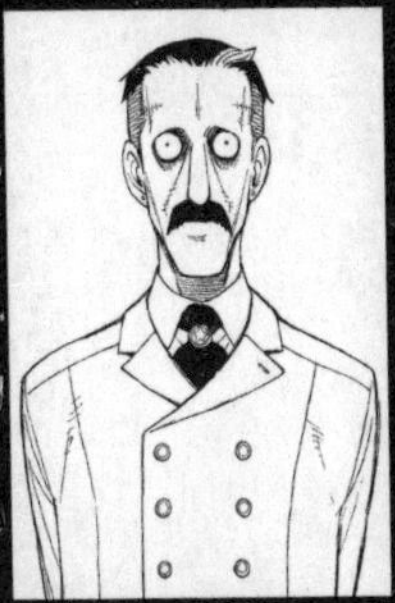

MISSION

OPERATION STRIX

Spy on Donovan Desmond, a dangerous figure who threatens to disrupt peace between the East and West. Must gain entry into the prestigious Eden Academy to breach the target's inner circle.

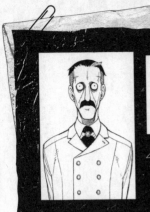

TARGET

DONOVAN DESMOND

The focus of Operation Strix. Chairman of Ostania's National Unity Party.

KEY PEOPLE

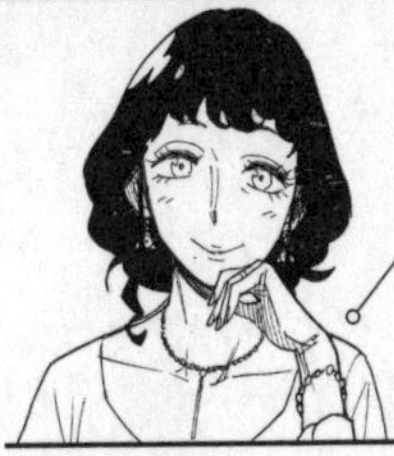

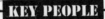

MELINDA DESMOND

Wife of Donovan Desmond.

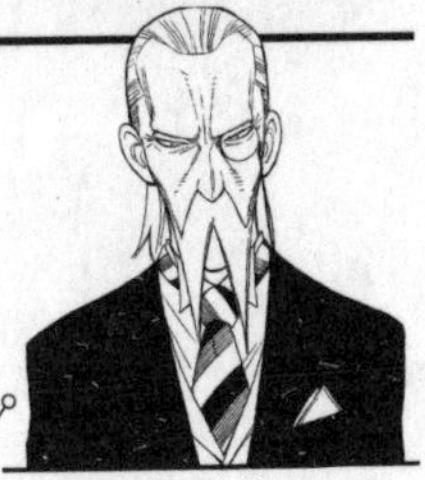

HENRY HENDERSON

Housemaster at Eden Academy.

BECKY BLACKBELL

Anya's friend.

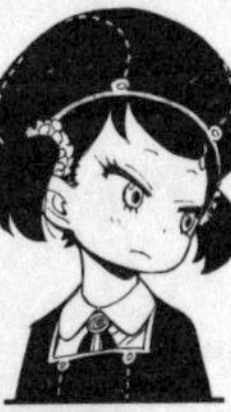

DAMIAN DESMOND

Second son of Donovan Desmond.

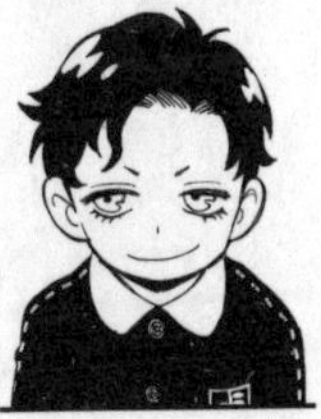

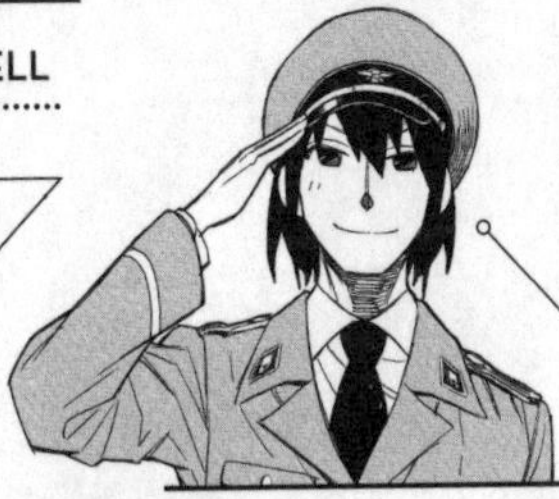

YURI BRIAR

Yor's younger brother, a secret police officer.

STORY

Westalis secret agent Twilight receives orders to uncover the plans of Donovan Desmond, the war-mongering chairman of Ostania's National Unity Party. To do so, Twilight must pose as Loid Forger, create a fake family, and enroll his child at the prestigious Eden Academy. However, by sheer coincidence, the daughter he selects from an orphanage is secretly a telepath! Also, the woman who agrees to be in a sham marriage with him is secretly an assassin! While concealing their true identities from one another, the three now find themselves living together as a family.

After reliving old memories of his wartime childhood and his journey to becoming a spy, Loid resolves anew to fight for peace. Around the same time, Yor has a chance encounter with Melinda Desmond, the wife of Loid's target. The two become friends, and Loid ponders how to exploit their relationship as part of a new "mommy friends" scheme, spurring Anya to get serious about her own friendship scheme with Damian!

CONTENTS

SPY×FAMILY 11

MISSION 67

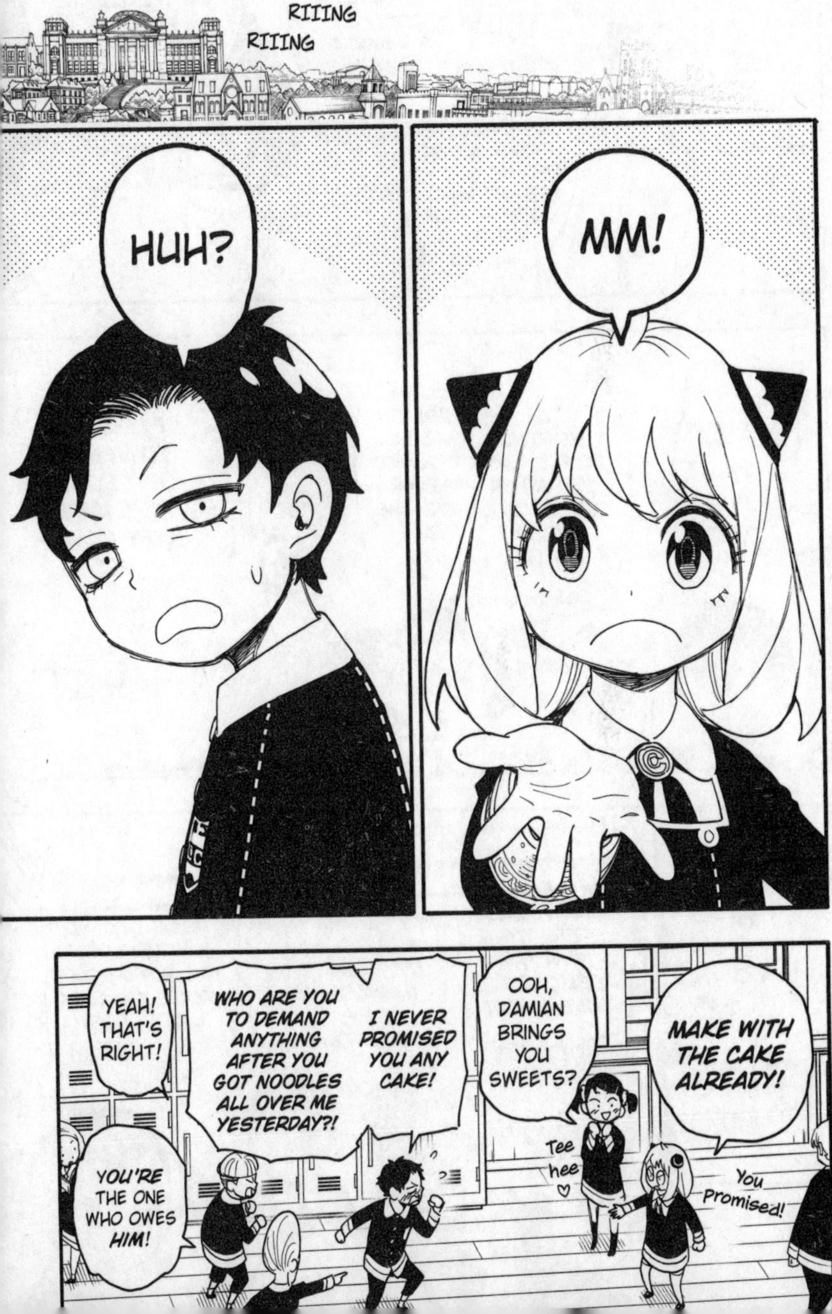
RIIING
RIIING
MM!
HUH?
MAKE WITH THE CAKE ALREADY!
You Promised!
OOH, DAMIAN BRINGS YOU SWEETS?
Tee hee
I NEVER PROMISED YOU ANY CAKE!
WHO ARE YOU TO DEMAND ANYTHING AFTER YOU GOT NOODLES ALL OVER ME YESTERDAY?!
YEAH! THAT'S RIGHT!
YOU'RE THE ONE WHO OWES HIM!

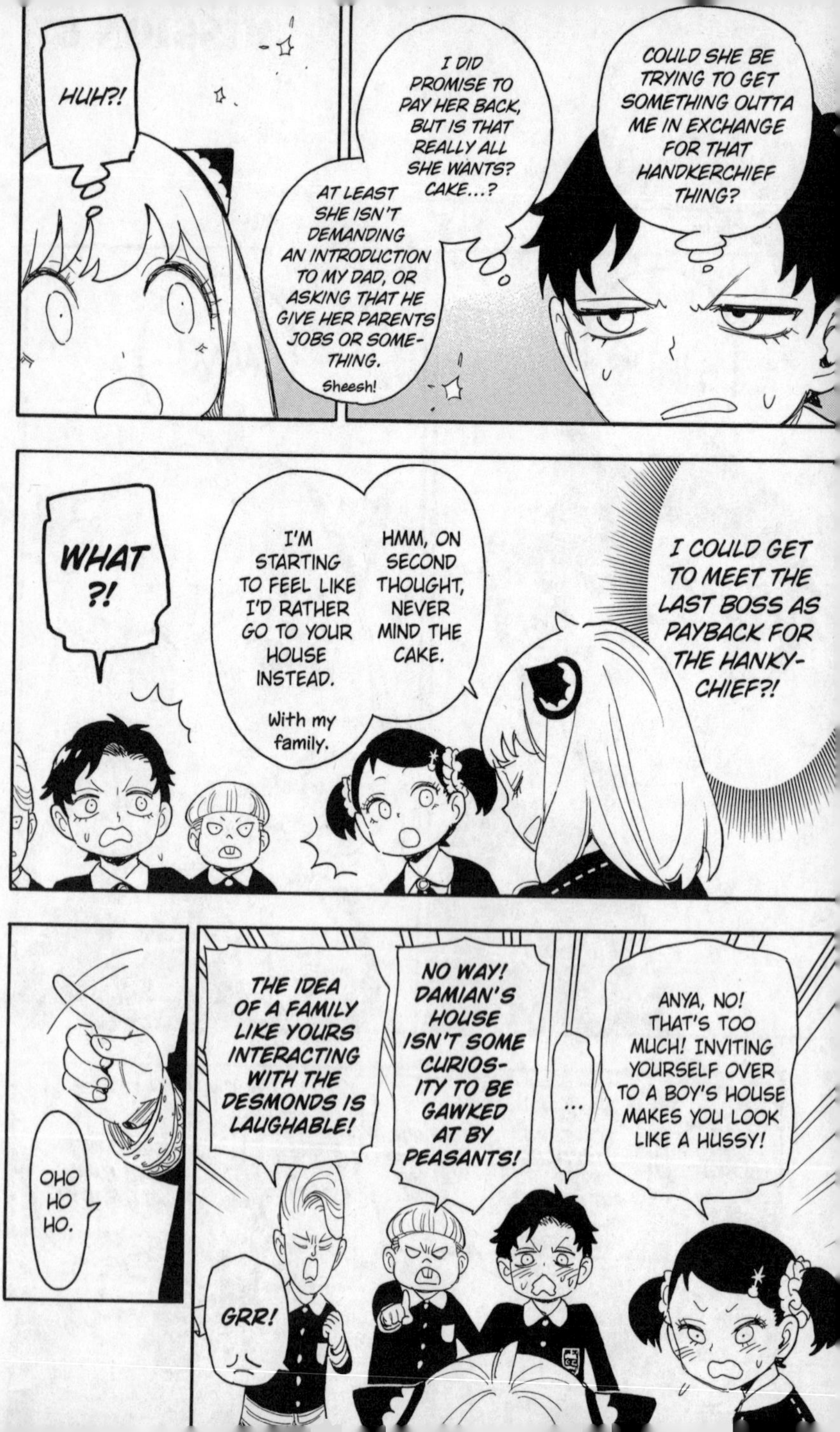
COULD SHE BE TRYING TO GET SOMETHING OUTTA ME IN EXCHANGE FOR THAT HANDKERCHIEF THING?
I DID PROMISE TO PAY HER BACK, BUT IS THAT REALLY ALL SHE WANTS? CAKE...?
AT LEAST SHE ISN'T DEMANDING AN INTRODUCTION TO MY DAD, OR ASKING THAT HE GIVE HER PARENTS JOBS OR SOME-THING.
Sheesh!
HUH?!
I COULD GET TO MEET THE LAST BOSS AS PAYBACK FOR THE HANKY-CHIEF?!
HMM, ON SECOND THOUGHT, NEVER MIND THE CAKE.
I'M STARTING TO FEEL LIKE I'D RATHER GO TO YOUR HOUSE INSTEAD.
With my family.
WHAT ?!
ANYA, NO! THAT'S TOO MUCH! INVITING YOURSELF OVER TO A BOY'S HOUSE MAKES YOU LOOK LIKE A HUSSY!
...
NO WAY! DAMIAN'S HOUSE ISN'T SOME CURIOS-ITY TO BE GAWKED AT BY PEASANTS!
THE IDEA OF A FAMILY LIKE YOURS INTERACTING WITH THE DESMONDS IS LAUGHABLE!
GRR!
OHO HO HO.

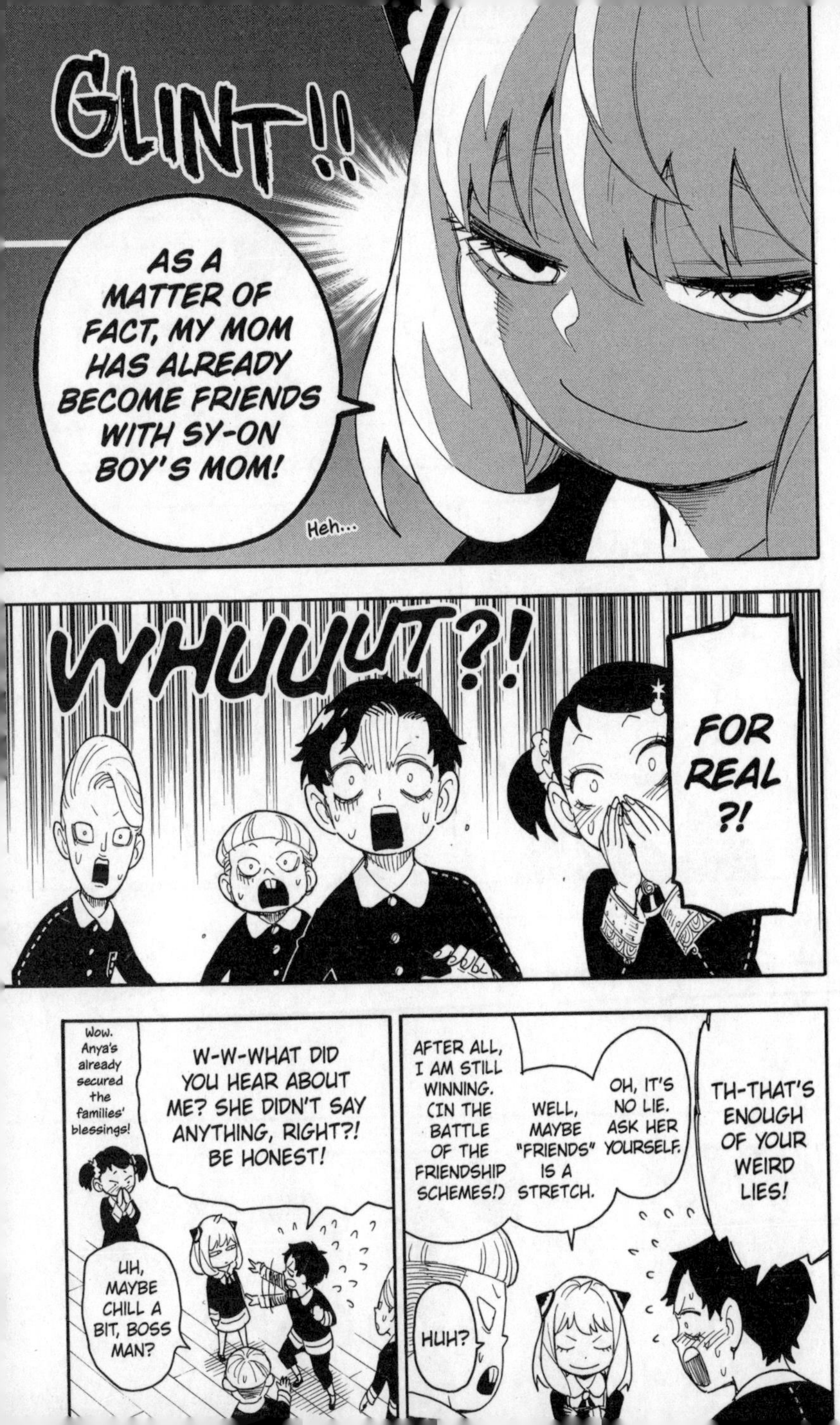
GLINT!!
AS A MATTER OF FACT, MY MOM HAS ALREADY BECOME FRIENDS WITH SY-ON BOY'S MOM!
Heh...
FOR REAL?!
WHUUUT?!
TH-THAT'S ENOUGH OF YOUR WEIRD LIES!
OH, IT'S NO LIE. ASK HER YOURSELF.
WELL, MAYBE "FRIENDS" IS A STRETCH.
AFTER ALL, I AM STILL WINNING. (IN THE BATTLE OF THE FRIENDSHIP SCHEMES!)
HUH?
W-W-WHAT DID YOU HEAR ABOUT ME? SHE DIDN'T SAY ANYTHING, RIGHT?! BE HONEST!
Wow. Anya's already secured the families' blessings!
UH, MAYBE CHILL A BIT, BOSS MAN?

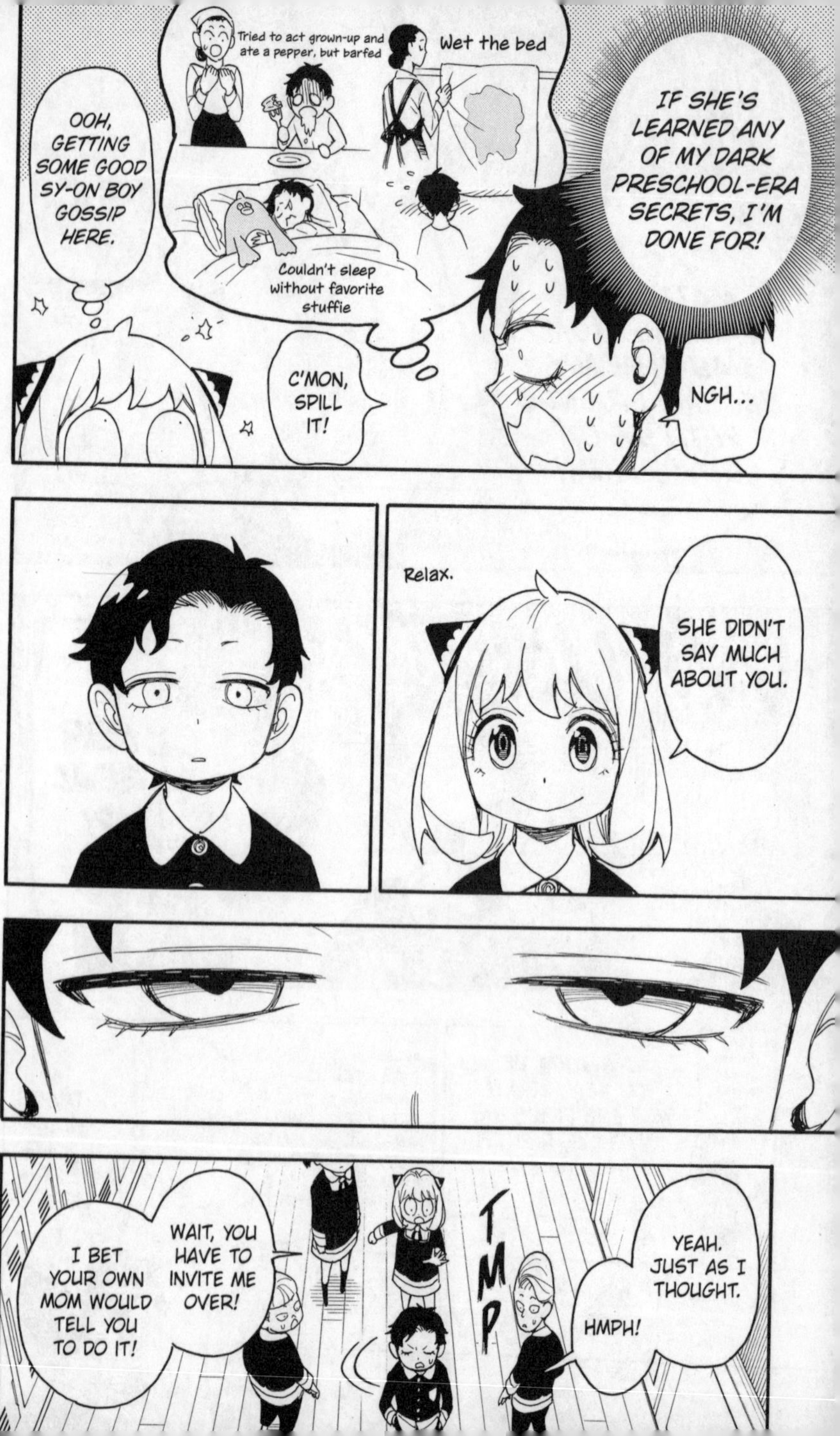
IF SHE'S LEARNED ANY OF MY DARK PRESCHOOL-ERA SECRETS, I'M DONE FOR!
Wet the bed
Tried to act grown-up and ate a pepper, but barfed
Couldn't sleep without favorite stuffie
NGH...
OOH, GETTING SOME GOOD SY-ON BOY GOSSIP HERE.
C'MON, SPILL IT!
SHE DIDN'T SAY MUCH ABOUT YOU.
Relax.
YEAH. JUST AS I THOUGHT.
HMPH!
TMP
WAIT, YOU HAVE TO INVITE ME OVER!
I BET YOUR OWN MOM WOULD TELL YOU TO DO IT!

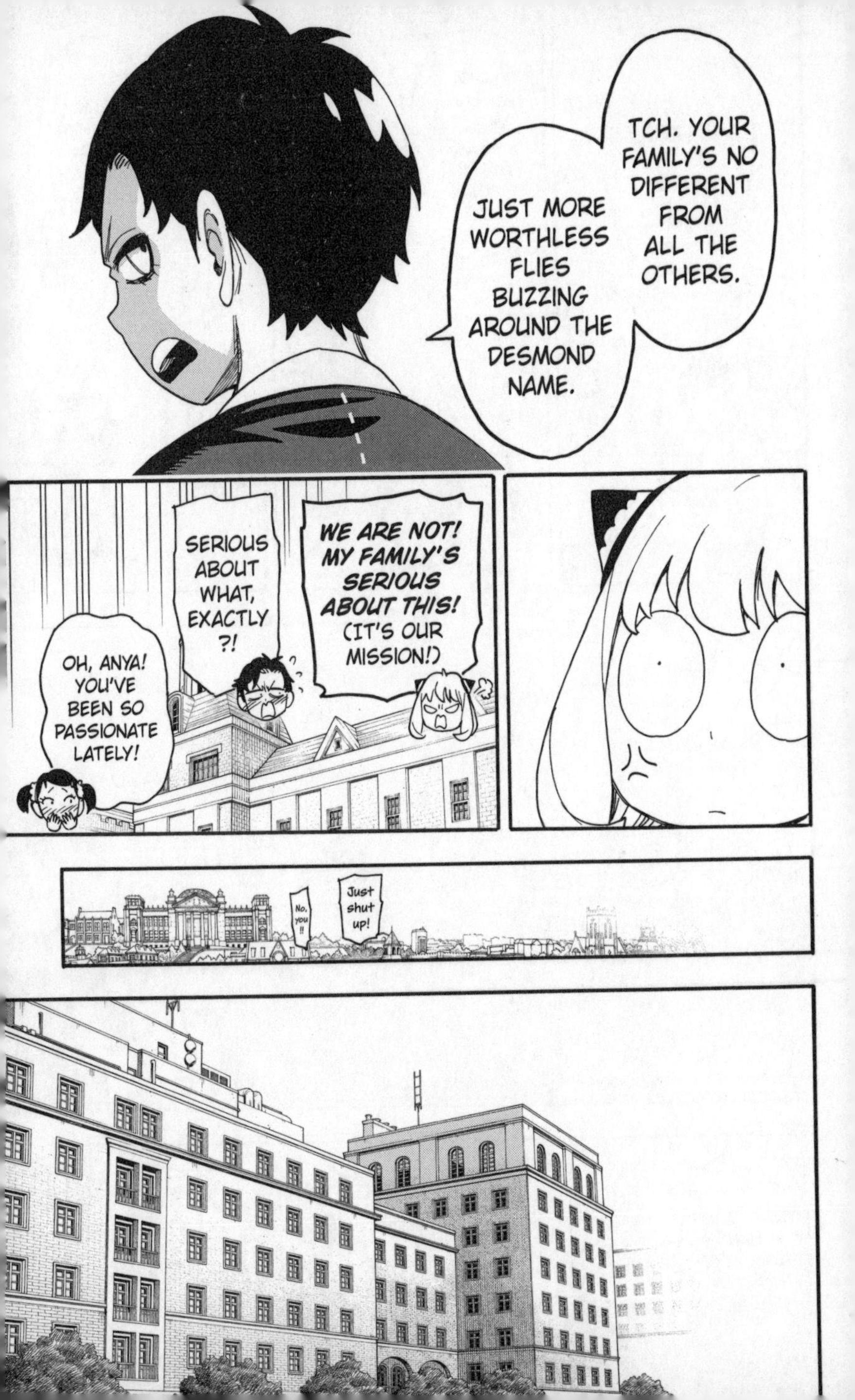
TCH. YOUR FAMILY'S NO DIFFERENT FROM ALL THE OTHERS.
JUST MORE WORTHLESS FLIES BUZZING AROUND THE DESMOND NAME.
WE ARE NOT! MY FAMILY'S SERIOUS ABOUT THIS! (IT'S OUR MISSION!)
SERIOUS ABOUT WHAT, EXACTLY?!
OH, ANYA! YOU'VE BEEN SO PASSIONATE LATELY!
Just shut up!
No, you!!

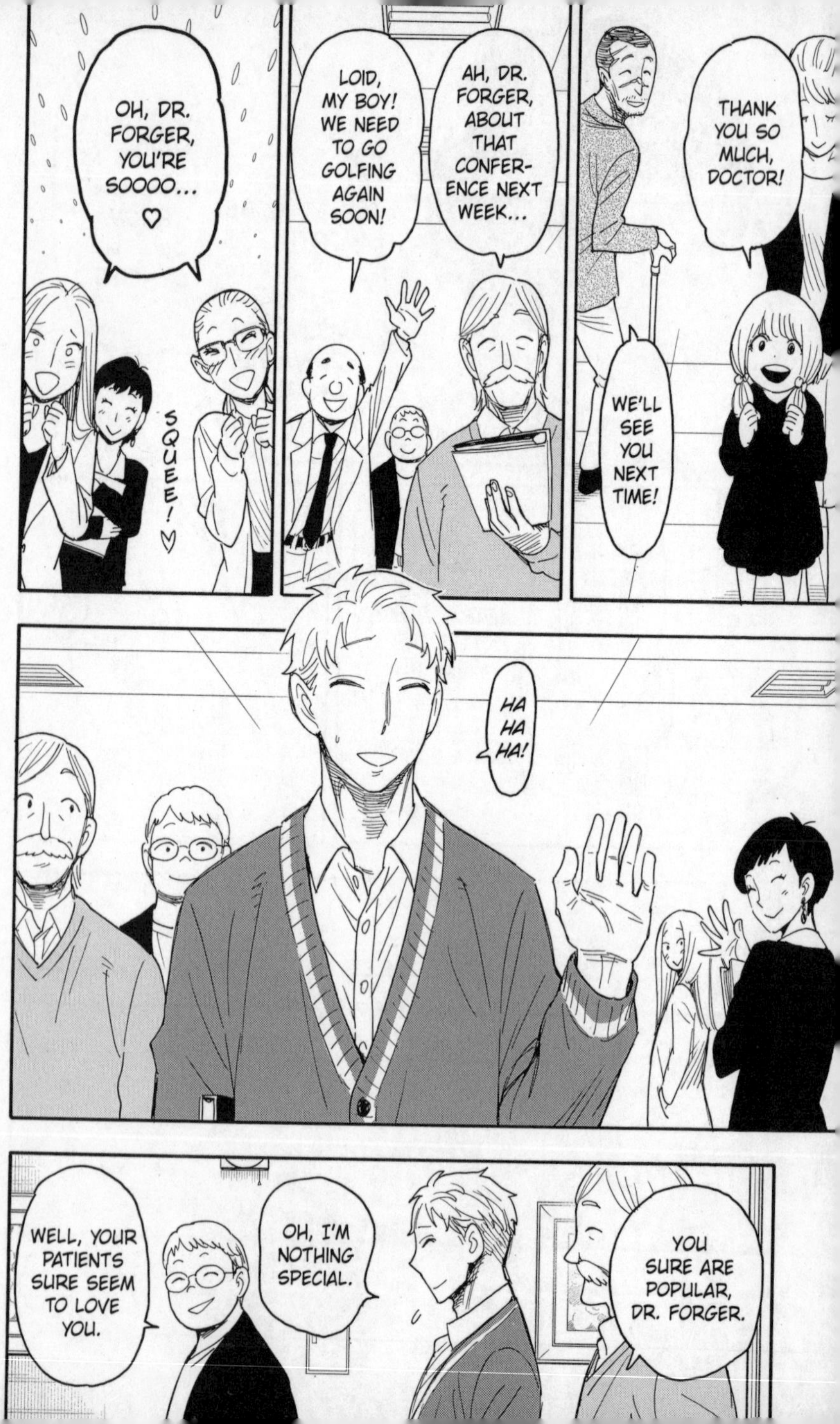
THANK YOU SO MUCH, DOCTOR!
WE'LL SEE YOU NEXT TIME!
AH, DR. FORGER, ABOUT THAT CONFER-ENCE NEXT WEEK...
LOID, MY BOY! WE NEED TO GO GOLFING AGAIN SOON!
OH, DR. FORGER, YOU'RE SOOOO... ♡
SQUEE! ♡
HA HA HA!
YOU SURE ARE POPULAR, DR. FORGER.
OH, I'M NOTHING SPECIAL.
WELL, YOUR PATIENTS SURE SEEM TO LOVE YOU.

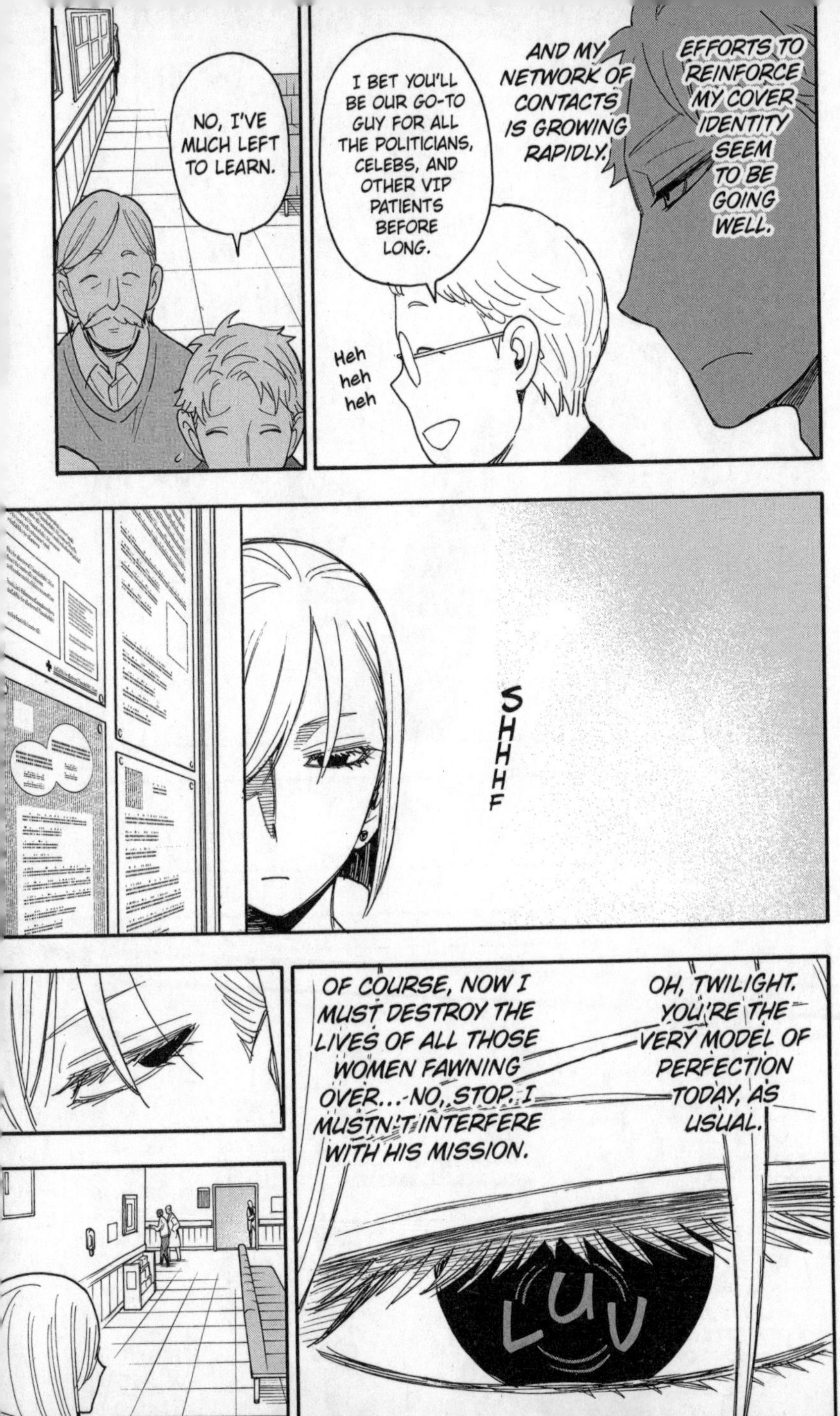
EFFORTS TO REINFORCE MY COVER IDENTITY SEEM TO BE GOING WELL.
AND MY NETWORK OF CONTACTS IS GROWING RAPIDLY.
I BET YOU'LL BE OUR GO-TO GUY FOR ALL THE POLITICIANS, CELEBS, AND OTHER VIP PATIENTS BEFORE LONG.
Heh heh heh
NO, I'VE MUCH LEFT TO LEARN.
SHHHF
OH, TWILIGHT. YOU'RE THE VERY MODEL OF PERFECTION TODAY, AS USUAL.
OF COURSE, NOW I MUST DESTROY THE LIVES OF ALL THOSE WOMEN FAWNING OVER... NO, STOP. I MUSTN'T INTERFERE WITH HIS MISSION.
LUV

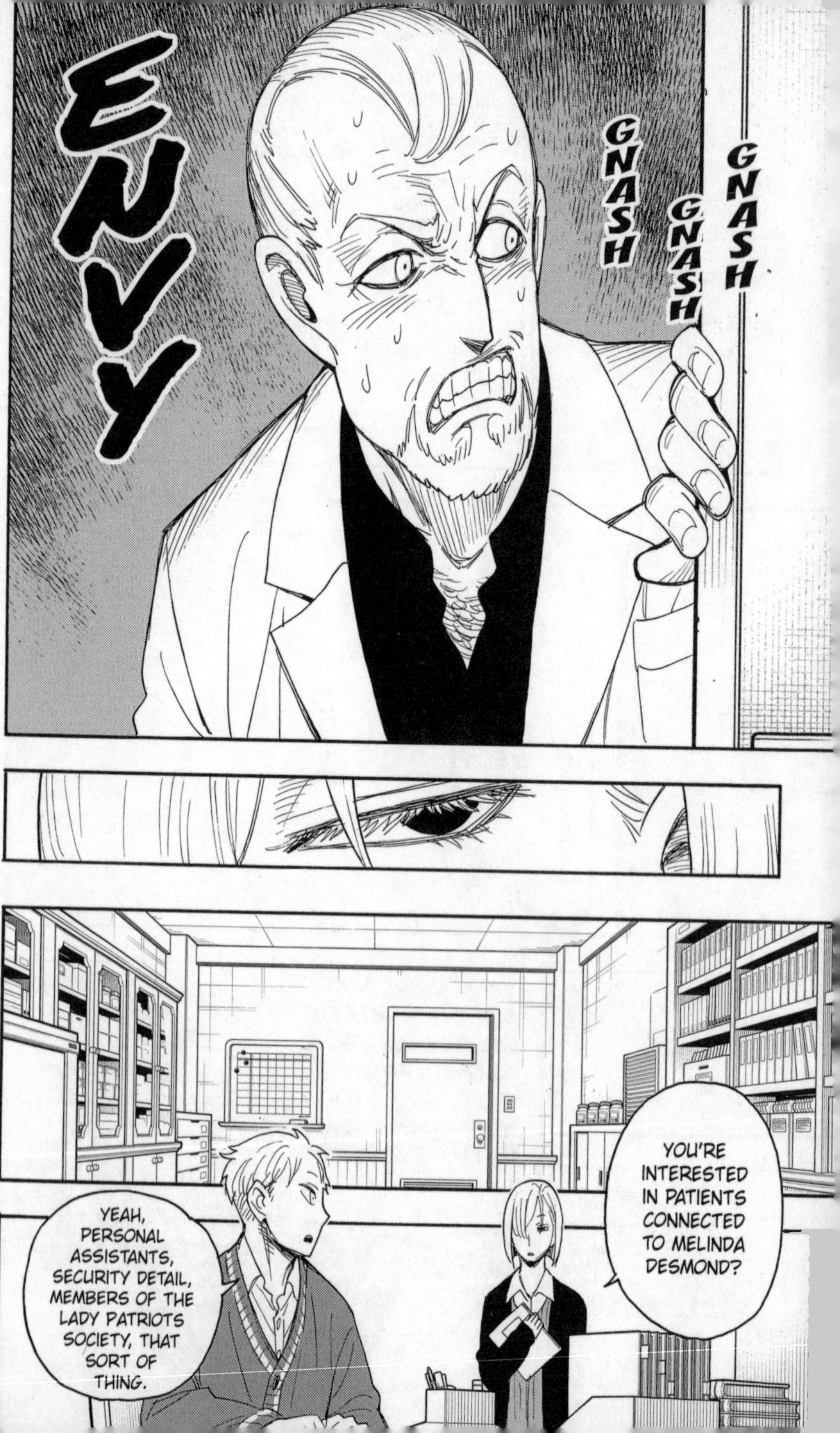
GNASH GNASH GNASH
ENVY
YOU'RE INTERESTED IN PATIENTS CONNECTED TO MELINDA DESMOND?
YEAH, PERSONAL ASSISTANTS, SECURITY DETAIL, MEMBERS OF THE LADY PATRIOTS SOCIETY, THAT SORT OF THING.

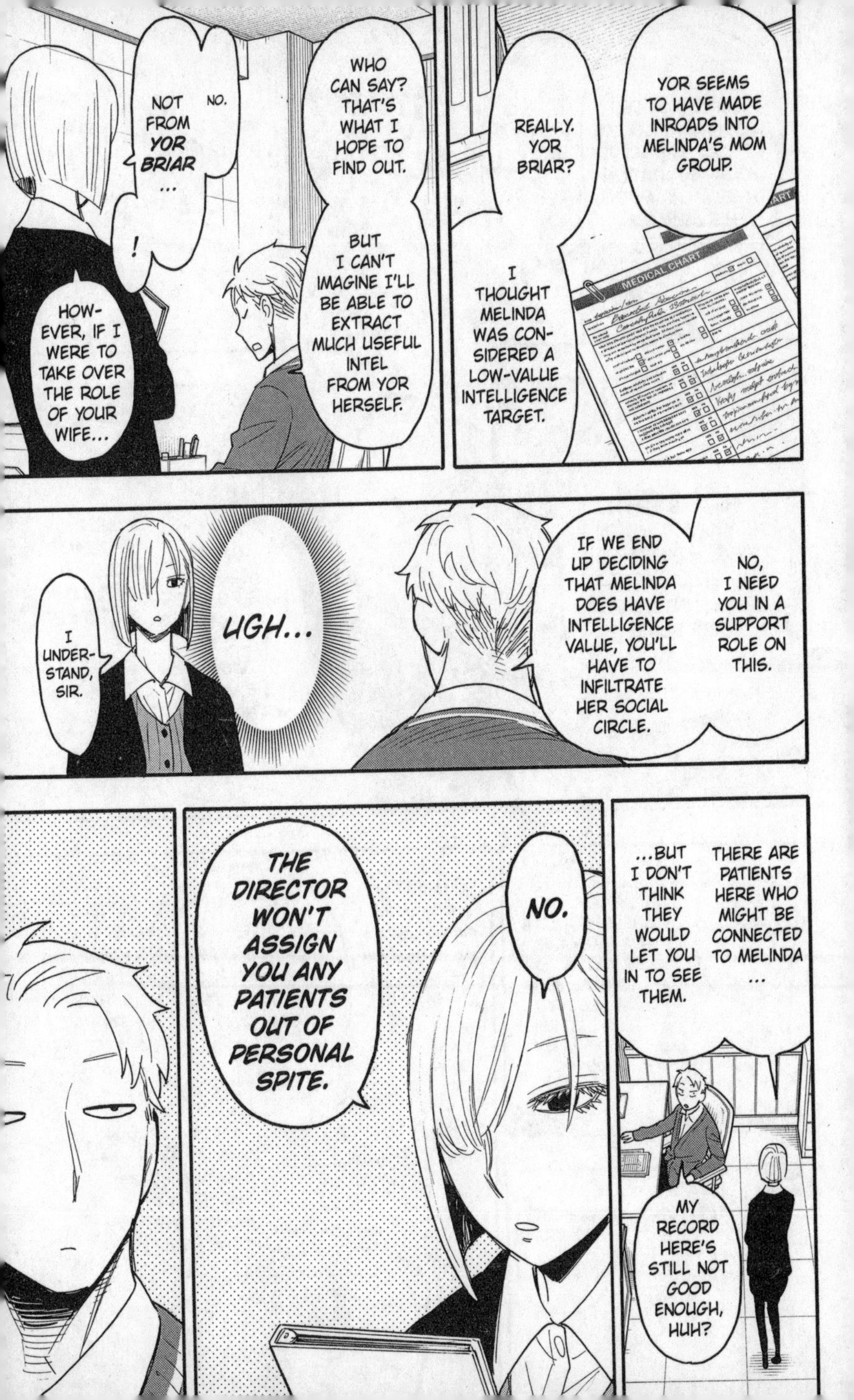
YOR SEEMS TO HAVE MADE INROADS INTO MELINDA'S MOM GROUP.
REALLY. YOR BRIAR?
I THOUGHT MELINDA WAS CONSIDERED A LOW-VALUE INTELLIGENCE TARGET.
MEDICAL CHART
WHO CAN SAY? THAT'S WHAT I HOPE TO FIND OUT.
BUT I CAN'T IMAGINE I'LL BE ABLE TO EXTRACT MUCH USEFUL INTEL FROM YOR HERSELF.
NO.
NOT FROM *YOR BRIAR*...
!
HOW-EVER, IF I WERE TO TAKE OVER THE ROLE OF YOUR WIFE...
NO, I NEED YOU IN A SUPPORT ROLE ON THIS.
IF WE END UP DECIDING THAT MELINDA DOES HAVE INTELLIGENCE VALUE, YOU'LL HAVE TO INFILTRATE HER SOCIAL CIRCLE.
UGH...
I UNDER-STAND, SIR.
THERE ARE PATIENTS HERE WHO MIGHT BE CONNECTED TO MELINDA...
...BUT I DON'T THINK THEY WOULD LET YOU IN TO SEE THEM.
MY RECORD HERE'S STILL NOT GOOD ENOUGH, HUH?
NO.
THE DIRECTOR WON'T ASSIGN YOU ANY PATIENTS OUT OF PERSONAL SPITE.

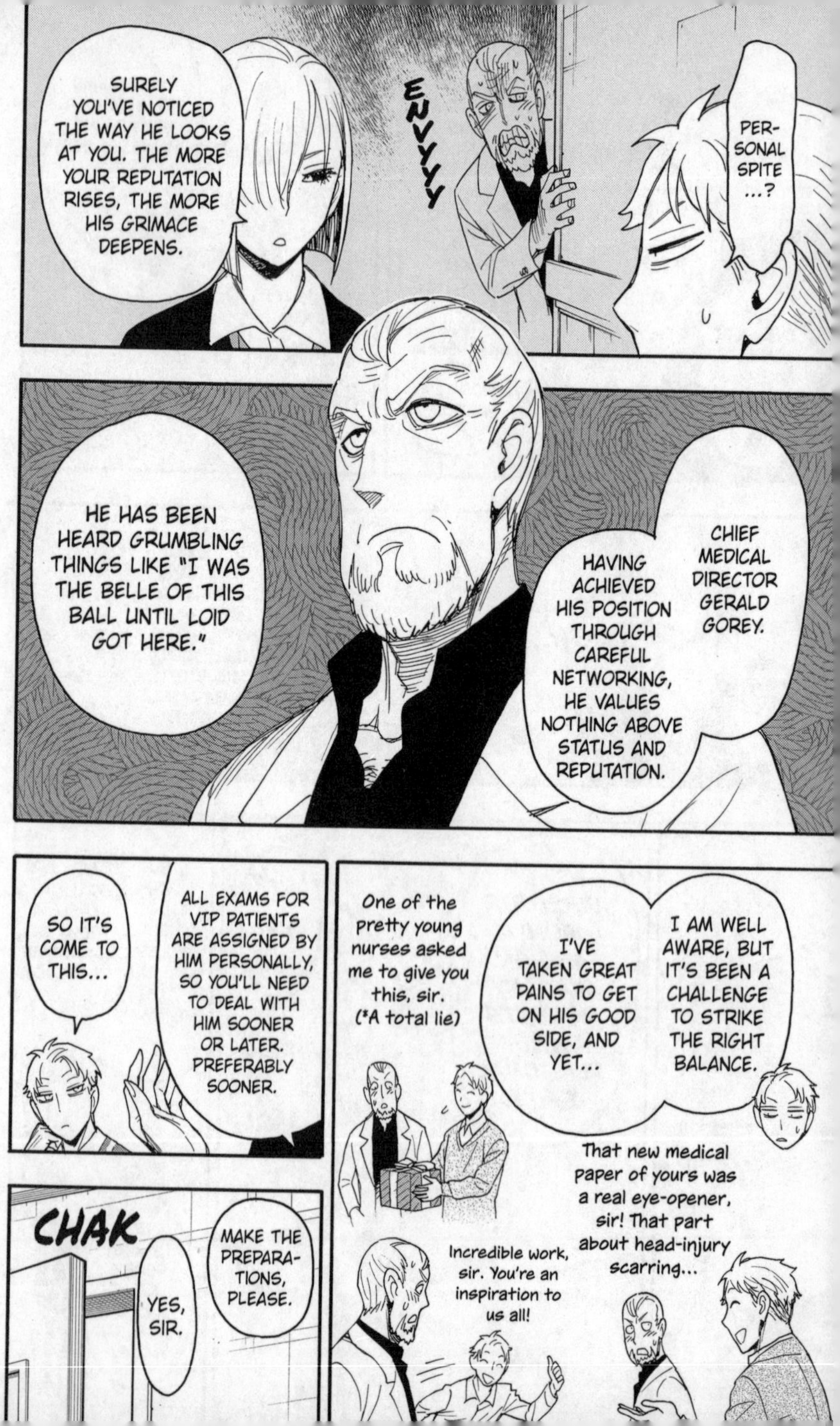
PER-SONAL SPITE...?
ENVYYY
SURELY YOU'VE NOTICED THE WAY HE LOOKS AT YOU. THE MORE YOUR REPUTATION RISES, THE MORE HIS GRIMACE DEEPENS.
CHIEF MEDICAL DIRECTOR GERALD GOREY.
HAVING ACHIEVED HIS POSITION THROUGH CAREFUL NETWORKING, HE VALUES NOTHING ABOVE STATUS AND REPUTATION.
HE HAS BEEN HEARD GRUMBLING THINGS LIKE "I WAS THE BELLE OF THIS BALL UNTIL LOID GOT HERE."
I AM WELL AWARE, BUT IT'S BEEN A CHALLENGE TO STRIKE THE RIGHT BALANCE.
I'VE TAKEN GREAT PAINS TO GET ON HIS GOOD SIDE, AND YET...
One of the pretty young nurses asked me to give you this, sir. (*A total lie)
That new medical paper of yours was a real eye-opener, sir! That part about head-injury scarring...
Incredible work, sir. You're an inspiration to us all!
ALL EXAMS FOR VIP PATIENTS ARE ASSIGNED BY HIM PERSONALLY, SO YOU'LL NEED TO DEAL WITH HIM SOONER OR LATER. PREFERABLY SOONER.
SO IT'S COME TO THIS...
MAKE THE PREPARA-TIONS, PLEASE.
YES, SIR.
CHAK

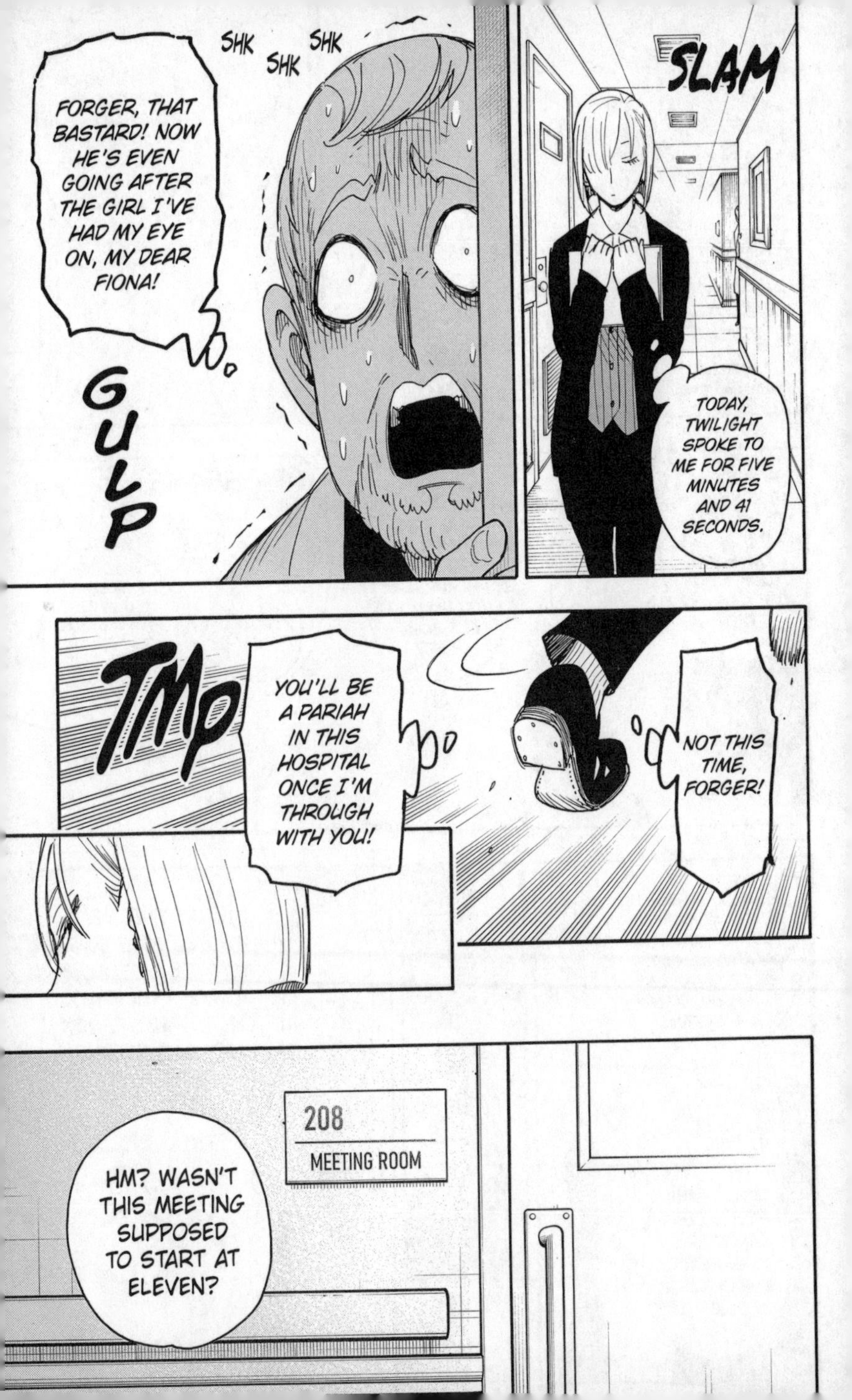
SLAM
TODAY, TWILIGHT SPOKE TO ME FOR FIVE MINUTES AND 41 SECONDS.
SHK SHK SHK
FORGER, THAT BASTARD! NOW HE'S EVEN GOING AFTER THE GIRL I'VE HAD MY EYE ON, MY DEAR FIONA!
GULP
NOT THIS TIME, FORGER!
YOU'LL BE A PARIAH IN THIS HOSPITAL ONCE I'M THROUGH WITH YOU!
TMP
208
MEETING ROOM
HM? WASN'T THIS MEETING SUPPOSED TO START AT ELEVEN?

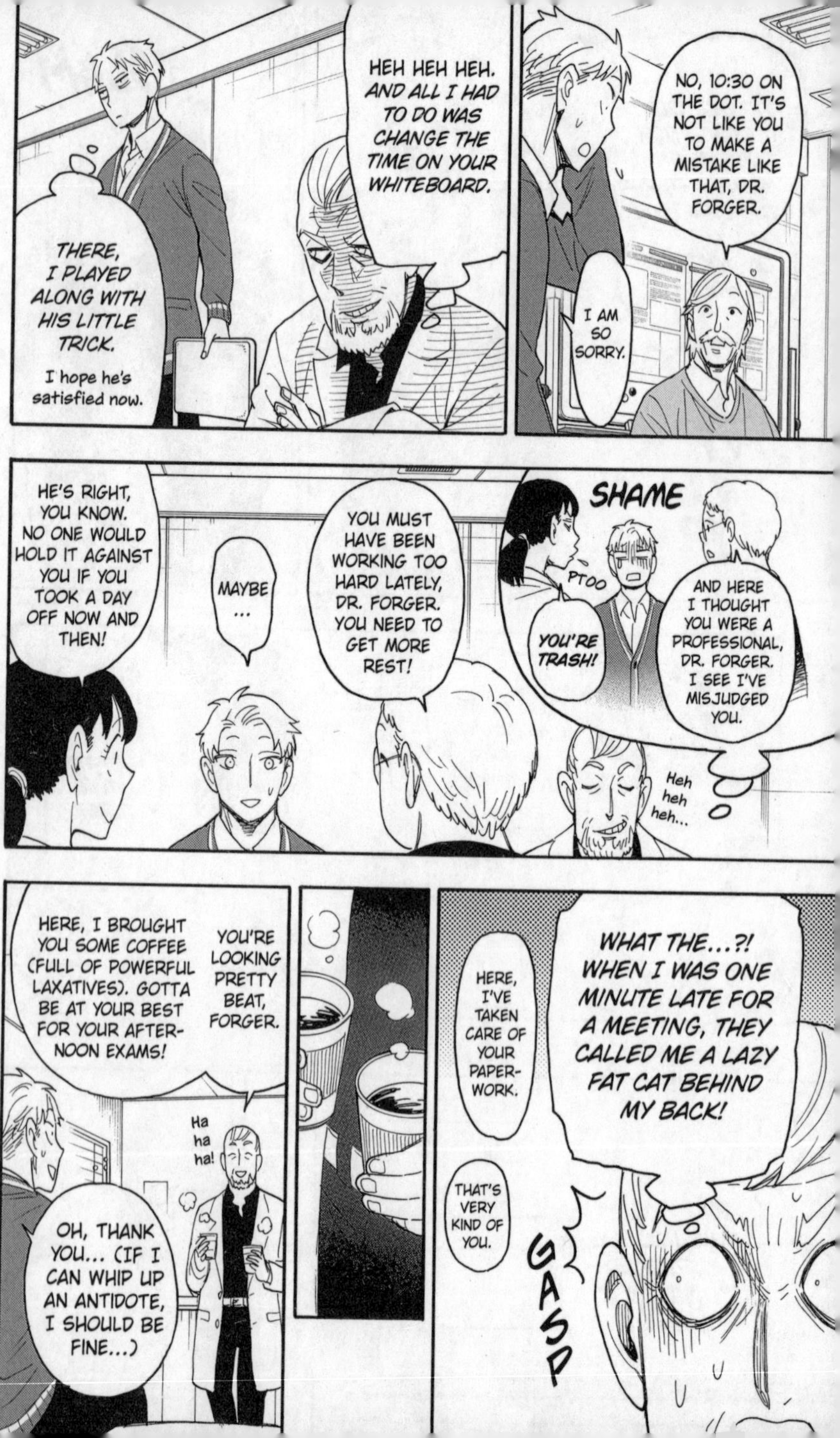
NO, 10:30 ON THE DOT. IT'S NOT LIKE YOU TO MAKE A MISTAKE LIKE THAT, DR. FORGER.
I AM SO SORRY.
HEH HEH HEH. AND ALL I HAD TO DO WAS CHANGE THE TIME ON YOUR WHITEBOARD.
THERE, I PLAYED ALONG WITH HIS LITTLE TRICK.
I hope he's satisfied now.
SHAME
AND HERE I THOUGHT YOU WERE A PROFESSIONAL, DR. FORGER. I SEE I'VE MISJUDGED YOU.
PTOO
YOU'RE TRASH!
YOU MUST HAVE BEEN WORKING TOO HARD LATELY, DR. FORGER. YOU NEED TO GET MORE REST!
MAYBE ...
HE'S RIGHT, YOU KNOW. NO ONE WOULD HOLD IT AGAINST YOU IF YOU TOOK A DAY OFF NOW AND THEN!
Heh heh heh...
WHAT THE...?! WHEN I WAS ONE MINUTE LATE FOR A MEETING, THEY CALLED ME A LAZY FAT CAT BEHIND MY BACK!
HERE, I'VE TAKEN CARE OF YOUR PAPER-WORK.
THAT'S VERY KIND OF YOU.
GASP
YOU'RE LOOKING PRETTY BEAT, FORGER.
HERE, I BROUGHT YOU SOME COFFEE (FULL OF POWERFUL LAXATIVES). GOTTA BE AT YOUR BEST FOR YOUR AFTER-NOON EXAMS!
Ha ha ha!
OH, THANK YOU... (IF I CAN WHIP UP AN ANTIDOTE, I SHOULD BE FINE...)

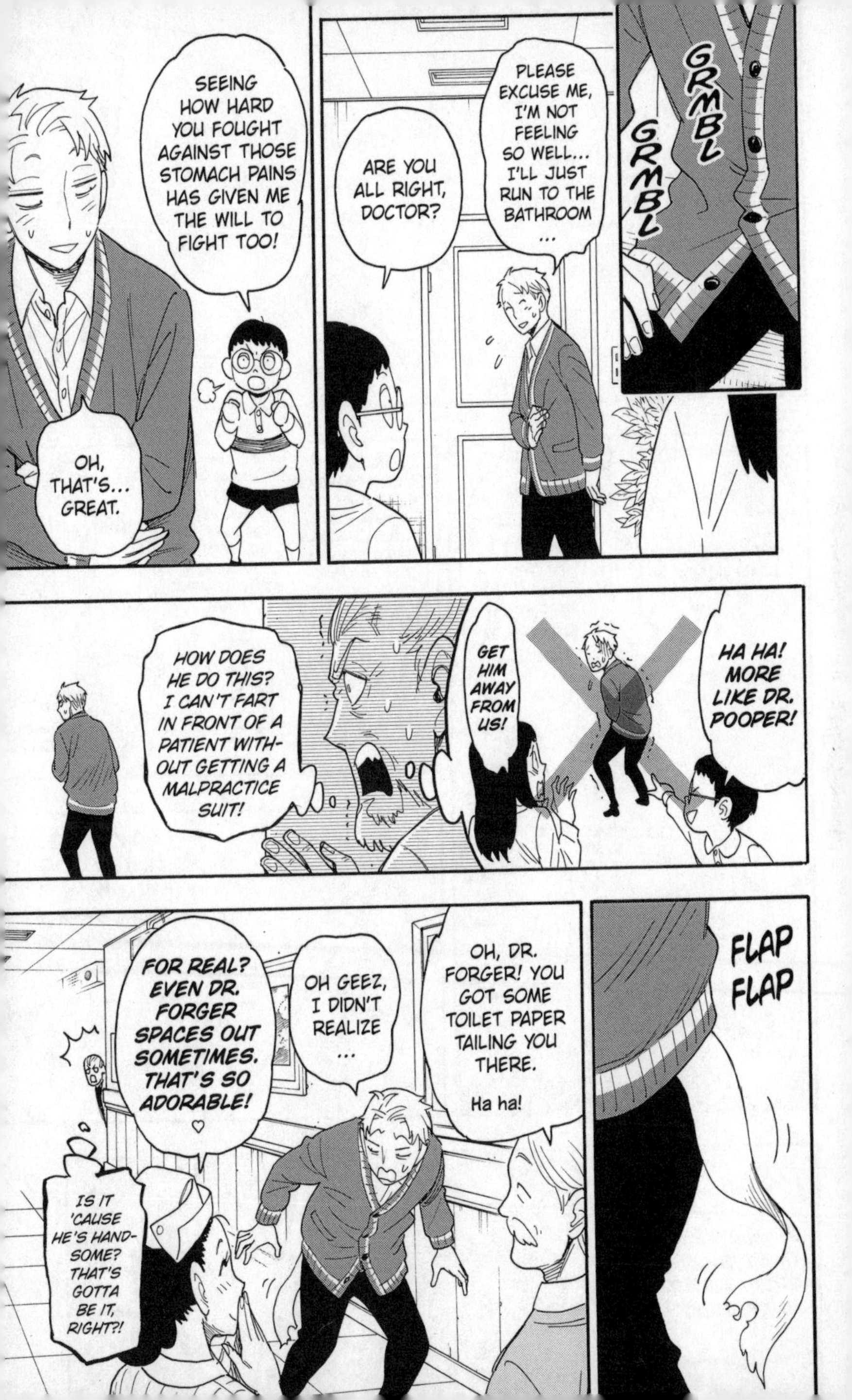
GRMBL
GRMBL
PLEASE EXCUSE ME, I'M NOT FEELING SO WELL... I'LL JUST RUN TO THE BATHROOM ...
ARE YOU ALL RIGHT, DOCTOR?
SEEING HOW HARD YOU FOUGHT AGAINST THOSE STOMACH PAINS HAS GIVEN ME THE WILL TO FIGHT TOO!
OH, THAT'S... GREAT.
HA HA! MORE LIKE DR. POOPER!
GET HIM AWAY FROM US!
HOW DOES HE DO THIS? I CAN'T FART IN FRONT OF A PATIENT WITH-OUT GETTING A MALPRACTICE SUIT!
FLAP FLAP
OH, DR. FORGER! YOU GOT SOME TOILET PAPER TAILING YOU THERE.
Ha ha!
OH GEEZ, I DIDN'T REALIZE ...
FOR REAL? EVEN DR. FORGER SPACES OUT SOMETIMES. THAT'S SO ADORABLE! ♡
IS IT 'CAUSE HE'S HAND-SOME? THAT'S GOTTA BE IT, RIGHT?!

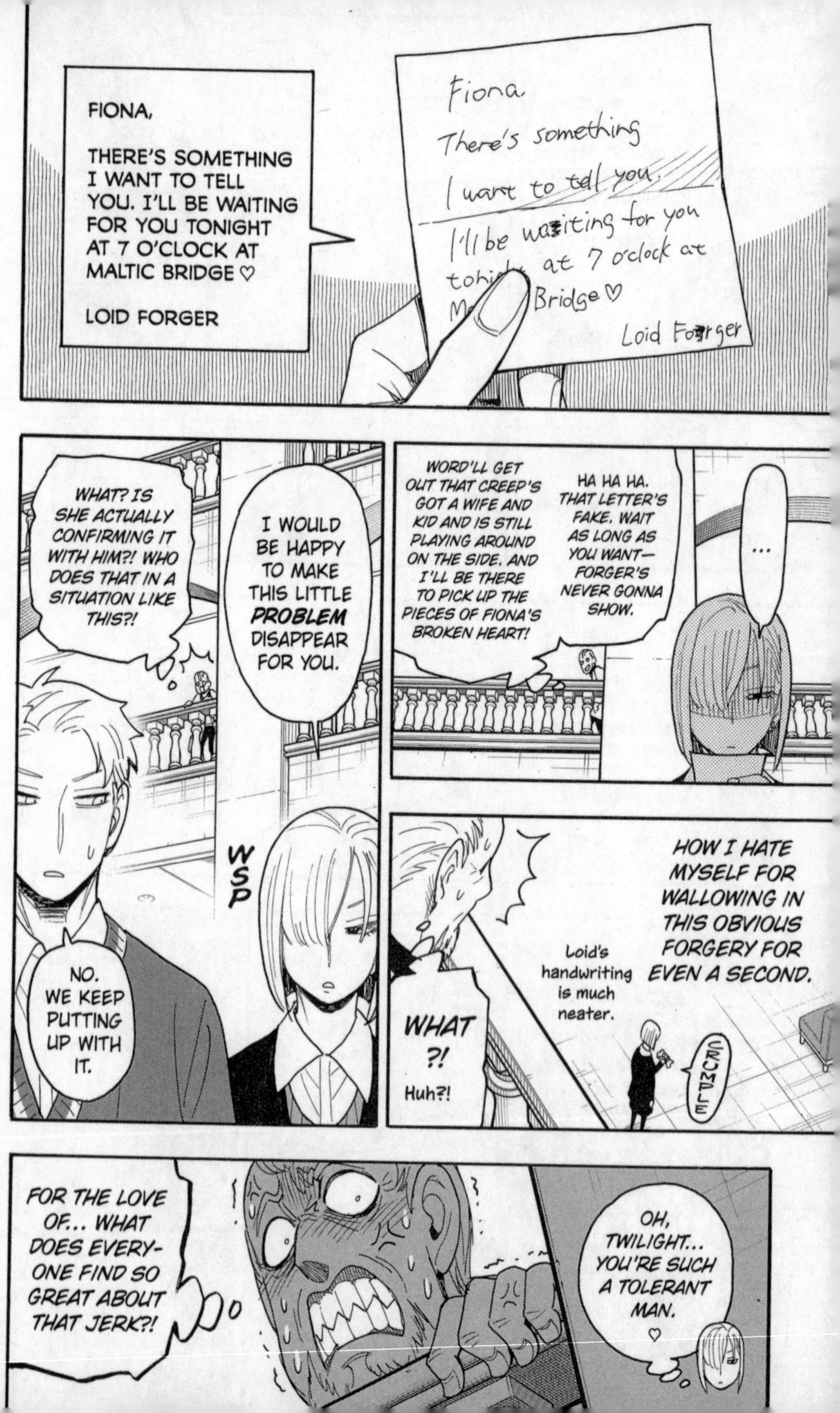

Fiona
There's something I want to tell you.
I'll be waiting for you at 7 o'clock at
Bridge♡
Loid Forger
FIONA, THERE'S SOMETHING I WANT TO TELL YOU. I'LL BE WAITING FOR YOU TONIGHT AT 7 O'CLOCK AT MALTIC BRIDGE♡ LOID FORGER
...
HA HA HA. THAT LETTER'S FAKE. WAIT AS LONG AS YOU WANT—FORGER'S NEVER GONNA SHOW.
WORD'LL GET OUT THAT CREEP'S GOT A WIFE AND KID AND IS STILL PLAYING AROUND ON THE SIDE. AND I'LL BE THERE TO PICK UP THE PIECES OF FIONA'S BROKEN HEART!
HOW I HATE MYSELF FOR WALLOWING IN THIS OBVIOUS FORGERY FOR EVEN A SECOND.
Loid's handwriting is much neater.
CRUMPLE
WHAT?!
Huh?!
WSP
I WOULD BE HAPPY TO MAKE THIS LITTLE PROBLEM DISAPPEAR FOR YOU.
WHAT? IS SHE ACTUALLY CONFIRMING IT WITH HIM?! WHO DOES THAT IN A SITUATION LIKE THIS?!
NO. WE KEEP PUTTING UP WITH IT.
OH, TWILIGHT... YOU'RE SUCH A TOLERANT MAN. ♡
FOR THE LOVE OF... WHAT DOES EVERYONE FIND SO GREAT ABOUT THAT JERK?!

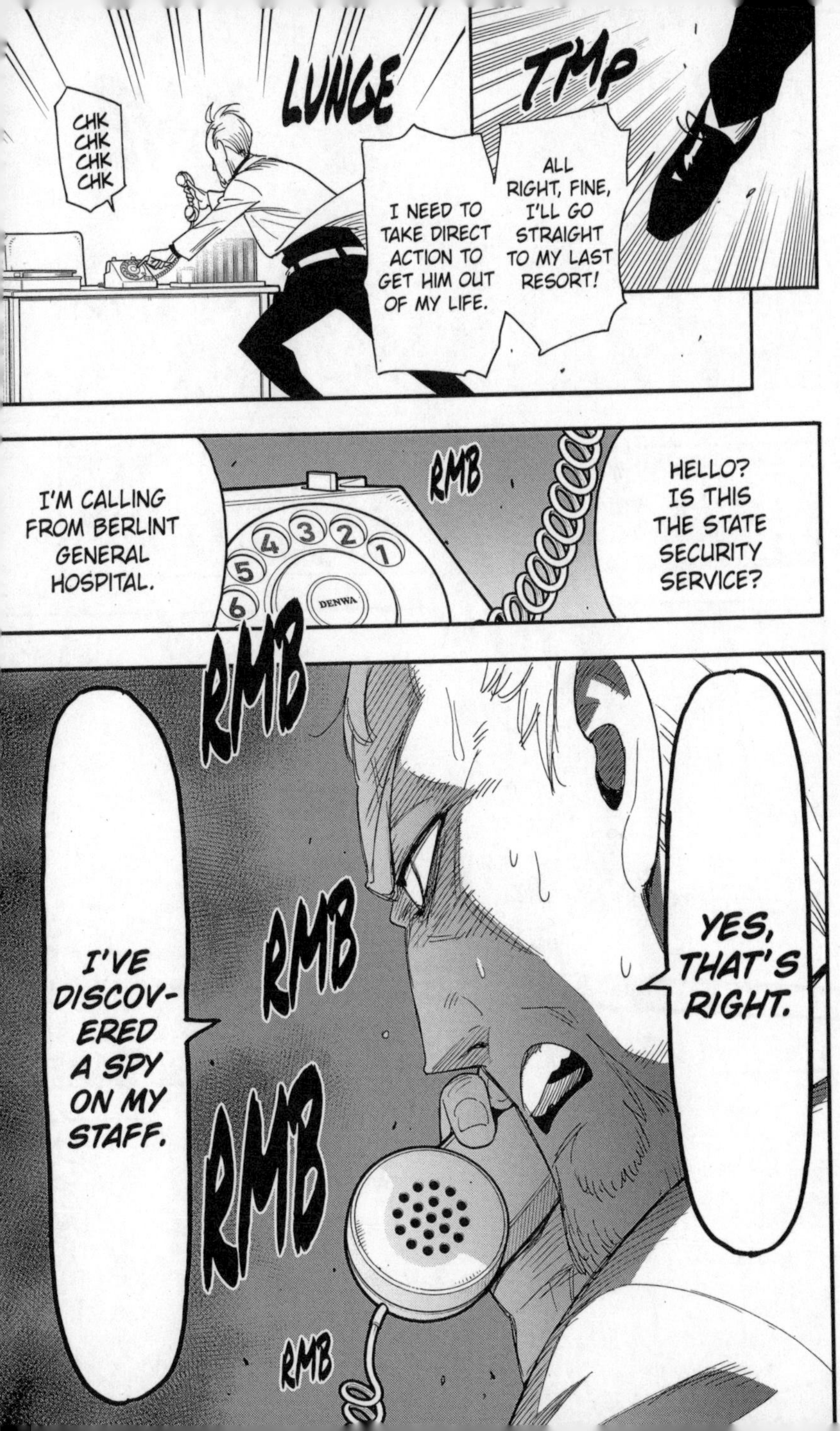
TMP
ALL RIGHT, FINE, I'LL GO STRAIGHT TO MY LAST RESORT!
I NEED TO TAKE DIRECT ACTION TO GET HIM OUT OF MY LIFE.
LUNGE
CHK CHK CHK CHK
HELLO? IS THIS THE STATE SECURITY SERVICE?
RMB
DENWA
I'M CALLING FROM BERLINT GENERAL HOSPITAL.
YES, THAT'S RIGHT.
RMB
RMB
RMB
RMB
I'VE DISCOVERED A SPY ON MY STAFF.

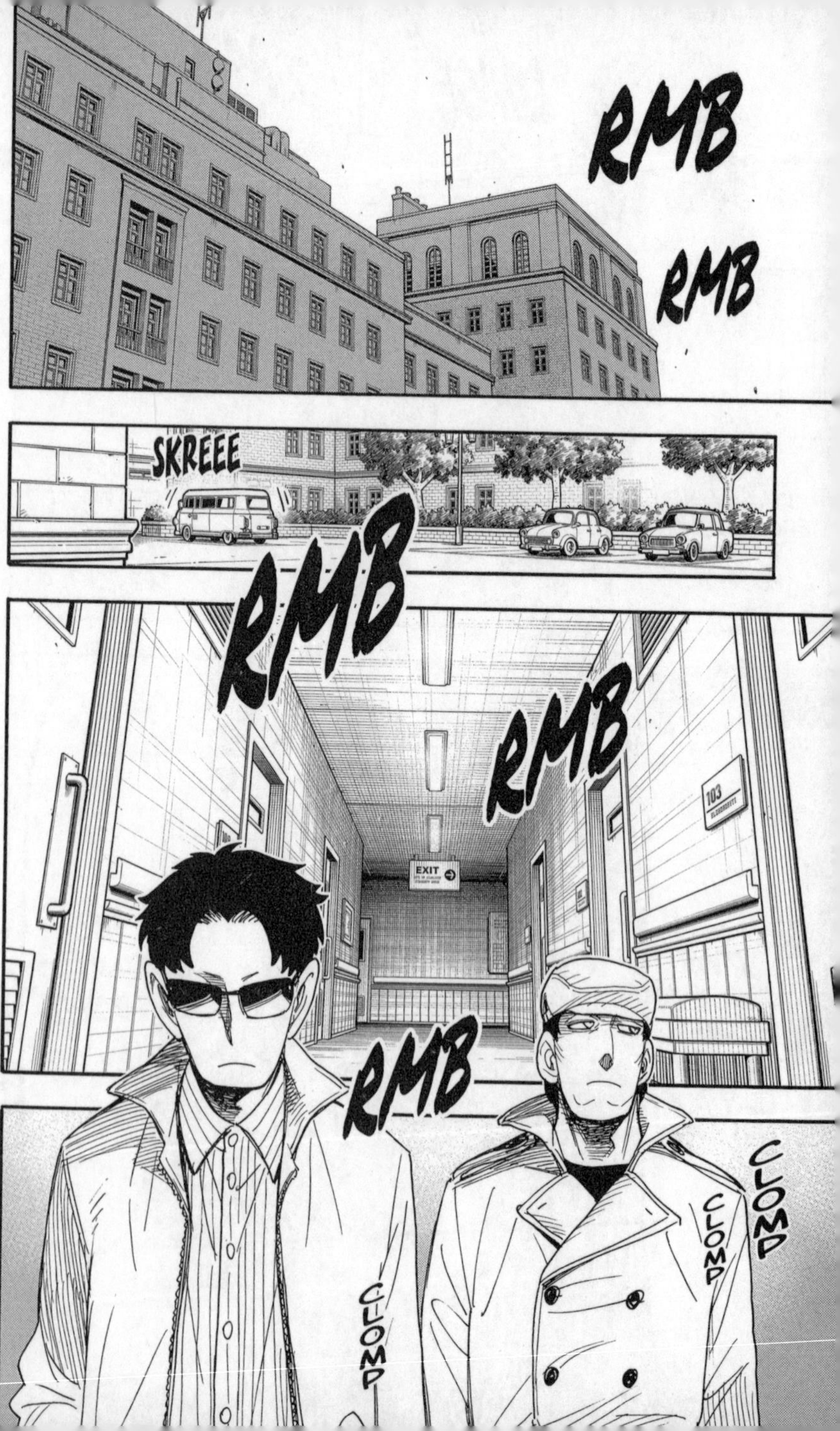
RMB
RMB
SKREEE
RMB
RMB
103
EXIT
RMB
CLOMP
CLOMP
CLOMP

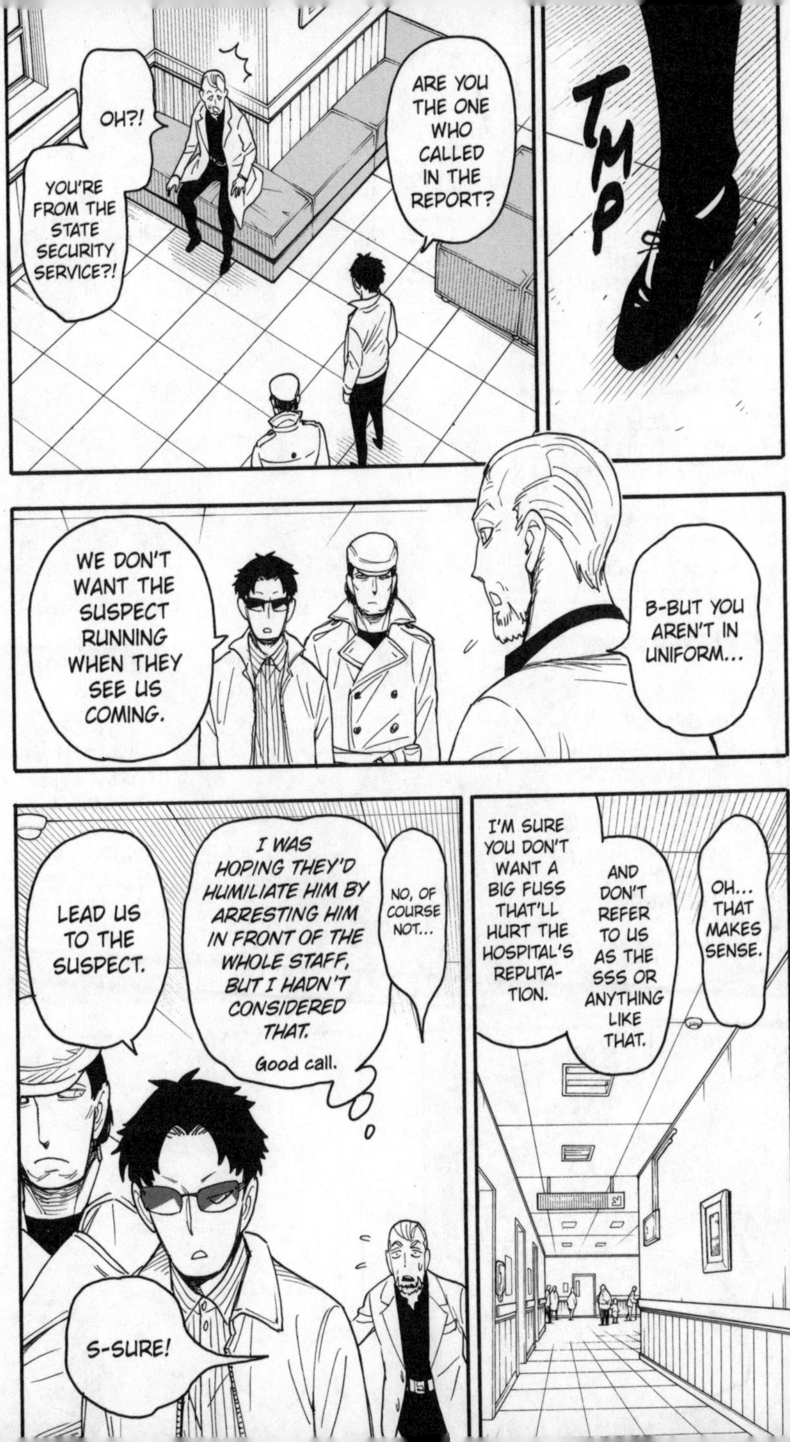
TMP
ARE YOU THE ONE WHO CALLED IN THE REPORT?
OH?!
YOU'RE FROM THE STATE SECURITY SERVICE?!
B-BUT YOU AREN'T IN UNIFORM...
WE DON'T WANT THE SUSPECT RUNNING WHEN THEY SEE US COMING.
OH... THAT MAKES SENSE.
I'M SURE YOU DON'T WANT A BIG FUSS THAT'LL HURT THE HOSPITAL'S REPUTA-TION.
AND DON'T REFER TO US AS THE SSS OR ANYTHING LIKE THAT.
NO, OF COURSE NOT...
I WAS HOPING THEY'D HUMILIATE HIM BY ARRESTING HIM IN FRONT OF THE WHOLE STAFF, BUT I HADN'T CONSIDERED THAT.
Good call.
LEAD US TO THE SUSPECT.
S-SURE!

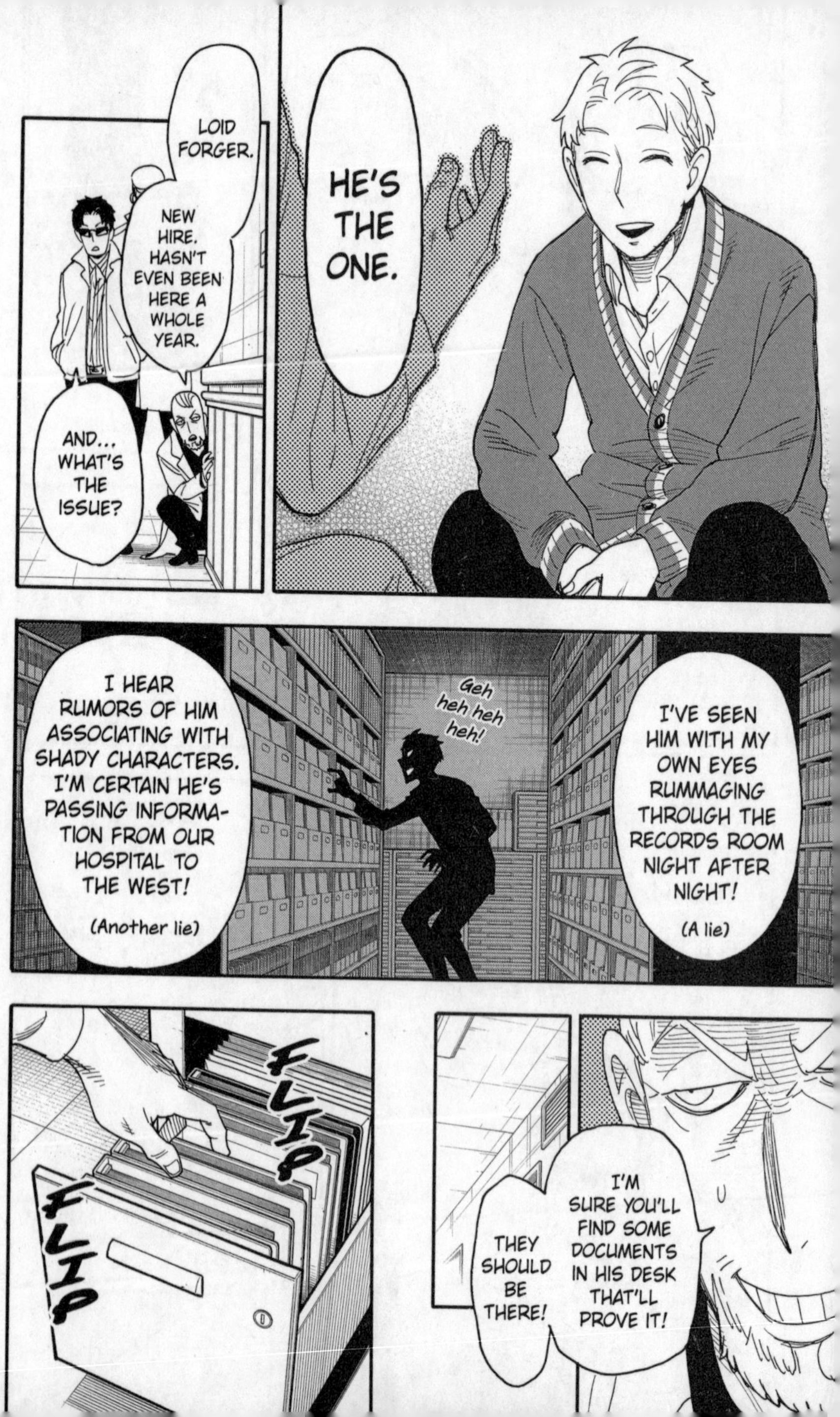
HE'S THE ONE.
LOID FORGER.
NEW HIRE. HASN'T EVEN BEEN HERE A WHOLE YEAR.
AND... WHAT'S THE ISSUE?
I'VE SEEN HIM WITH MY OWN EYES RUMMAGING THROUGH THE RECORDS ROOM NIGHT AFTER NIGHT!
(A lie)
Geh heh heh heh!
I HEAR RUMORS OF HIM ASSOCIATING WITH SHADY CHARACTERS. I'M CERTAIN HE'S PASSING INFORMATION FROM OUR HOSPITAL TO THE WEST!
(Another lie)
I'M SURE YOU'LL FIND SOME DOCUMENTS IN HIS DESK THAT'LL PROVE IT!
THEY SHOULD BE THERE!
FLIP
FLIP

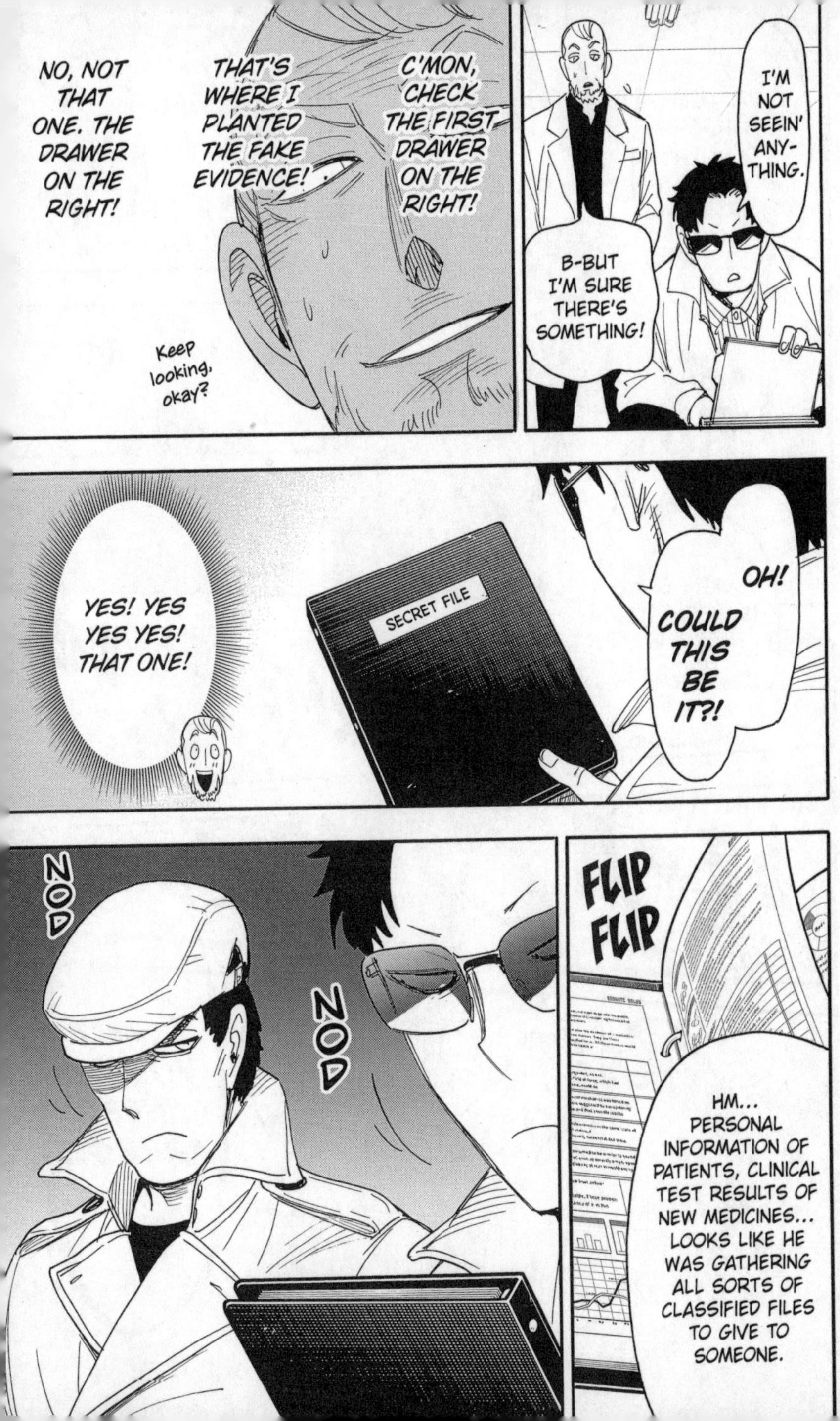
I'M NOT SEEIN' ANYTHING.
B-BUT I'M SURE THERE'S SOMETHING!
C'MON, CHECK THE FIRST DRAWER ON THE RIGHT!
THAT'S WHERE I PLANTED THE FAKE EVIDENCE!
NO, NOT THAT ONE. THE DRAWER ON THE RIGHT!
Keep looking, okay?
OH!
COULD THIS BE IT?!
SECRET FILE
YES! YES YES YES! THAT ONE!
FLIP FLIP
HM... PERSONAL INFORMATION OF PATIENTS, CLINICAL TEST RESULTS OF NEW MEDICINES... LOOKS LIKE HE WAS GATHERING ALL SORTS OF CLASSIFIED FILES TO GIVE TO SOMEONE.
NOD
NOD

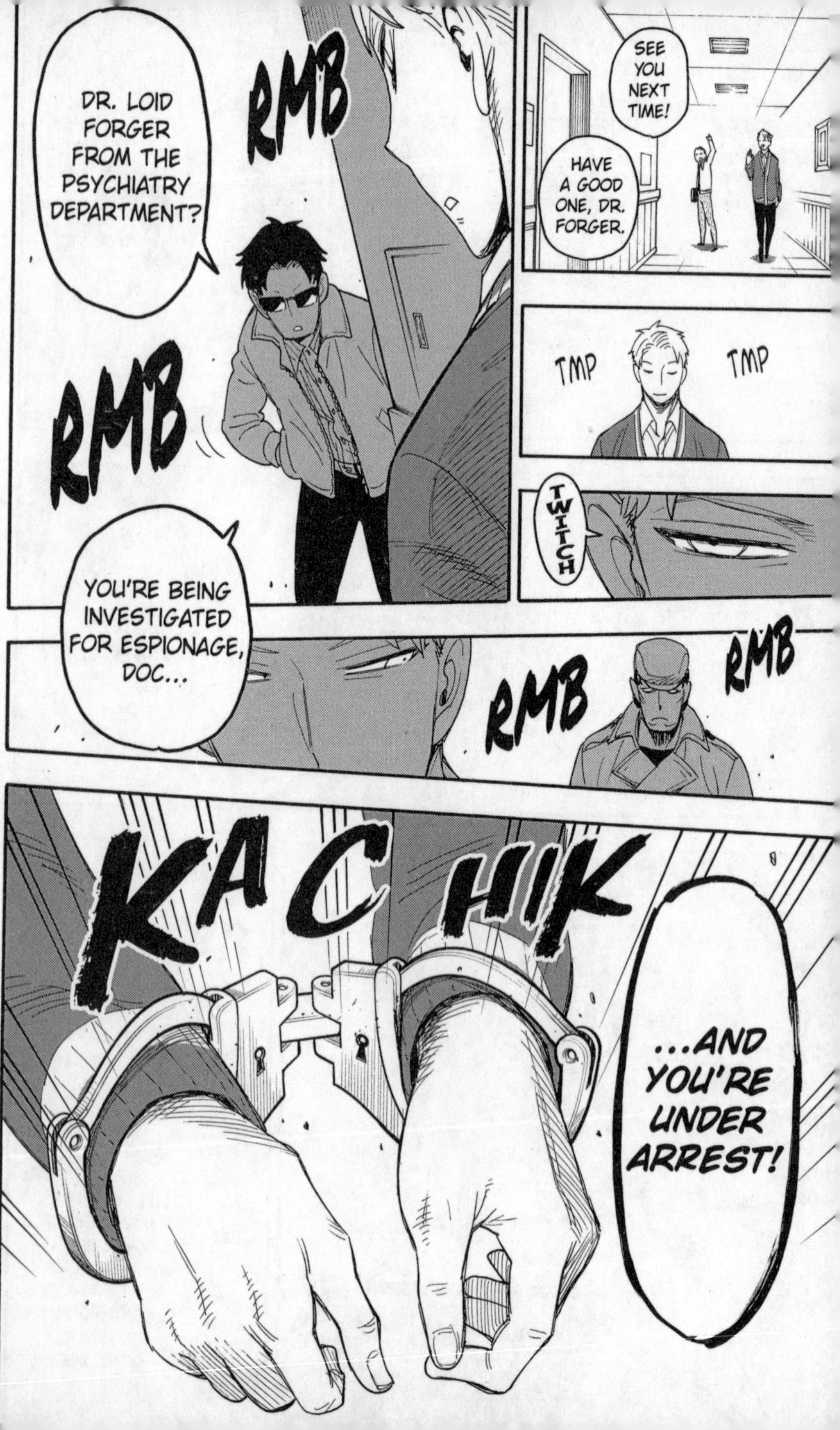
SEE YOU NEXT TIME!
HAVE A GOOD ONE, DR. FORGER.
TMP
TMP
TWITCH
RMB
DR. LOID FORGER FROM THE PSYCHIATRY DEPARTMENT?
RMB
YOU'RE BEING INVESTIGATED FOR ESPIONAGE, DOC...
RMB
RMB
KACHIK
...AND YOU'RE UNDER ARREST!

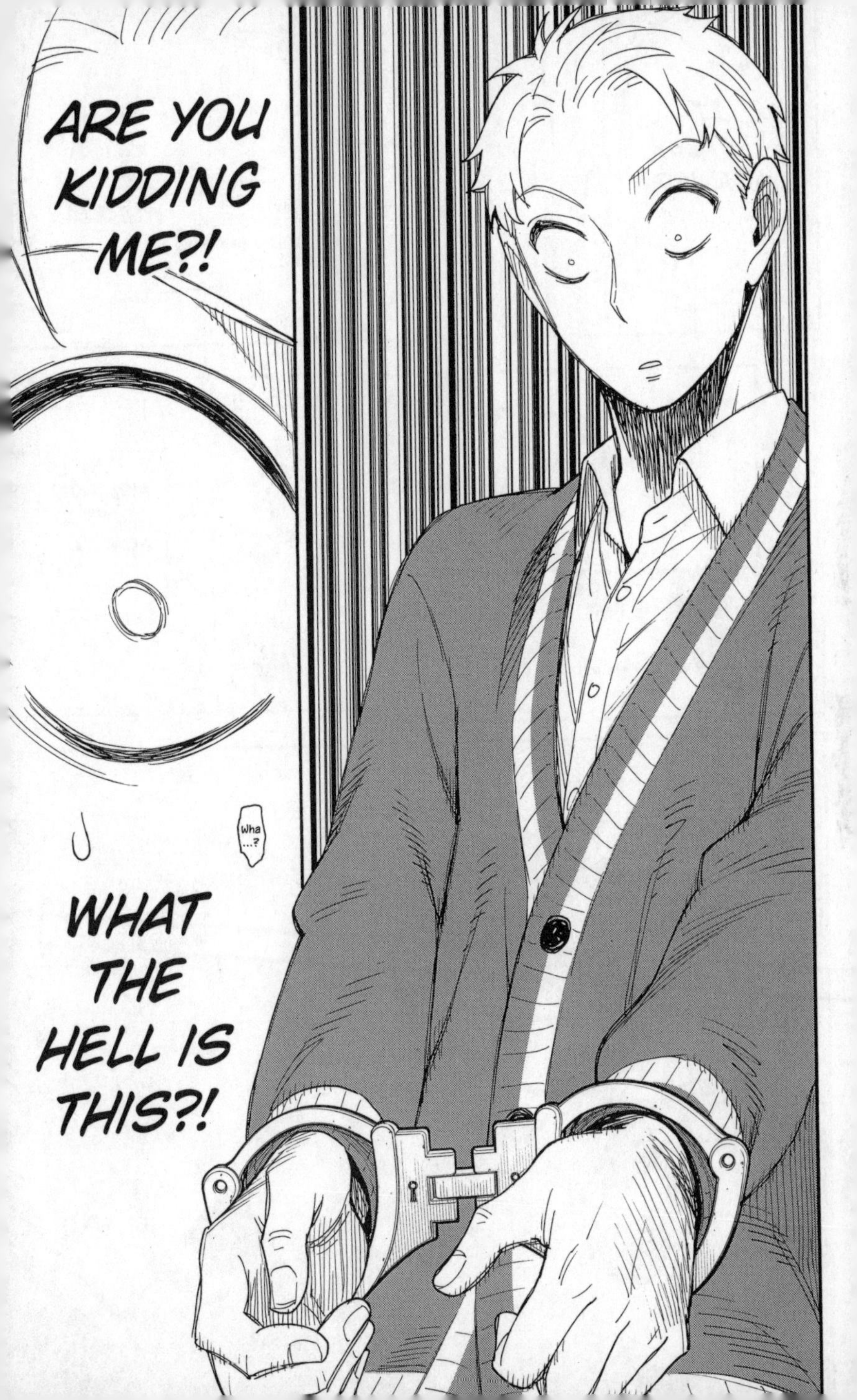
ARE YOU KIDDING ME?!
Wha ...?
WHAT THE HELL IS THIS?!

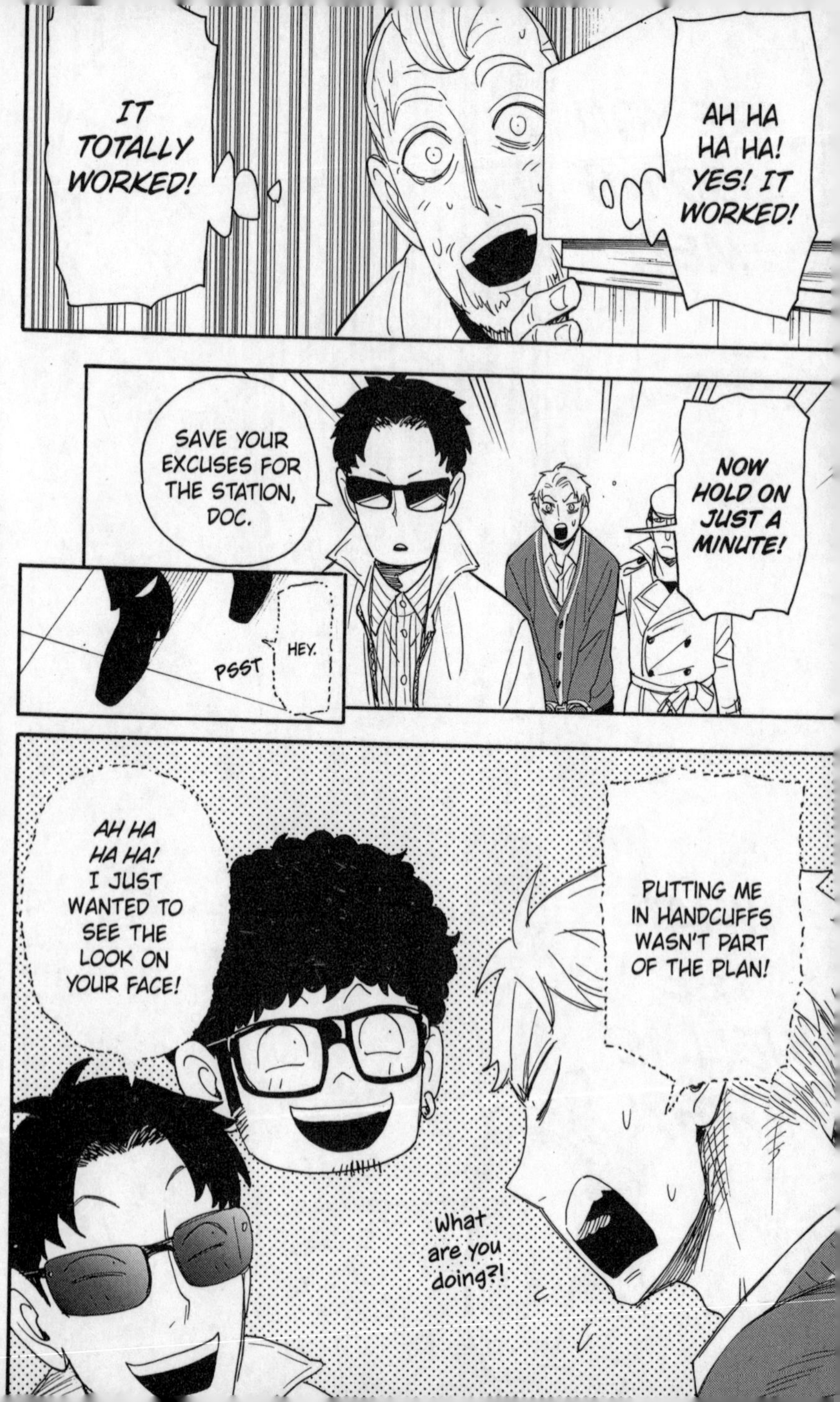
AH HA HA HA! YES! IT WORKED!
IT TOTALLY WORKED!
NOW HOLD ON JUST A MINUTE!
SAVE YOUR EXCUSES FOR THE STATION, DOC.
HEY.
PSST
PUTTING ME IN HANDCUFFS WASN'T PART OF THE PLAN!
AH HA HA HA! I JUST WANTED TO SEE THE LOOK ON YOUR FACE!
What are you doing?!

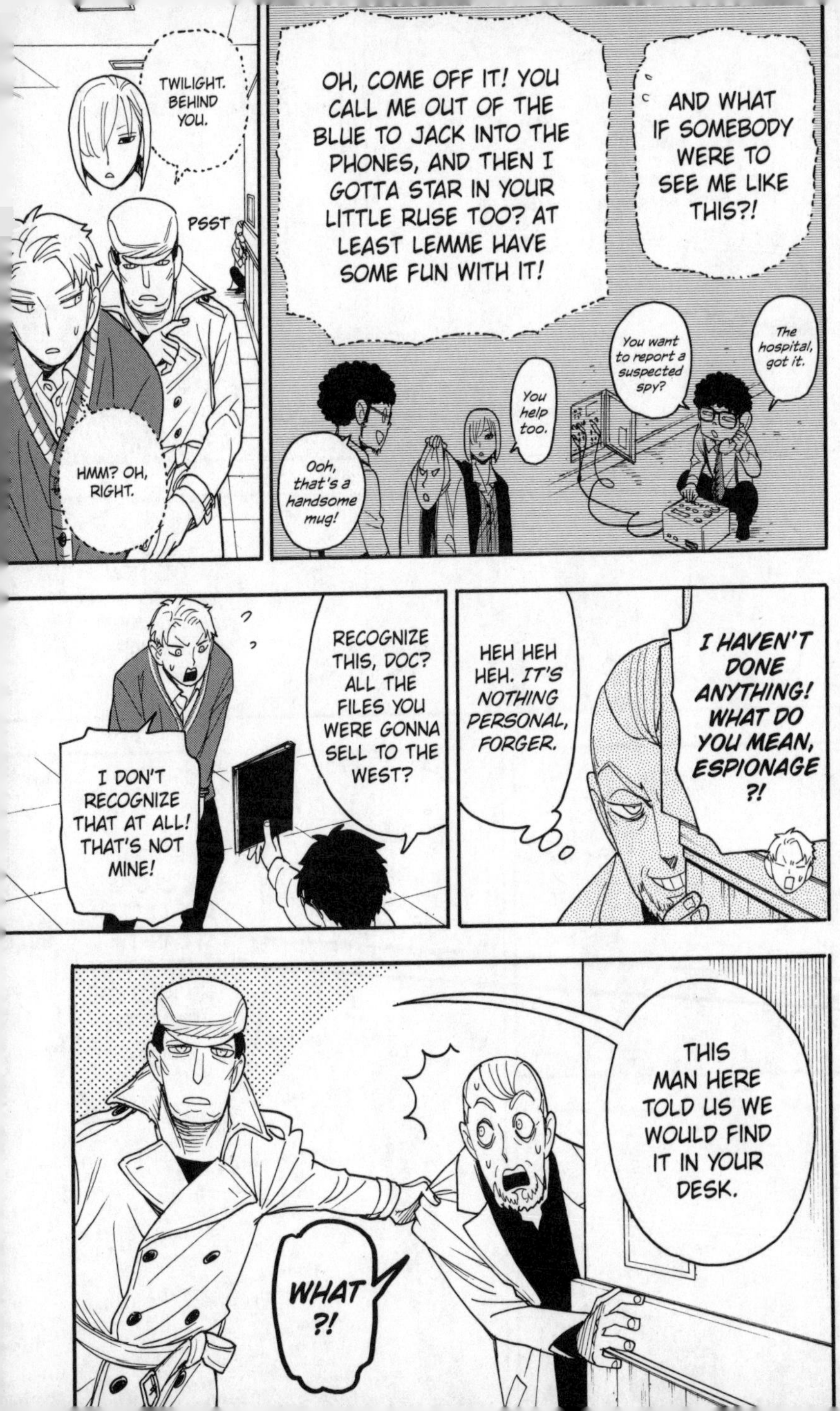
AND WHAT IF SOMEBODY WERE TO SEE ME LIKE THIS?!
OH, COME OFF IT! YOU CALL ME OUT OF THE BLUE TO JACK INTO THE PHONES, AND THEN I GOTTA STAR IN YOUR LITTLE RUSE TOO? AT LEAST LEMME HAVE SOME FUN WITH IT!
The hospital, got it.
You want to report a suspected spy?
You help too.
Ooh, that's a handsome mug!
TWILIGHT. BEHIND YOU.
PSST
HMM? OH, RIGHT.
I HAVEN'T DONE ANYTHING! WHAT DO YOU MEAN, ESPIONAGE?!
HEH HEH HEH. IT'S NOTHING PERSONAL, FORGER.
RECOGNIZE THIS, DOC? ALL THE FILES YOU WERE GONNA SELL TO THE WEST?
I DON'T RECOGNIZE THAT AT ALL! THAT'S NOT MINE!
THIS MAN HERE TOLD US WE WOULD FIND IT IN YOUR DESK.
WHAT?!

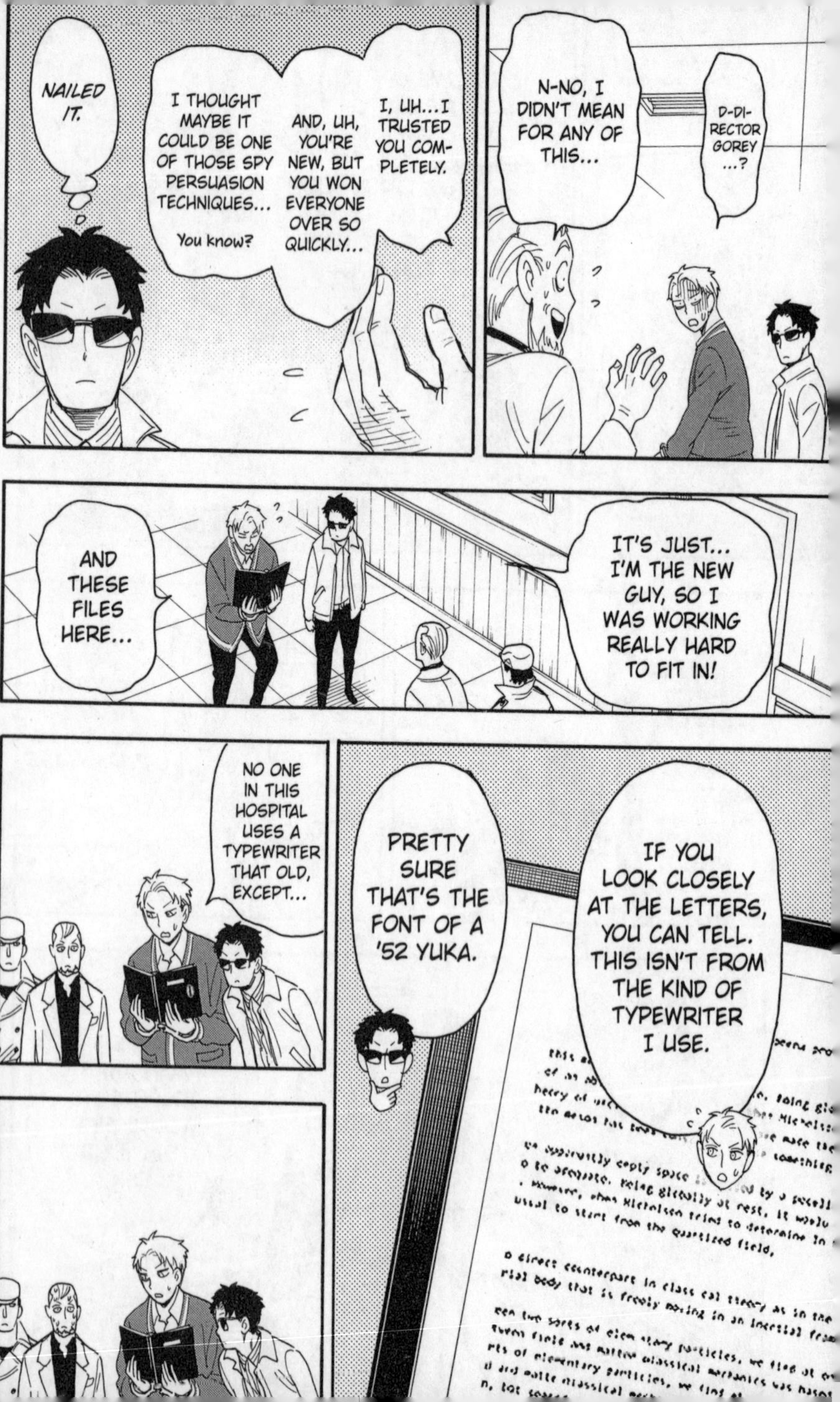
D-DIRECTOR GOREY...?
N-NO, I DIDN'T MEAN FOR ANY OF THIS...
I, UH...I TRUSTED YOU COMPLETELY.
AND, UH, YOU'RE NEW, BUT YOU WON EVERYONE OVER SO QUICKLY...
I THOUGHT MAYBE IT COULD BE ONE OF THOSE SPY PERSUASION TECHNIQUES... You know?
NAILED IT.
IT'S JUST... I'M THE NEW GUY, SO I WAS WORKING REALLY HARD TO FIT IN!
AND THESE FILES HERE...
IF YOU LOOK CLOSELY AT THE LETTERS, YOU CAN TELL. THIS ISN'T FROM THE KIND OF TYPEWRITER I USE.
PRETTY SURE THAT'S THE FONT OF A '52 YUKA.
NO ONE IN THIS HOSPITAL USES A TYPEWRITER THAT OLD, EXCEPT...

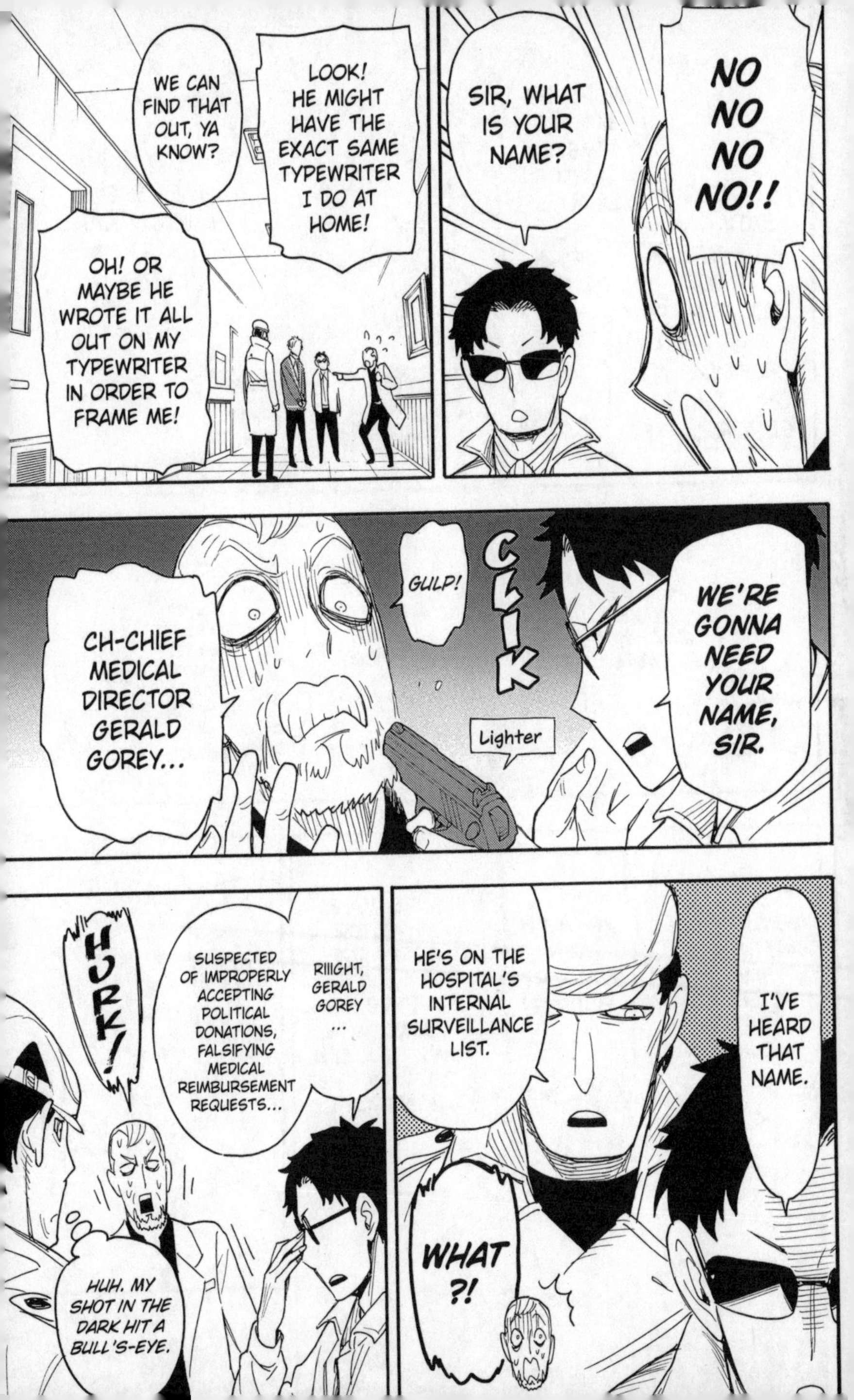
NO NO NO NO!!
SIR, WHAT IS YOUR NAME?
LOOK! HE MIGHT HAVE THE EXACT SAME TYPEWRITER I DO AT HOME!
WE CAN FIND THAT OUT, YA KNOW?
OH! OR MAYBE HE WROTE IT ALL OUT ON MY TYPEWRITER IN ORDER TO FRAME ME!
WE'RE GONNA NEED YOUR NAME, SIR.
CLIK
Lighter
GULP!
CH-CHIEF MEDICAL DIRECTOR GERALD GOREY...
I'VE HEARD THAT NAME.
HE'S ON THE HOSPITAL'S INTERNAL SURVEILLANCE LIST.
WHAT?!
RIIIGHT, GERALD GOREY ...
SUSPECTED OF IMPROPERLY ACCEPTING POLITICAL DONATIONS, FALSIFYING MEDICAL REIMBURSEMENT REQUESTS...
HURK!
HUH. MY SHOT IN THE DARK HIT A BULL'S-EYE.

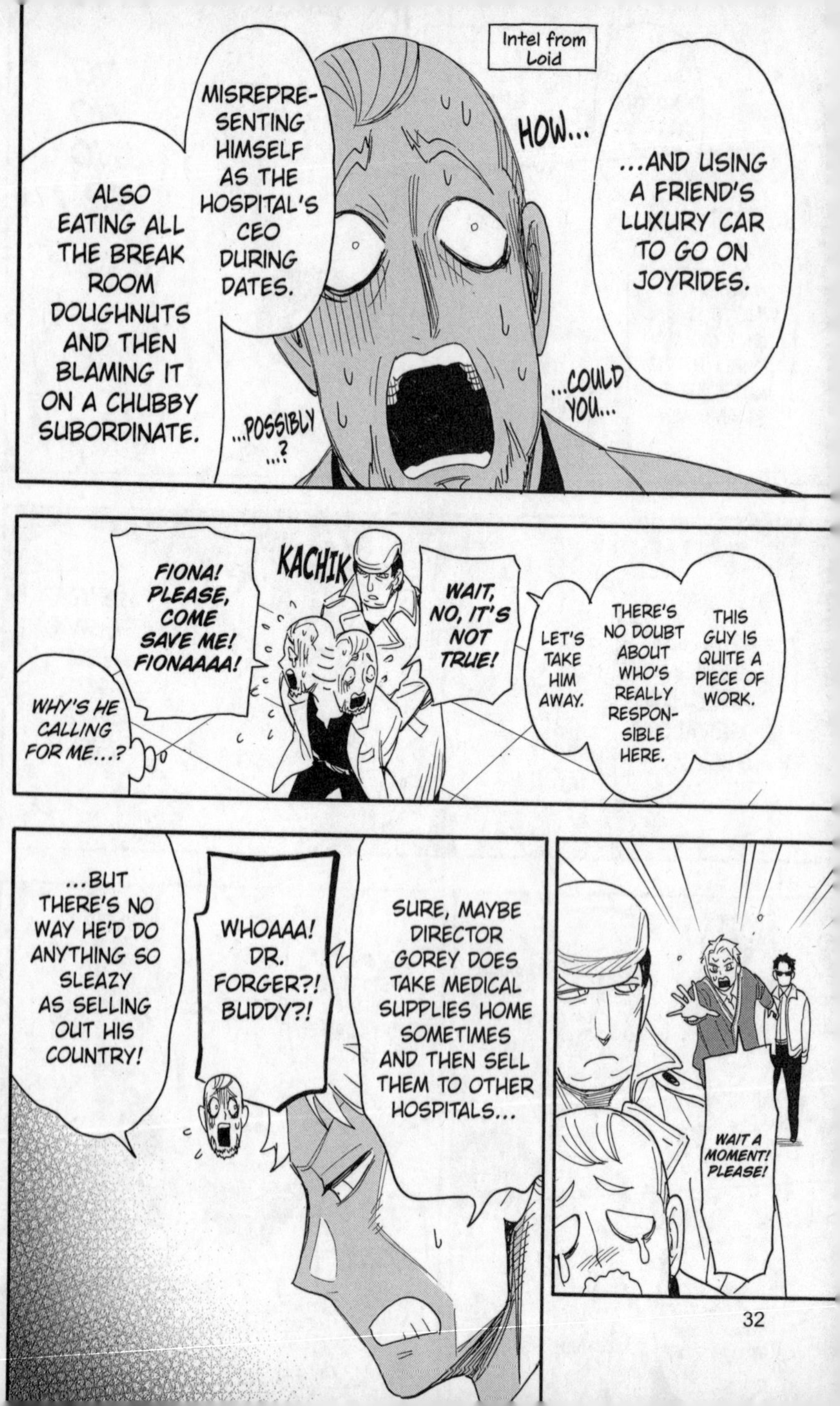
Intel from Loid
...AND USING A FRIEND'S LUXURY CAR TO GO ON JOYRIDES.
HOW...
MISREPRESENTING HIMSELF AS THE HOSPITAL'S CEO DURING DATES.
...COULD YOU...
ALSO EATING ALL THE BREAK ROOM DOUGHNUTS AND THEN BLAMING IT ON A CHUBBY SUBORDINATE.
...POSSIBLY ...?
THIS GUY IS QUITE A PIECE OF WORK.
THERE'S NO DOUBT ABOUT WHO'S REALLY RESPONSIBLE HERE.
LET'S TAKE HIM AWAY.
WAIT, NO, IT'S NOT TRUE!
KACHIK
FIONA! PLEASE, COME SAVE ME! FIONAAAA!
WHY'S HE CALLING FOR ME...?
WAIT A MOMENT! PLEASE!
SURE, MAYBE DIRECTOR GOREY DOES TAKE MEDICAL SUPPLIES HOME SOMETIMES AND THEN SELL THEM TO OTHER HOSPITALS...
WHOAAA! DR. FORGER?! BUDDY?!
...BUT THERE'S NO WAY HE'D DO ANYTHING SO SLEAZY AS SELLING OUT HIS COUNTRY!

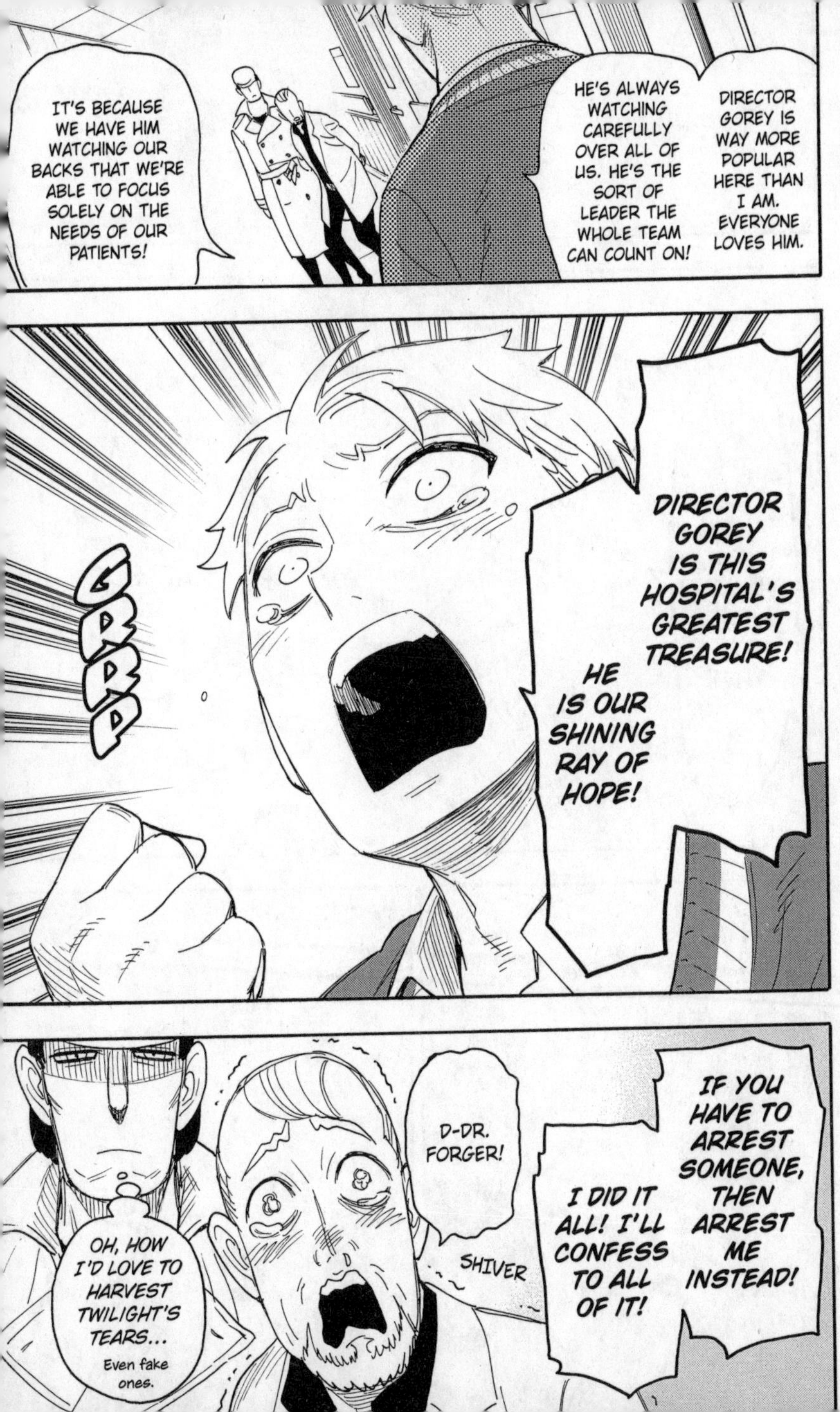
DIRECTOR GOREY IS WAY MORE POPULAR HERE THAN I AM. EVERYONE LOVES HIM.
HE'S ALWAYS WATCHING CAREFULLY OVER ALL OF US. HE'S THE SORT OF LEADER THE WHOLE TEAM CAN COUNT ON!
IT'S BECAUSE WE HAVE HIM WATCHING OUR BACKS THAT WE'RE ABLE TO FOCUS SOLELY ON THE NEEDS OF OUR PATIENTS!
DIRECTOR GOREY IS THIS HOSPITAL'S GREATEST TREASURE!
HE IS OUR SHINING RAY OF HOPE!
GRRP
IF YOU HAVE TO ARREST SOMEONE, THEN ARREST ME INSTEAD!
I DID IT ALL! I'LL CONFESS TO ALL OF IT!
D-DR. FORGER!
SHIVER
OH, HOW I'D LOVE TO HARVEST TWILIGHT'S TEARS...
Even fake ones.

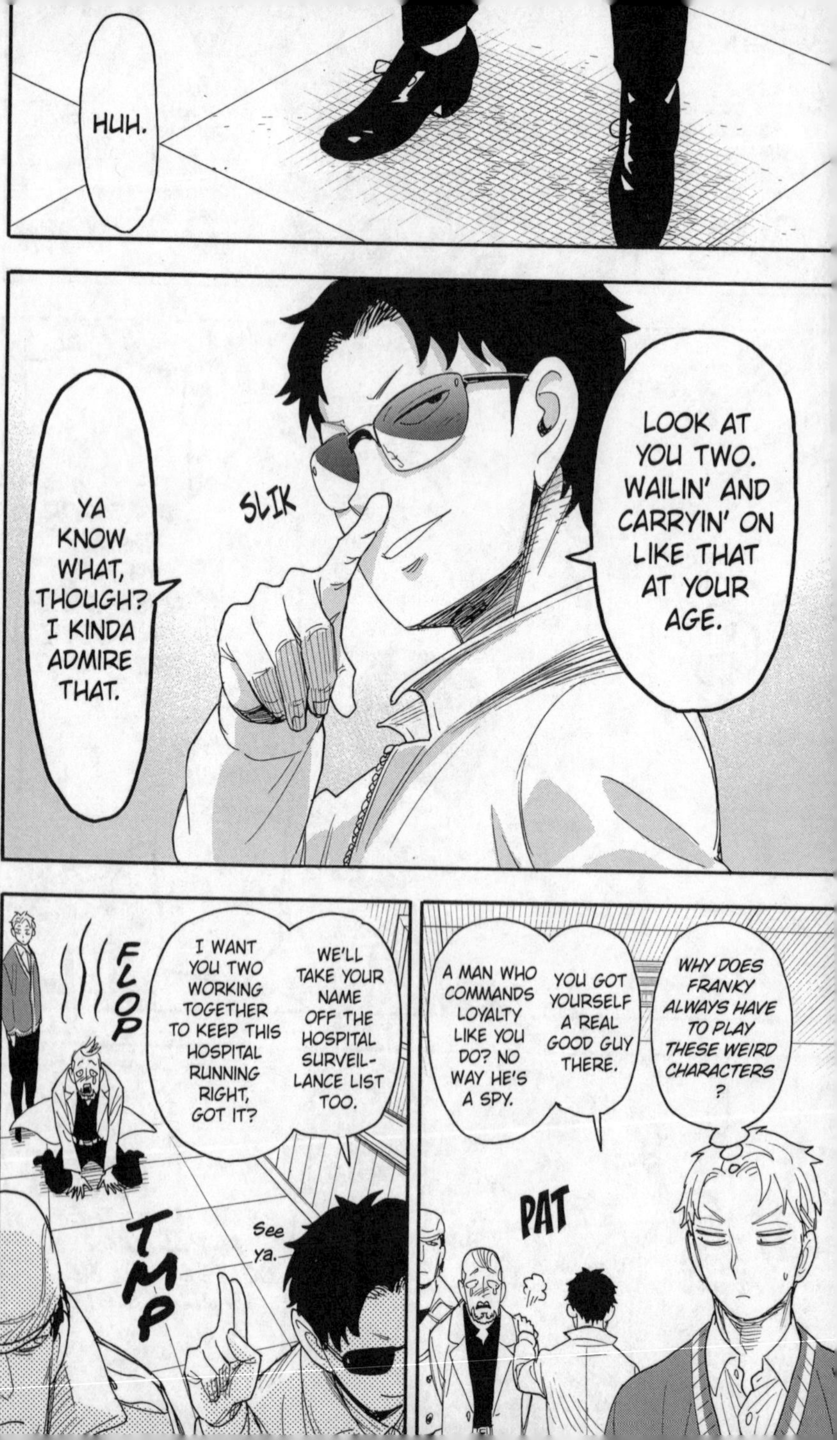
HUH.
LOOK AT YOU TWO. WAILIN' AND CARRYIN' ON LIKE THAT AT YOUR AGE.
SLIK
YA KNOW WHAT, THOUGH? I KINDA ADMIRE THAT.
WHY DOES FRANKY ALWAYS HAVE TO PLAY THESE WEIRD CHARACTERS?
YOU GOT YOURSELF A REAL GOOD GUY THERE.
A MAN WHO COMMANDS LOYALTY LIKE YOU DO? NO WAY HE'S A SPY.
PAT
WE'LL TAKE YOUR NAME OFF THE HOSPITAL SURVEIL-LANCE LIST TOO.
I WANT YOU TWO WORKING TOGETHER TO KEEP THIS HOSPITAL RUNNING RIGHT, GOT IT?
FLOP
See ya.
TMP

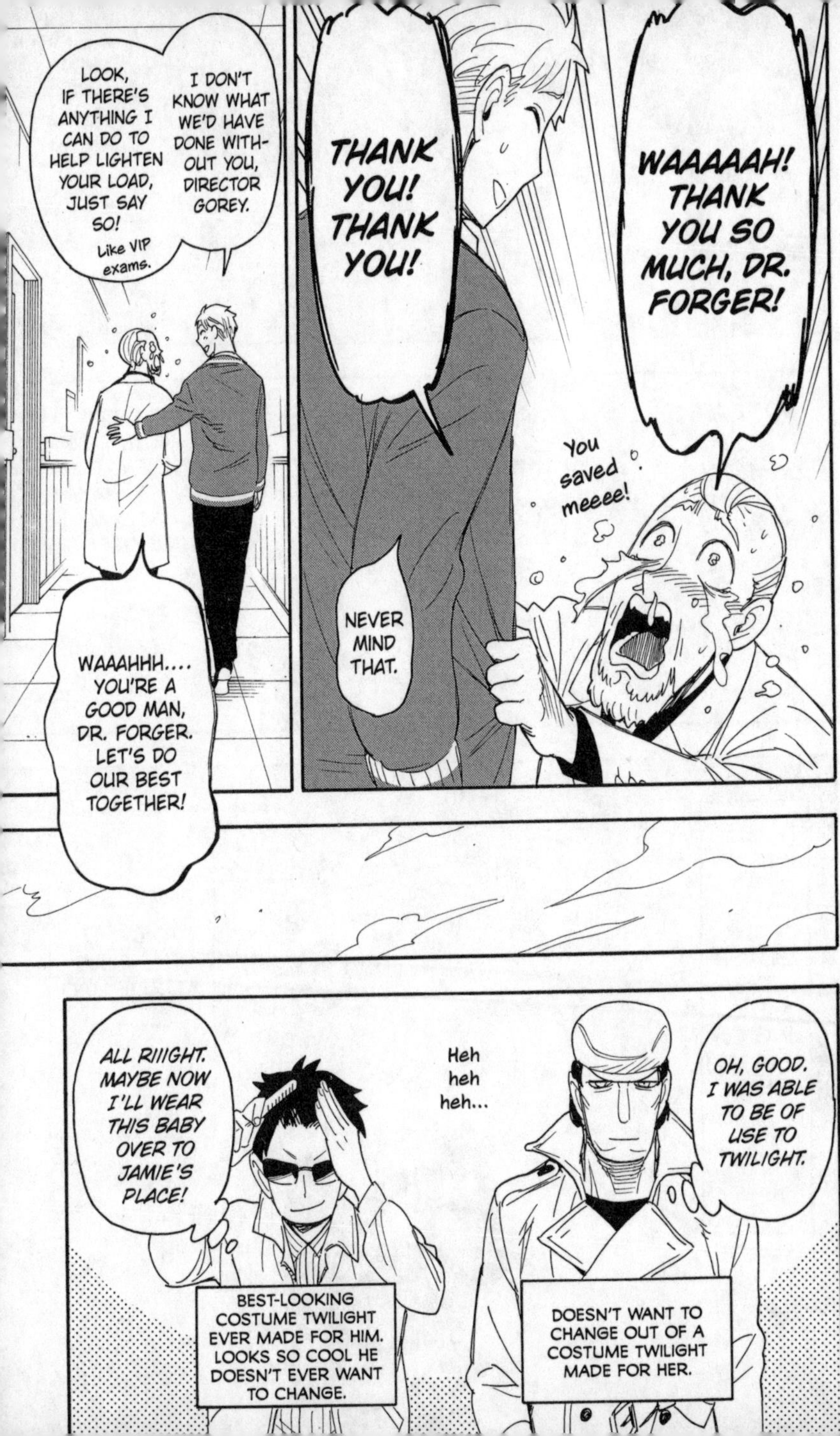
WAAAAAH! THANK YOU SO MUCH, DR. FORGER!
You saved meeee!
THANK YOU! THANK YOU!
NEVER MIND THAT.
I DON'T KNOW WHAT WE'D HAVE DONE WITH-OUT YOU, DIRECTOR GOREY.
LOOK, IF THERE'S ANYTHING I CAN DO TO HELP LIGHTEN YOUR LOAD, JUST SAY SO!
Like VIP exams.
WAAAHHH.... YOU'RE A GOOD MAN, DR. FORGER. LET'S DO OUR BEST TOGETHER!
OH, GOOD. I WAS ABLE TO BE OF USE TO TWILIGHT.
DOESN'T WANT TO CHANGE OUT OF A COSTUME TWILIGHT MADE FOR HER.
Heh heh heh...
ALL RIIIGHT. MAYBE NOW I'LL WEAR THIS BABY OVER TO JAMIE'S PLACE!
BEST-LOOKING COSTUME TWILIGHT EVER MADE FOR HIM. LOOKS SO COOL HE DOESN'T EVER WANT TO CHANGE.

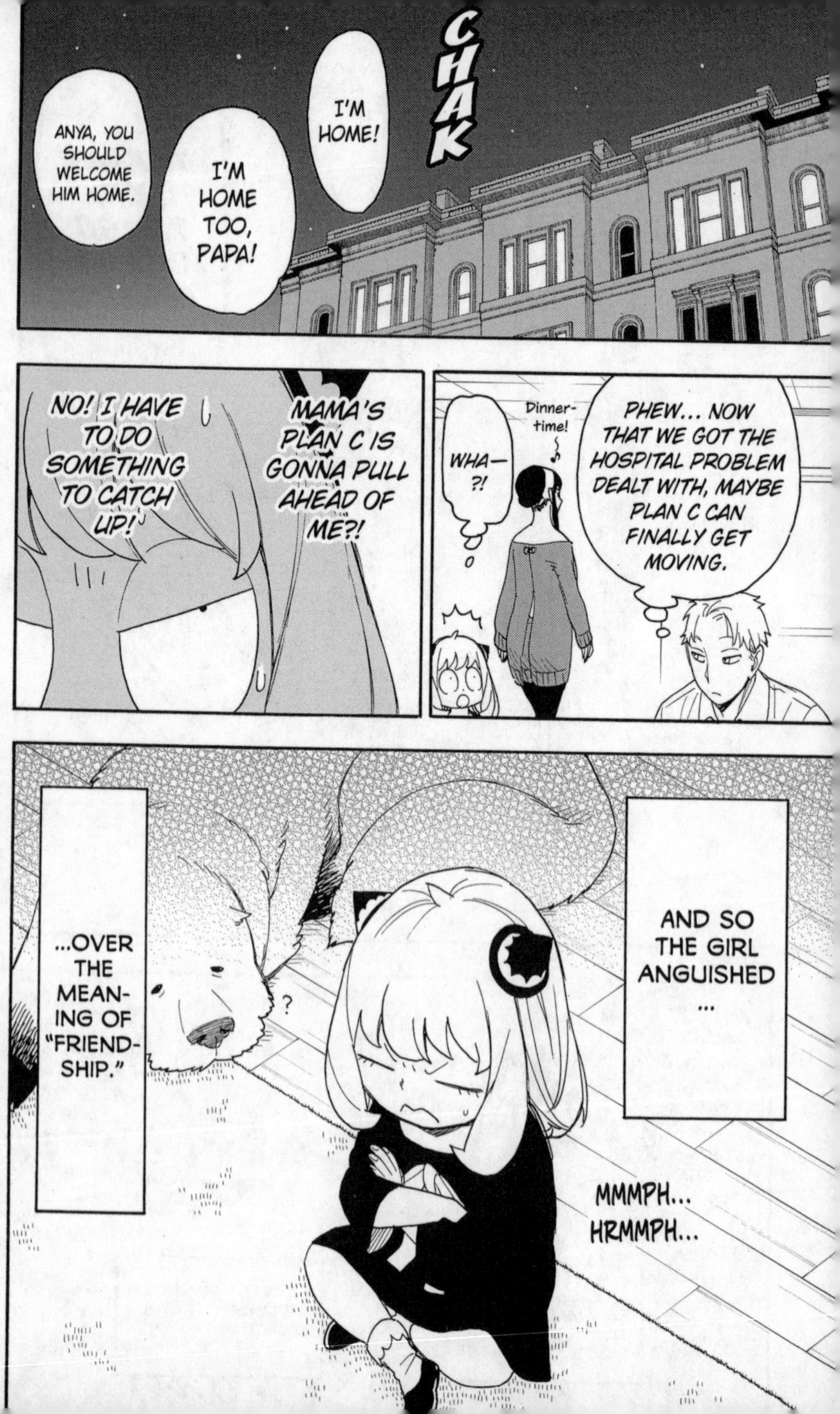
CHAK
I'M HOME!
I'M HOME TOO, PAPA!
ANYA, YOU SHOULD WELCOME HIM HOME.
PHEW... NOW THAT WE GOT THE HOSPITAL PROBLEM DEALT WITH, MAYBE PLAN C CAN FINALLY GET MOVING.
Dinner-time!
WHA—?!
MAMA'S PLAN C IS GONNA PULL AHEAD OF ME?!
NO! I HAVE TO DO SOMETHING TO CATCH UP!
AND SO THE GIRL ANGUISHED...
MMMPH... HRMMPH...
...OVER THE MEANING OF "FRIENDSHIP."

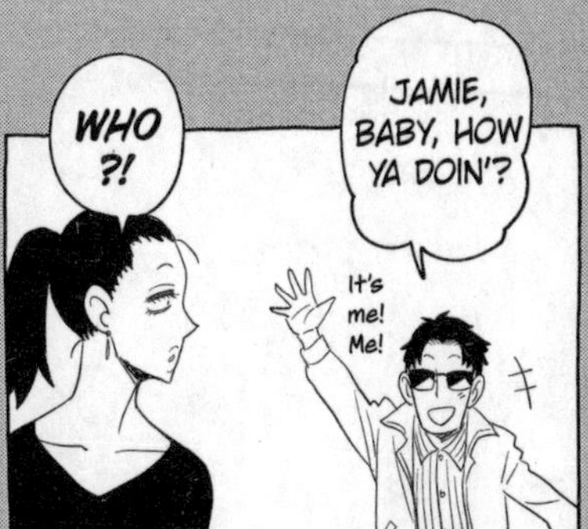
JAMIE, BABY, HOW YA DOIN'?
It's me! Me!
WHO ?!

SPY×FAMILY

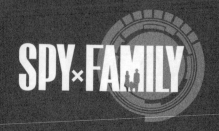

MISSION 68

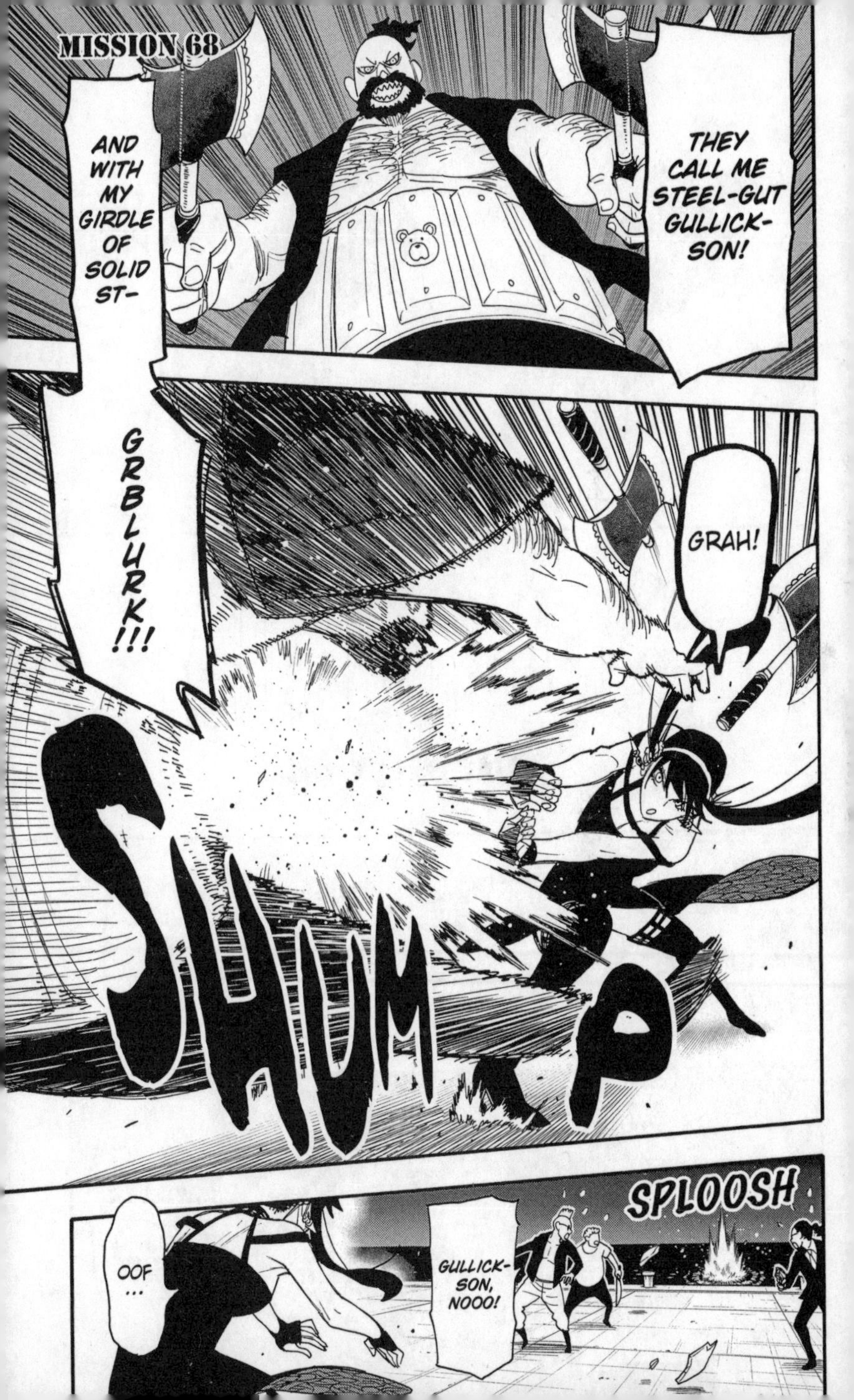
THEY CALL ME STEEL-GUT GULLICK-SON!
AND WITH MY GIRDLE OF SOLID ST-
GRAH!
GRBLURK!!!
SHUMP
SPLOOSH
GULLICK-SON, NOOO!
OOF...

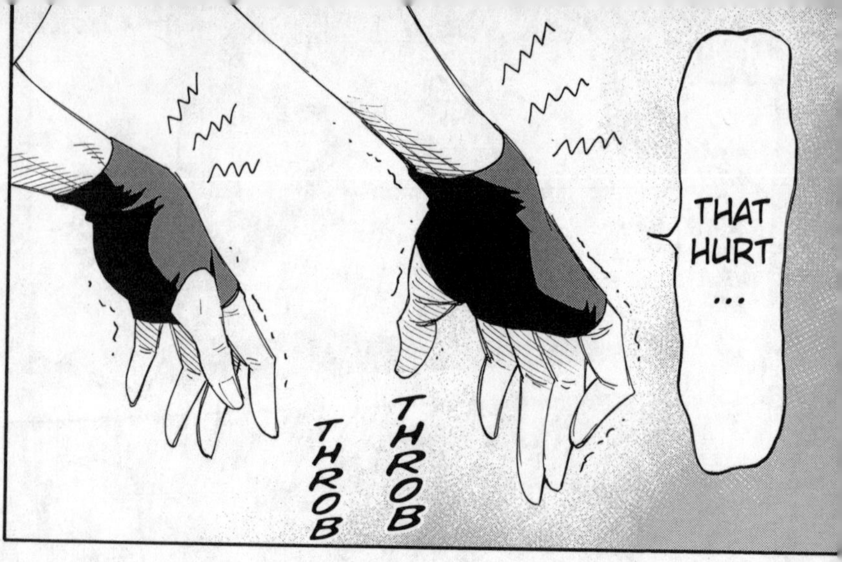
THAT HURT...
THROB
THROB

SPY×FAMILY

MISSION 68

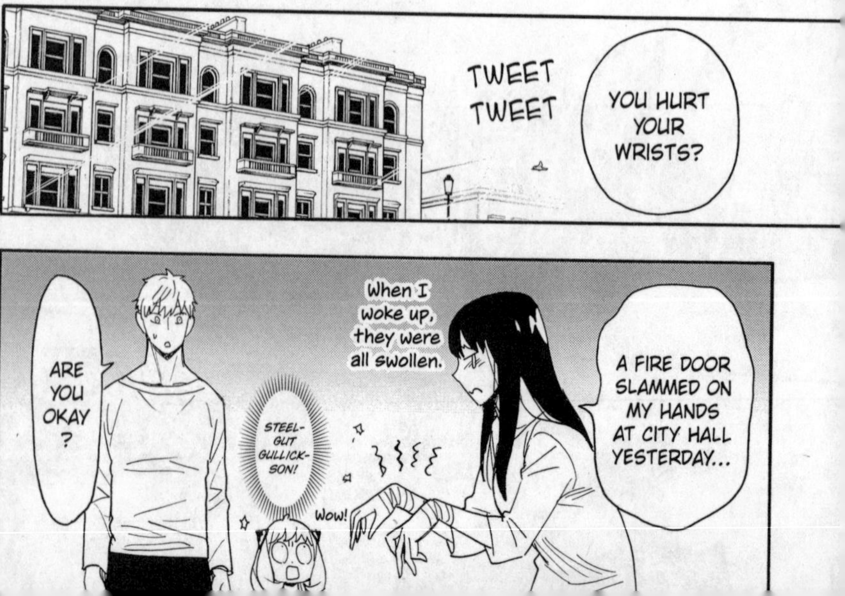
YOU HURT YOUR WRISTS?
TWEET TWEET
A FIRE DOOR SLAMMED ON MY HANDS AT CITY HALL YESTERDAY...
When I woke up, they were all swollen.
STEEL-GUT GULLICK-SON!
Wow!
ARE YOU OKAY?

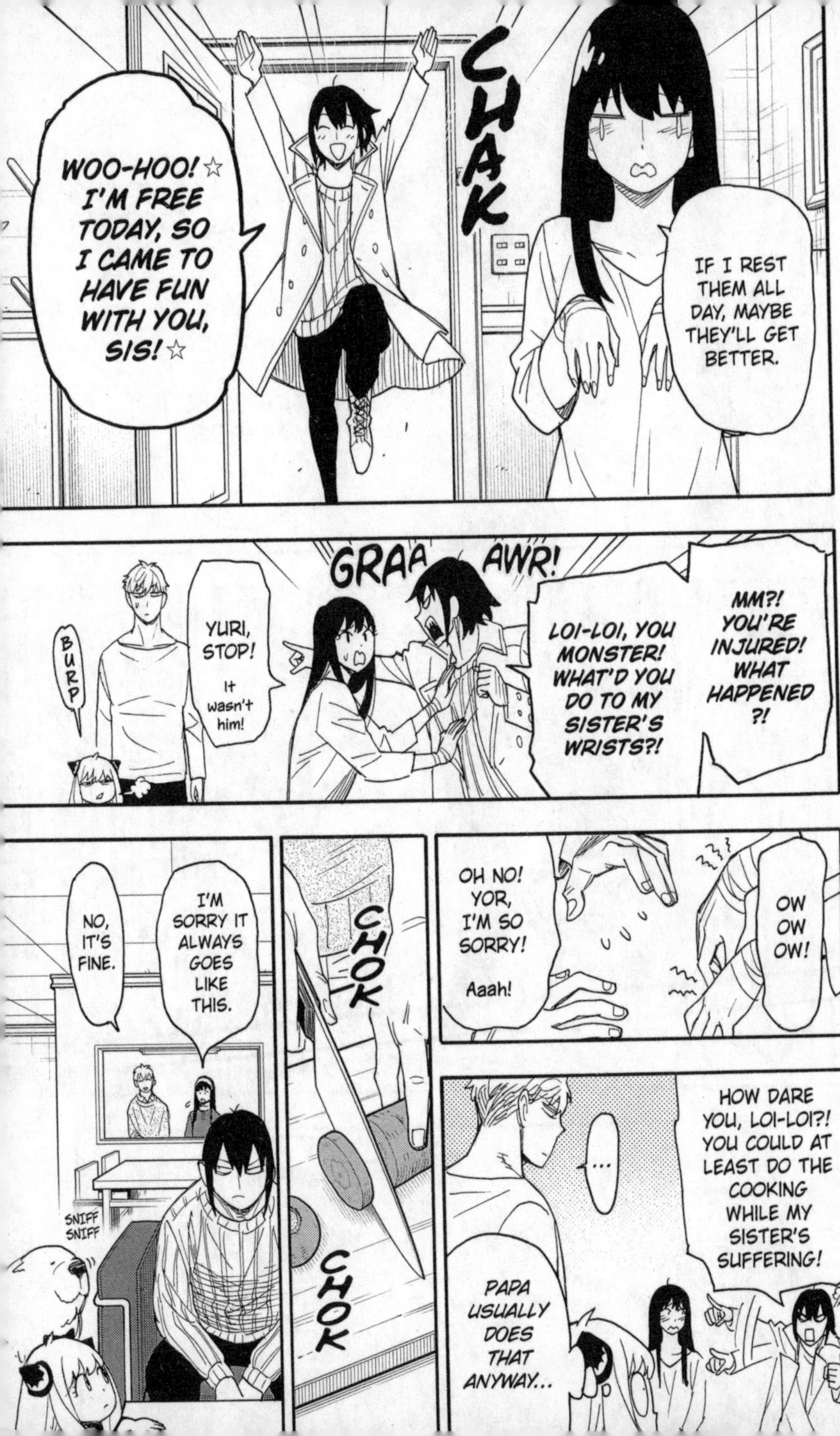
IF I REST THEM ALL DAY, MAYBE THEY'LL GET BETTER.
CHAK
WOO-HOO! ☆ I'M FREE TODAY, SO I CAME TO HAVE FUN WITH YOU, SIS! ☆
MM?! YOU'RE INJURED! WHAT HAPPENED?!
GRAAAWR!
LOI-LOI, YOU MONSTER! WHAT'D YOU DO TO MY SISTER'S WRISTS?!
YURI, STOP!
It wasn't him!
BURP
OW OW OW!
OH NO! YOR, I'M SO SORRY!
Aaah!
HOW DARE YOU, LOI-LOI?! YOU COULD AT LEAST DO THE COOKING WHILE MY SISTER'S SUFFERING!
...
PAPA USUALLY DOES THAT ANYWAY...
CHOK
CHOK
CHOK
I'M SORRY IT ALWAYS GOES LIKE THIS.
NO, IT'S FINE.
SNIFF SNIFF

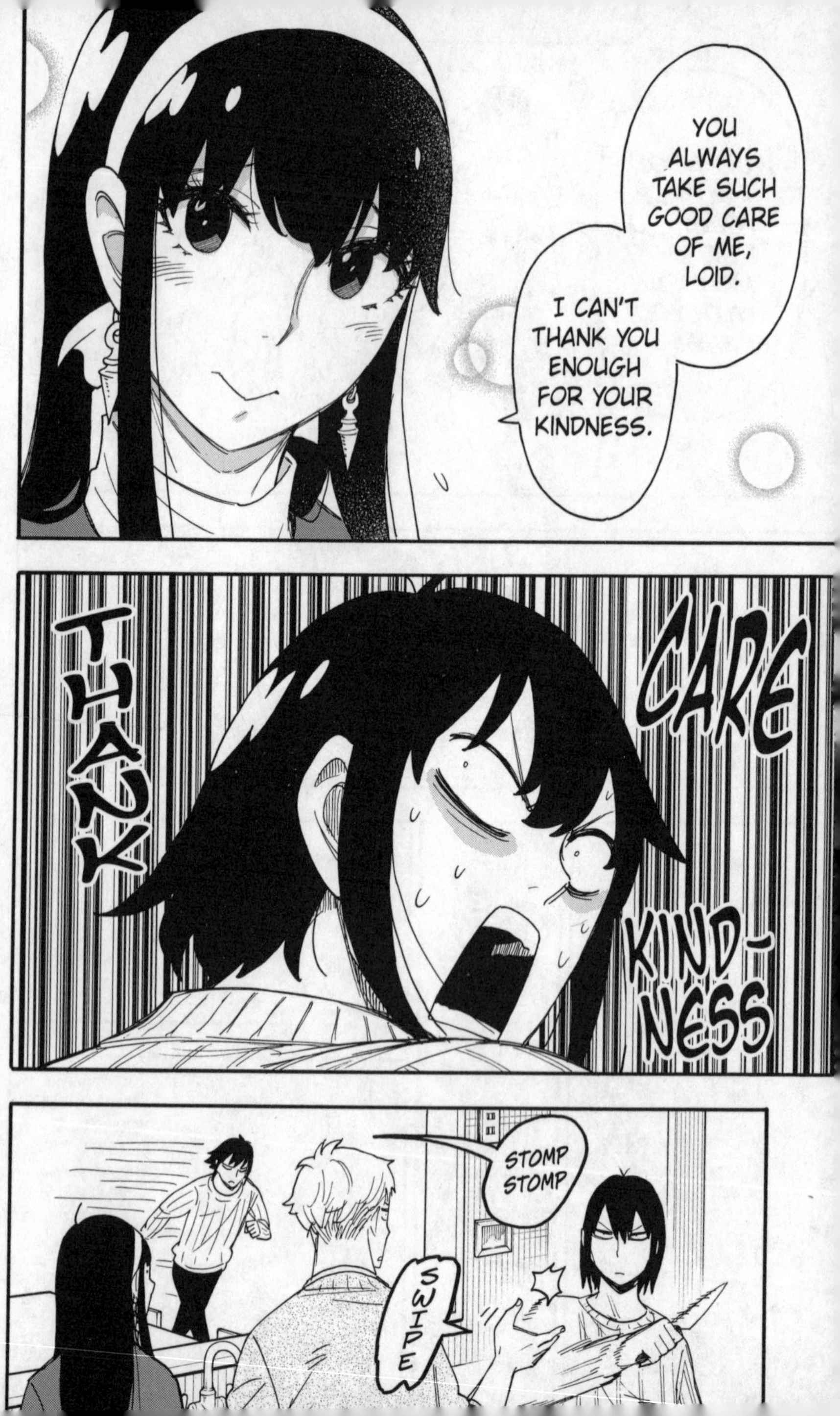
YOU ALWAYS TAKE SUCH GOOD CARE OF ME, LOID.
I CAN'T THANK YOU ENOUGH FOR YOUR KINDNESS.
CARE
KIND-NESS
THANK
STOMP STOMP
SWIPE

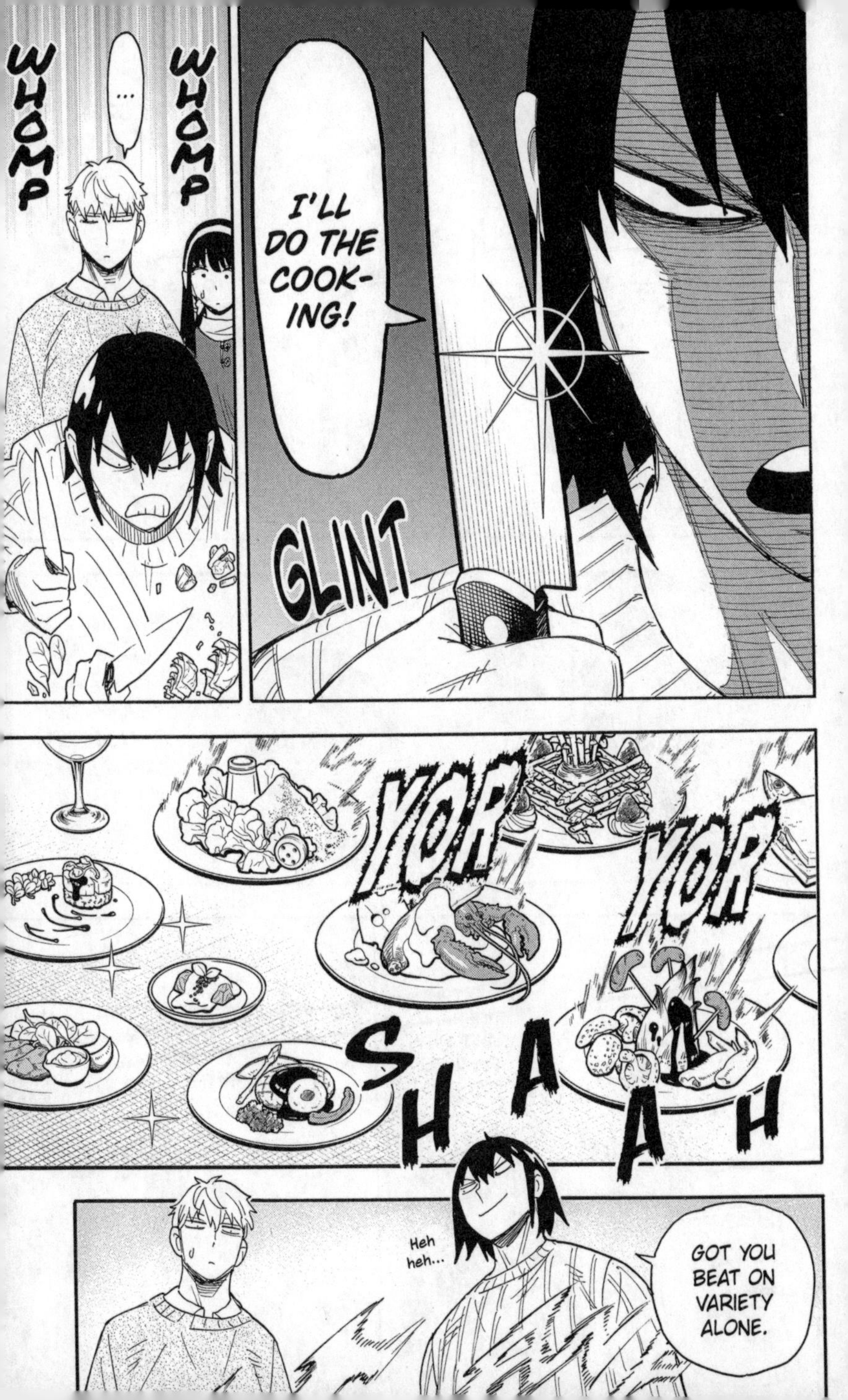
I'LL DO THE COOK-ING!
GLINT
WHOMP
...
WHOMP
YOR
YOR
SHAAH
Heh heh...
GOT YOU BEAT ON VARIETY ALONE.

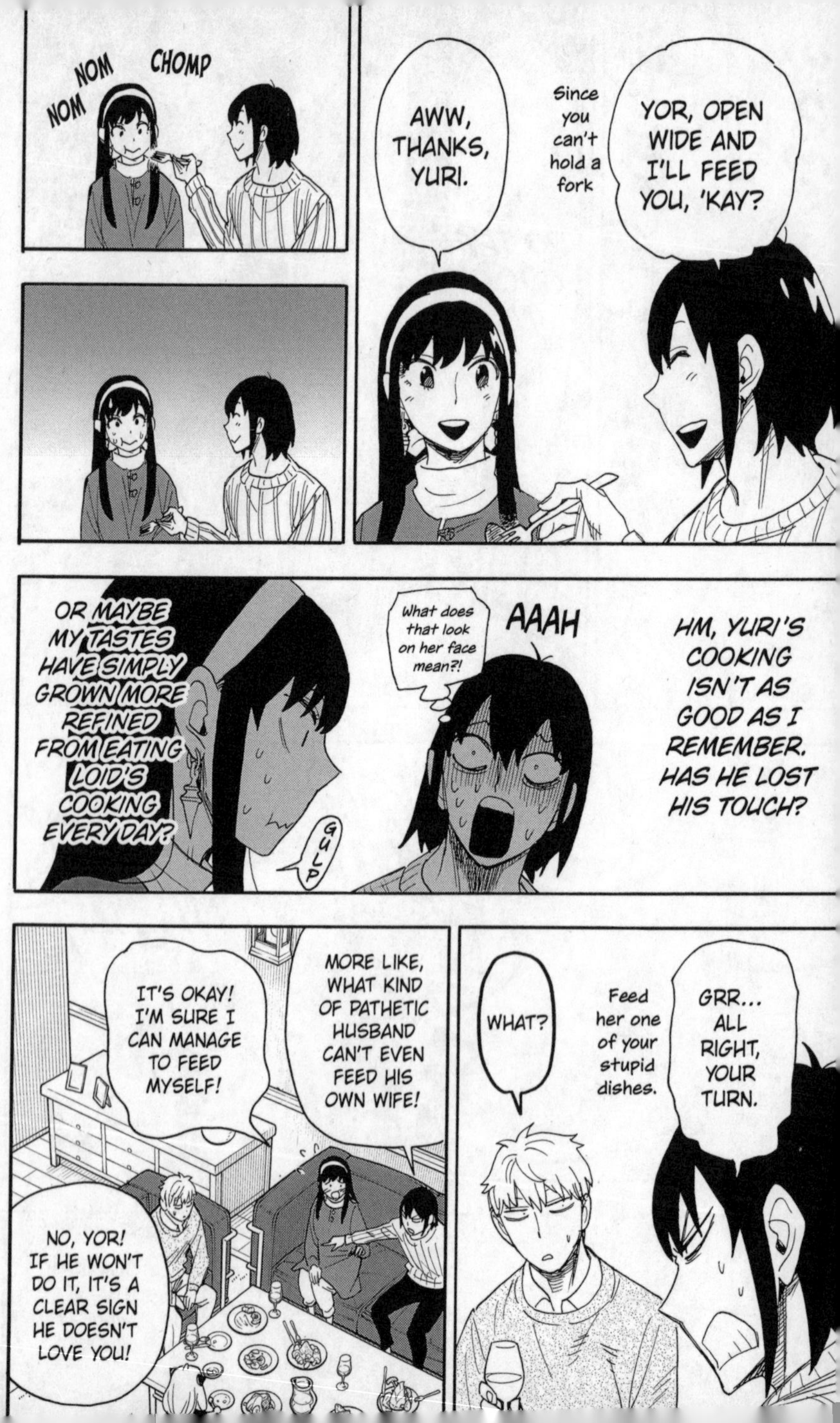
YOR, OPEN WIDE AND I'LL FEED YOU, 'KAY?
Since you can't hold a fork
AWW, THANKS, YURI.
CHOMP
NOM NOM
HM, YURI'S COOKING ISN'T AS GOOD AS I REMEMBER. HAS HE LOST HIS TOUCH?
AAAH
What does that look on her face mean?!
GULP
OR MAYBE MY TASTES HAVE SIMPLY GROWN MORE REFINED FROM EATING LOID'S COOKING EVERY DAY?
GRR... ALL RIGHT, YOUR TURN.
Feed her one of your stupid dishes.
WHAT?
MORE LIKE, WHAT KIND OF PATHETIC HUSBAND CAN'T EVEN FEED HIS OWN WIFE!
IT'S OKAY! I'M SURE I CAN MANAGE TO FEED MYSELF!
NO, YOR! IF HE WON'T DO IT, IT'S A CLEAR SIGN HE DOESN'T LOVE YOU!

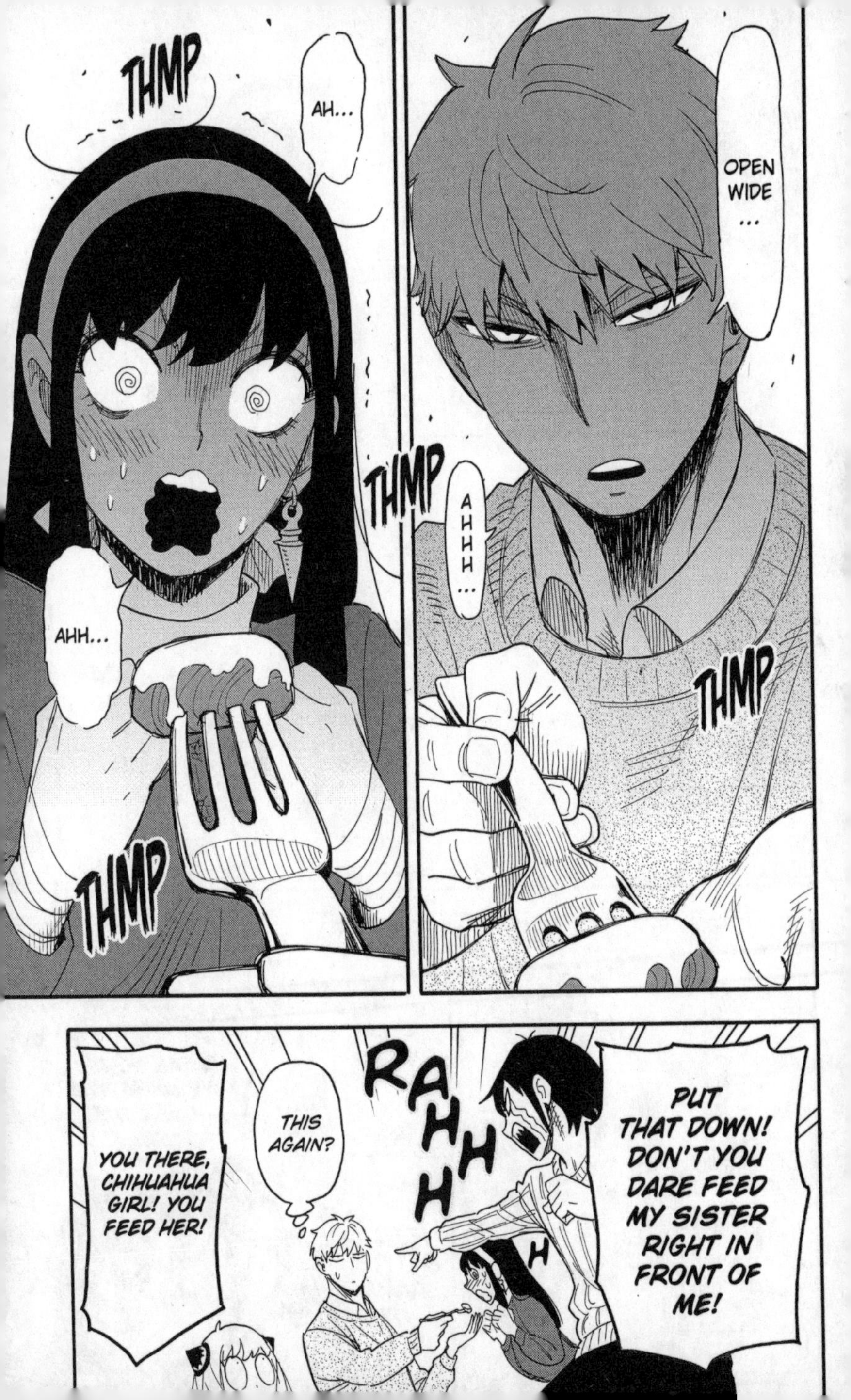
OPEN WIDE ...
THMP
AHHH...
THMP
THMP
AH...
AHH...
THMP
PUT THAT DOWN! DON'T YOU DARE FEED MY SISTER RIGHT IN FRONT OF ME!
RAHHHHH
THIS AGAIN?
YOU THERE, CHIHUAHUA GIRL! YOU FEED HER!

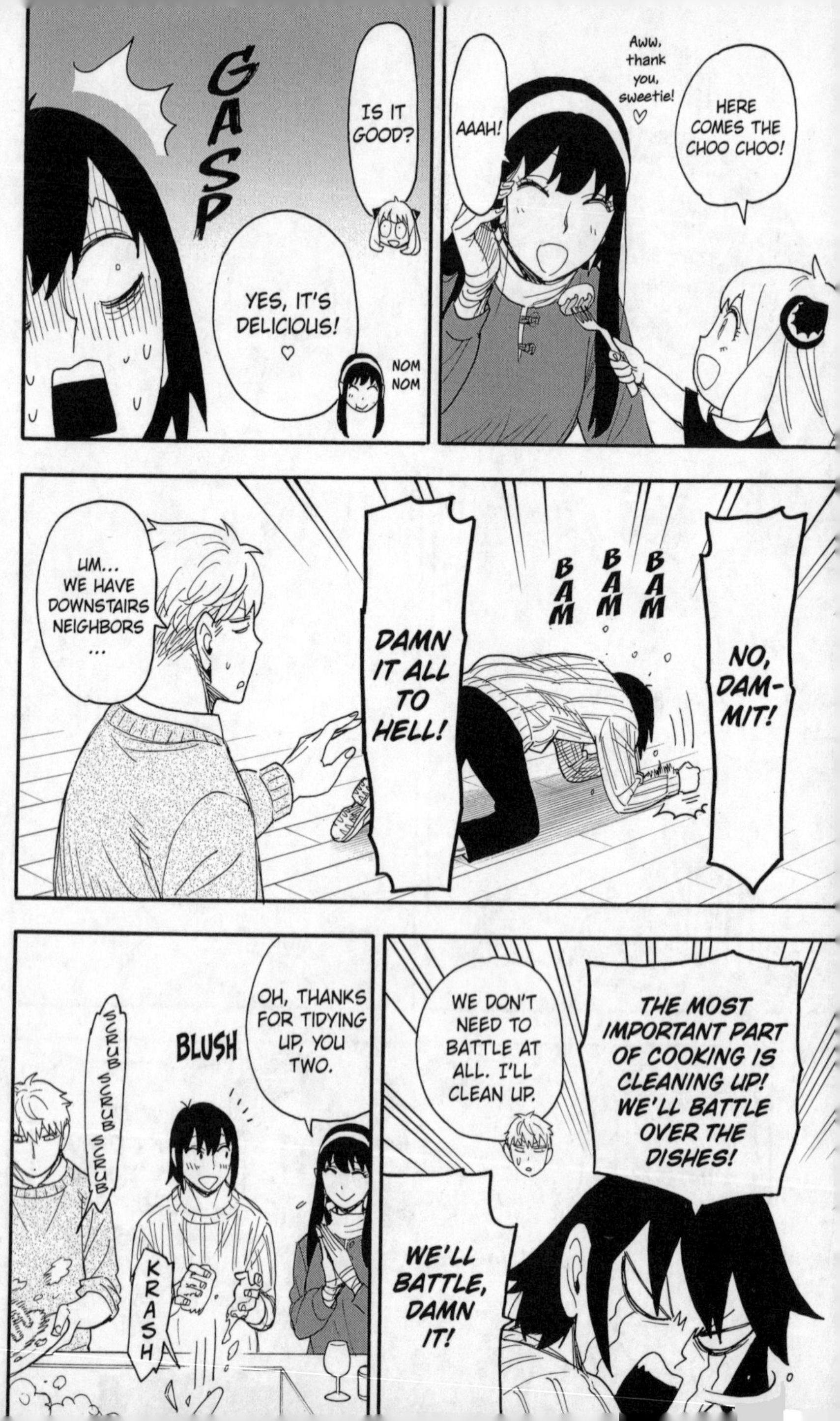
HERE COMES THE CHOO CHOO!
Aww, thank you, sweetie! ♡
AAAH!
IS IT GOOD?
GASP
YES, IT'S DELICIOUS! ♡
NOM NOM
NO, DAM-MIT!
BAM BAM BAM
DAMN IT ALL TO HELL!
UM... WE HAVE DOWNSTAIRS NEIGHBORS...
THE MOST IMPORTANT PART OF COOKING IS CLEANING UP! WE'LL BATTLE OVER THE DISHES!
WE DON'T NEED TO BATTLE AT ALL. I'LL CLEAN UP.
WE'LL BATTLE, DAMN IT!
OH, THANKS FOR TIDYING UP, YOU TWO.
BLUSH
SCRUB SCRUB SCRUB
KRASH

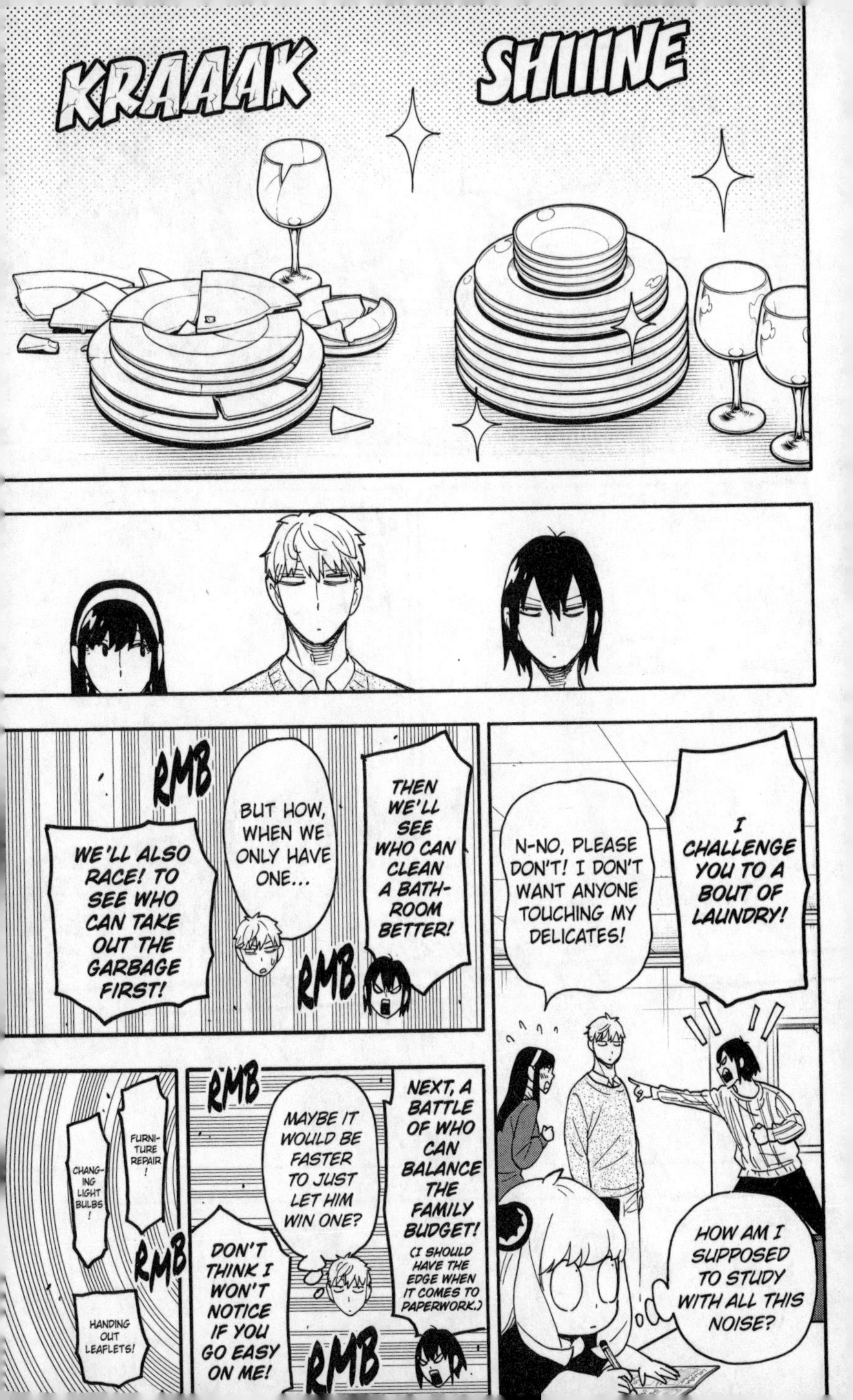
SHIIINE
KRAAAK
I CHALLENGE YOU TO A BOUT OF LAUNDRY!
N-NO, PLEASE DON'T! I DON'T WANT ANYONE TOUCHING MY DELICATES!
HOW AM I SUPPOSED TO STUDY WITH ALL THIS NOISE?
THEN WE'LL SEE WHO CAN CLEAN A BATH-ROOM BETTER!
RMB
BUT HOW, WHEN WE ONLY HAVE ONE...
WE'LL ALSO RACE! TO SEE WHO CAN TAKE OUT THE GARBAGE FIRST!
RMB
NEXT, A BATTLE OF WHO CAN BALANCE THE FAMILY BUDGET!
(I SHOULD HAVE THE EDGE WHEN IT COMES TO PAPERWORK.)
MAYBE IT WOULD BE FASTER TO JUST LET HIM WIN ONE?
RMB
DON'T THINK I WON'T NOTICE IF YOU GO EASY ON ME!
RMB
FURNI-TURE REPAIR!
CHANG-ING LIGHT BULBS!
RMB
HANDING OUT LEAFLETS!

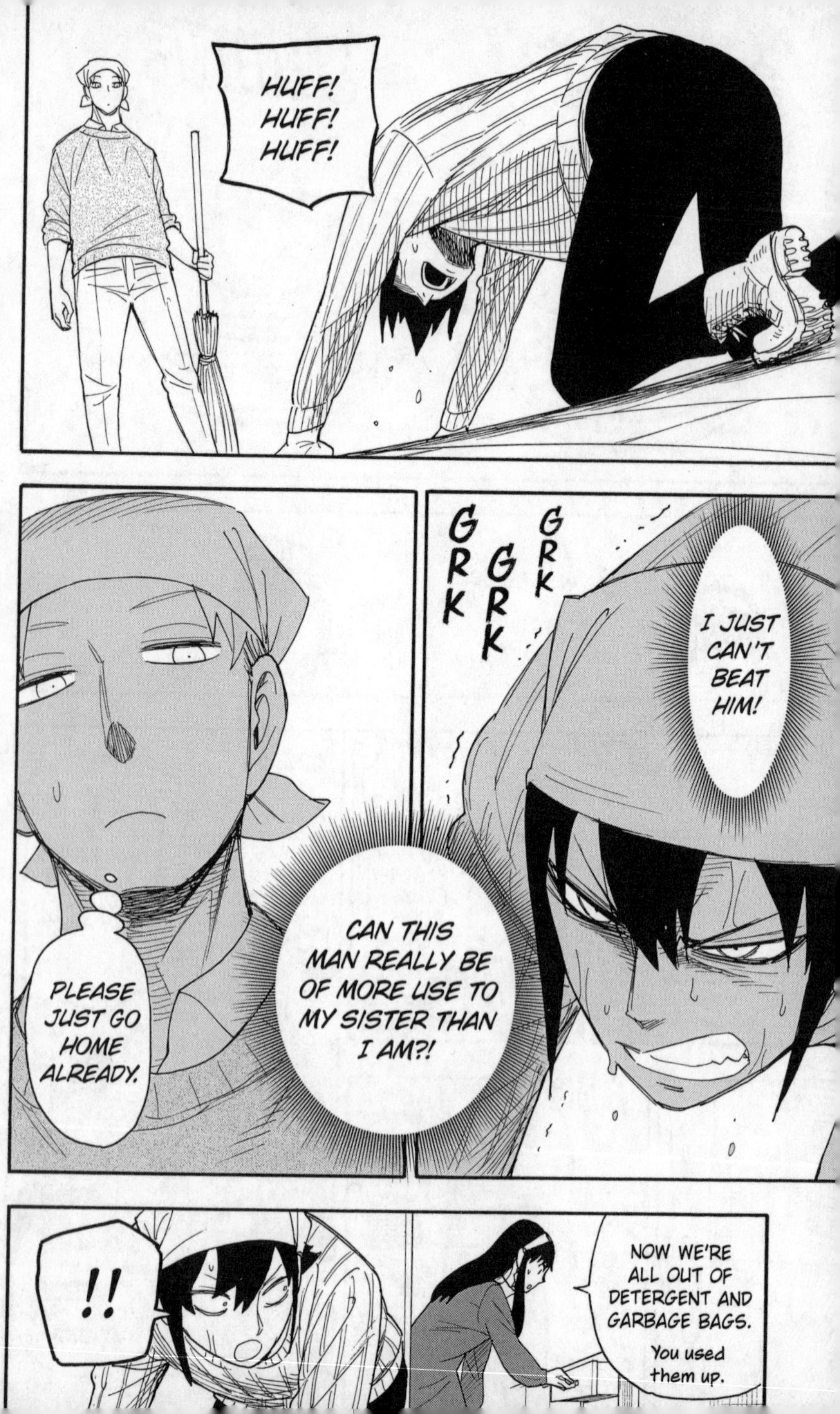
HUFF! HUFF! HUFF!
GRK GRK GRK
I JUST CAN'T BEAT HIM!
CAN THIS MAN REALLY BE OF MORE USE TO MY SISTER THAN I AM?!
PLEASE JUST GO HOME ALREADY.
NOW WE'RE ALL OUT OF DETERGENT AND GARBAGE BAGS.
You used them up.
!!

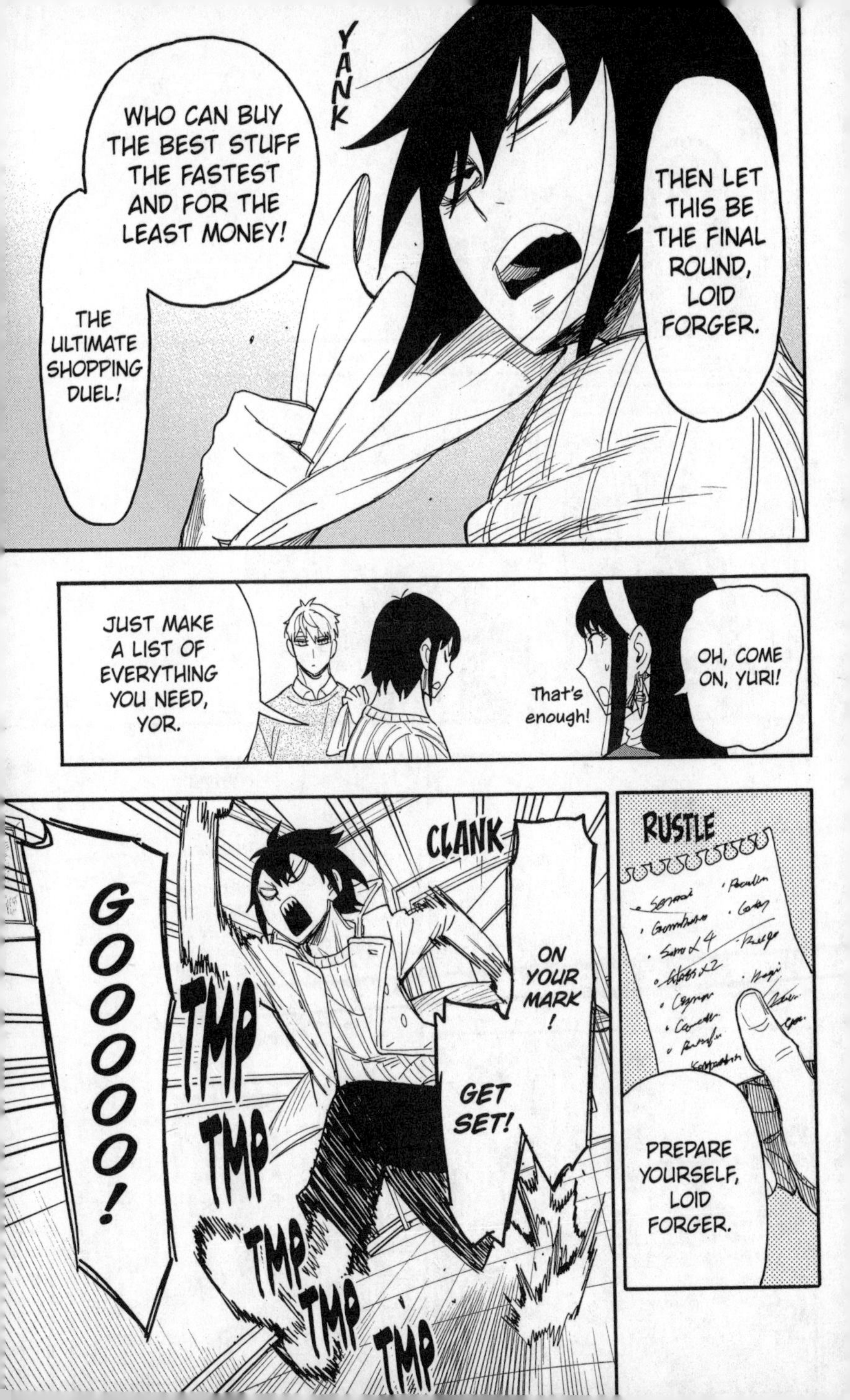
THEN LET THIS BE THE FINAL ROUND, LOID FORGER.
YANK
WHO CAN BUY THE BEST STUFF THE FASTEST AND FOR THE LEAST MONEY!
THE ULTIMATE SHOPPING DUEL!
OH, COME ON, YURI!
That's enough!
JUST MAKE A LIST OF EVERYTHING YOU NEED, YOR.
RUSTLE
PREPARE YOURSELF, LOID FORGER.
CLANK
ON YOUR MARK!
GET SET!
GOOOOOO!
TMP
TMP
TMP
TMP
TMP

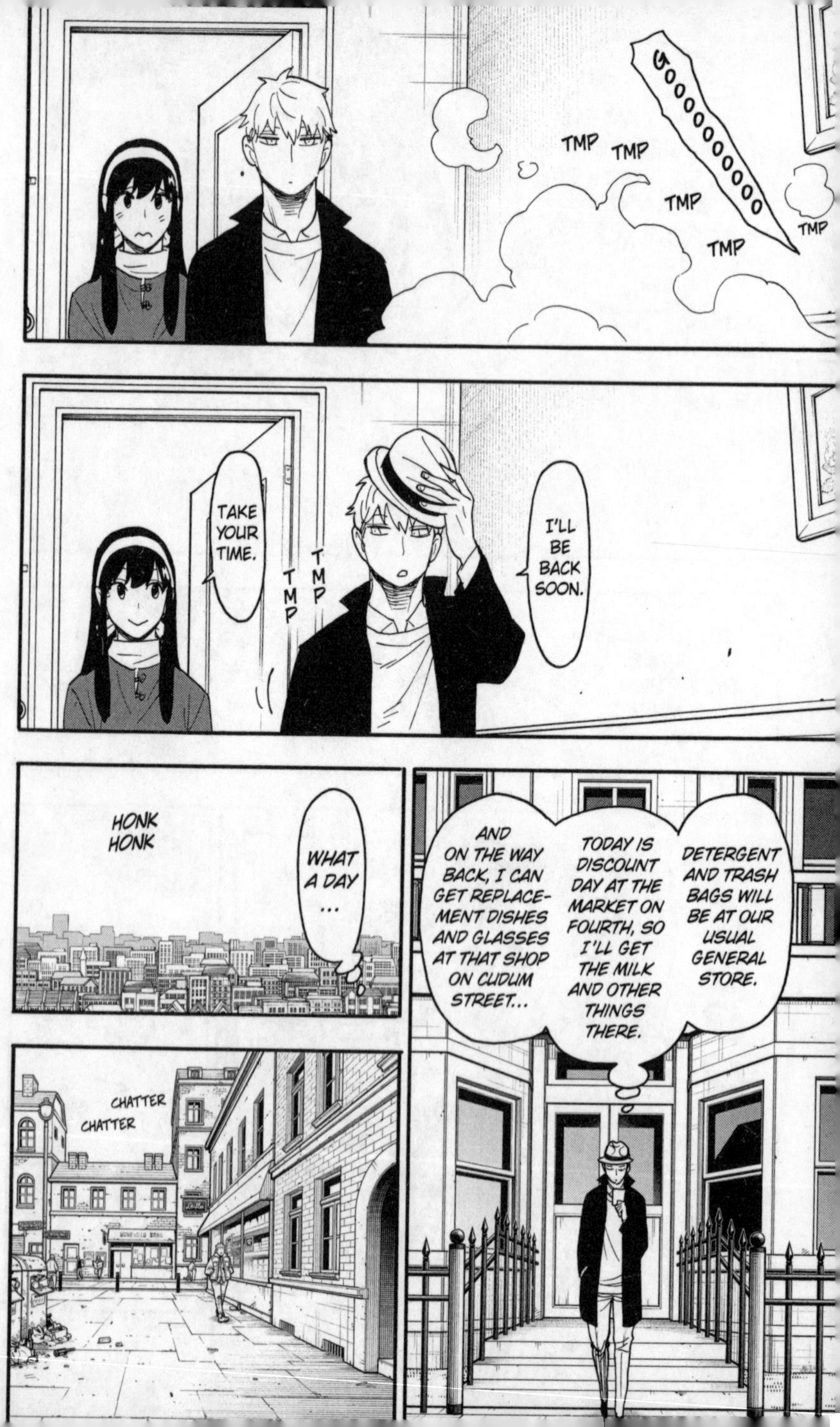
GOOOOOOOOOO
TMP
TMP
TMP
TMP
TMP
I'LL BE BACK SOON.
TMP
TMP
TAKE YOUR TIME.
DETERGENT AND TRASH BAGS WILL BE AT OUR USUAL GENERAL STORE.
TODAY IS DISCOUNT DAY AT THE MARKET ON FOURTH, SO I'LL GET THE MILK AND OTHER THINGS THERE.
AND ON THE WAY BACK, I CAN GET REPLACEMENT DISHES AND GLASSES AT THAT SHOP ON CUDUM STREET...
WHAT A DAY ...
HONK HONK
CHATTER
CHATTER

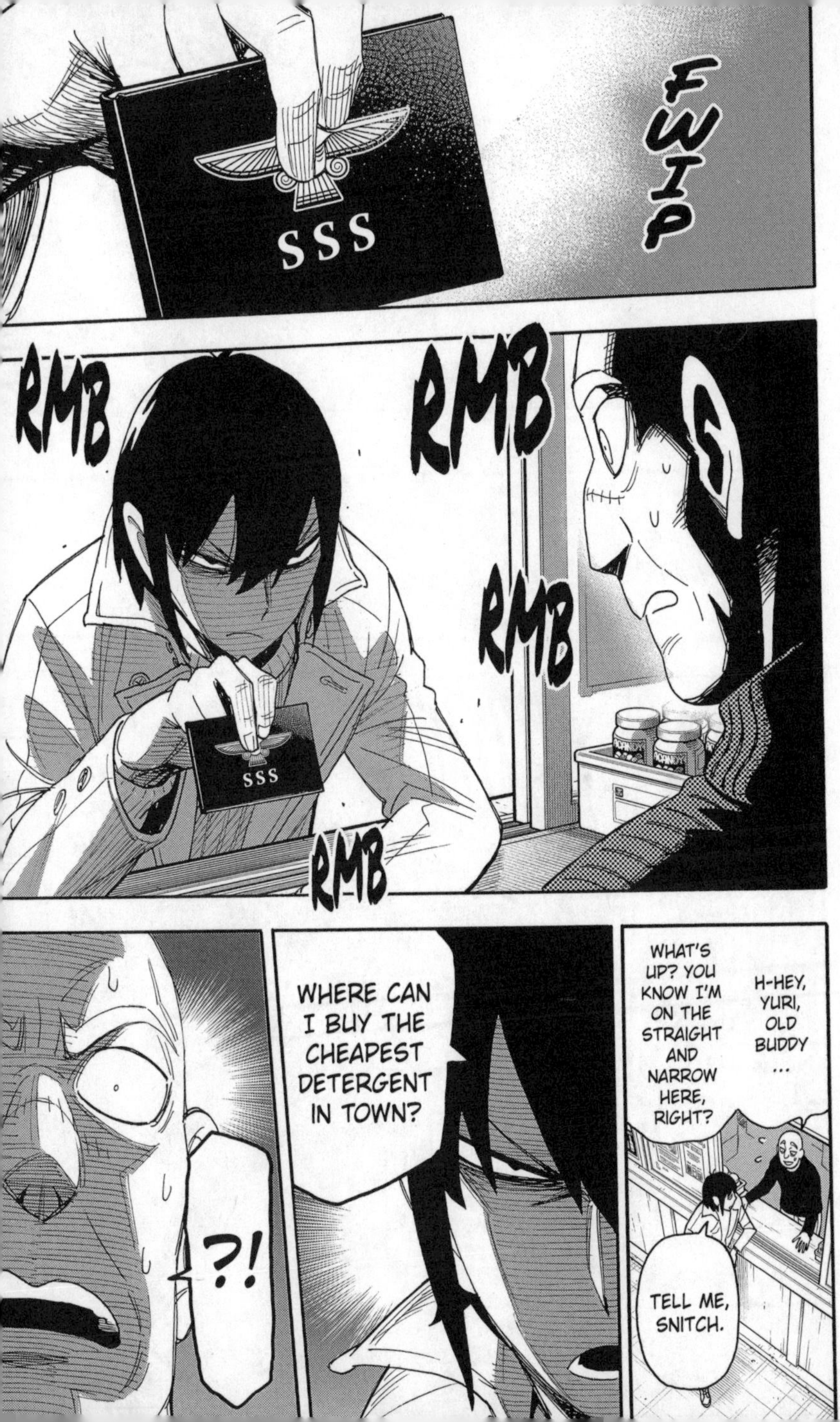
FWIP
RMB
RMB
RMB
RMB
H-HEY, YURI, OLD BUDDY...
WHAT'S UP? YOU KNOW I'M ON THE STRAIGHT AND NARROW HERE, RIGHT?
TELL ME, SNITCH.
WHERE CAN I BUY THE CHEAPEST DETERGENT IN TOWN?
?!

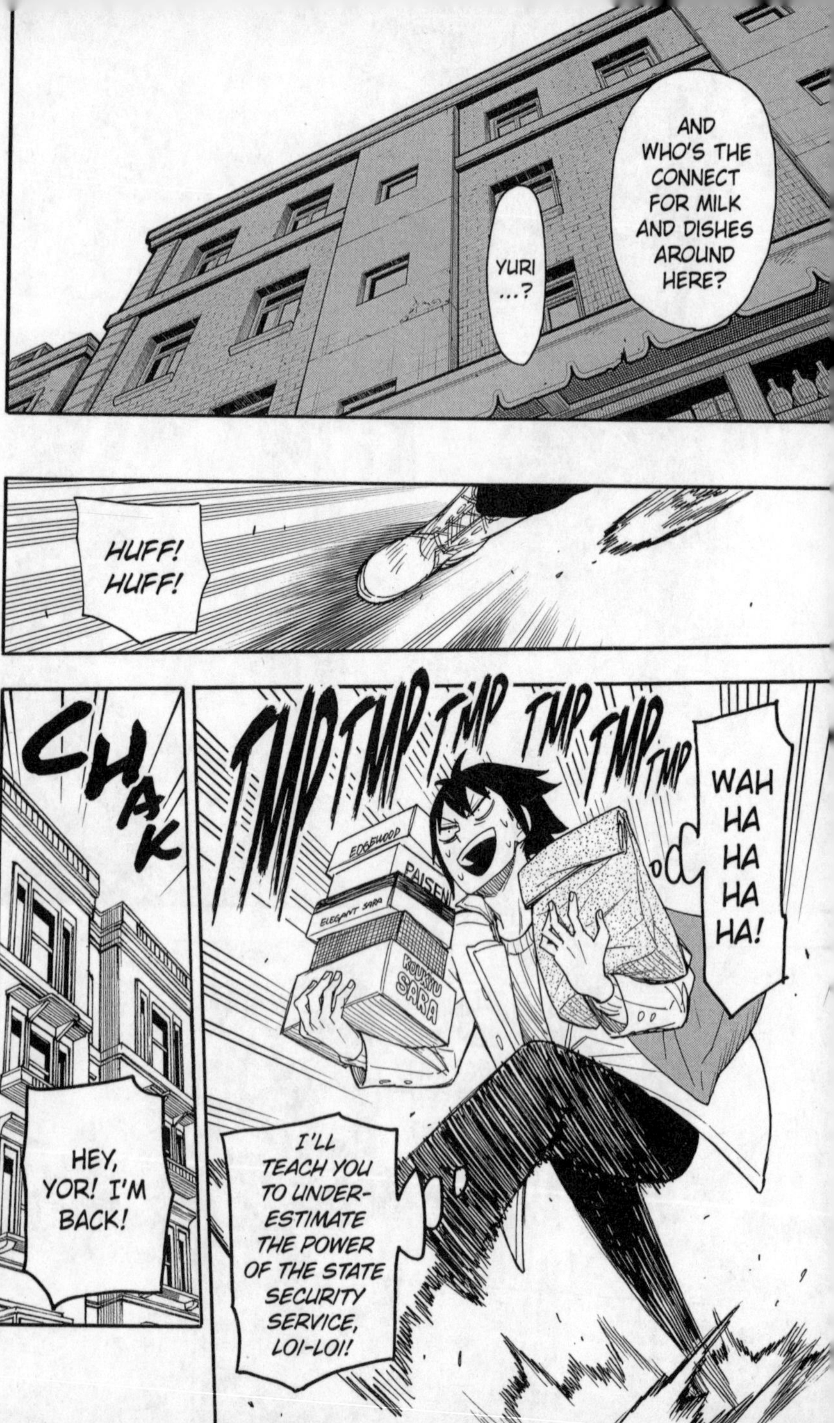
AND WHO'S THE CONNECT FOR MILK AND DISHES AROUND HERE?
YURI ...?
HUFF! HUFF!
TMP TMP TMP TMP TMP TMP
WAH HA HA HA HA!
EDGEWOOD
PAISEN
ELEGANT SARA
KOUKYU SARA
I'LL TEACH YOU TO UNDER-ESTIMATE THE POWER OF THE STATE SECURITY SERVICE, LOI-LOI!
CHAK
HEY, YOR! I'M BACK!

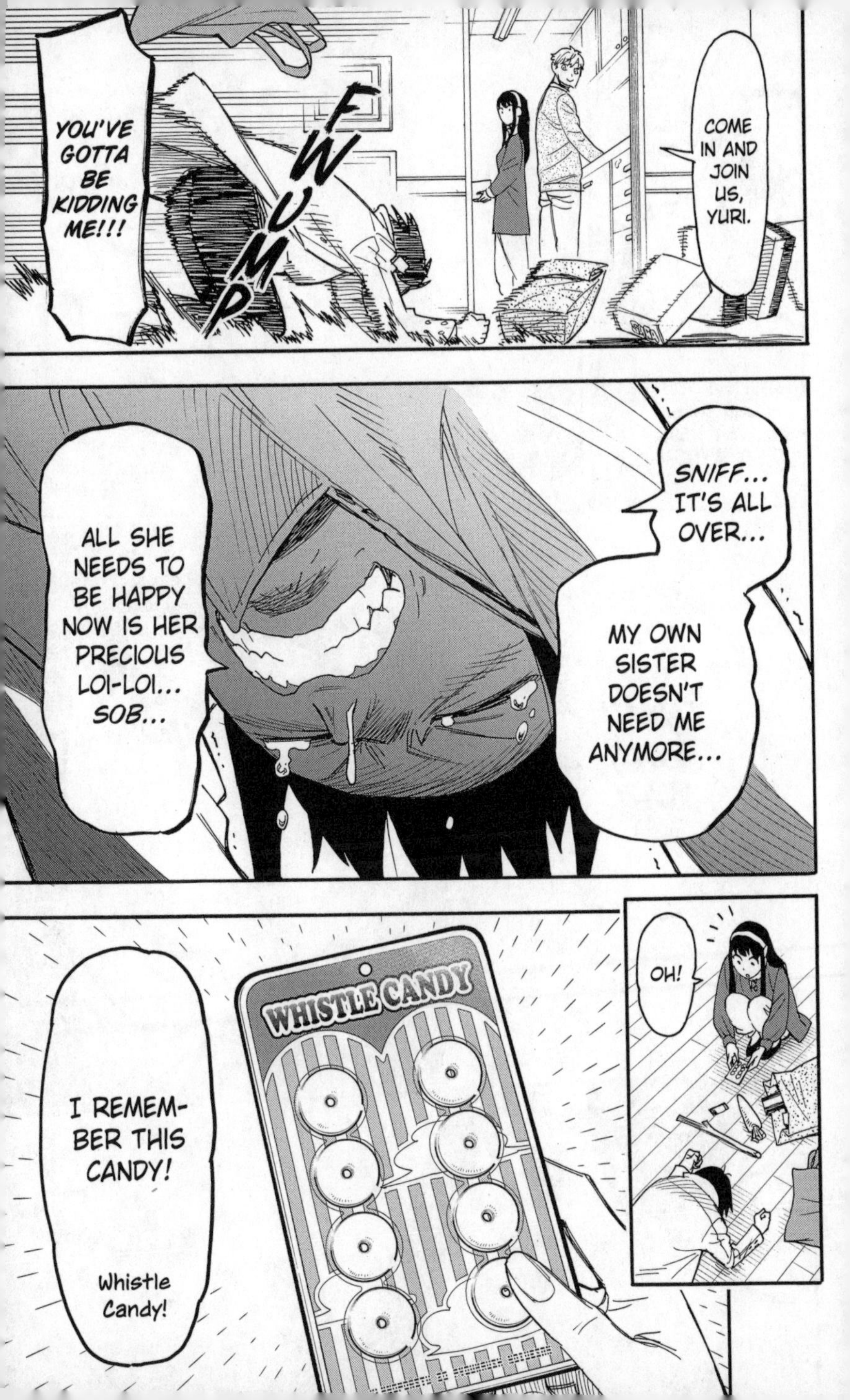
COME IN AND JOIN US, YURI.
FWUMP
YOU'VE GOTTA BE KIDDING ME!!!
SNIFF... IT'S ALL OVER...
MY OWN SISTER DOESN'T NEED ME ANYMORE...
ALL SHE NEEDS TO BE HAPPY NOW IS HER PRECIOUS LOI-LOI... SOB...
OH!
WHISTLE CANDY
I REMEM-BER THIS CANDY!
Whistle Candy!

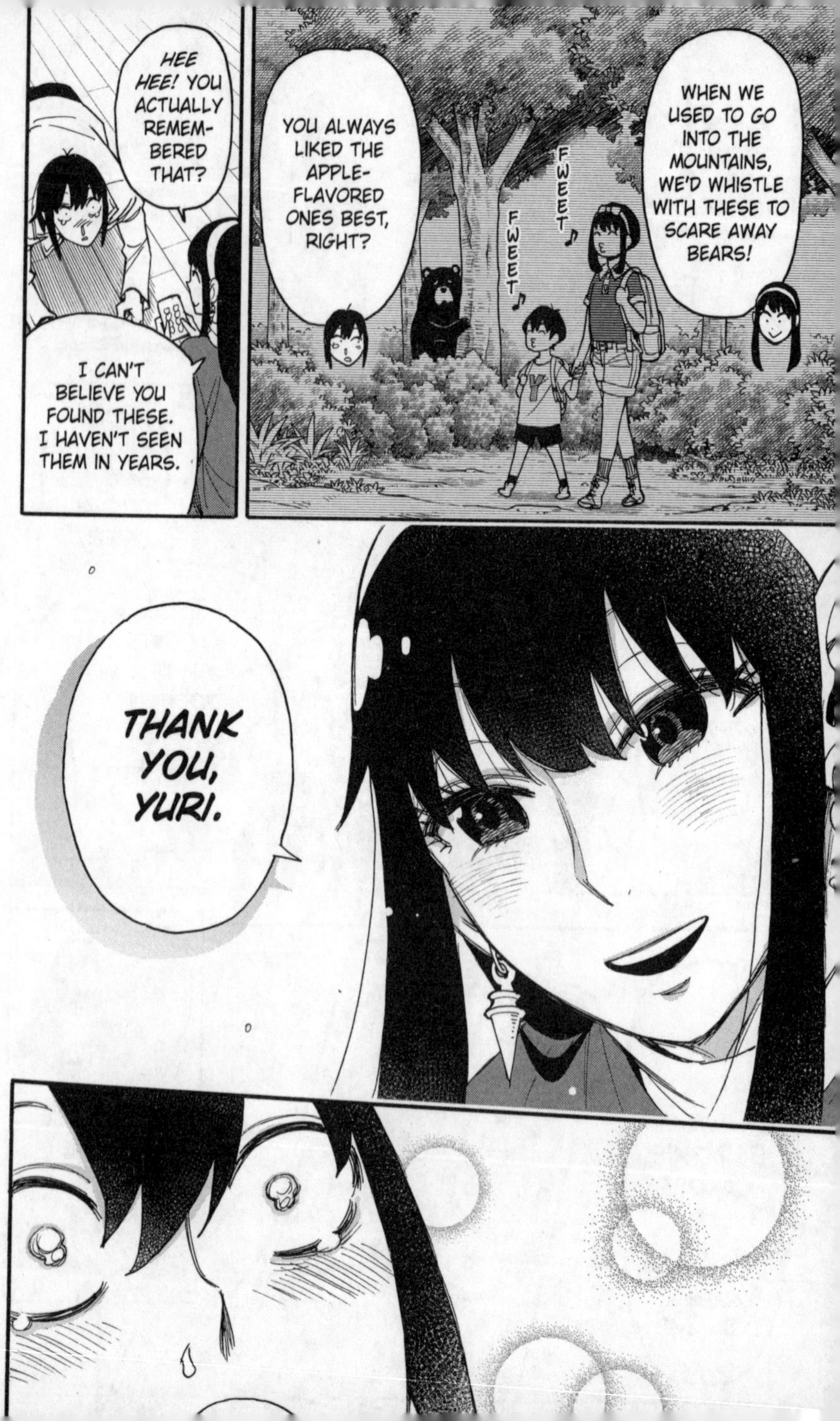
WHEN WE USED TO GO INTO THE MOUNTAINS, WE'D WHISTLE WITH THESE TO SCARE AWAY BEARS!
FWEET
FWEET
YOU ALWAYS LIKED THE APPLE-FLAVORED ONES BEST, RIGHT?
HEE HEE! YOU ACTUALLY REMEMBERED THAT?
I CAN'T BELIEVE YOU FOUND THESE. I HAVEN'T SEEN THEM IN YEARS.
THANK YOU, YURI.

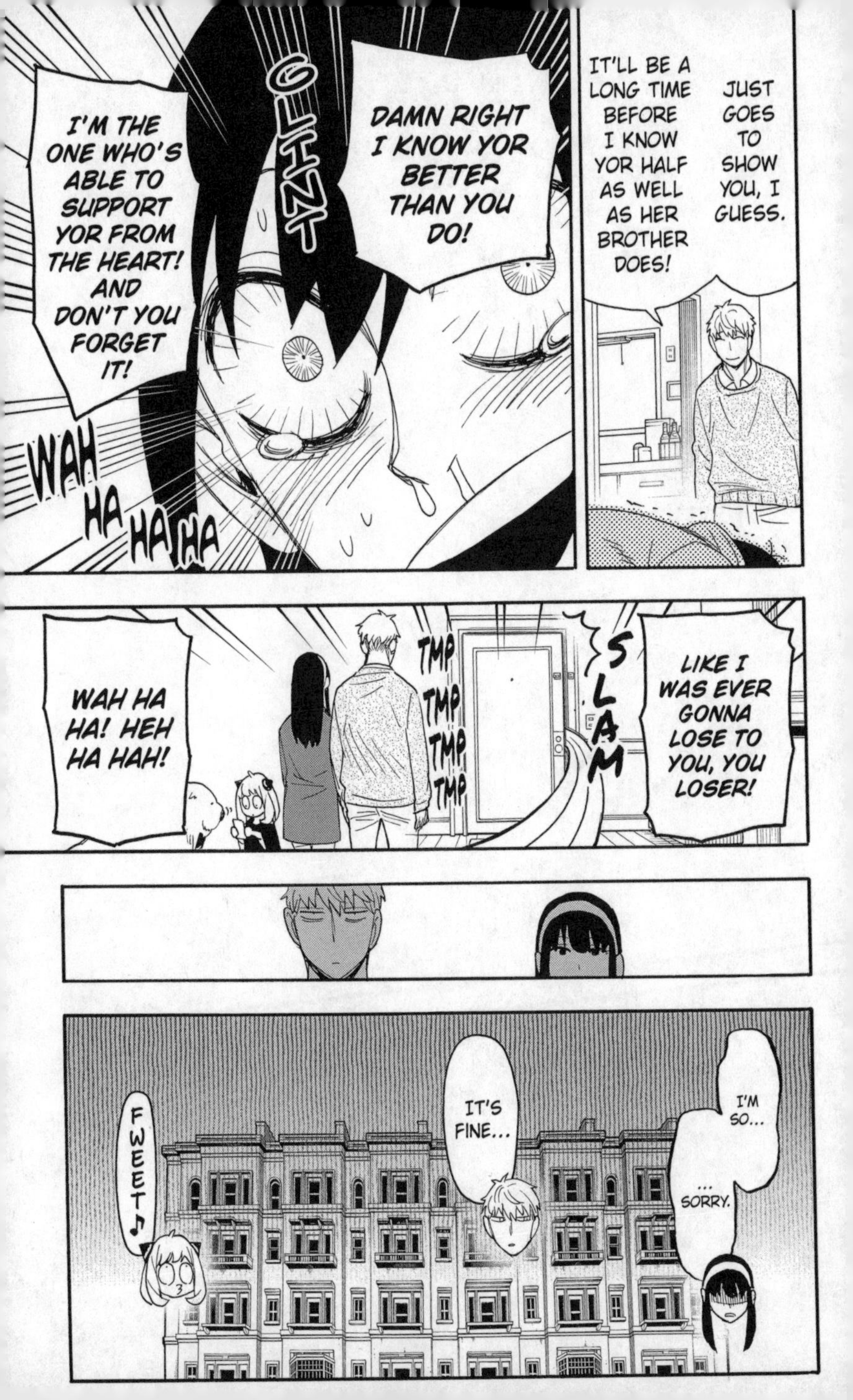
JUST GOES TO SHOW YOU, I GUESS.
IT'LL BE A LONG TIME BEFORE I KNOW YOR HALF AS WELL AS HER BROTHER DOES!
DAMN RIGHT I KNOW YOR BETTER THAN YOU DO!
GLINT
I'M THE ONE WHO'S ABLE TO SUPPORT YOR FROM THE HEART! AND DON'T YOU FORGET IT!
WAH HA HA HA
LIKE I WAS EVER GONNA LOSE TO YOU, YOU LOSER!
SLAM
TMP TMP TMP TMP
WAH HA HA! HEH HA HAH!
I'M SO...
...SORRY.
IT'S FINE...
FWEET♪

SPY×FAMILY

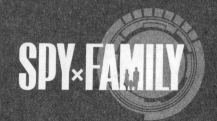

MISSION 69

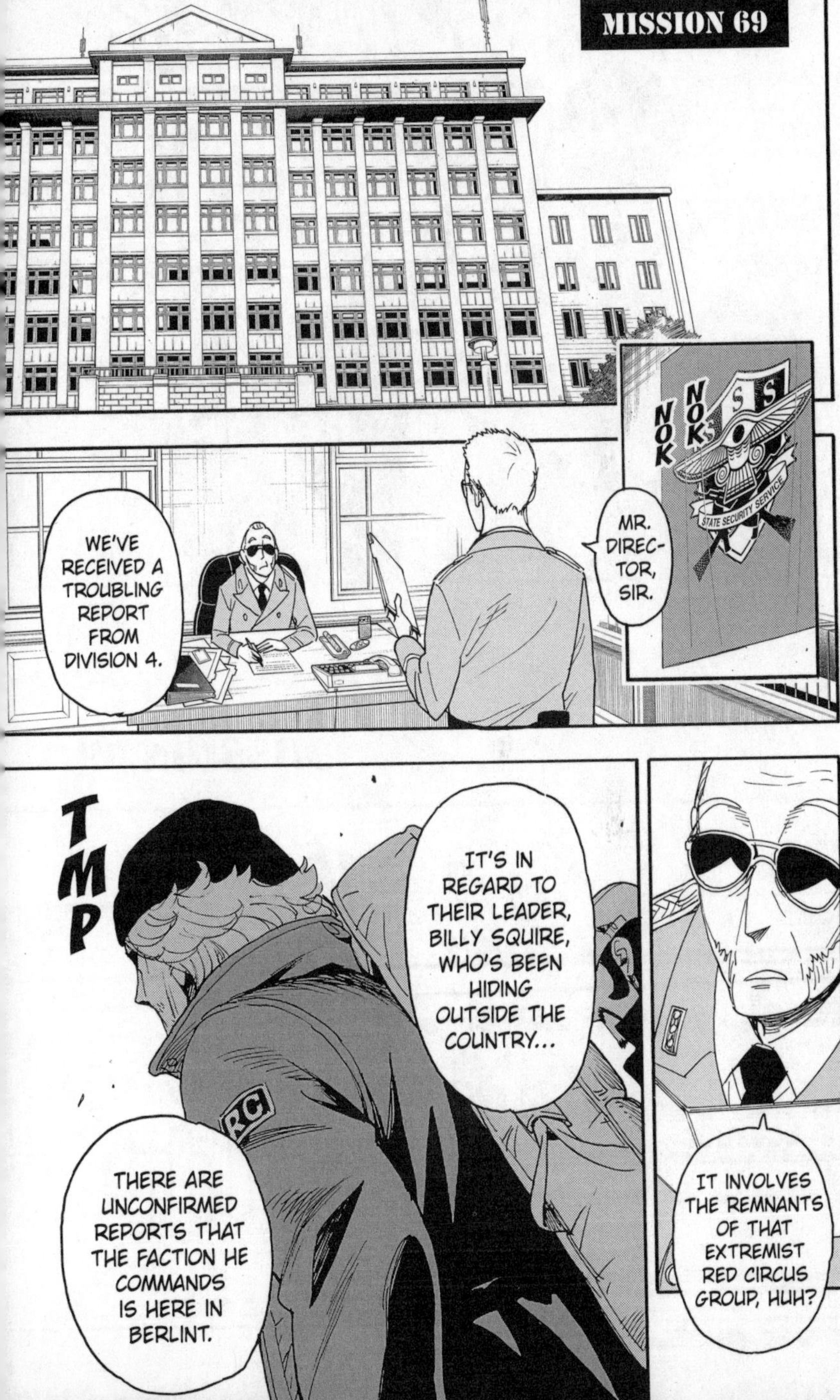
NOK NOK
STATE SECURITY SERVICE
MR. DIRECTOR, SIR.
WE'VE RECEIVED A TROUBLING REPORT FROM DIVISION 4.
IT INVOLVES THE REMNANTS OF THAT EXTREMIST RED CIRCUS GROUP, HUH?
TMP
IT'S IN REGARD TO THEIR LEADER, BILLY SQUIRE, WHO'S BEEN HIDING OUTSIDE THE COUNTRY...
RC
THERE ARE UNCONFIRMED REPORTS THAT THE FACTION HE COMMANDS IS HERE IN BERLINT.

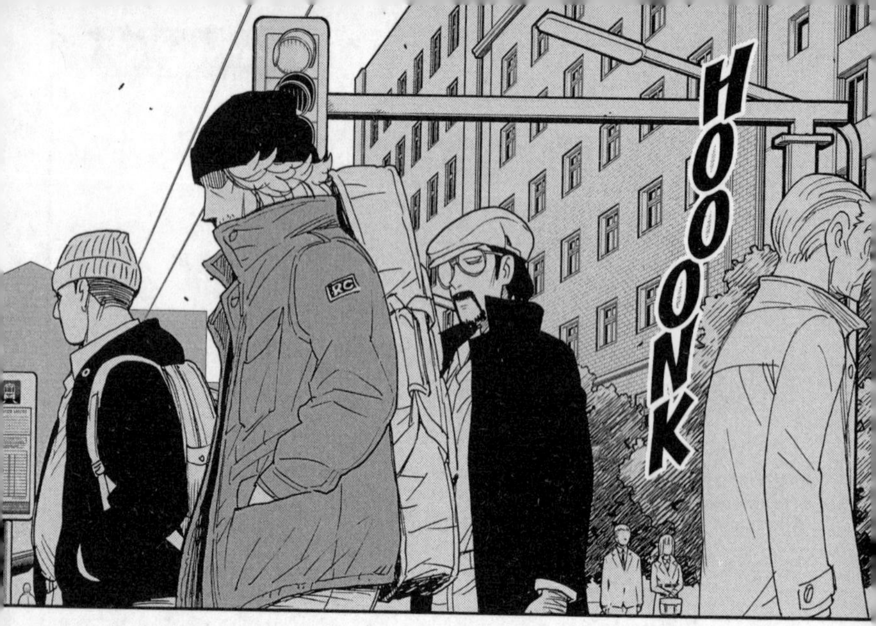
HOOONK

MISSION 69

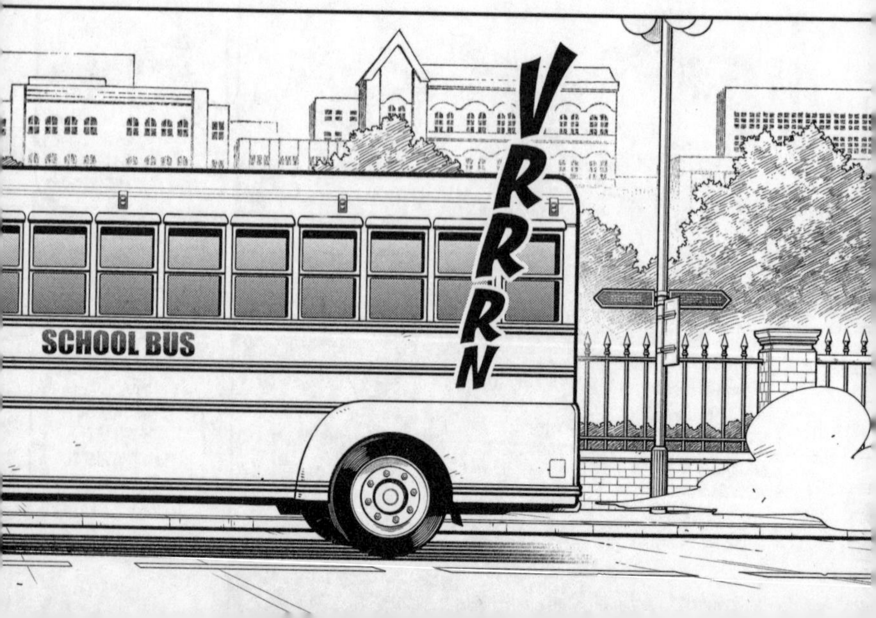
VRRRN
SCHOOL BUS

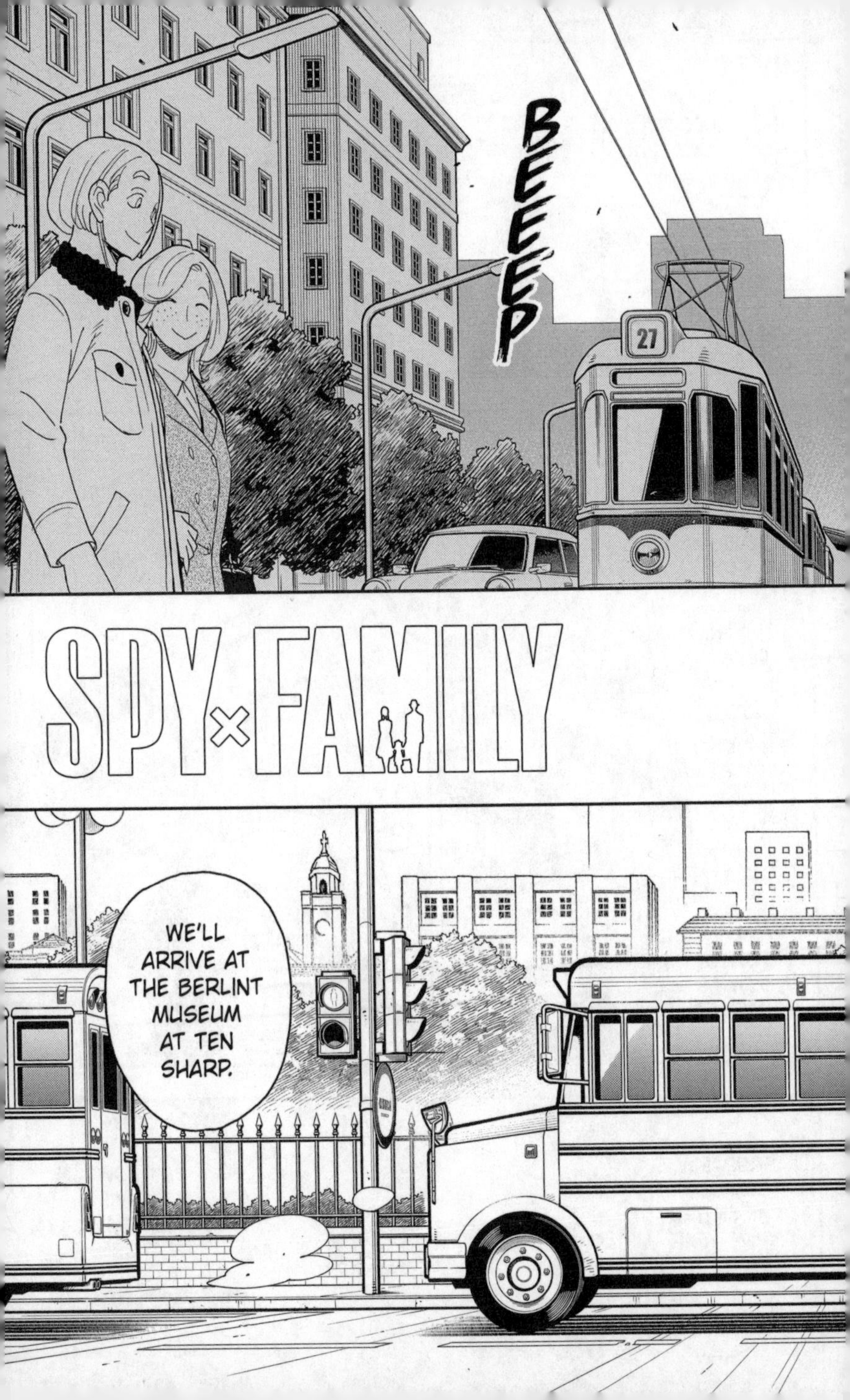
BEEEEP
SPY×FAMILY
WE'LL ARRIVE AT THE BERLINT MUSEUM AT TEN SHARP.

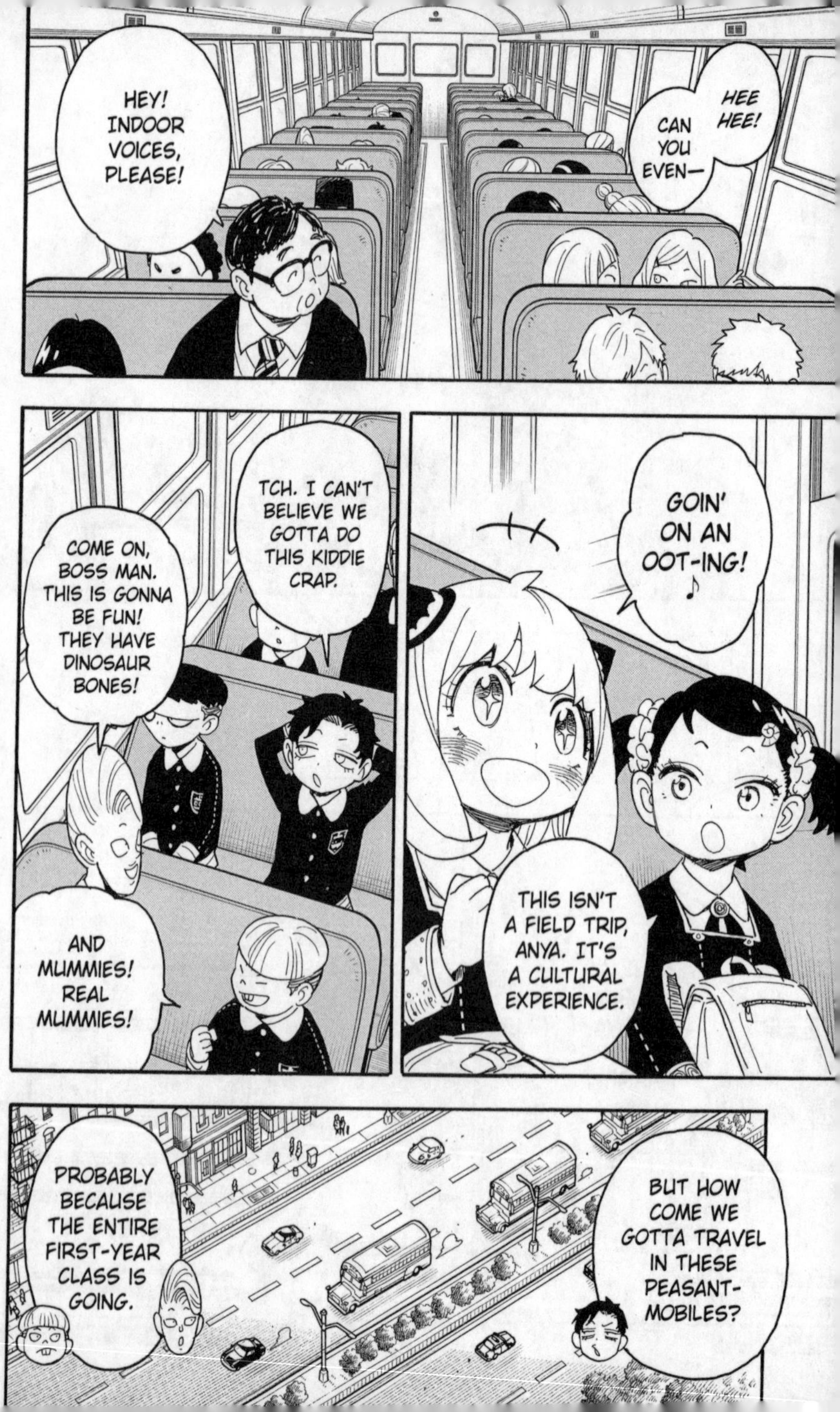
HEE HEE! CAN YOU EVEN—
HEY! INDOOR VOICES, PLEASE!
GOIN' ON AN OOT-ING! ♪
THIS ISN'T A FIELD TRIP, ANYA. IT'S A CULTURAL EXPERIENCE.
TCH. I CAN'T BELIEVE WE GOTTA DO THIS KIDDIE CRAP.
COME ON, BOSS MAN. THIS IS GONNA BE FUN! THEY HAVE DINOSAUR BONES!
AND MUMMIES! REAL MUMMIES!
BUT HOW COME WE GOTTA TRAVEL IN THESE PEASANT-MOBILES?
PROBABLY BECAUSE THE ENTIRE FIRST-YEAR CLASS IS GOING.

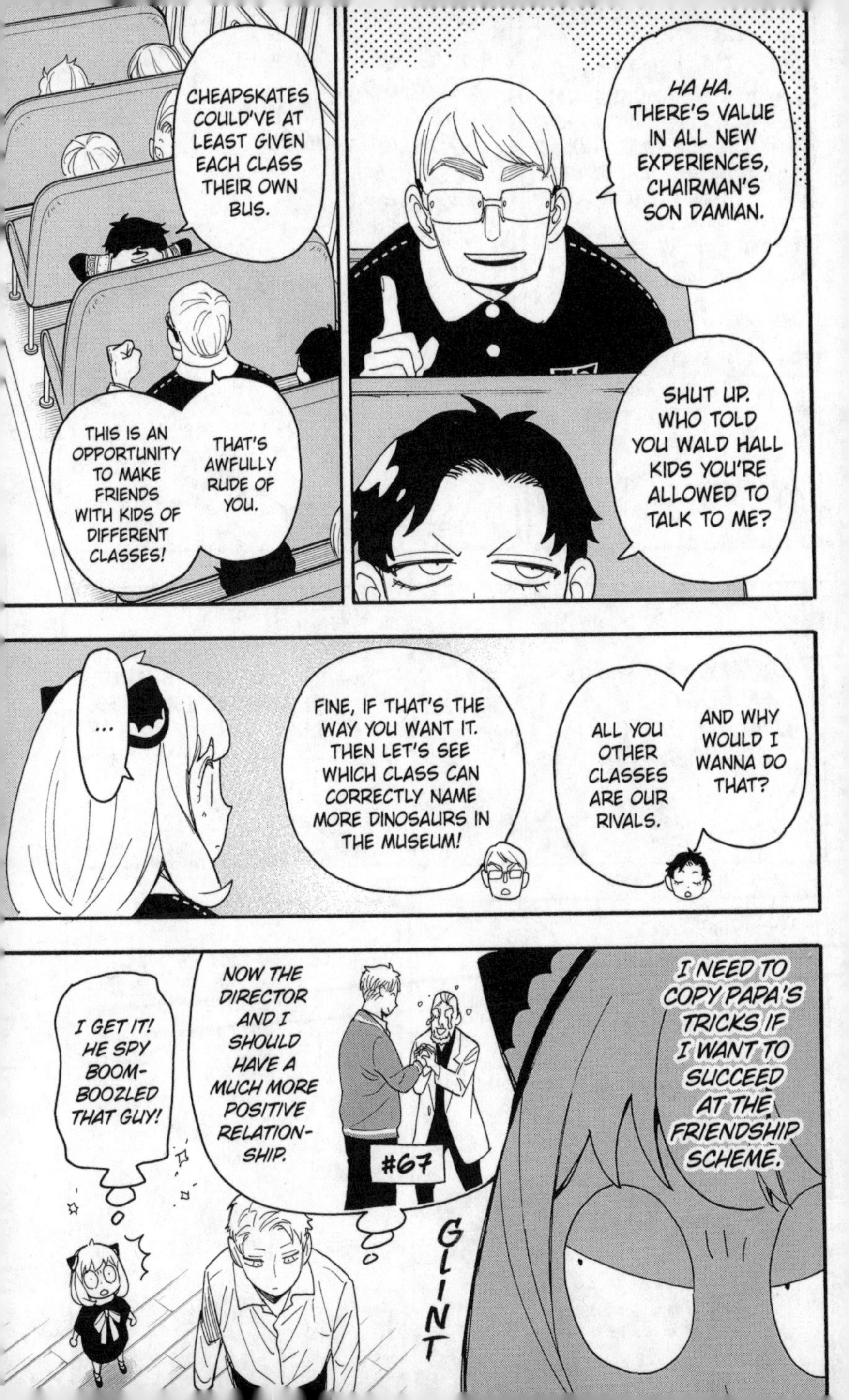
HA HA. THERE'S VALUE IN ALL NEW EXPERIENCES, CHAIRMAN'S SON DAMIAN.
SHUT UP. WHO TOLD YOU WALD HALL KIDS YOU'RE ALLOWED TO TALK TO ME?
CHEAPSKATES COULD'VE AT LEAST GIVEN EACH CLASS THEIR OWN BUS.
THAT'S AWFULLY RUDE OF YOU.
THIS IS AN OPPORTUNITY TO MAKE FRIENDS WITH KIDS OF DIFFERENT CLASSES!
AND WHY WOULD I WANNA DO THAT?
ALL YOU OTHER CLASSES ARE OUR RIVALS.
FINE, IF THAT'S THE WAY YOU WANT IT. THEN LET'S SEE WHICH CLASS CAN CORRECTLY NAME MORE DINOSAURS IN THE MUSEUM!
...
I NEED TO COPY PAPA'S TRICKS IF I WANT TO SUCCEED AT THE FRIENDSHIP SCHEME.
GLINT
NOW THE DIRECTOR AND I SHOULD HAVE A MUCH MORE POSITIVE RELATIONSHIP.
#67
I GET IT! HE SPY BOOMBOOZLED THAT GUY!

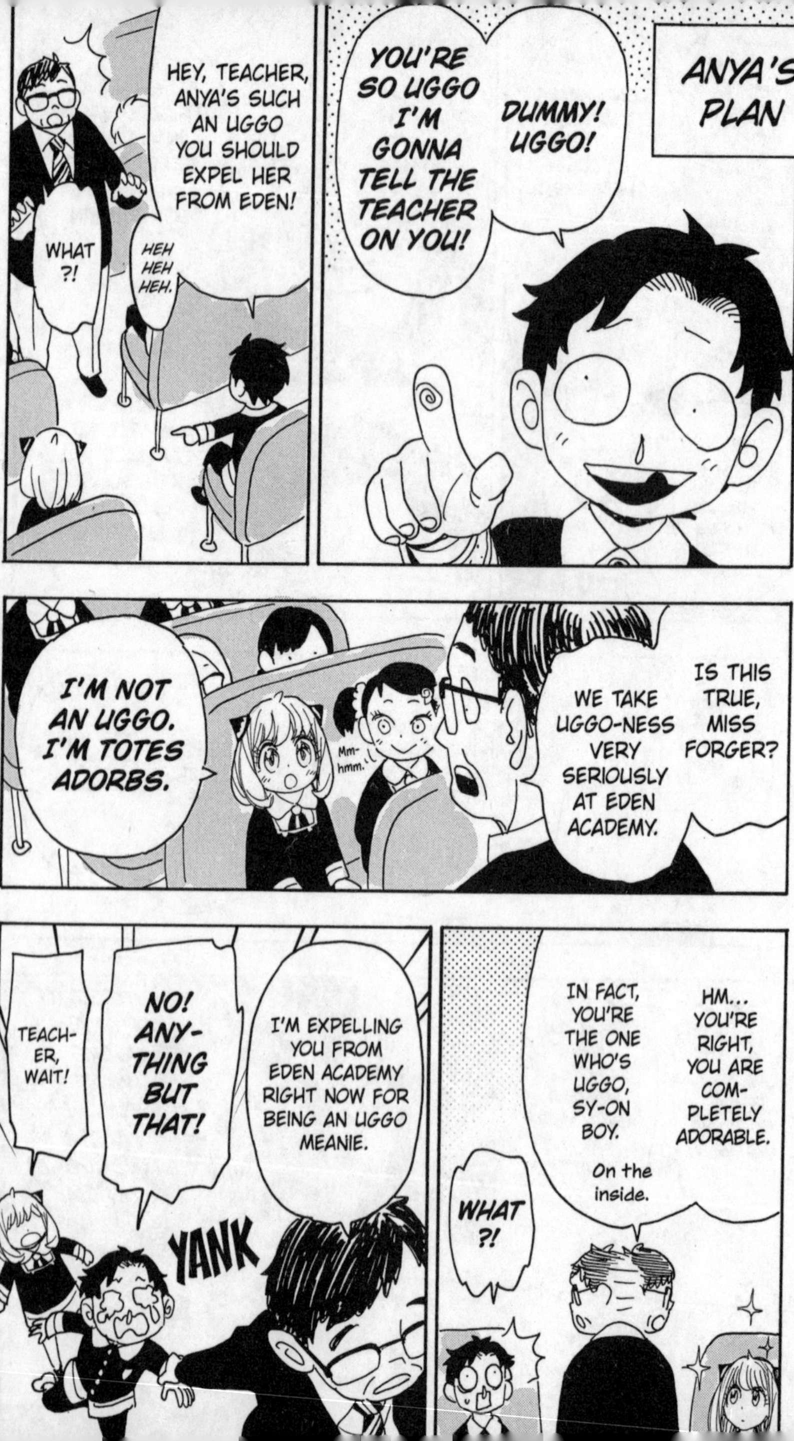
ANYA'S PLAN
DUMMY! UGGO!
YOU'RE SO UGGO I'M GONNA TELL THE TEACHER ON YOU!
HEY, TEACHER, ANYA'S SUCH AN UGGO YOU SHOULD EXPEL HER FROM EDEN!
HEH HEH HEH.
WHAT ?!
IS THIS TRUE, MISS FORGER?
WE TAKE UGGO-NESS VERY SERIOUSLY AT EDEN ACADEMY.
Mm-hmm.
I'M NOT AN UGGO. I'M TOTES ADORBS.
HM... YOU'RE RIGHT, YOU ARE COM-PLETELY ADORABLE.
IN FACT, YOU'RE THE ONE WHO'S UGGO, SY-ON BOY.
On the inside.
WHAT ?!
I'M EXPELLING YOU FROM EDEN ACADEMY RIGHT NOW FOR BEING AN UGGO MEANIE.
NO! ANY-THING BUT THAT!
TEACH-ER, WAIT!
YANK

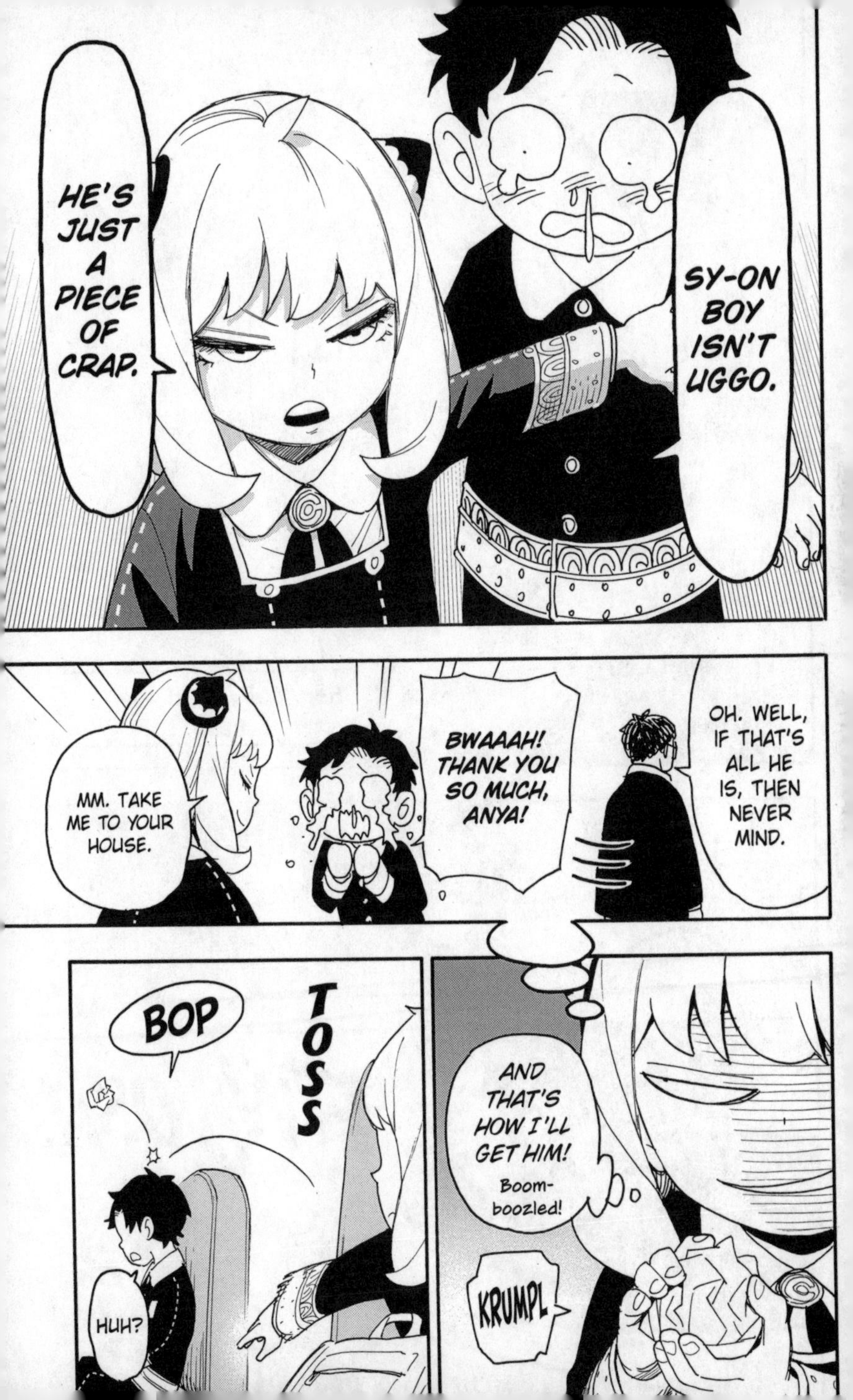
SY-ON BOY ISN'T UGGO.
HE'S JUST A PIECE OF CRAP.
OH. WELL, IF THAT'S ALL HE IS, THEN NEVER MIND.
BWAAAH! THANK YOU SO MUCH, ANYA!
MM. TAKE ME TO YOUR HOUSE.
AND THAT'S HOW I'LL GET HIM!
Boom-boozled!
KRUMPL
TOSS
BOP
HUH?

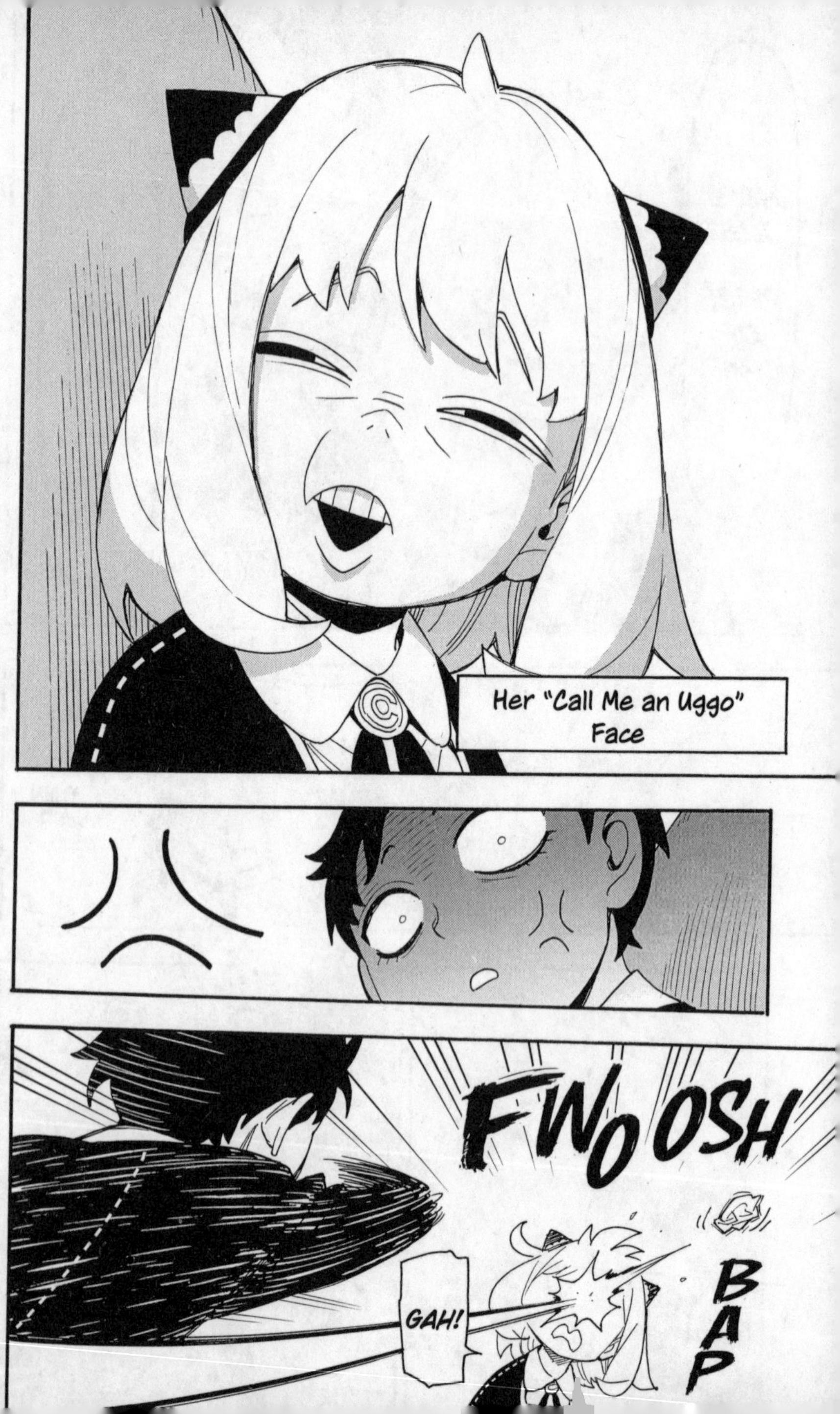
Her "Call Me an Uggo" Face
FWOOSH
BAP
GAH!

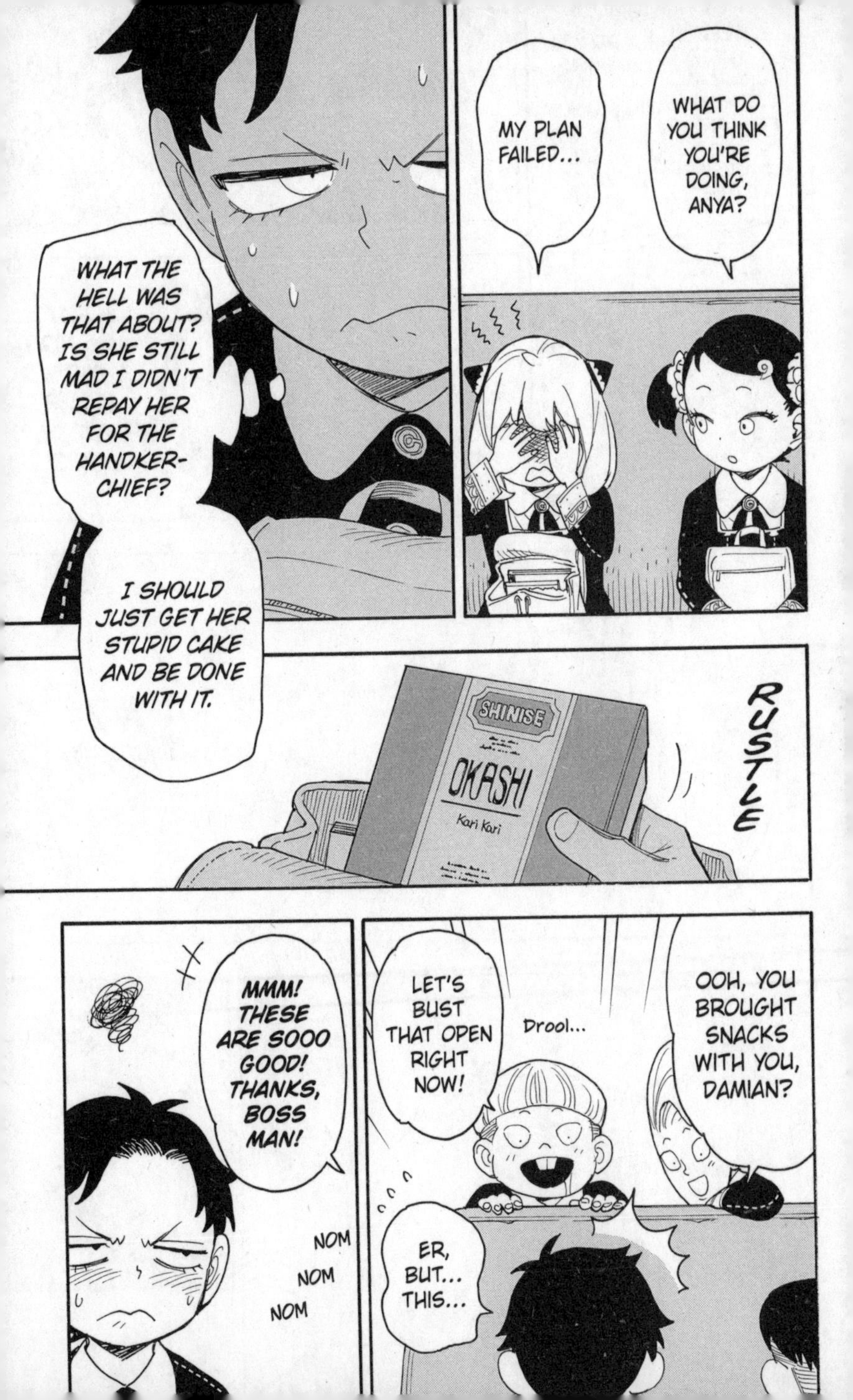
WHAT DO YOU THINK YOU'RE DOING, ANYA?
MY PLAN FAILED...
WHAT THE HELL WAS THAT ABOUT? IS SHE STILL MAD I DIDN'T REPAY HER FOR THE HANDKER-CHIEF?
I SHOULD JUST GET HER STUPID CAKE AND BE DONE WITH IT.
RUSTLE
SHINISE
OKASHI
Kari Kari
OOH, YOU BROUGHT SNACKS WITH YOU, DAMIAN?
Drool...
LET'S BUST THAT OPEN RIGHT NOW!
ER, BUT... THIS...
MMM! THESE ARE SOOO GOOD! THANKS, BOSS MAN!
NOM
NOM
NOM

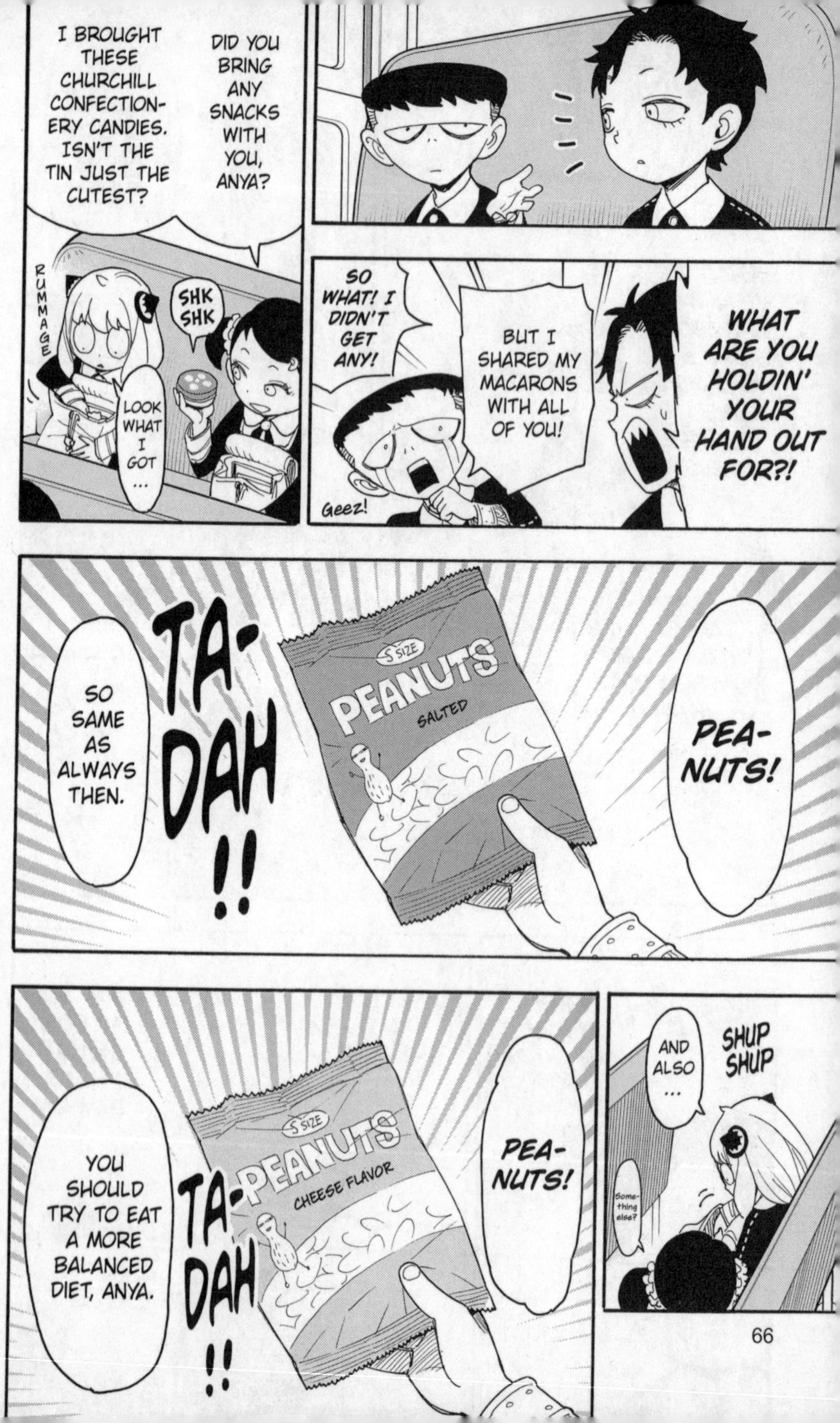
WHAT ARE YOU HOLDIN' YOUR HAND OUT FOR?!
BUT I SHARED MY MACARONS WITH ALL OF YOU!
SO WHAT! I DIDN'T GET ANY!
Geez!
DID YOU BRING ANY SNACKS WITH YOU, ANYA?
I BROUGHT THESE CHURCHILL CONFECTIONERY CANDIES. ISN'T THE TIN JUST THE CUTEST?
SHK SHK
RUMMAGE
LOOK WHAT I GOT ...
PEA-NUTS!
TA-DAH!!
S SIZE
PEANUTS
SALTED
SO SAME AS ALWAYS THEN.
SHUP SHUP
AND ALSO ...
Some-thing else?
PEA-NUTS!
TA-DAH!!
S SIZE
PEANUTS
CHEESE FLAVOR
YOU SHOULD TRY TO EAT A MORE BALANCED DIET, ANYA.

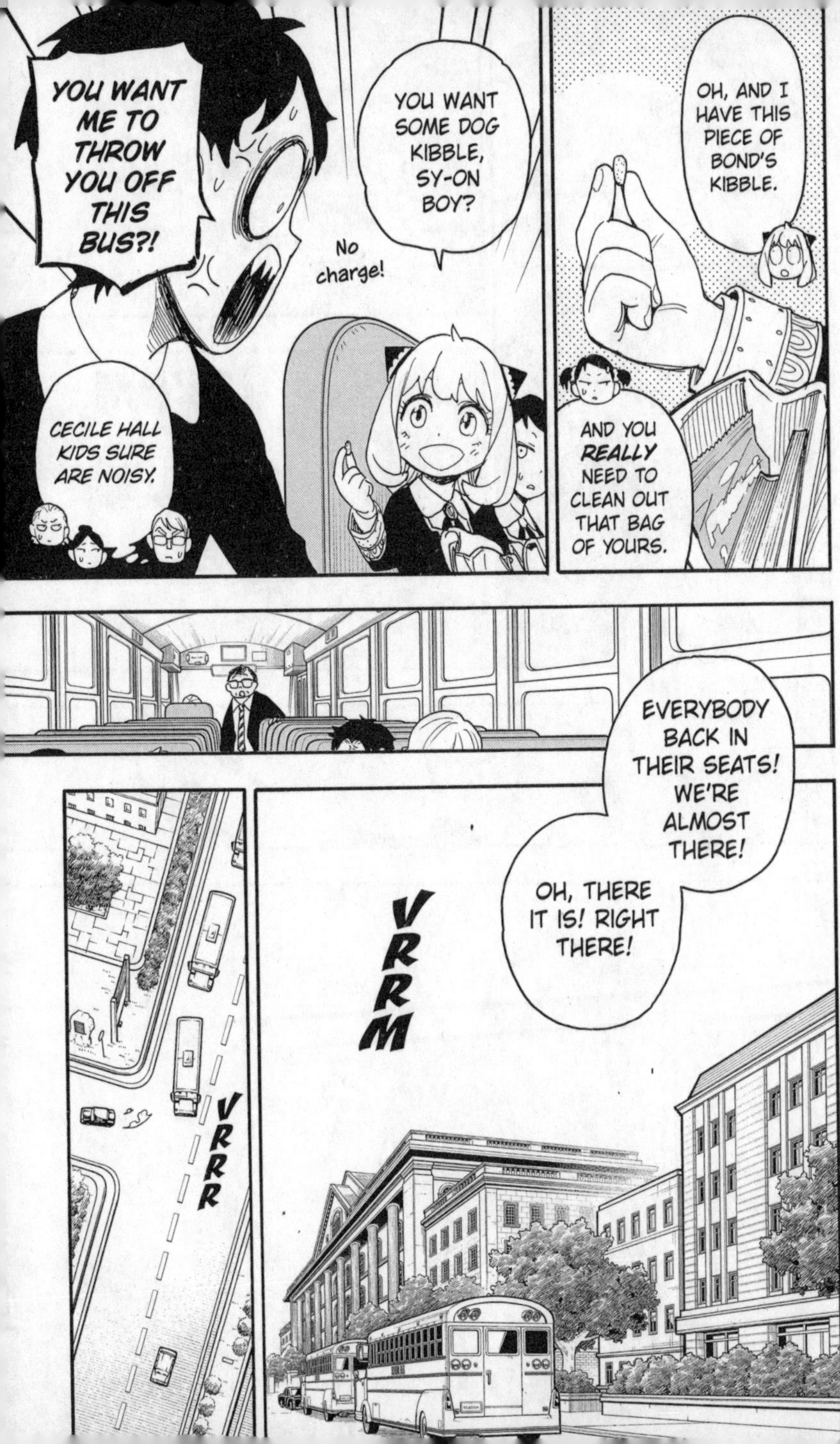
OH, AND I HAVE THIS PIECE OF BOND'S KIBBLE.
AND YOU **REALLY** NEED TO CLEAN OUT THAT BAG OF YOURS.
YOU WANT SOME DOG KIBBLE, SY-ON BOY?
No charge!
YOU WANT ME TO THROW YOU OFF THIS BUS?!
CECILE HALL KIDS SURE ARE NOISY.
EVERYBODY BACK IN THEIR SEATS! WE'RE ALMOST THERE!
OH, THERE IT IS! RIGHT THERE!
VRRM
VRRR

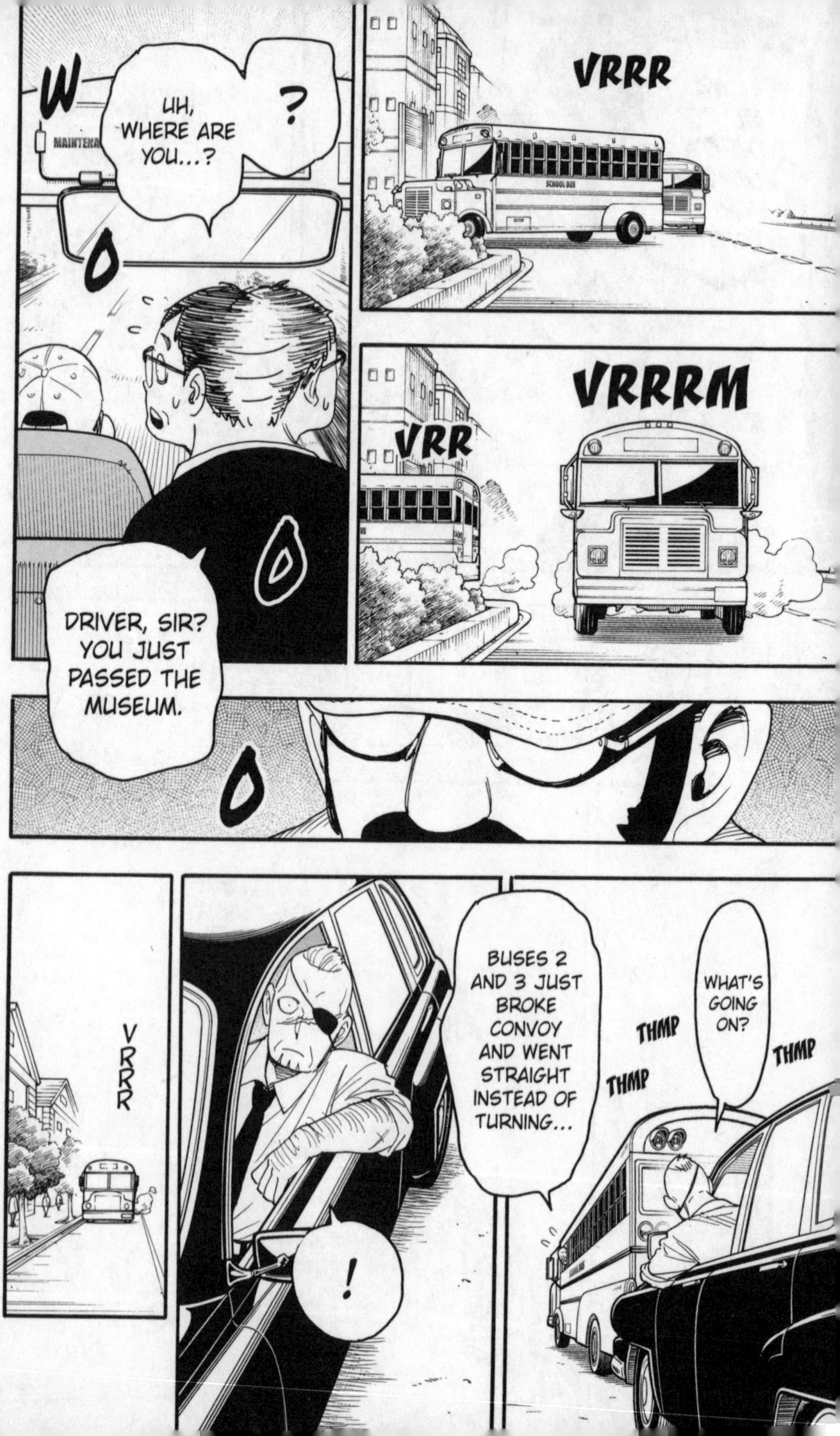
VRRR
VRRRM
VRR
UH, WHERE ARE YOU...?
?
DRIVER, SIR? YOU JUST PASSED THE MUSEUM.
WHAT'S GOING ON?
THMP
THMP
THMP
BUSES 2 AND 3 JUST BROKE CONVOY AND WENT STRAIGHT INSTEAD OF TURNING...
!
VRRR

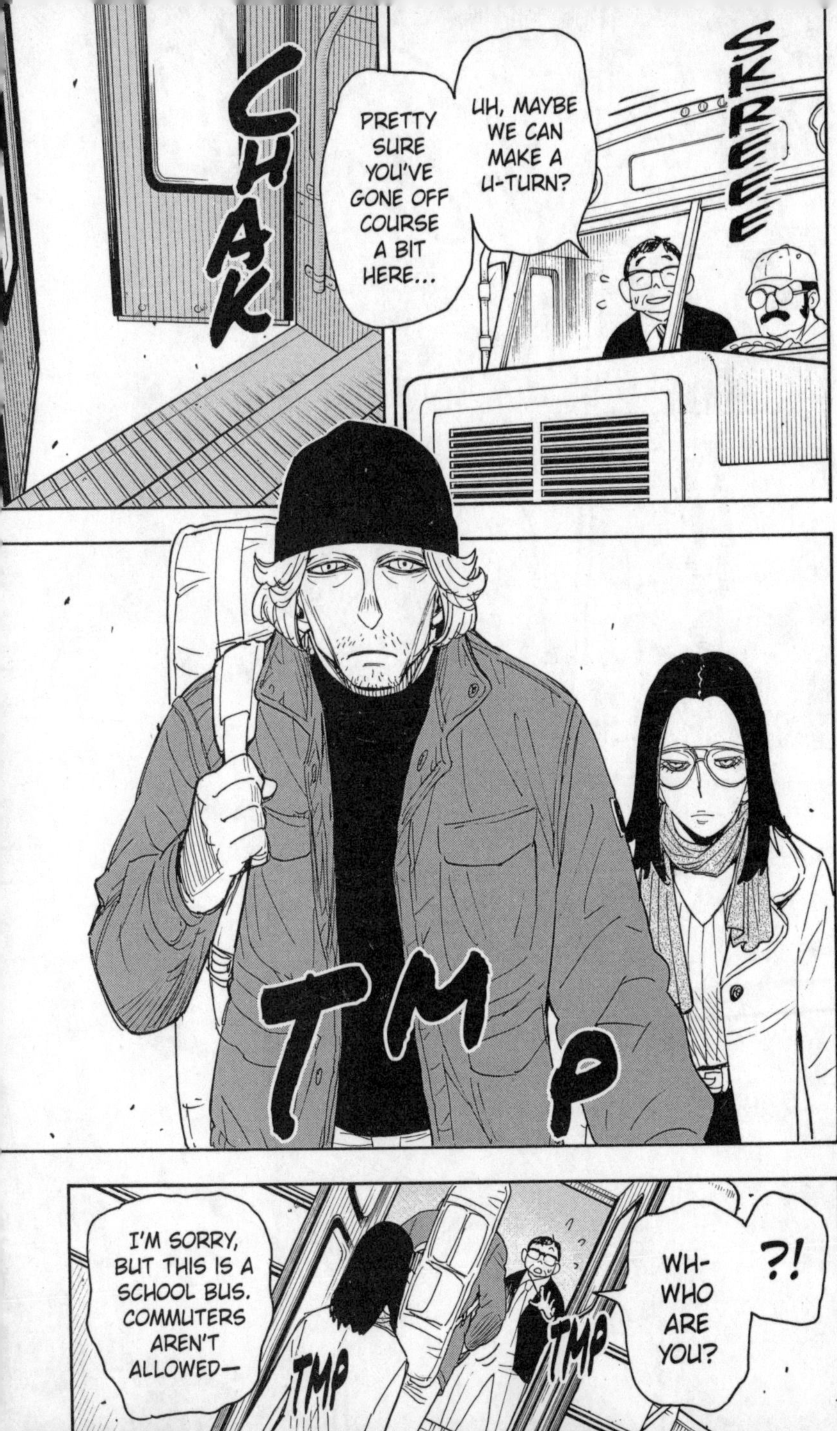
SKREEEE
UH, MAYBE WE CAN MAKE A U-TURN?
PRETTY SURE YOU'VE GONE OFF COURSE A BIT HERE...
CHAK
TMP
?!
WH-WHO ARE YOU?
TMP
I'M SORRY, BUT THIS IS A SCHOOL BUS. COMMUTERS AREN'T ALLOWED—
TMP

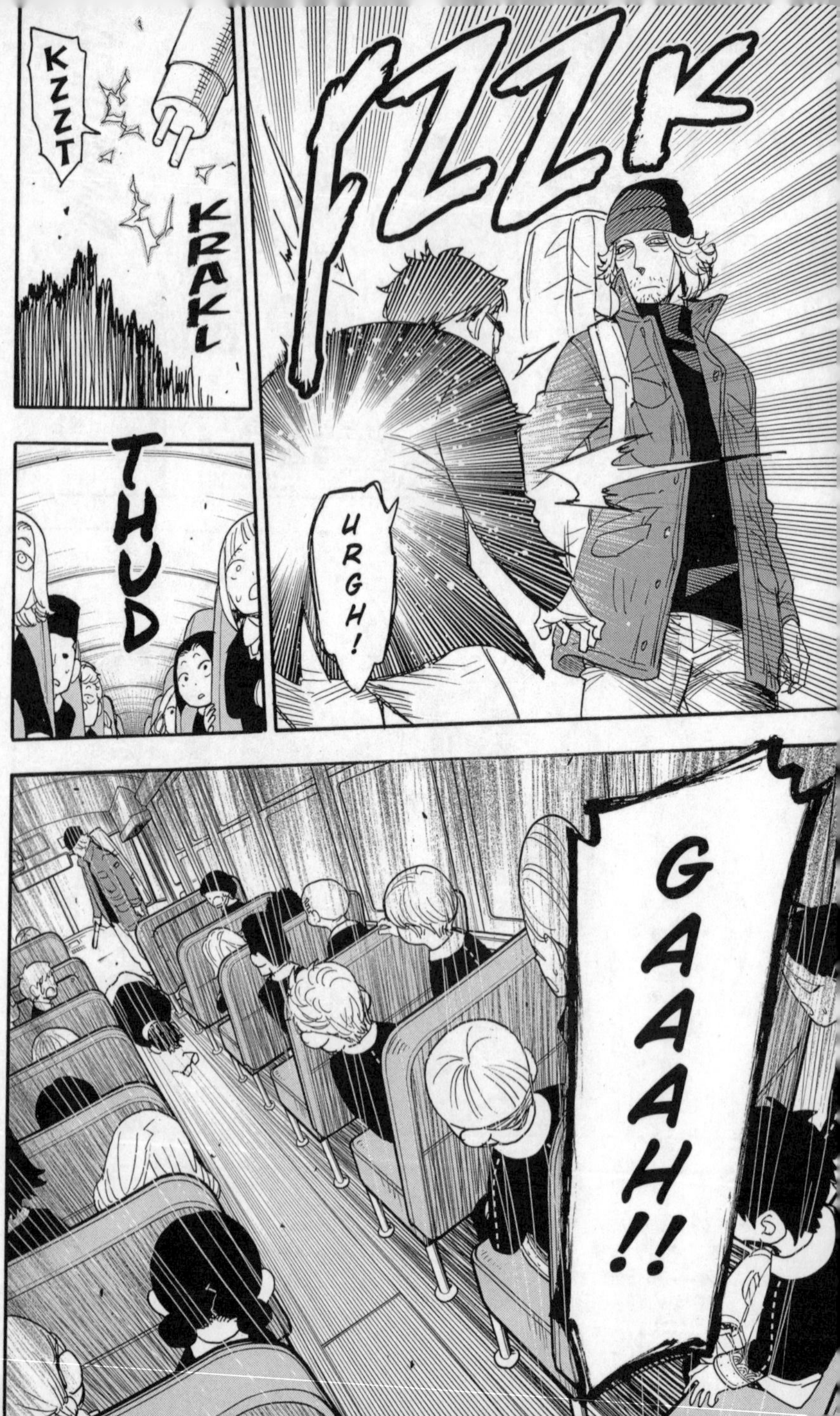
FZZK
KZZT
KRAKL
URGH!
THUD
GAAAAH!!

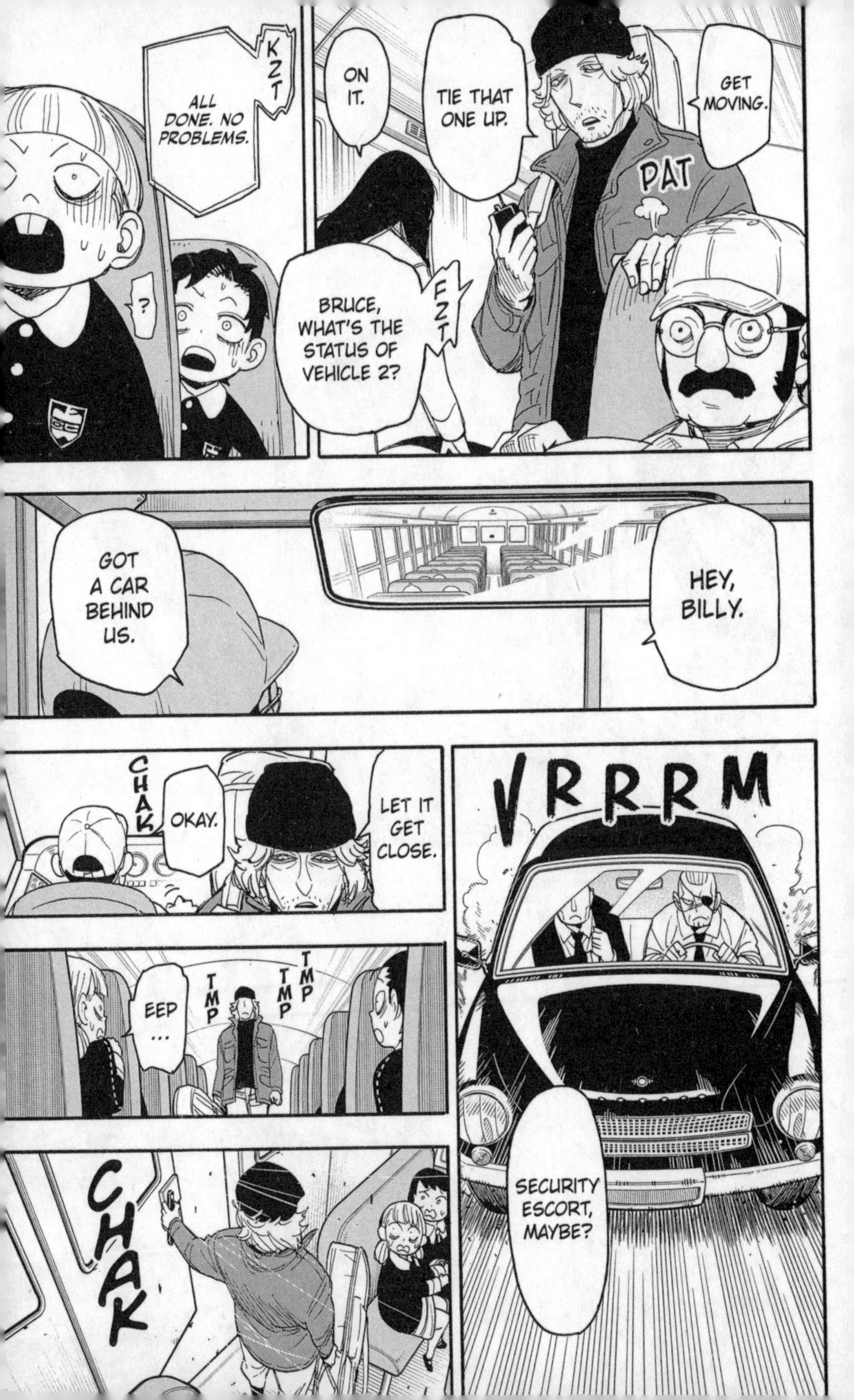
GET MOVING.
PAT
TIE THAT ONE UP.
ON IT.
FZT
BRUCE, WHAT'S THE STATUS OF VEHICLE 2?
KZT
ALL DONE. NO PROBLEMS.
?
HEY, BILLY.
GOT A CAR BEHIND US.
VRRRM
SECURITY ESCORT, MAYBE?
LET IT GET CLOSE.
OKAY.
CHAK
TMP TMP TMP
EEP ...
CHAK

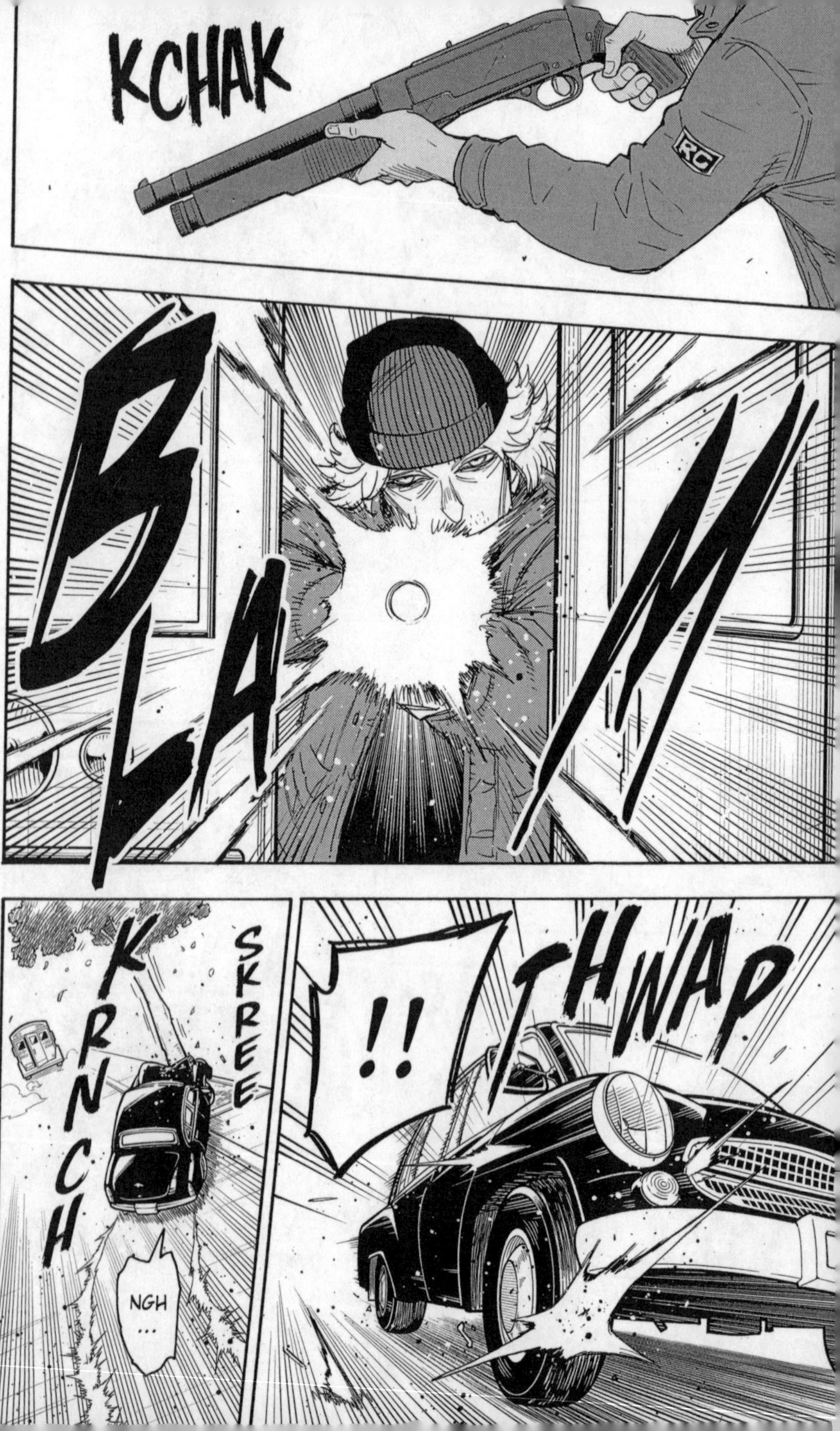
KCHAK
RC
BLAM
THWAP
!!
SKREE
KRNCH
NGH...

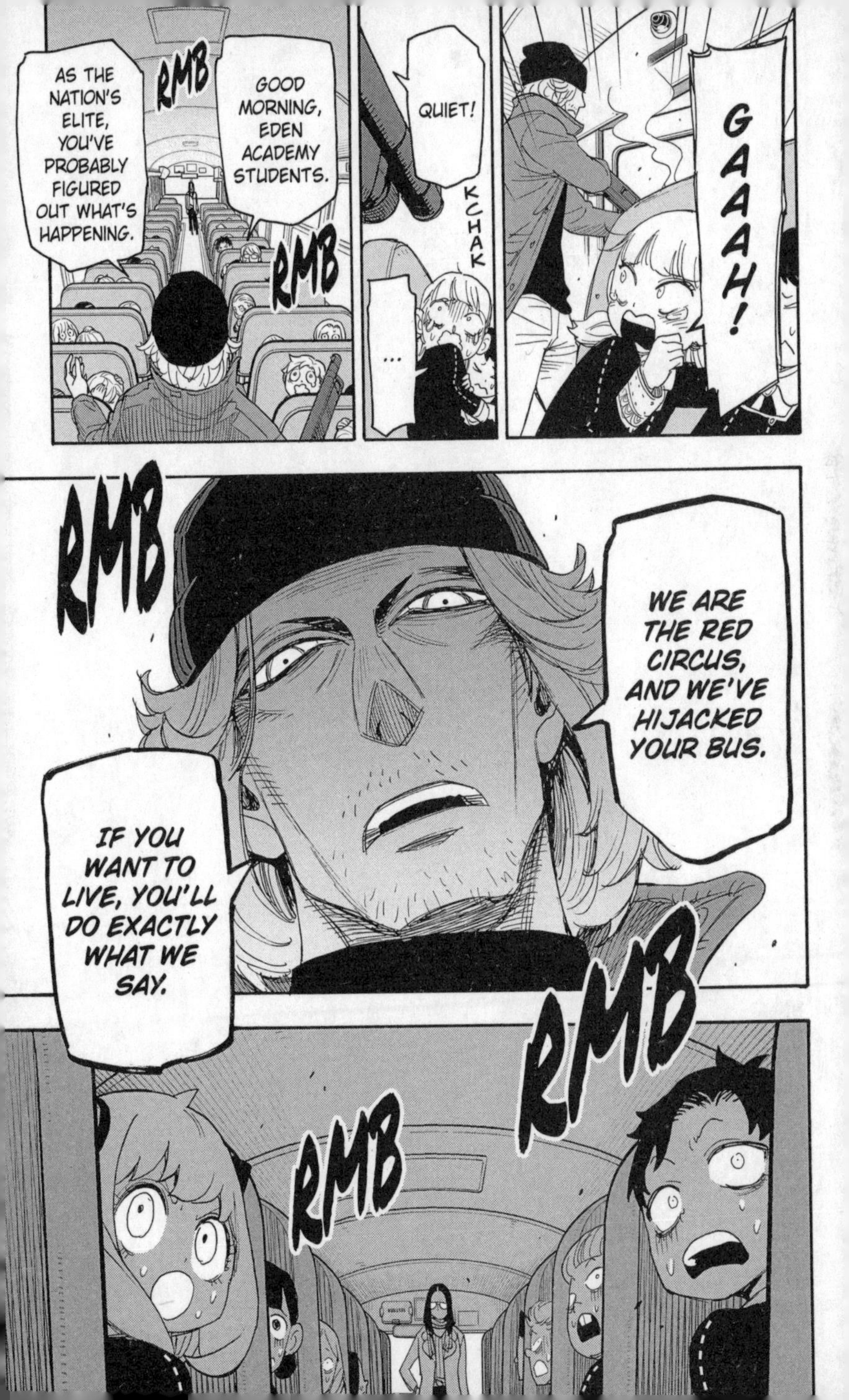
GAAAAH!
QUIET!
KCHAK
...
GOOD MORNING, EDEN ACADEMY STUDENTS.
RMB
AS THE NATION'S ELITE, YOU'VE PROBABLY FIGURED OUT WHAT'S HAPPENING.
RMB
WE ARE THE RED CIRCUS, AND WE'VE HIJACKED YOUR BUS.
RMB
IF YOU WANT TO LIVE, YOU'LL DO EXACTLY WHAT WE SAY.
RMB
RMB

SPY×FAMILY

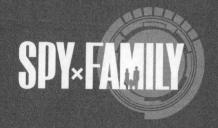

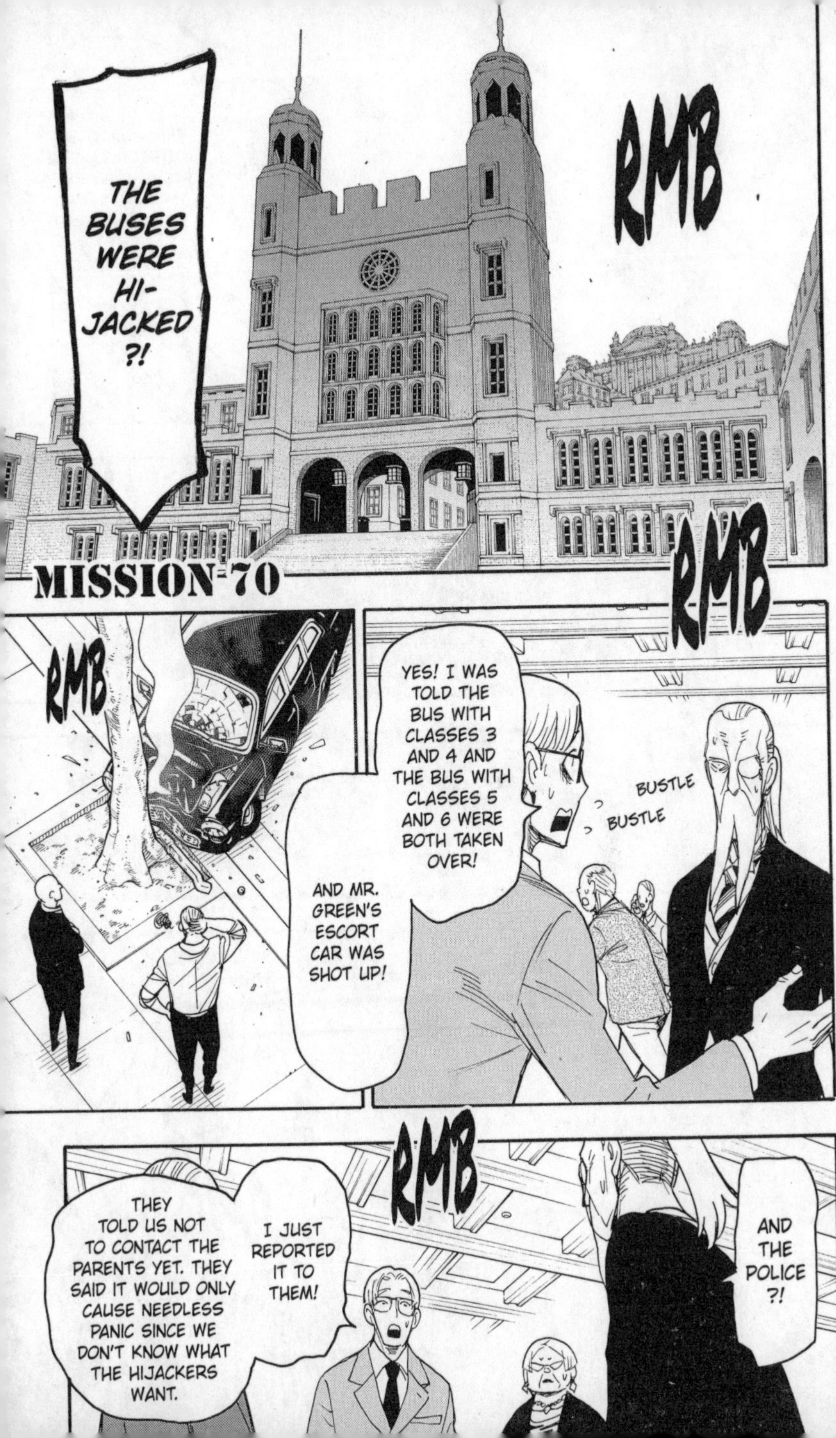
RMB
THE BUSES WERE HI-JACKED?!
RMB
MISSION 70
YES! I WAS TOLD THE BUS WITH CLASSES 3 AND 4 AND THE BUS WITH CLASSES 5 AND 6 WERE BOTH TAKEN OVER!
AND MR. GREEN'S ESCORT CAR WAS SHOT UP!
BUSTLE
BUSTLE
RMB
AND THE POLICE?!
RMB
I JUST REPORTED IT TO THEM!
THEY TOLD US NOT TO CONTACT THE PARENTS YET. THEY SAID IT WOULD ONLY CAUSE NEEDLESS PANIC SINCE WE DON'T KNOW WHAT THE HIJACKERS WANT.

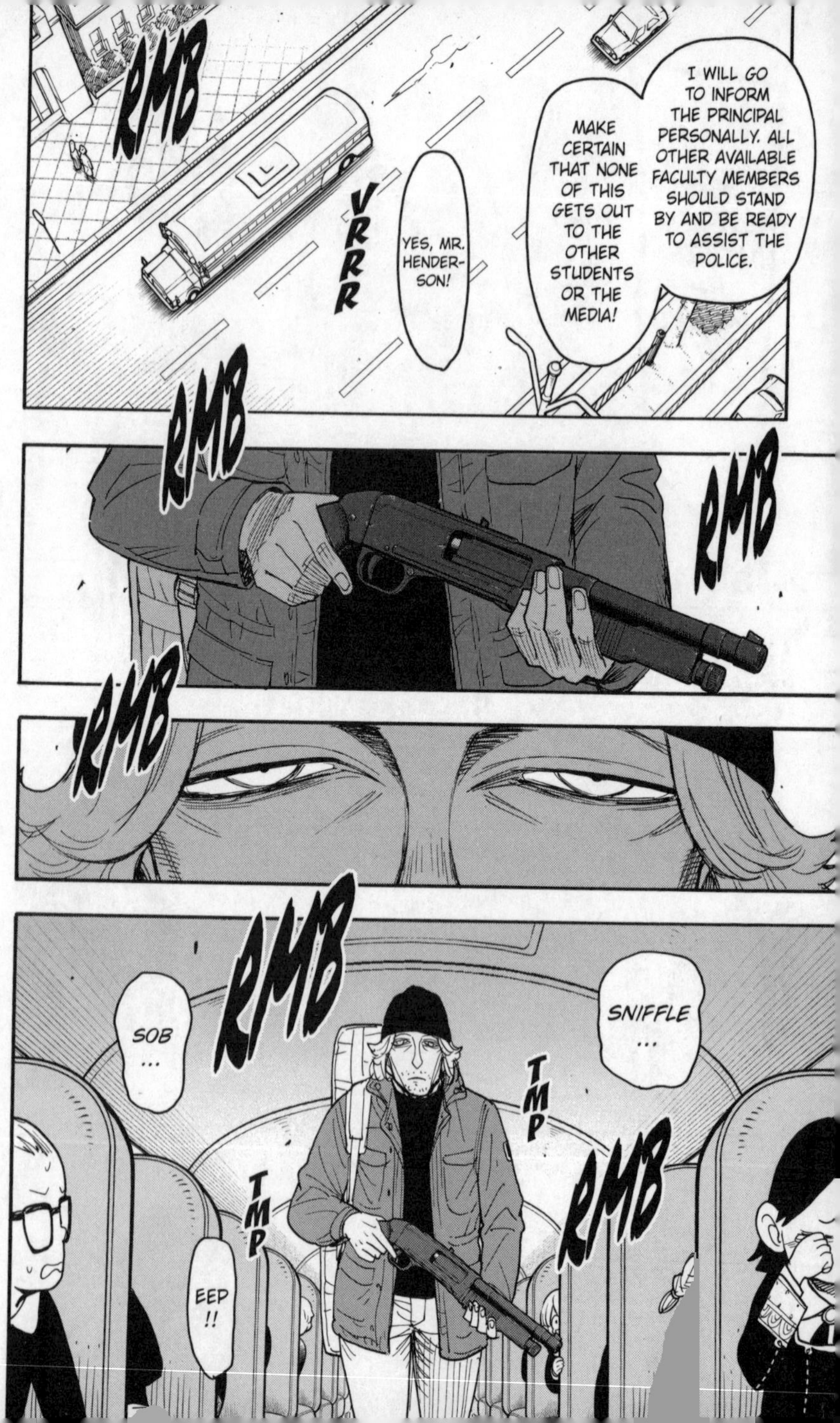
I WILL GO TO INFORM THE PRINCIPAL PERSONALLY. ALL OTHER AVAILABLE FACULTY MEMBERS SHOULD STAND BY AND BE READY TO ASSIST THE POLICE.
MAKE CERTAIN THAT NONE OF THIS GETS OUT TO THE OTHER STUDENTS OR THE MEDIA!
VRRR
YES, MR. HENDER-SON!
RMB
RMB
RMB
RMB
SNIFFLE ...
RMB
TMP
RMB
SOB ...
TMP
EEP !!

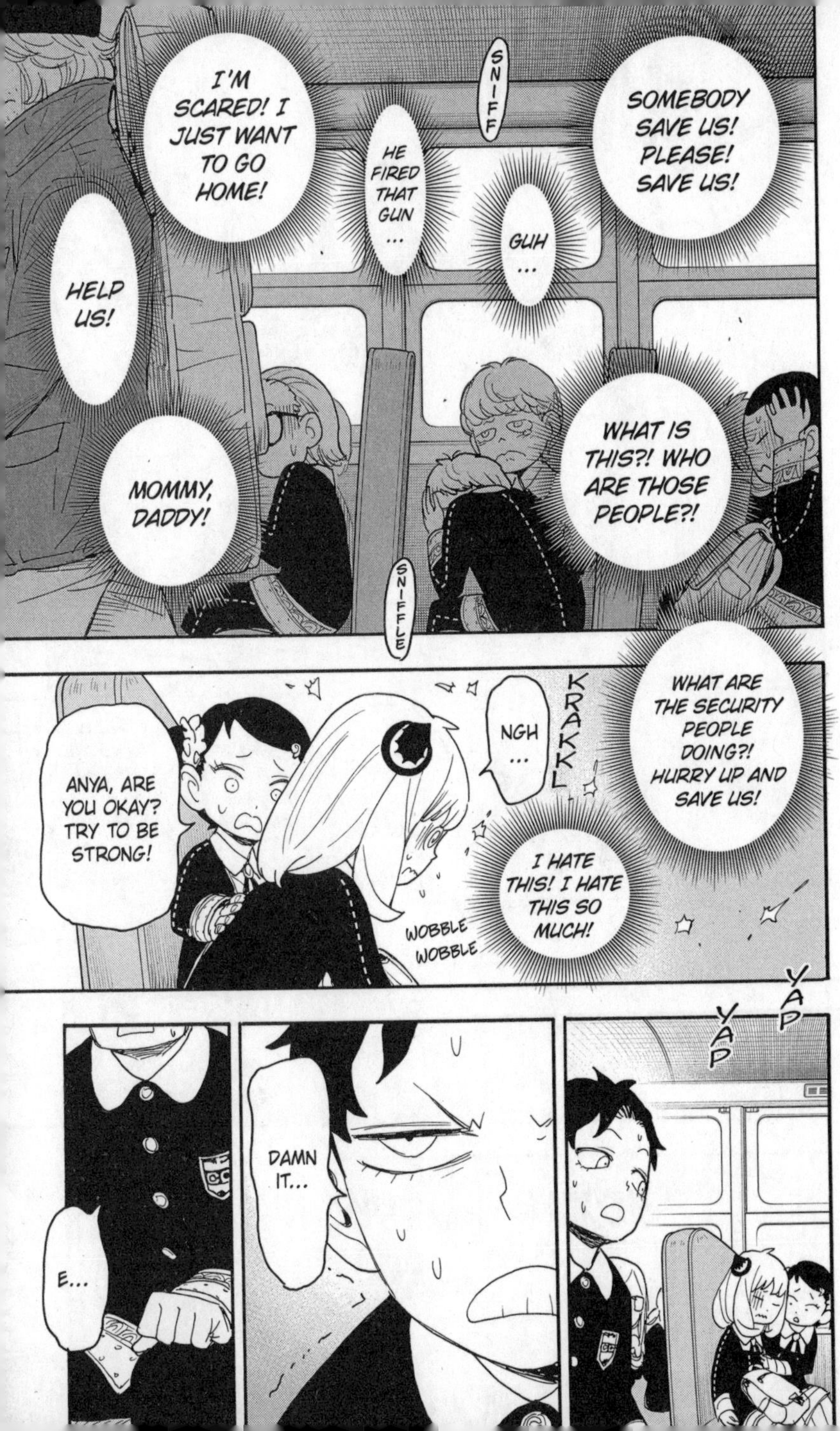
SOMEBODY SAVE US! PLEASE! SAVE US!
SNIFF
GUH...
HE FIRED THAT GUN...
I'M SCARED! I JUST WANT TO GO HOME!
WHAT IS THIS?! WHO ARE THOSE PEOPLE?!
HELP US!
SNIFFLE
MOMMY, DADDY!
WHAT ARE THE SECURITY PEOPLE DOING?! HURRY UP AND SAVE US!
KRAKKL
NGH...
I HATE THIS! I HATE THIS SO MUCH!
ANYA, ARE YOU OKAY? TRY TO BE STRONG!
WOBBLE WOBBLE
YAP YAP
DAMN IT...
E...

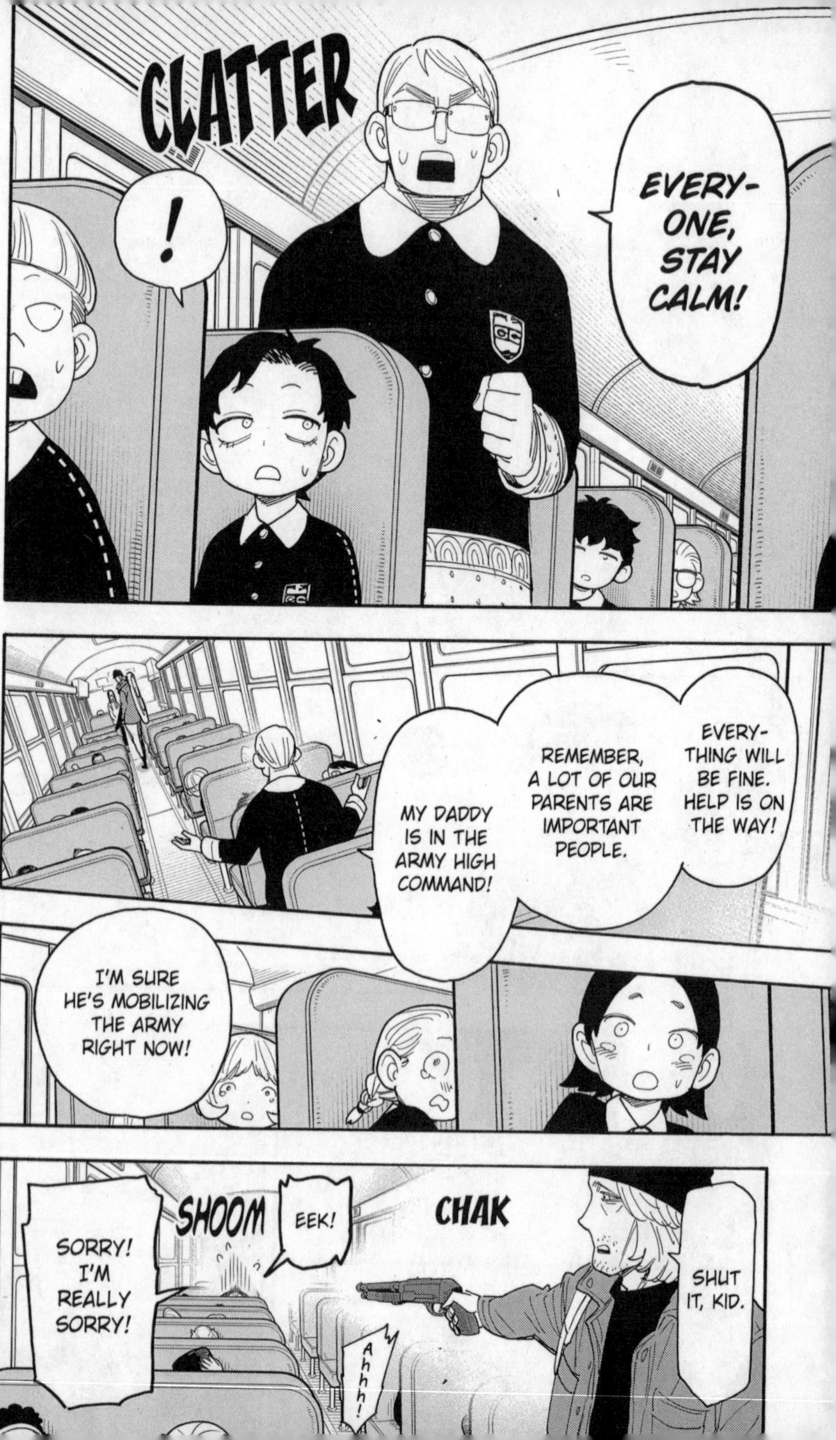
EVERY-ONE, STAY CALM!
CLATTER
!
EVERY-THING WILL BE FINE. HELP IS ON THE WAY!
REMEMBER, A LOT OF OUR PARENTS ARE IMPORTANT PEOPLE.
MY DADDY IS IN THE ARMY HIGH COMMAND!
I'M SURE HE'S MOBILIZING THE ARMY RIGHT NOW!
SHUT IT, KID.
CHAK
EEK!
SHOOM
SORRY! I'M REALLY SORRY!
Ahhh!

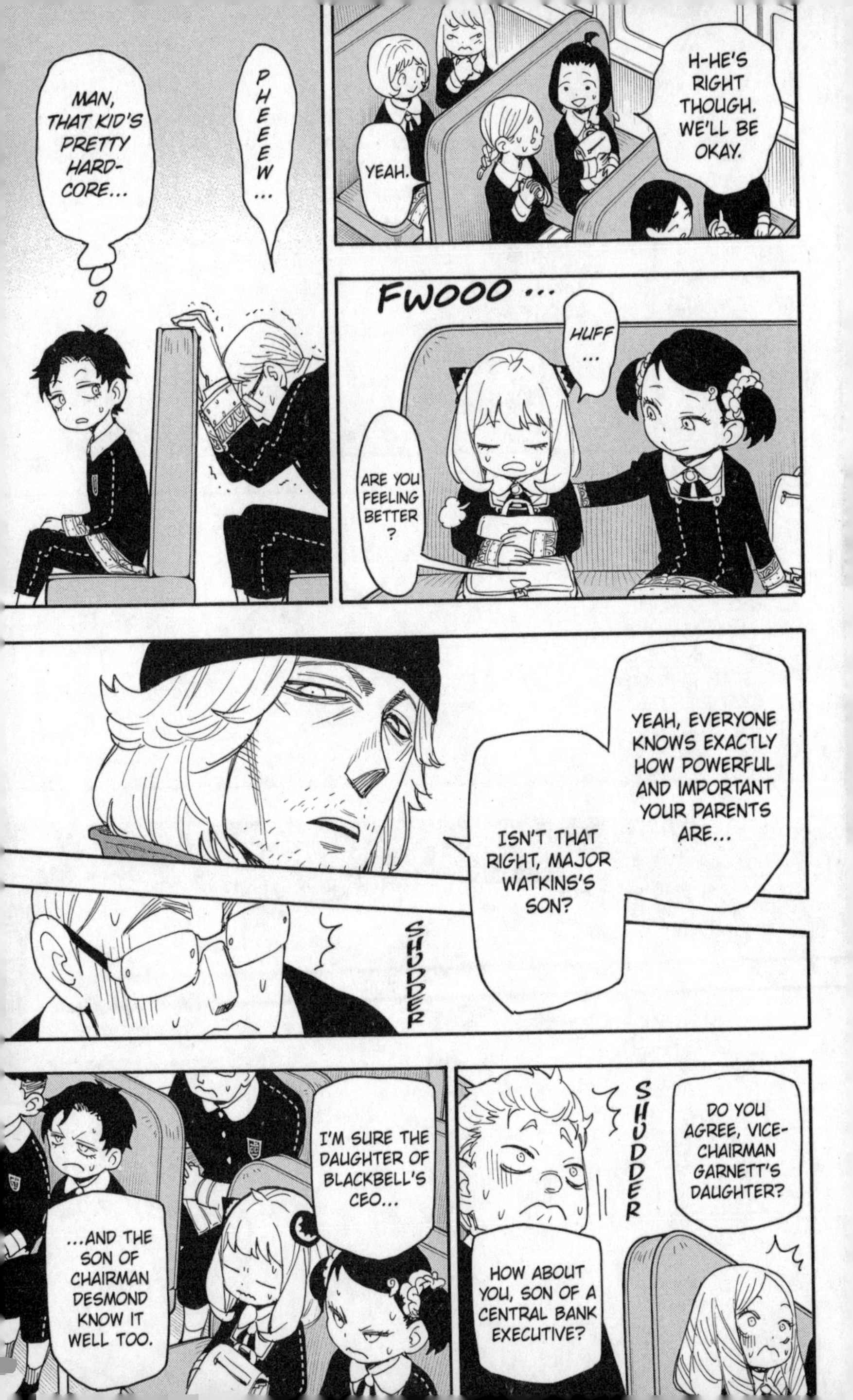
H-HE'S RIGHT THOUGH. WE'LL BE OKAY.
YEAH.
FWOOO...
HUFF...
ARE YOU FEELING BETTER?
PHEEEW...
MAN, THAT KID'S PRETTY HARD-CORE...
YEAH, EVERYONE KNOWS EXACTLY HOW POWERFUL AND IMPORTANT YOUR PARENTS ARE...
ISN'T THAT RIGHT, MAJOR WATKINS'S SON?
SHUDDER
DO YOU AGREE, VICE-CHAIRMAN GARNETT'S DAUGHTER?
SHUDDER
HOW ABOUT YOU, SON OF A CENTRAL BANK EXECUTIVE?
I'M SURE THE DAUGHTER OF BLACKBELL'S CEO...
...AND THE SON OF CHAIRMAN DESMOND KNOW IT WELL TOO.

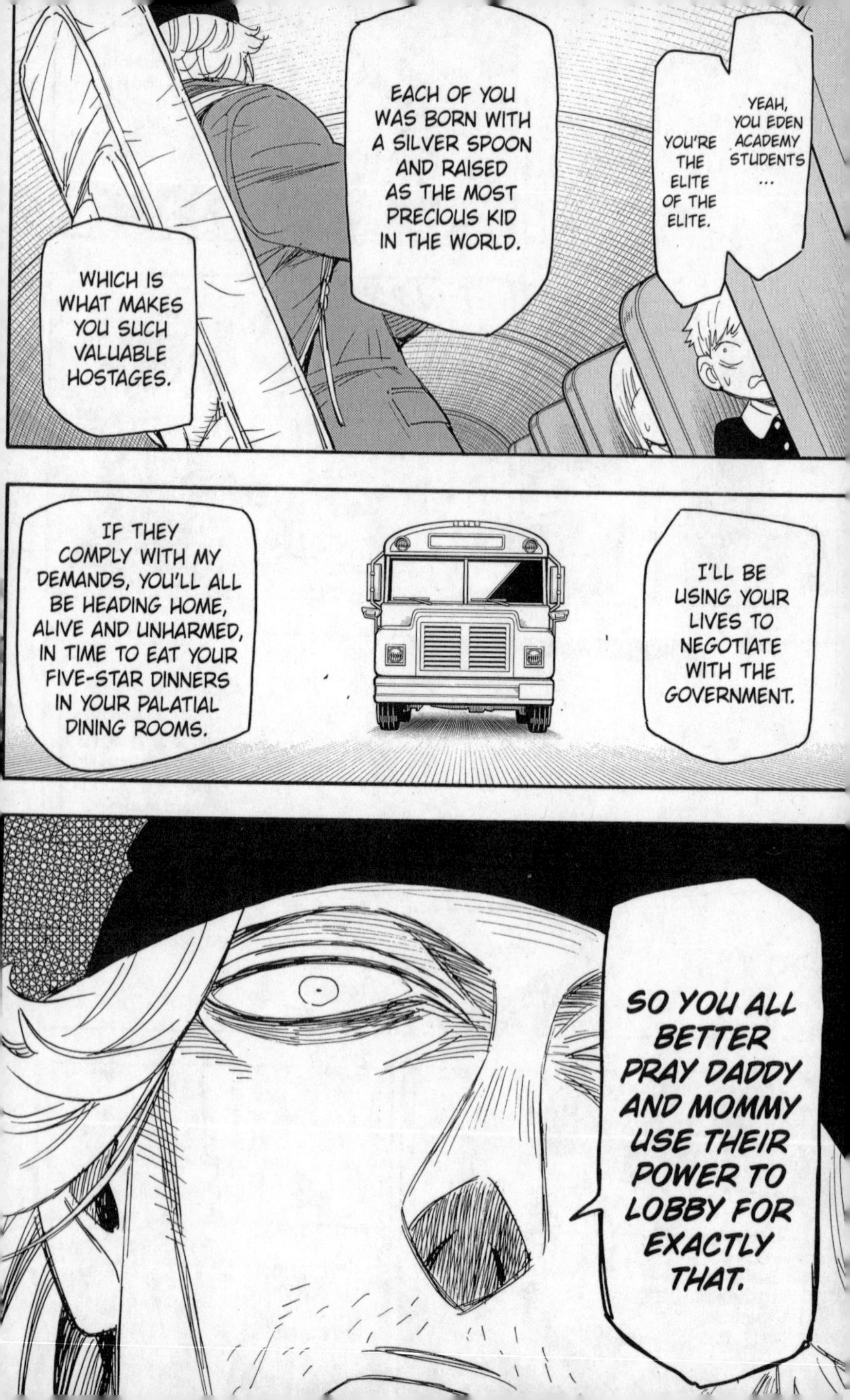
YEAH, YOU EDEN ACADEMY STUDENTS...
YOU'RE THE ELITE OF THE ELITE.
EACH OF YOU WAS BORN WITH A SILVER SPOON AND RAISED AS THE MOST PRECIOUS KID IN THE WORLD.
WHICH IS WHAT MAKES YOU SUCH VALUABLE HOSTAGES.
I'LL BE USING YOUR LIVES TO NEGOTIATE WITH THE GOVERNMENT.
IF THEY COMPLY WITH MY DEMANDS, YOU'LL ALL BE HEADING HOME, ALIVE AND UNHARMED, IN TIME TO EAT YOUR FIVE-STAR DINNERS IN YOUR PALATIAL DINING ROOMS.
SO YOU ALL BETTER PRAY DADDY AND MOMMY USE THEIR POWER TO LOBBY FOR EXACTLY THAT.

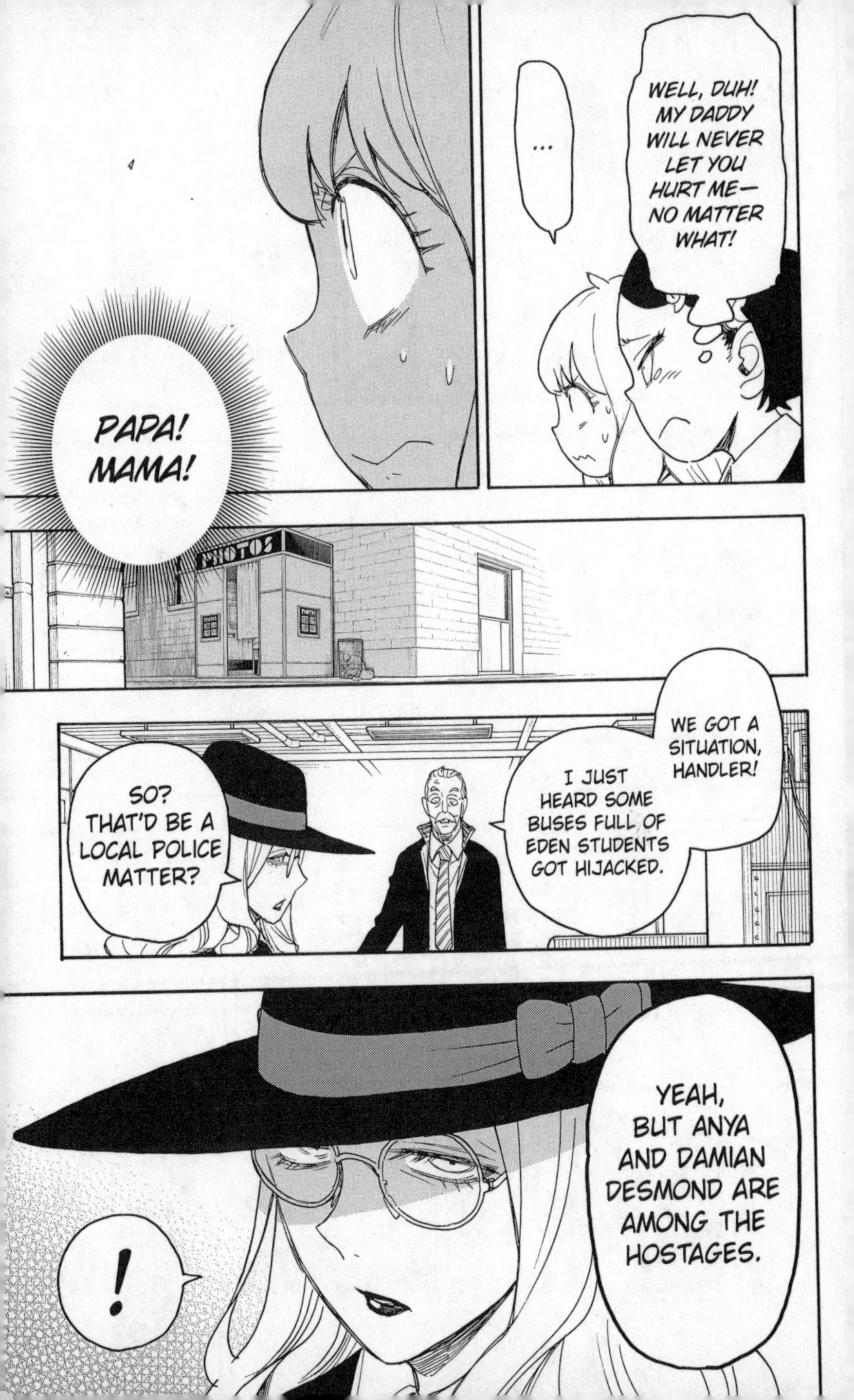
WELL, DUH! MY DADDY WILL NEVER LET YOU HURT ME— NO MATTER WHAT!
...
PAPA! MAMA!
PHOTOS
WE GOT A SITUATION, HANDLER!
I JUST HEARD SOME BUSES FULL OF EDEN STUDENTS GOT HIJACKED.
SO? THAT'D BE A LOCAL POLICE MATTER?
YEAH, BUT ANYA AND DAMIAN DESMOND ARE AMONG THE HOSTAGES.
!

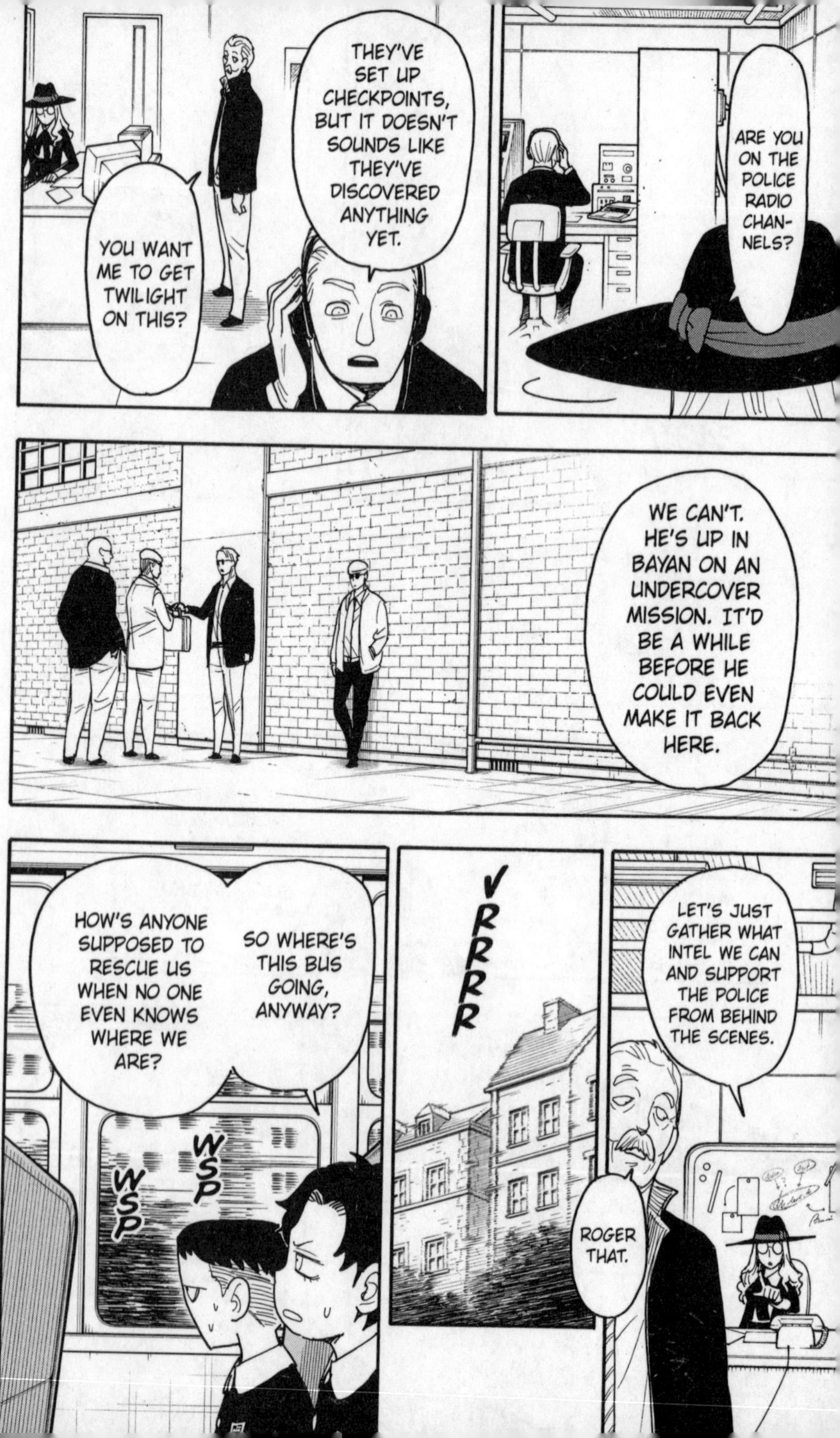
ARE YOU ON THE POLICE RADIO CHANNELS?
THEY'VE SET UP CHECKPOINTS, BUT IT DOESN'T SOUNDS LIKE THEY'VE DISCOVERED ANYTHING YET.
YOU WANT ME TO GET TWILIGHT ON THIS?
WE CAN'T. HE'S UP IN BAYAN ON AN UNDERCOVER MISSION. IT'D BE A WHILE BEFORE HE COULD EVEN MAKE IT BACK HERE.
LET'S JUST GATHER WHAT INTEL WE CAN AND SUPPORT THE POLICE FROM BEHIND THE SCENES.
ROGER THAT.
VRRRR
SO WHERE'S THIS BUS GOING, ANYWAY?
HOW'S ANYONE SUPPOSED TO RESCUE US WHEN NO ONE EVEN KNOWS WHERE WE ARE?
WSP
WSP

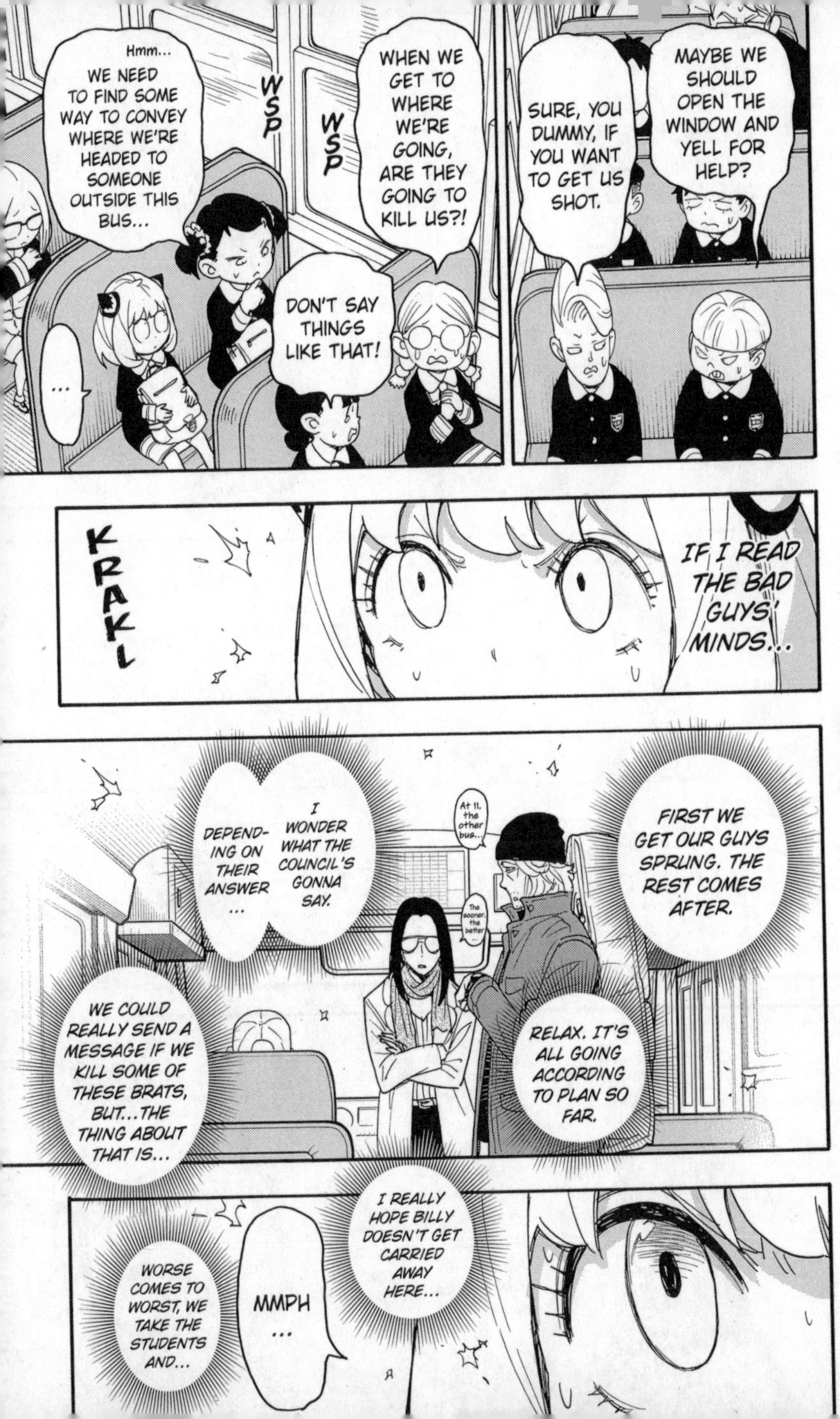

MAYBE WE SHOULD OPEN THE WINDOW AND YELL FOR HELP?
SURE, YOU DUMMY, IF YOU WANT TO GET US SHOT.
WHEN WE GET TO WHERE WE'RE GOING, ARE THEY GOING TO KILL US?!
WSP
WSP
Hmm... WE NEED TO FIND SOME WAY TO CONVEY WHERE WE'RE HEADED TO SOMEONE OUTSIDE THIS BUS...
DON'T SAY THINGS LIKE THAT!
...
IF I READ THE BAD GUYS' MINDS...
KRAKL
FIRST WE GET OUR GUYS SPRUNG. THE REST COMES AFTER.
At 11, the other bus...
The sooner, the better...
I WONDER WHAT THE COUNCIL'S GONNA SAY.
DEPENDING ON THEIR ANSWER...
RELAX. IT'S ALL GOING ACCORDING TO PLAN SO FAR.
WE COULD REALLY SEND A MESSAGE IF WE KILL SOME OF THESE BRATS, BUT...THE THING ABOUT THAT IS...
I REALLY HOPE BILLY DOESN'T GET CARRIED AWAY HERE...
MMPH ...
WORSE COMES TO WORST, WE TAKE THE STUDENTS AND...

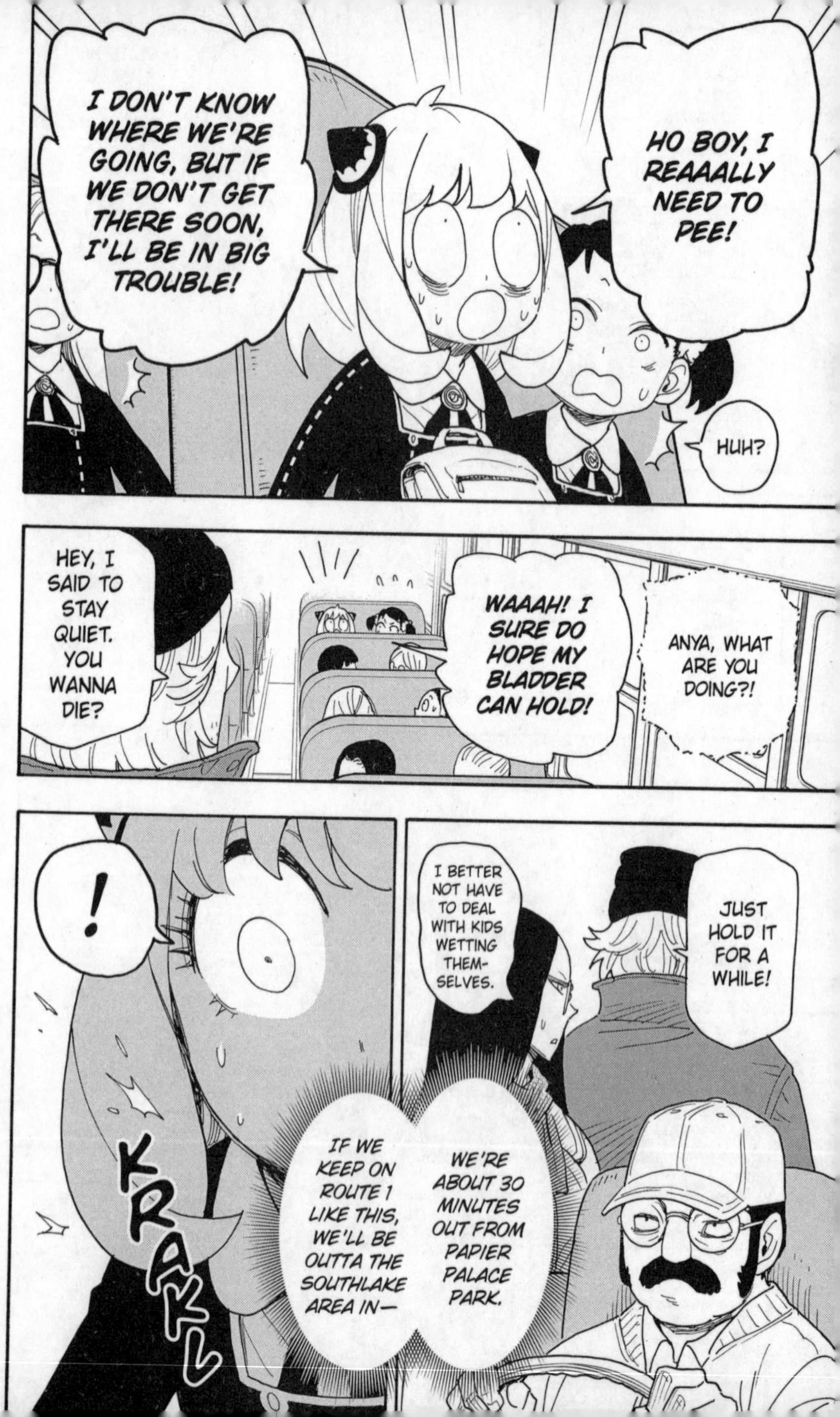
HO BOY, I REAAALLY NEED TO PEE!
I DON'T KNOW WHERE WE'RE GOING, BUT IF WE DON'T GET THERE SOON, I'LL BE IN BIG TROUBLE!
HUH?
ANYA, WHAT ARE YOU DOING?!
WAAAH! I SURE DO HOPE MY BLADDER CAN HOLD!
HEY, I SAID TO STAY QUIET. YOU WANNA DIE?
JUST HOLD IT FOR A WHILE!
I BETTER NOT HAVE TO DEAL WITH KIDS WETTING THEM-SELVES.
!
WE'RE ABOUT 30 MINUTES OUT FROM PAPIER PALACE PARK.
IF WE KEEP ON ROUTE 1 LIKE THIS, WE'LL BE OUTTA THE SOUTHLAKE AREA IN—

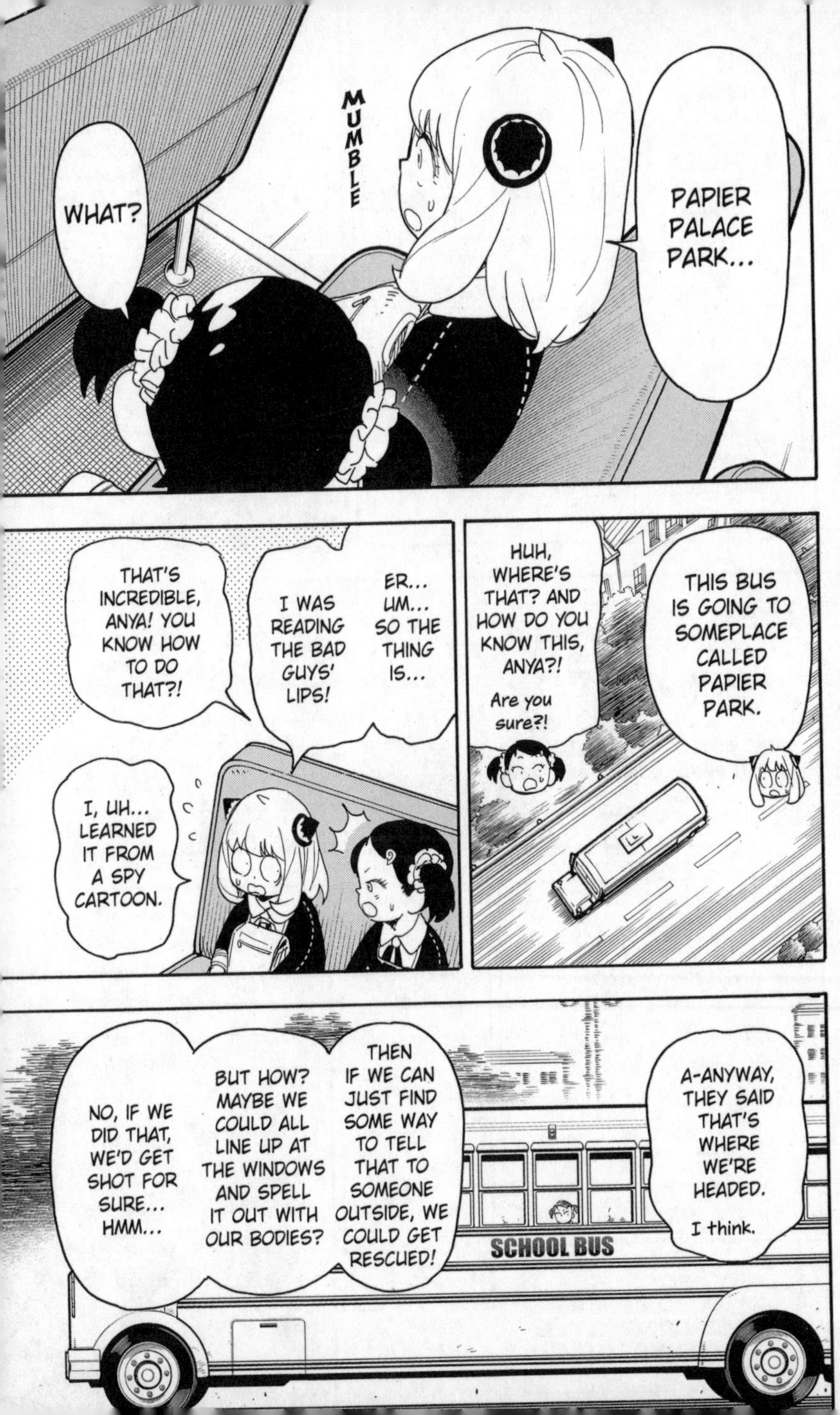
PAPIER PALACE PARK...
MUMBLE
WHAT?
THIS BUS IS GOING TO SOMEPLACE CALLED PAPIER PARK.
HUH, WHERE'S THAT? AND HOW DO YOU KNOW THIS, ANYA?!
Are you sure?!
ER... UM... SO THE THING IS...
I WAS READING THE BAD GUYS' LIPS!
THAT'S INCREDIBLE, ANYA! YOU KNOW HOW TO DO THAT?!
I, UH... LEARNED IT FROM A SPY CARTOON.
A-ANYWAY, THEY SAID THAT'S WHERE WE'RE HEADED.
I think.
SCHOOL BUS
THEN IF WE CAN JUST FIND SOME WAY TO TELL THAT TO SOMEONE OUTSIDE, WE COULD GET RESCUED!
BUT HOW? MAYBE WE COULD ALL LINE UP AT THE WINDOWS AND SPELL IT OUT WITH OUR BODIES?
NO, IF WE DID THAT, WE'D GET SHOT FOR SURE... HMM...

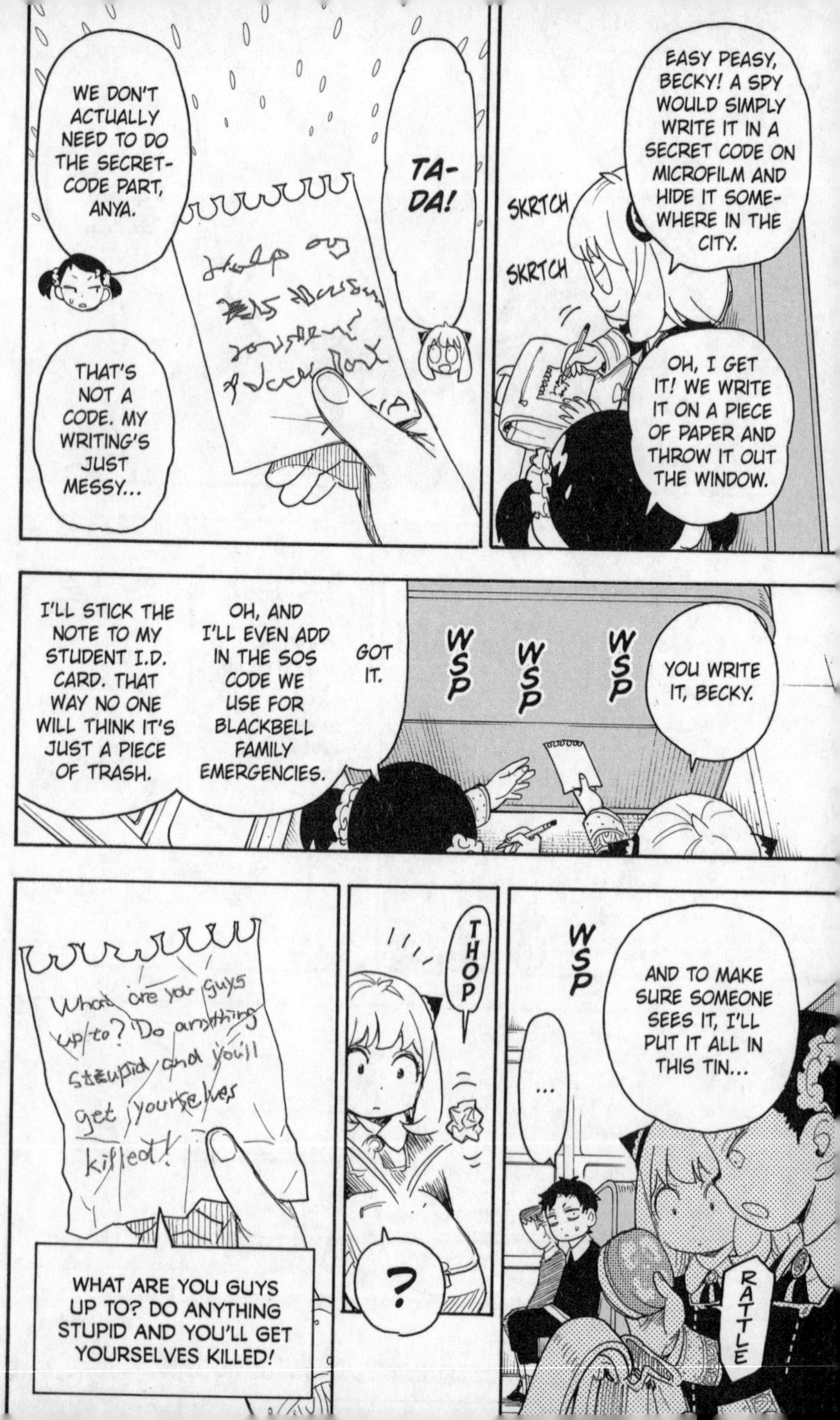
EASY PEASY, BECKY! A SPY WOULD SIMPLY WRITE IT IN A SECRET CODE ON MICROFILM AND HIDE IT SOMEWHERE IN THE CITY.
SKRTCH
SKRTCH
OH, I GET IT! WE WRITE IT ON A PIECE OF PAPER AND THROW IT OUT THE WINDOW.
TA-DA!
WE DON'T ACTUALLY NEED TO DO THE SECRET-CODE PART, ANYA.
THAT'S NOT A CODE. MY WRITING'S JUST MESSY...
YOU WRITE IT, BECKY.
WSP
WSP
WSP
GOT IT.
OH, AND I'LL EVEN ADD IN THE SOS CODE WE USE FOR BLACKBELL FAMILY EMERGENCIES.
I'LL STICK THE NOTE TO MY STUDENT I.D. CARD. THAT WAY NO ONE WILL THINK IT'S JUST A PIECE OF TRASH.
AND TO MAKE SURE SOMEONE SEES IT, I'LL PUT IT ALL IN THIS TIN...
WSP
...
RATTLE
THOP
?
What are you guys up to? Do anything stupid and you'll get yourselves killed!
WHAT ARE YOU GUYS UP TO? DO ANYTHING STUPID AND YOU'LL GET YOURSELVES KILLED!

THOP

? ?

...

We know where the
bad guys are going!
So we need to tell
our rescuers!
It's our only hope!

WE KNOW WHERE THE
BAD GUYS ARE GOING, SO WE
NEED TO TELL OUR RESCUERS!
IT'S OUR ONLY HOPE!

THOP

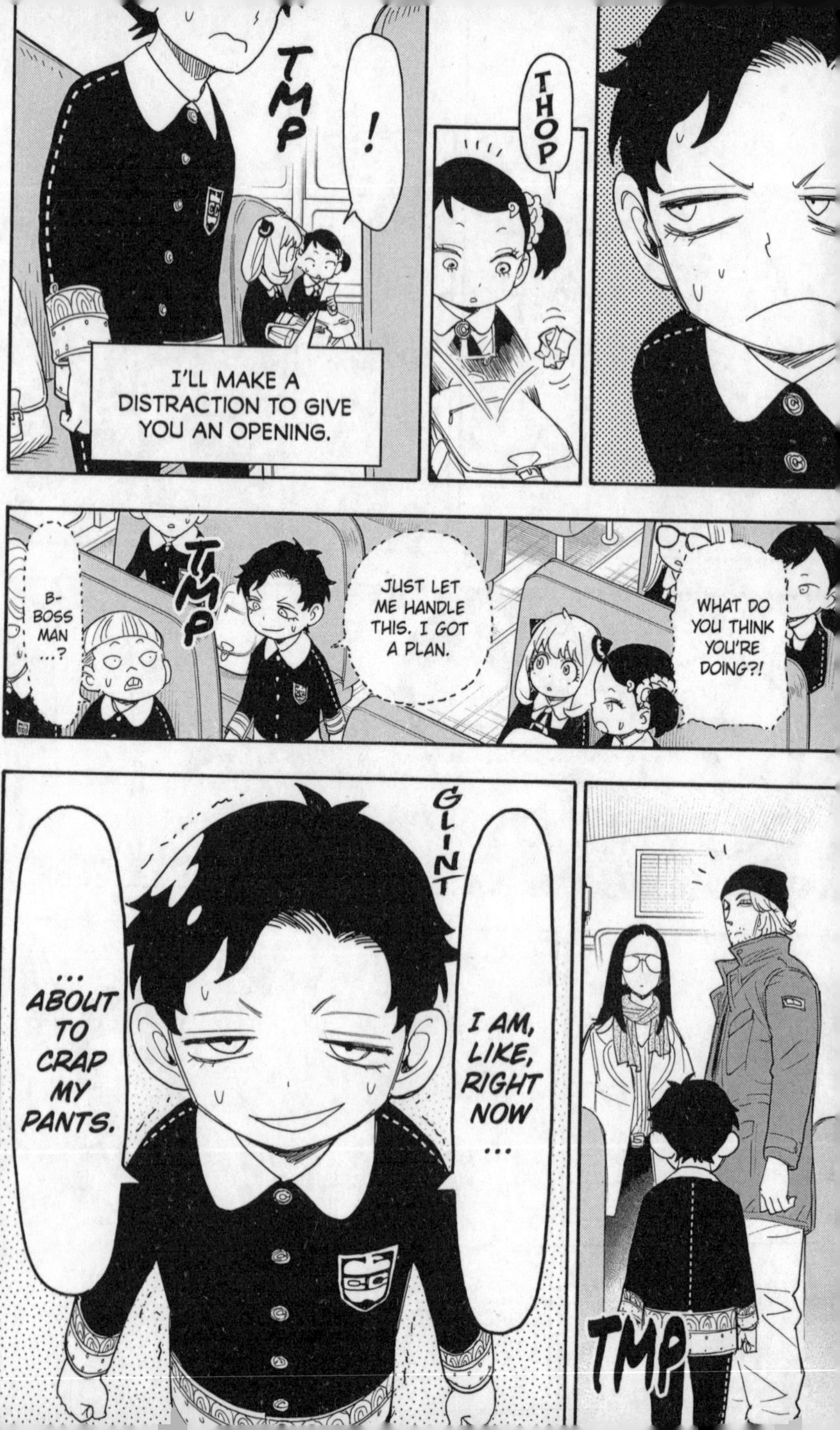
THOP
TMP
!
I'LL MAKE A DISTRACTION TO GIVE YOU AN OPENING.
WHAT DO YOU THINK YOU'RE DOING?!
JUST LET ME HANDLE THIS. I GOT A PLAN.
TMP
B-BOSS MAN ...?
TMP
GLINT
I AM, LIKE, RIGHT NOW ...
... ABOUT TO CRAP MY PANTS.

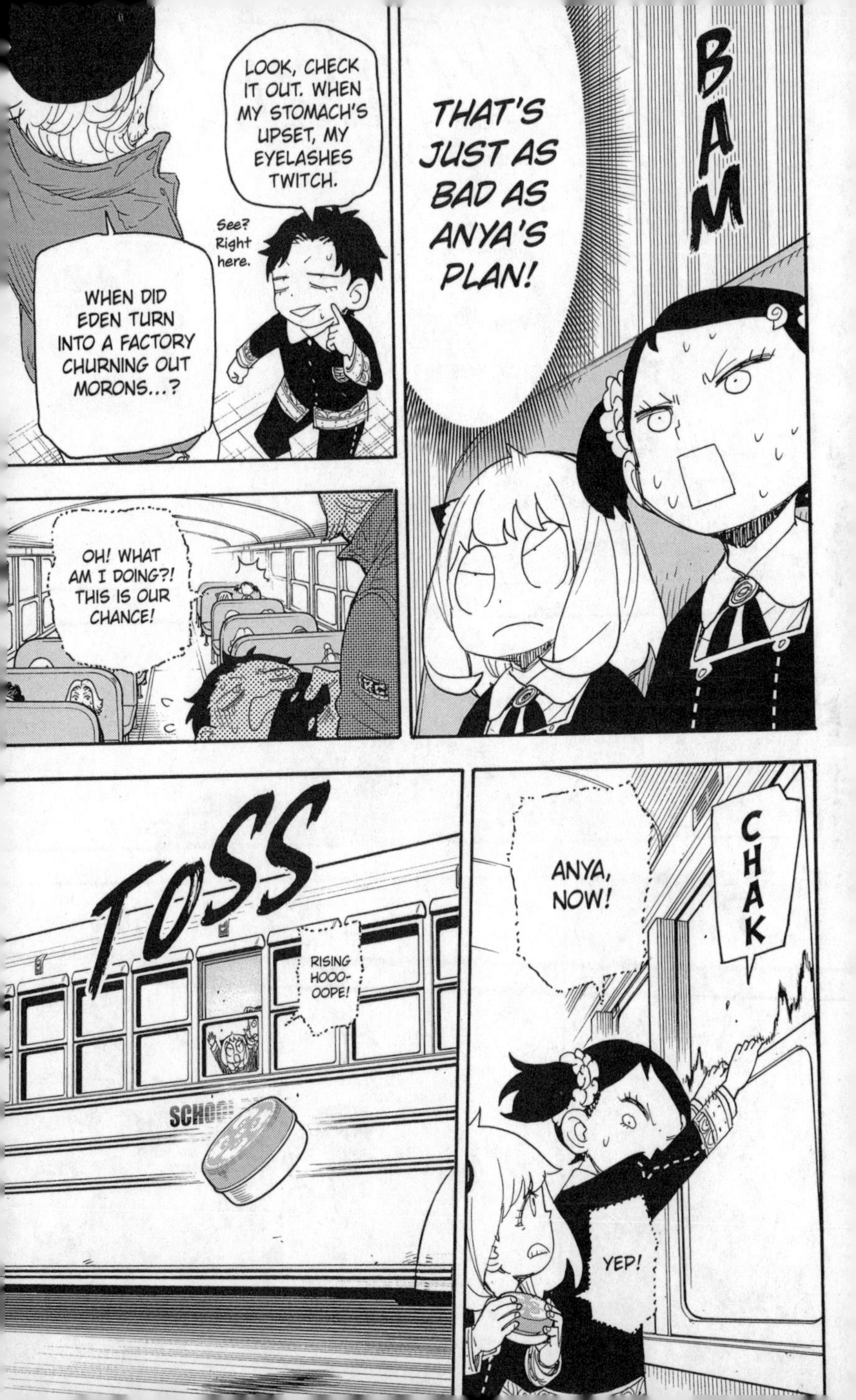
BAM
THAT'S JUST AS BAD AS ANYA'S PLAN!
LOOK, CHECK IT OUT. WHEN MY STOMACH'S UPSET, MY EYELASHES TWITCH.
See? Right here.
WHEN DID EDEN TURN INTO A FACTORY CHURNING OUT MORONS...?
OH! WHAT AM I DOING?! THIS IS OUR CHANCE!
CHAK
ANYA, NOW!
YEP!
TOSS
RISING HOOOO-OOPE!
SCHOO

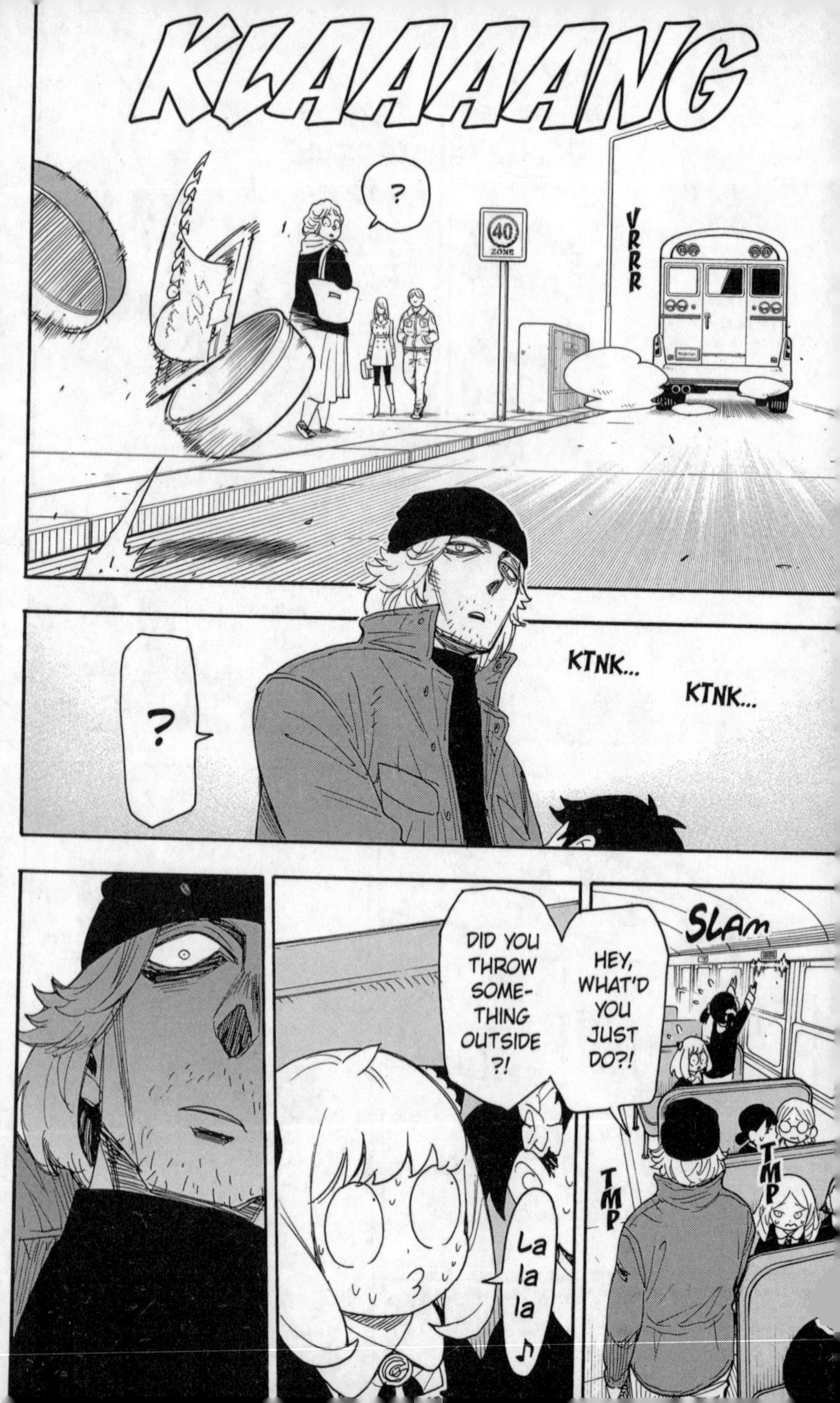
KLAAAANG
VRRR
?
40
ZONE
KTNK...
KTNK...
?
SLAM
HEY, WHAT'D YOU JUST DO?!
TMP
TMP
DID YOU THROW SOME-THING OUTSIDE?!
La la la ♪

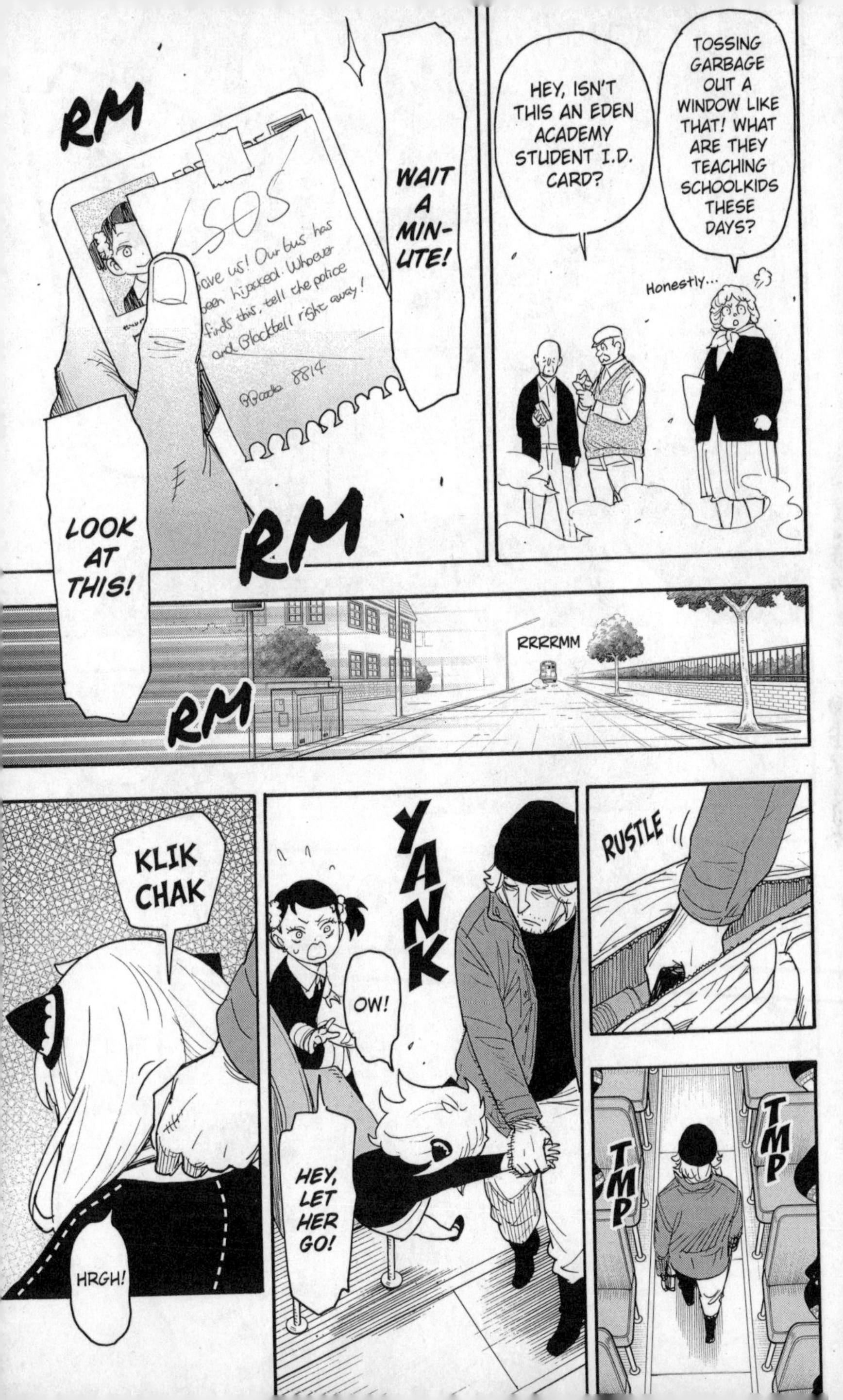
TOSSING GARBAGE OUT A WINDOW LIKE THAT! WHAT ARE THEY TEACHING SCHOOLKIDS THESE DAYS?
HEY, ISN'T THIS AN EDEN ACADEMY STUDENT I.D. CARD?
Honestly...
RM
WAIT A MIN-UTE!
SOS
Save us! Our bus has been hijacked. Whoever finds this, tell the police and Blackbell right away!
8814
LOOK AT THIS!
RM
RRRRMM
RM
RUSTLE
TMP
TMP
YANK
OW!
HEY, LET HER GO!
KLIK CHAK
HRGH!

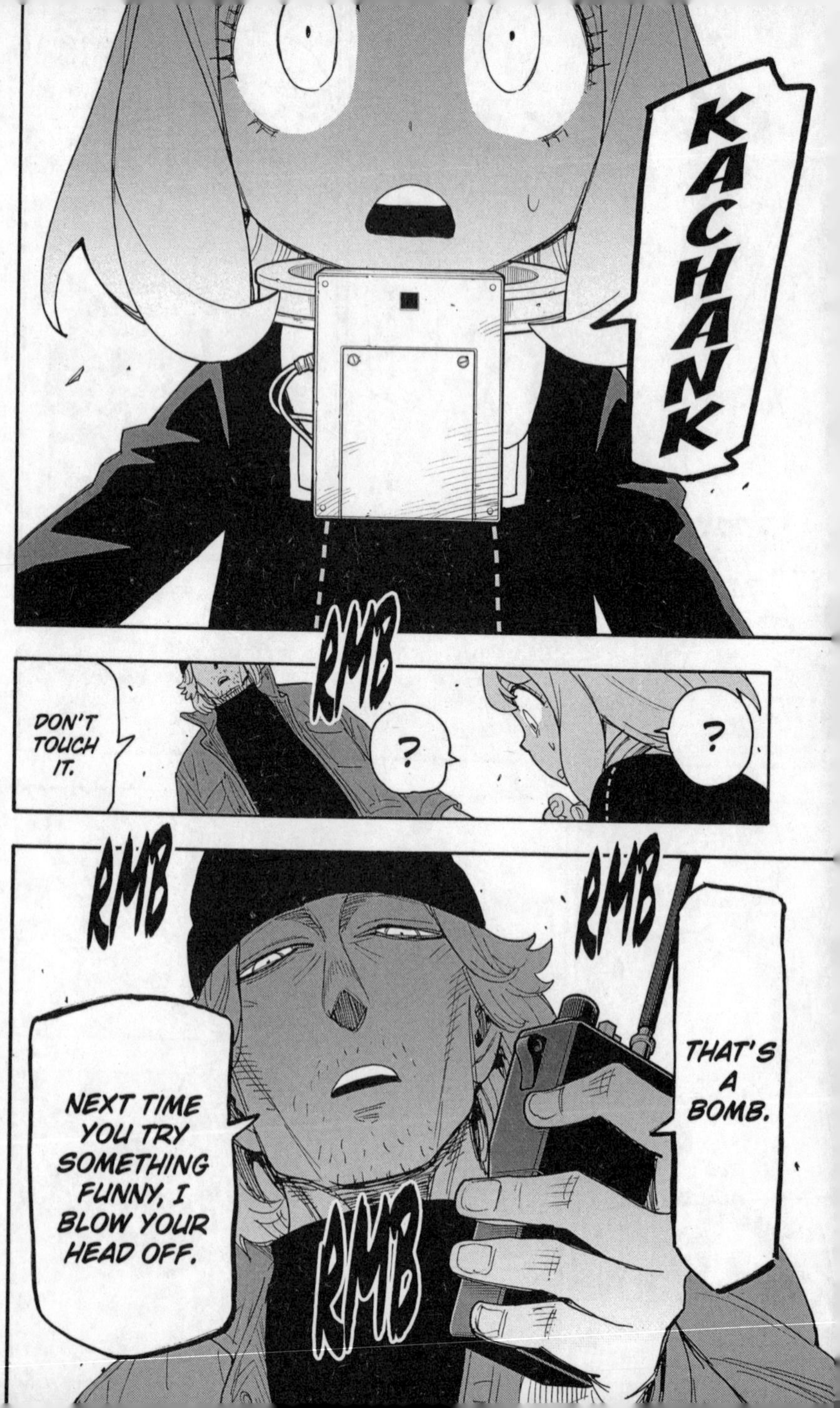
KACHANK
RMB
?
?
DON'T TOUCH IT.
RMB
RMB
THAT'S A BOMB.
NEXT TIME YOU TRY SOMETHING FUNNY, I BLOW YOUR HEAD OFF.
RMB

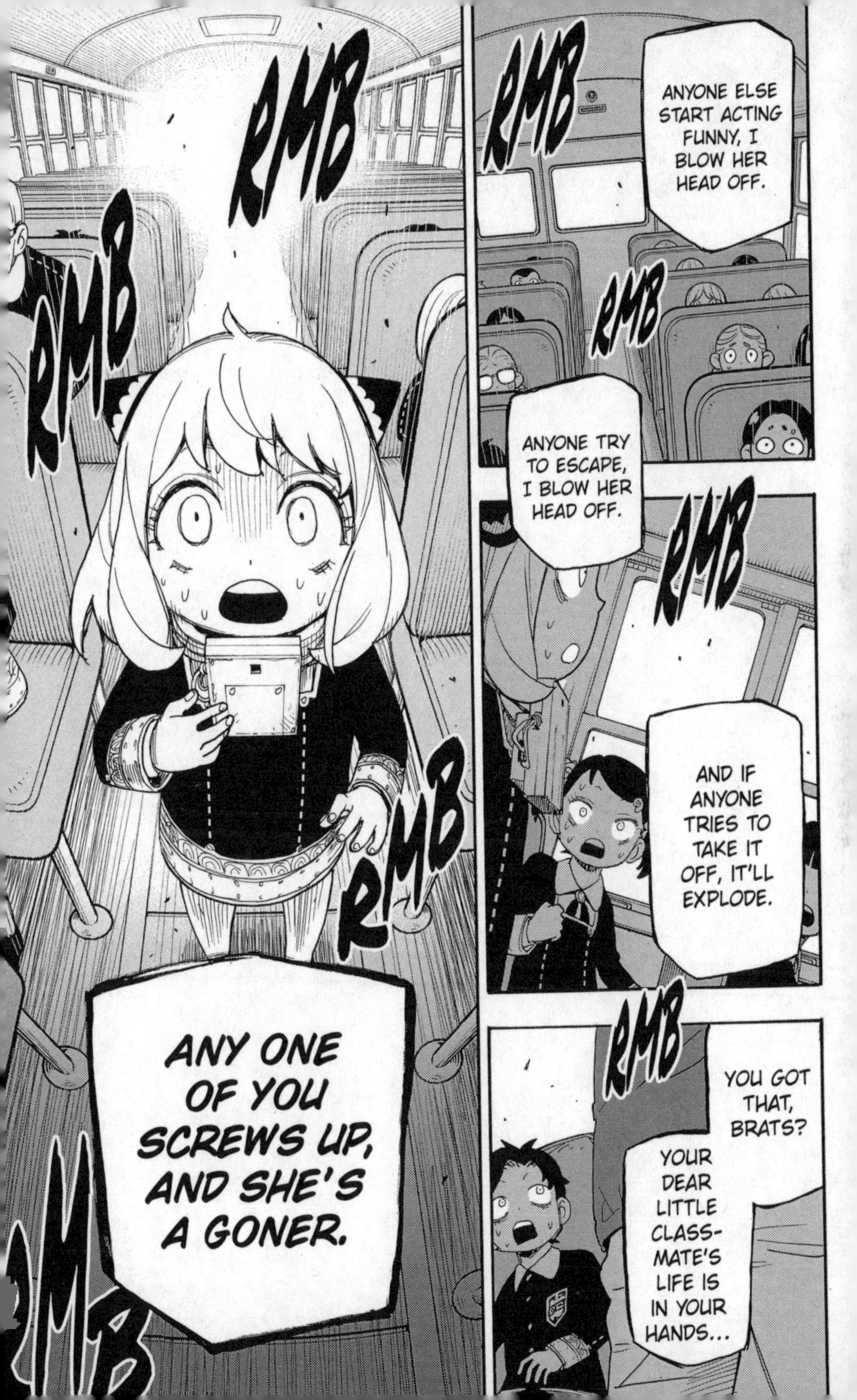
RMB
ANYONE ELSE START ACTING FUNNY, I BLOW HER HEAD OFF.
RMB
ANYONE TRY TO ESCAPE, I BLOW HER HEAD OFF.
RMB
AND IF ANYONE TRIES TO TAKE IT OFF, IT'LL EXPLODE.
RMB
YOU GOT THAT, BRATS?
YOUR DEAR LITTLE CLASS-MATE'S LIFE IS IN YOUR HANDS...
RMB
RMB
RMB
ANY ONE OF YOU SCREWS UP, AND SHE'S A GONER.
RMB

SPY×FAMILY

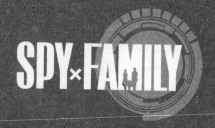

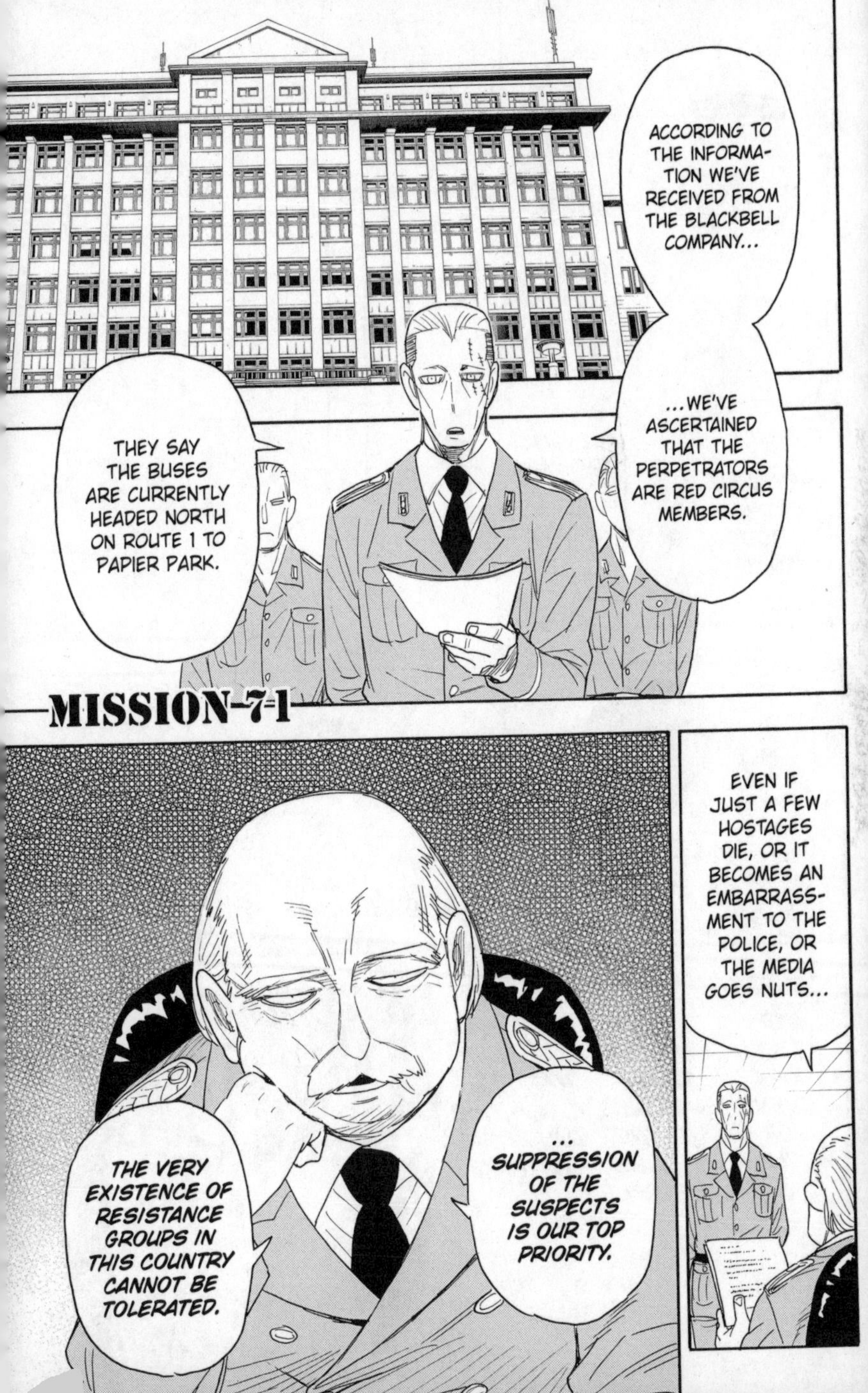
ACCORDING TO THE INFORMATION WE'VE RECEIVED FROM THE BLACKBELL COMPANY...
...WE'VE ASCERTAINED THAT THE PERPETRATORS ARE RED CIRCUS MEMBERS.
THEY SAY THE BUSES ARE CURRENTLY HEADED NORTH ON ROUTE 1 TO PAPIER PARK.
MISSION 7-1
EVEN IF JUST A FEW HOSTAGES DIE, OR IT BECOMES AN EMBARRASSMENT TO THE POLICE, OR THE MEDIA GOES NUTS...
...SUPPRESSION OF THE SUSPECTS IS OUR TOP PRIORITY.
THE VERY EXISTENCE OF RESISTANCE GROUPS IN THIS COUNTRY CANNOT BE TOLERATED.

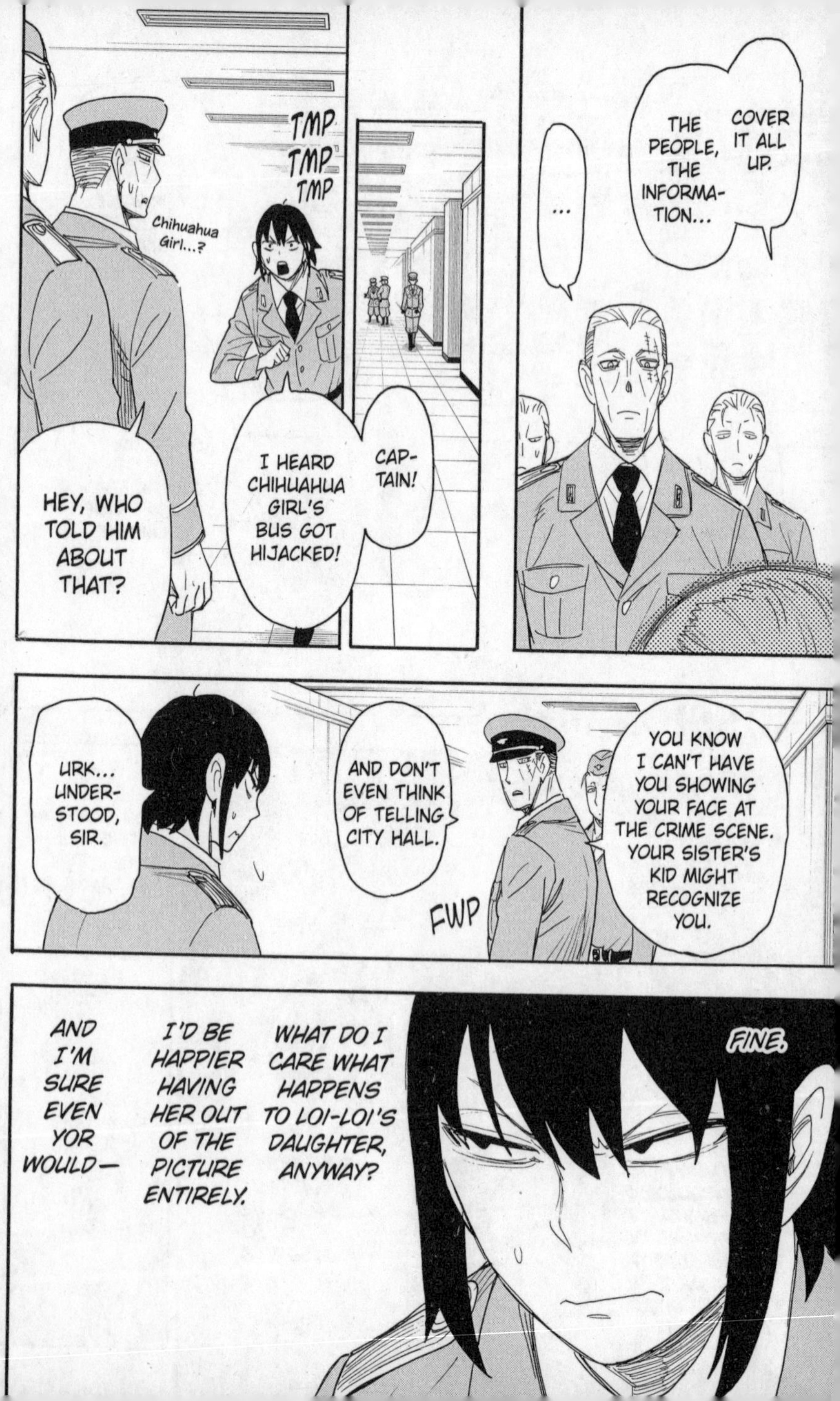
COVER IT ALL UP.
THE PEOPLE, THE INFORMATION...
...
TMP TMP TMP
CAPTAIN!
I HEARD CHIHUAHUA GIRL'S BUS GOT HIJACKED!
Chihuahua Girl...?
HEY, WHO TOLD HIM ABOUT THAT?
YOU KNOW I CAN'T HAVE YOU SHOWING YOUR FACE AT THE CRIME SCENE. YOUR SISTER'S KID MIGHT RECOGNIZE YOU.
FWP
AND DON'T EVEN THINK OF TELLING CITY HALL.
URK... UNDERSTOOD, SIR.
FINE.
WHAT DO I CARE WHAT HAPPENS TO LOI-LOI'S DAUGHTER, ANYWAY?
I'D BE HAPPIER HAVING HER OUT OF THE PICTURE ENTIRELY.
AND I'M SURE EVEN YOR WOULD—

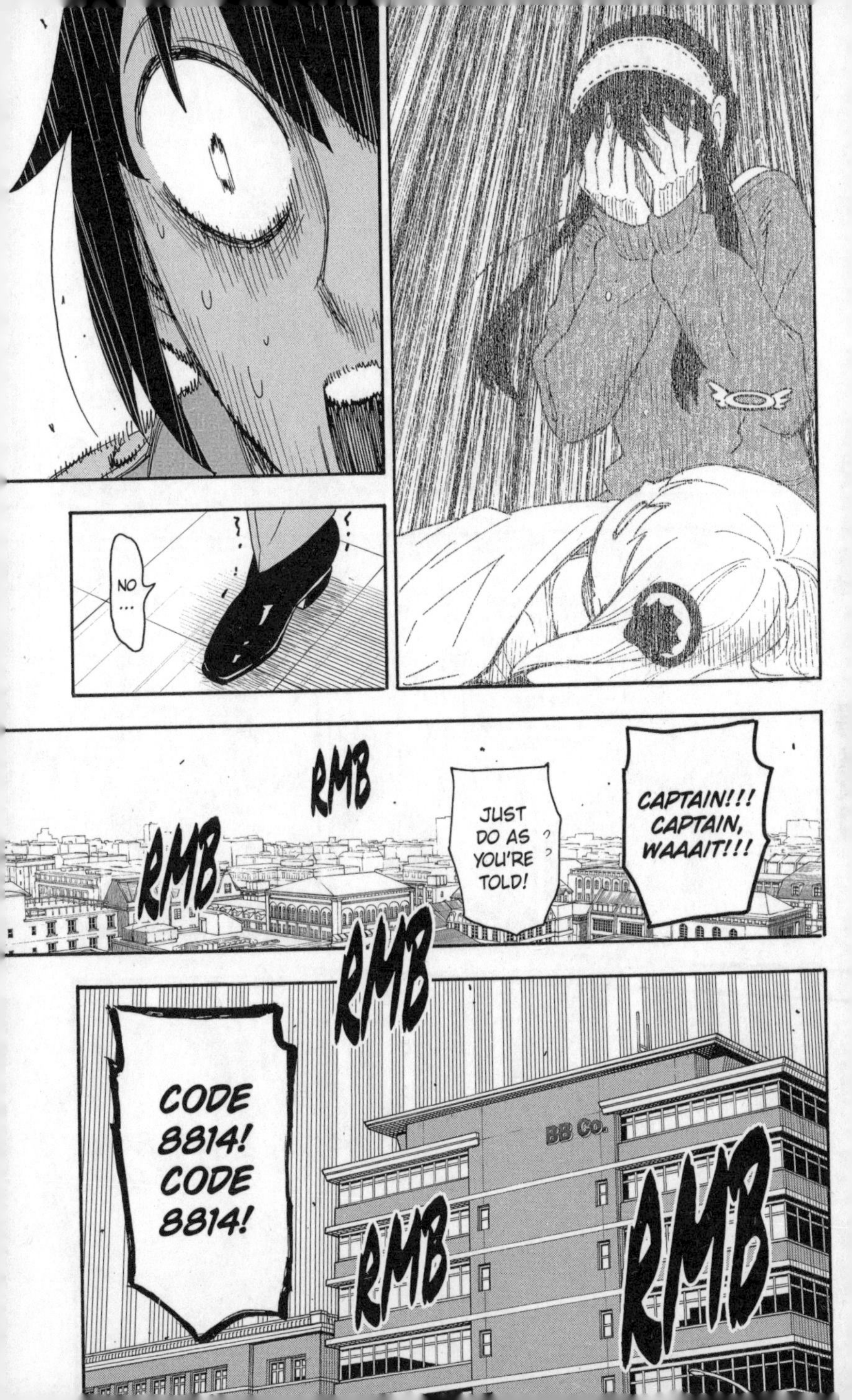
NO ...
CAPTAIN!!! CAPTAIN, WAAAIT!!!
JUST DO AS YOU'RE TOLD!
RMB
RMB
RMB
RMB
RMB
BB Co.
CODE 8814! CODE 8814!

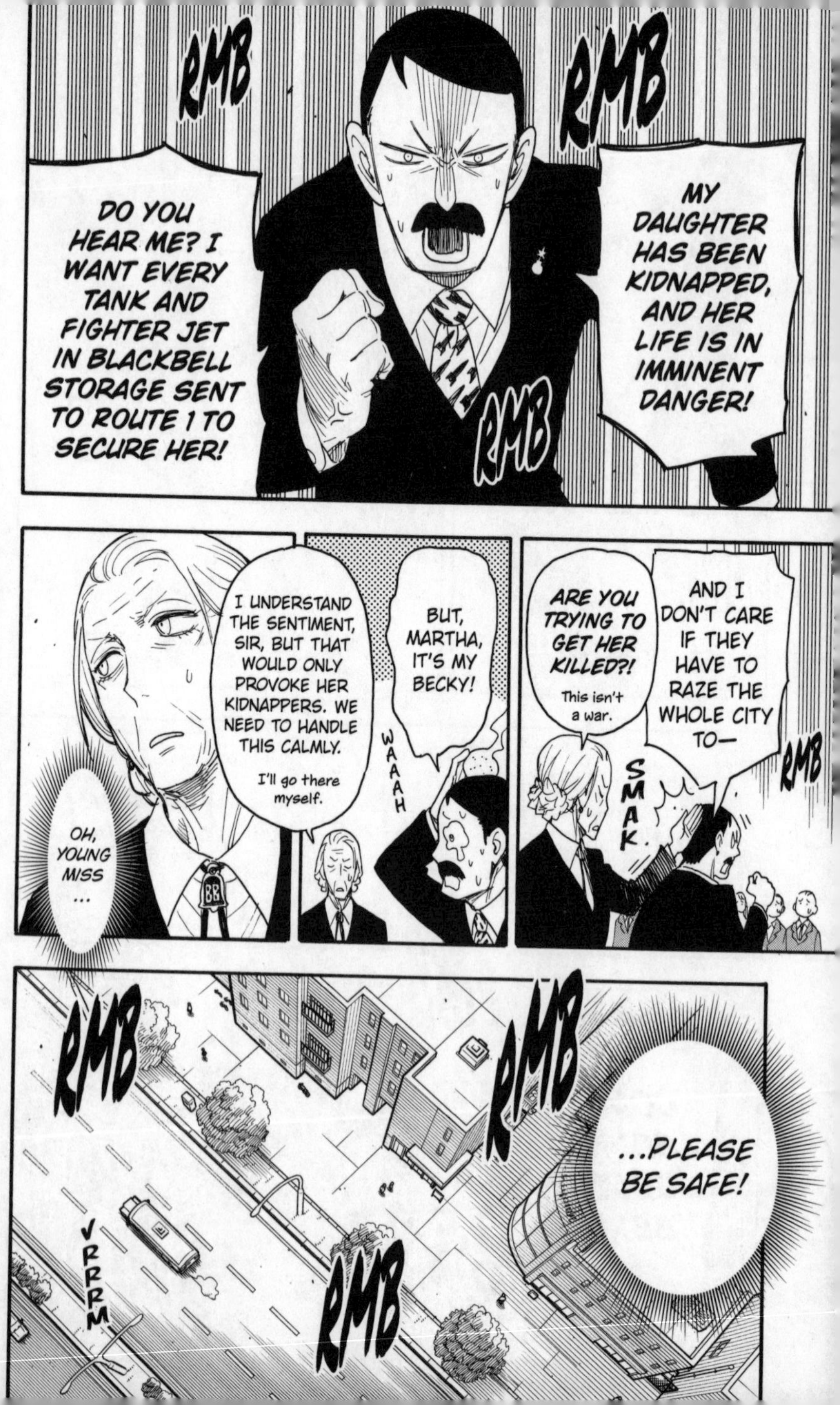
RMB
RMB
MY DAUGHTER HAS BEEN KIDNAPPED, AND HER LIFE IS IN IMMINENT DANGER!
DO YOU HEAR ME? I WANT EVERY TANK AND FIGHTER JET IN BLACKBELL STORAGE SENT TO ROUTE 1 TO SECURE HER!
RMB
AND I DON'T CARE IF THEY HAVE TO RAZE THE WHOLE CITY TO—
RMB
SMAK
ARE YOU TRYING TO GET HER KILLED?!
This isn't a war.
BUT, MARTHA, IT'S MY BECKY!
WAAAAH
I UNDERSTAND THE SENTIMENT, SIR, BUT THAT WOULD ONLY PROVOKE HER KIDNAPPERS. WE NEED TO HANDLE THIS CALMLY.
I'll go there myself.
OH, YOUNG MISS ...
RMB
...PLEASE BE SAFE!
RMB
RMB
VRRRM

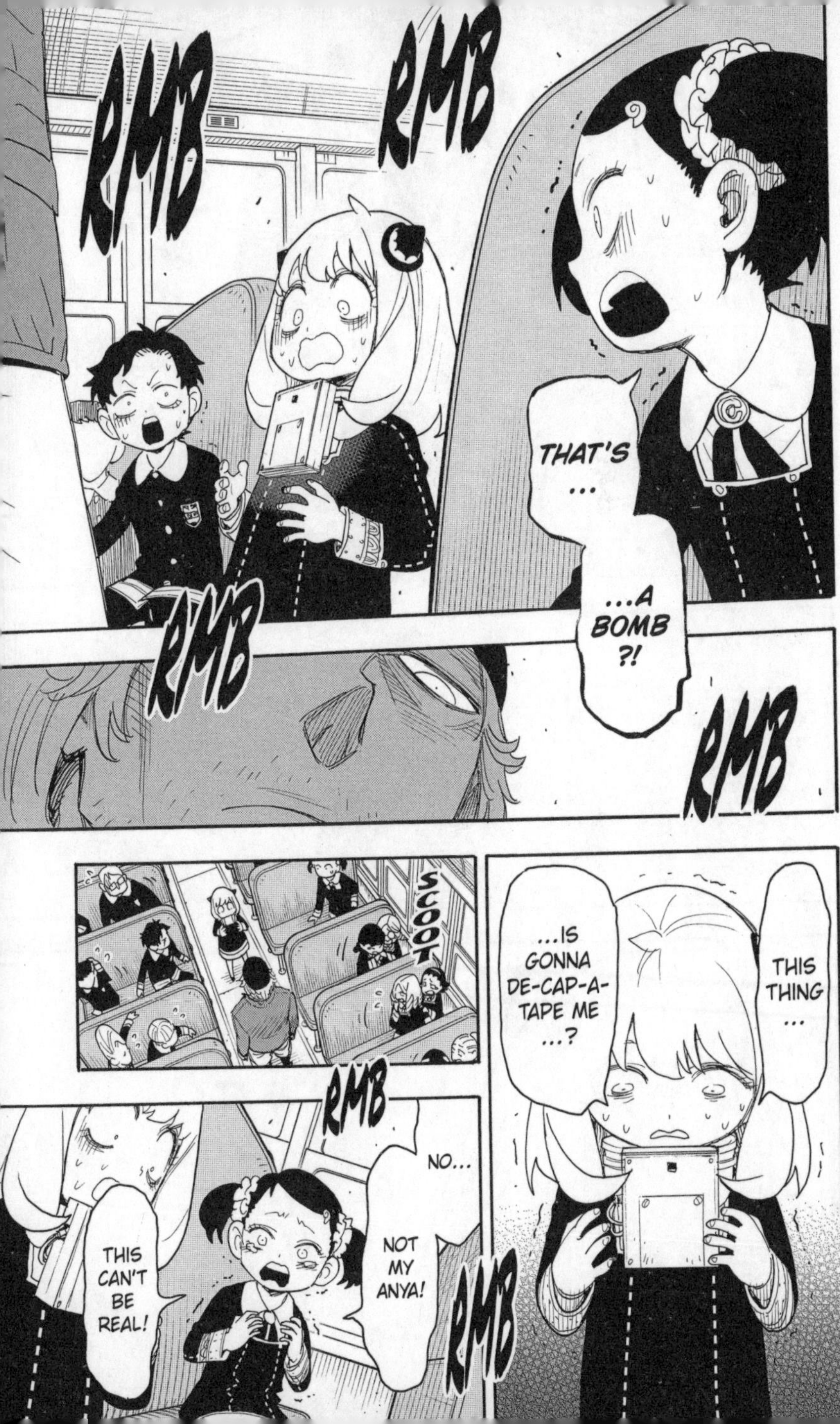
RMB
RMB
THAT'S ...
...A BOMB ?!
RMB
RMB
THIS THING ...
...IS GONNA DE-CAP-A-TAPE ME ...?
SCOOT
RMB
NO...
NOT MY ANYA!
THIS CAN'T BE REAL!
RMB

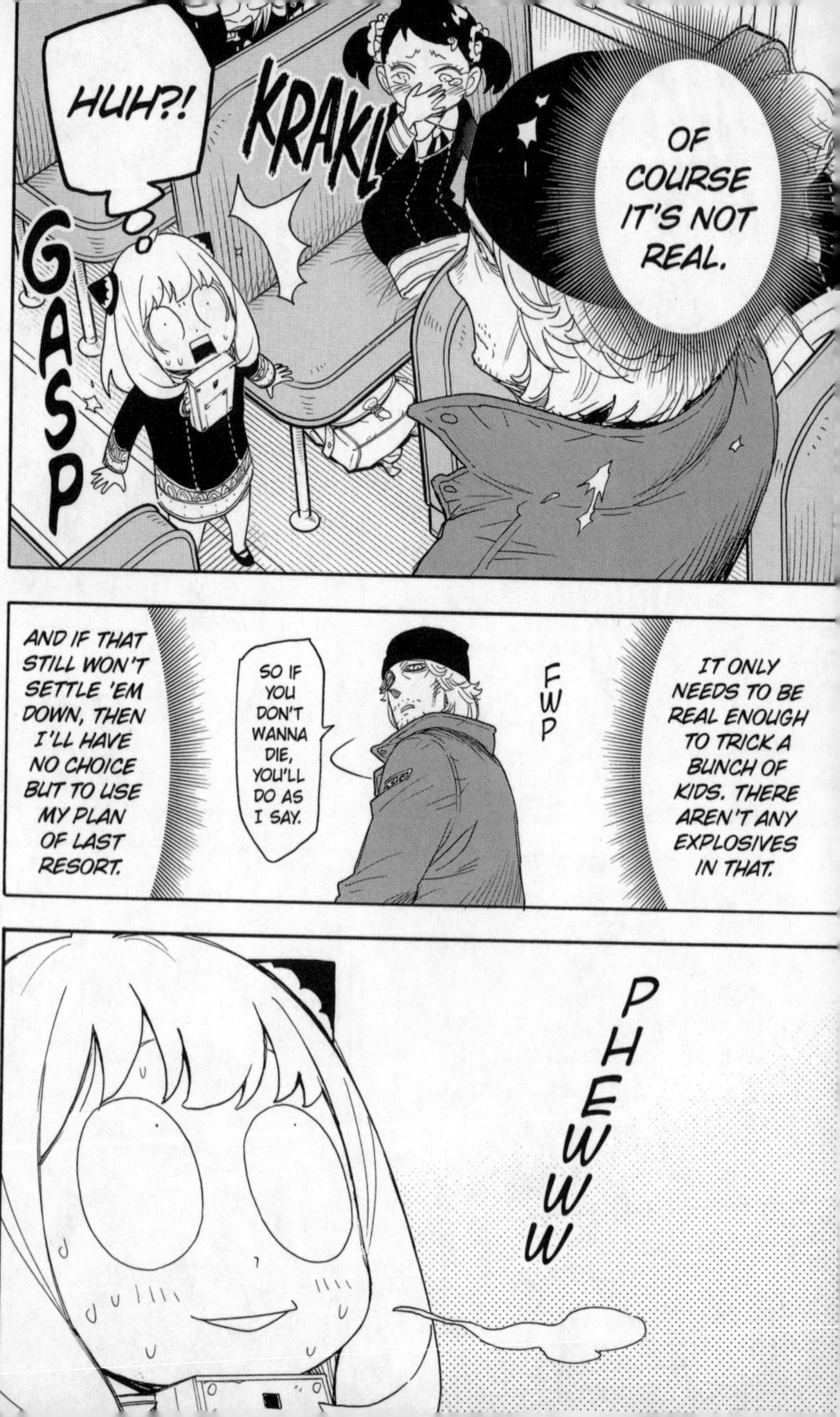
OF COURSE IT'S NOT REAL.
KRAKL
HUH?!
GASP
IT ONLY NEEDS TO BE REAL ENOUGH TO TRICK A BUNCH OF KIDS. THERE AREN'T ANY EXPLOSIVES IN THAT.
FWP
SO IF YOU DON'T WANNA DIE, YOU'LL DO AS I SAY.
AND IF THAT STILL WON'T SETTLE 'EM DOWN, THEN I'LL HAVE NO CHOICE BUT TO USE MY PLAN OF LAST RESORT.
PHEWWW

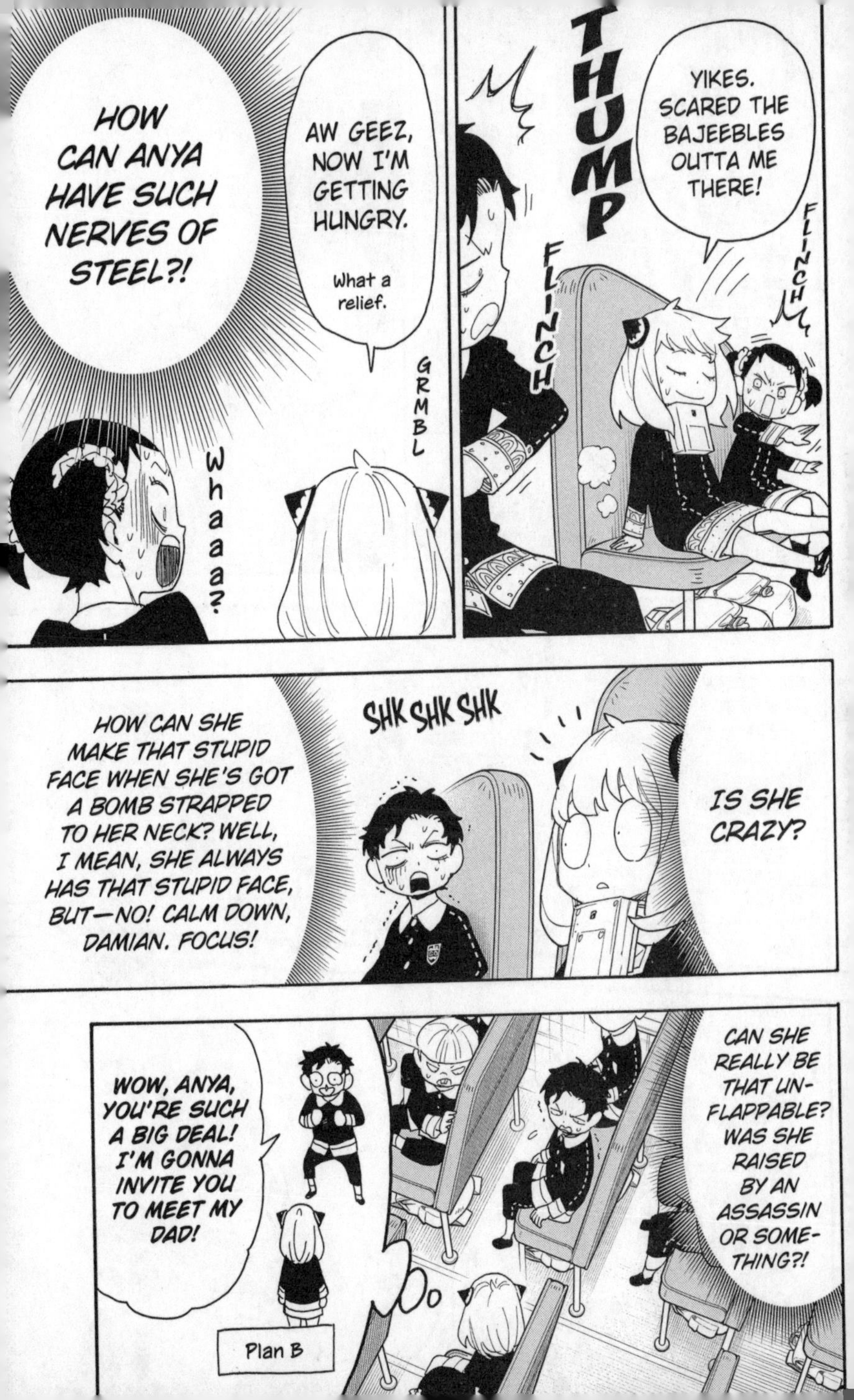

YIKES. SCARED THE BAJEEBLES OUTTA ME THERE!
THUMP
FLINCH
FLINCH
AW GEEZ, NOW I'M GETTING HUNGRY.
What a relief.
GRMBL
Whaaaa?
HOW CAN ANYA HAVE SUCH NERVES OF STEEL?!
IS SHE CRAZY?
SHK SHK SHK
HOW CAN SHE MAKE THAT STUPID FACE WHEN SHE'S GOT A BOMB STRAPPED TO HER NECK? WELL, I MEAN, SHE ALWAYS HAS THAT STUPID FACE, BUT—NO! CALM DOWN, DAMIAN. FOCUS!
CAN SHE REALLY BE THAT UN-FLAPPABLE? WAS SHE RAISED BY AN ASSASSIN OR SOME-THING?!
WOW, ANYA, YOU'RE SUCH A BIG DEAL! I'M GONNA INVITE YOU TO MEET MY DAD!
Oo
Plan B

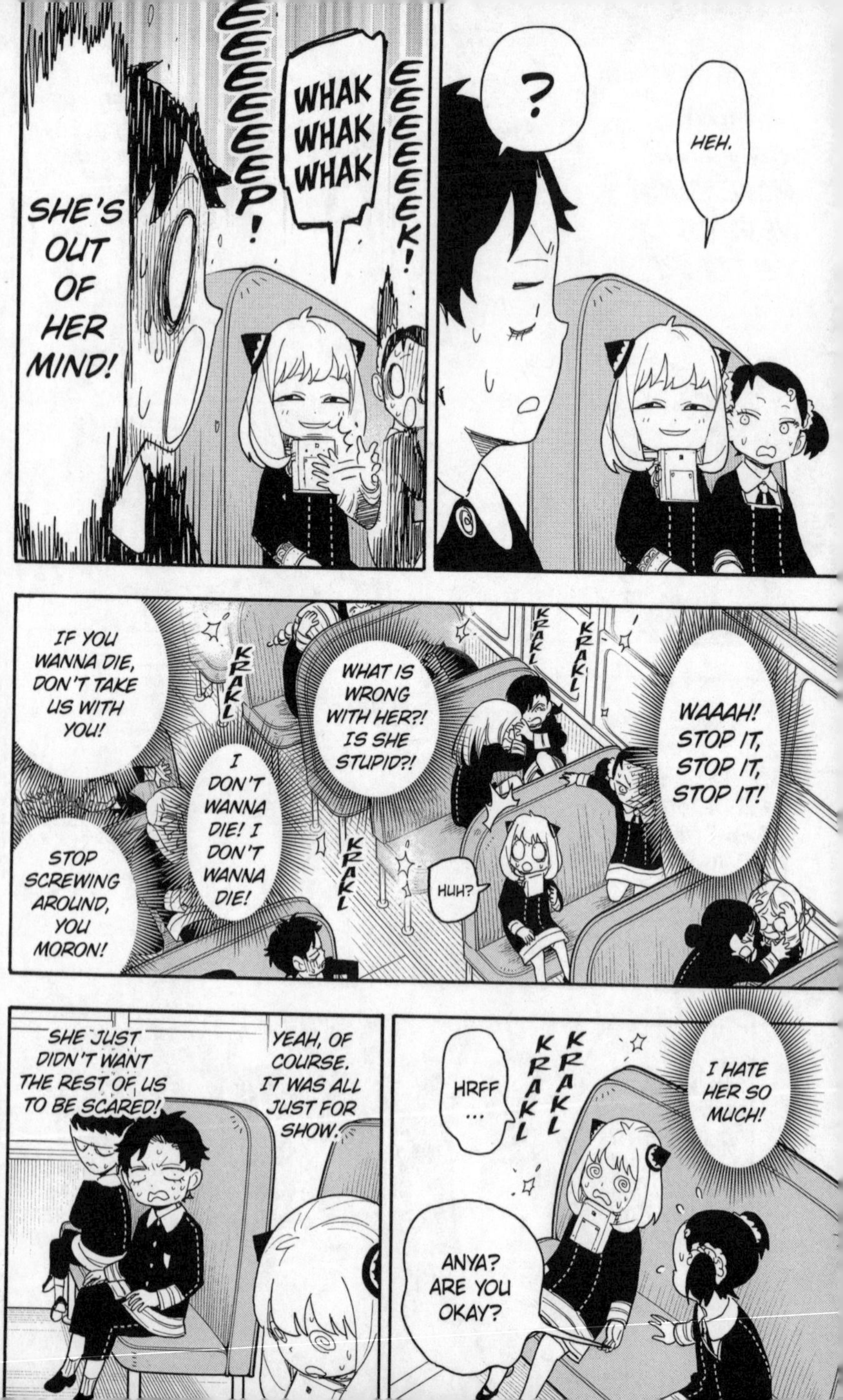
HEH.
?
EEEEEEEK!
WHAK WHAK WHAK
EEEEEEP!
SHE'S OUT OF HER MIND!
WAAAH! STOP IT, STOP IT, STOP IT!
KRAKL
KRAKL
WHAT IS WRONG WITH HER?! IS SHE STUPID?!
KRAKL
IF YOU WANNA DIE, DON'T TAKE US WITH YOU!
I DON'T WANNA DIE! I DON'T WANNA DIE!
KRAKL
HUH?
STOP SCREWING AROUND, YOU MORON!
I HATE HER SO MUCH!
KRAKL
KRAKL
HRFF ...
ANYA? ARE YOU OKAY?
YEAH, OF COURSE. IT WAS ALL JUST FOR SHOW.
SHE JUST DIDN'T WANT THE REST OF US TO BE SCARED!

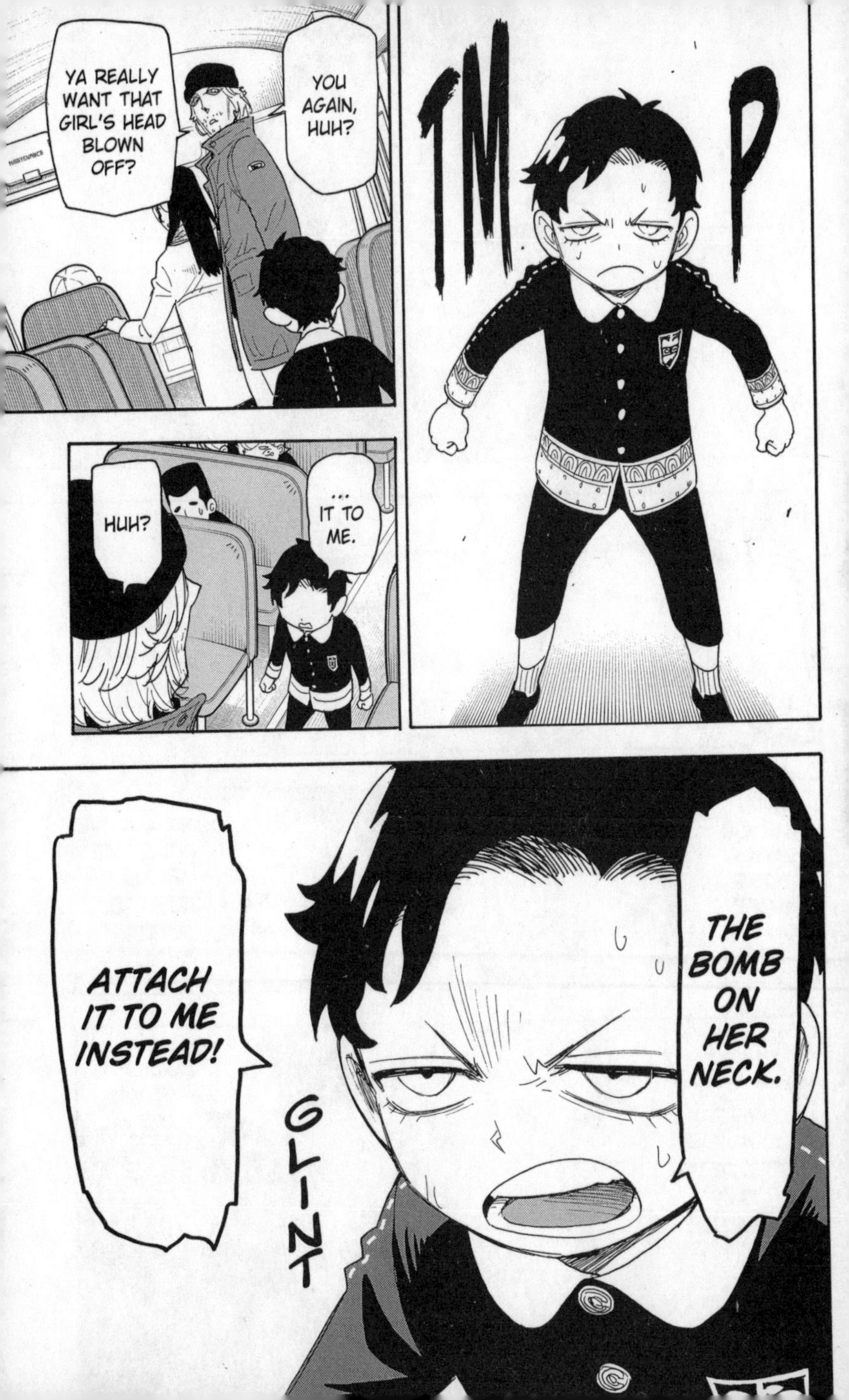
TMP
YOU AGAIN, HUH?
YA REALLY WANT THAT GIRL'S HEAD BLOWN OFF?
... IT TO ME.
HUH?
THE BOMB ON HER NECK.
GLINT
ATTACH IT TO ME INSTEAD!

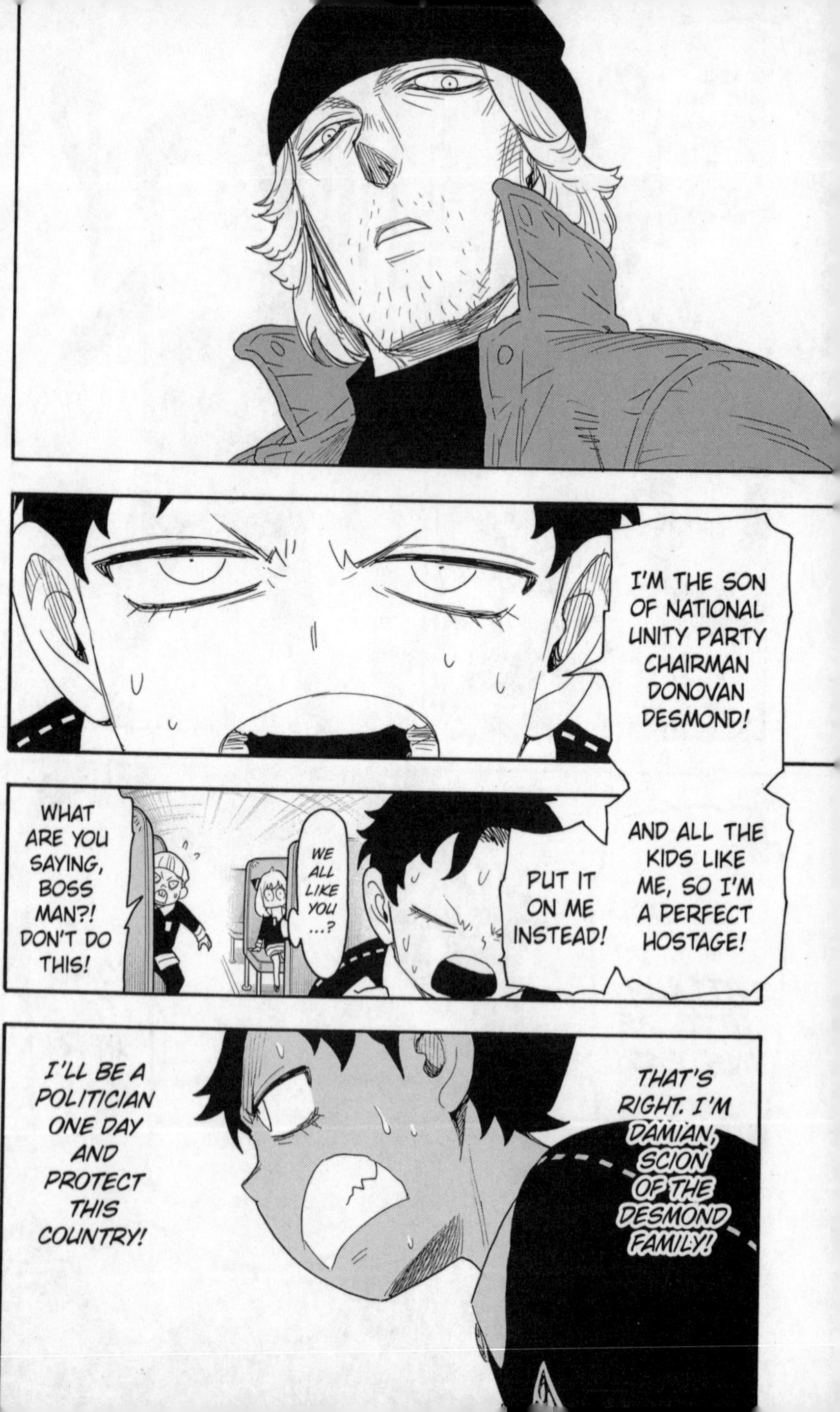
I'M THE SON OF NATIONAL UNITY PARTY CHAIRMAN DONOVAN DESMOND!
AND ALL THE KIDS LIKE ME, SO I'M A PERFECT HOSTAGE!
PUT IT ON ME INSTEAD!
WE ALL LIKE YOU ...?
WHAT ARE YOU SAYING, BOSS MAN?! DON'T DO THIS!
THAT'S RIGHT. I'M DAMIAN, SCION OF THE DESMOND FAMILY!
I'LL BE A POLITICIAN ONE DAY AND PROTECT THIS COUNTRY!

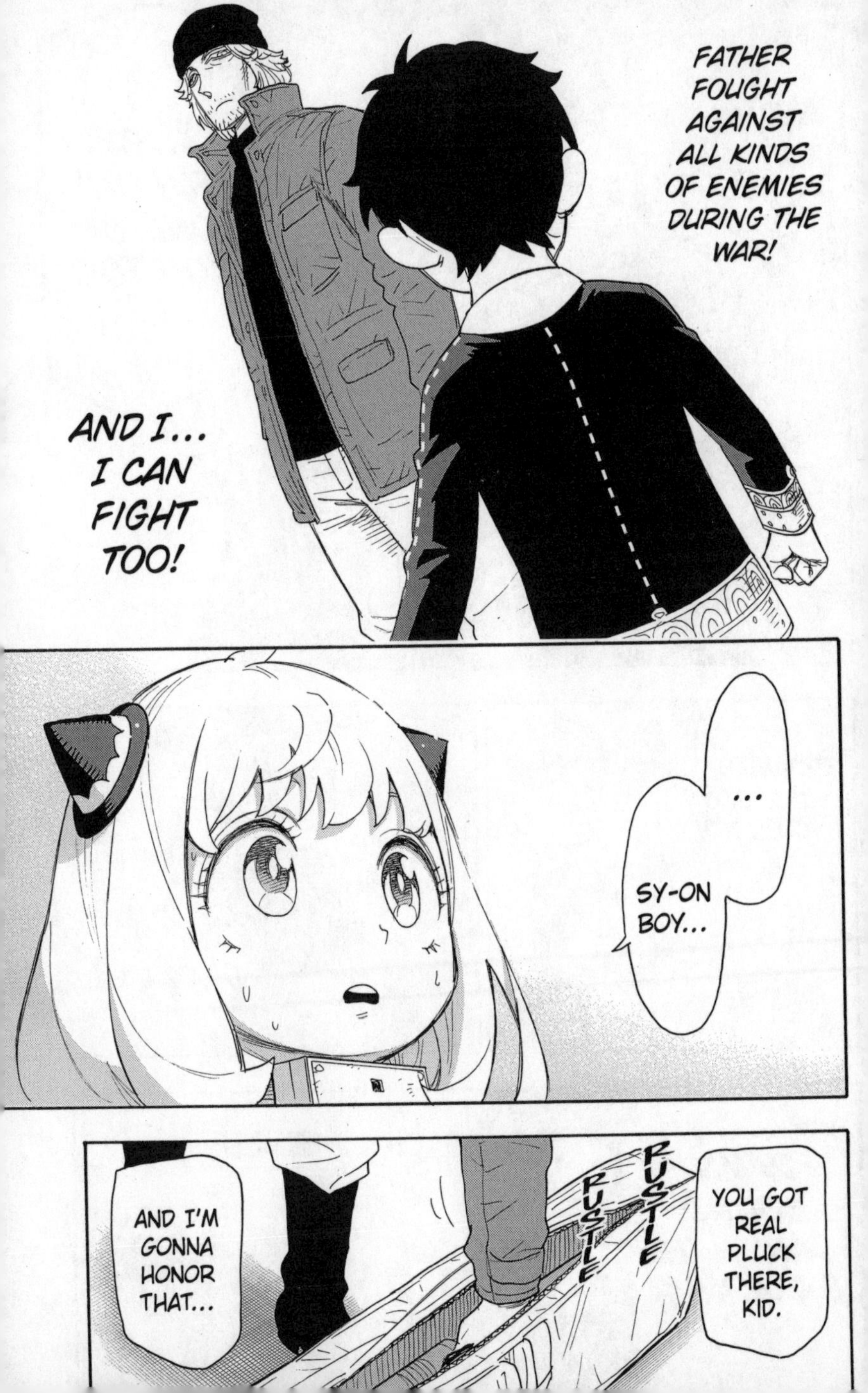
FATHER FOUGHT AGAINST ALL KINDS OF ENEMIES DURING THE WAR!
AND I... I CAN FIGHT TOO!
...
SY-ON BOY...
YOU GOT REAL PLUCK THERE, KID.
RUSTLE
RUSTLE
AND I'M GONNA HONOR THAT...

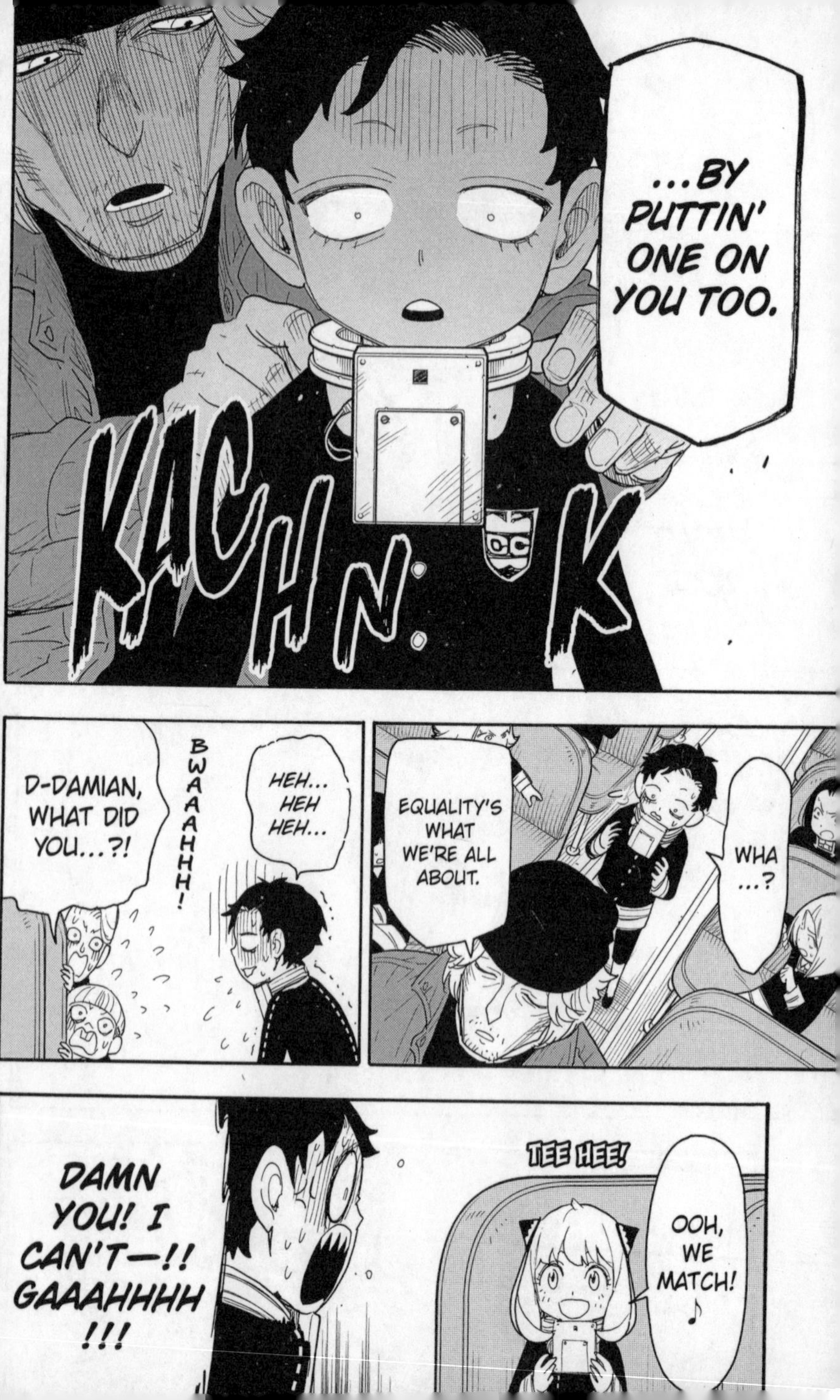
...BY PUTTIN' ONE ON YOU TOO.
KACHNK
WHA...?
EQUALITY'S WHAT WE'RE ALL ABOUT.
HEH... HEH HEH...
BWAAAAHHH!
D-DAMIAN, WHAT DID YOU...?!
TEE HEE!
OOH, WE MATCH! ♪
DAMN YOU! I CAN'T—!! GAAAHHHH!!!

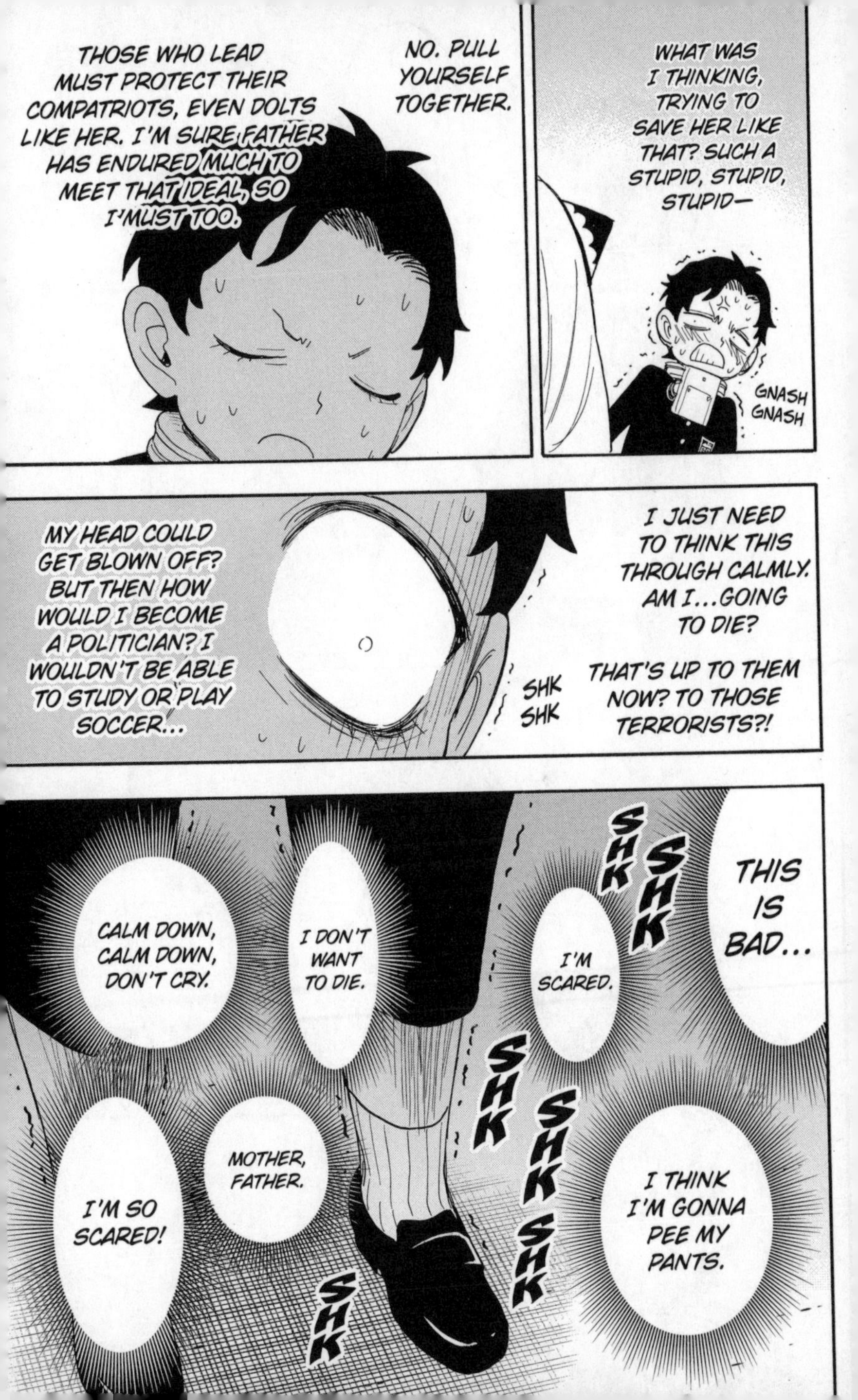
WHAT WAS I THINKING, TRYING TO SAVE HER LIKE THAT? SUCH A STUPID, STUPID, STUPID—
GNASH GNASH
NO. PULL YOURSELF TOGETHER.
THOSE WHO LEAD MUST PROTECT THEIR COMPATRIOTS, EVEN DOLTS LIKE HER. I'M SURE FATHER HAS ENDURED MUCH TO MEET THAT IDEAL, SO I MUST TOO.
I JUST NEED TO THINK THIS THROUGH CALMLY. AM I...GOING TO DIE?
THAT'S UP TO THEM NOW? TO THOSE TERRORISTS?!
SHK SHK
MY HEAD COULD GET BLOWN OFF? BUT THEN HOW WOULD I BECOME A POLITICIAN? I WOULDN'T BE ABLE TO STUDY OR PLAY SOCCER...
THIS IS BAD...
SHK SHK
I'M SCARED.
I DON'T WANT TO DIE.
CALM DOWN, CALM DOWN, DON'T CRY.
SHK SHK SHK
I THINK I'M GONNA PEE MY PANTS.
MOTHER, FATHER.
I'M SO SCARED!
SHK

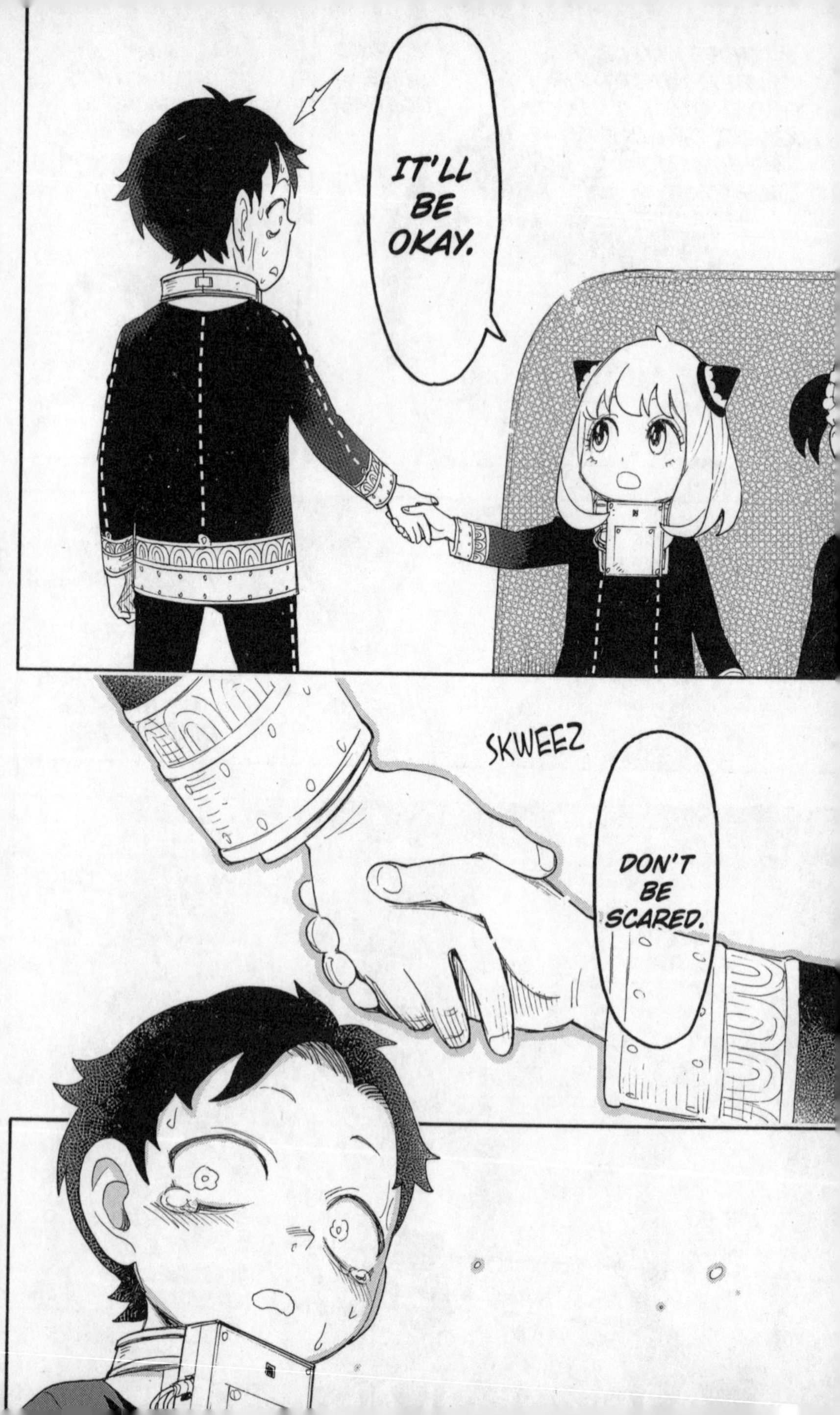
IT'LL BE OKAY.
SKWEEZ
DON'T BE SCARED.

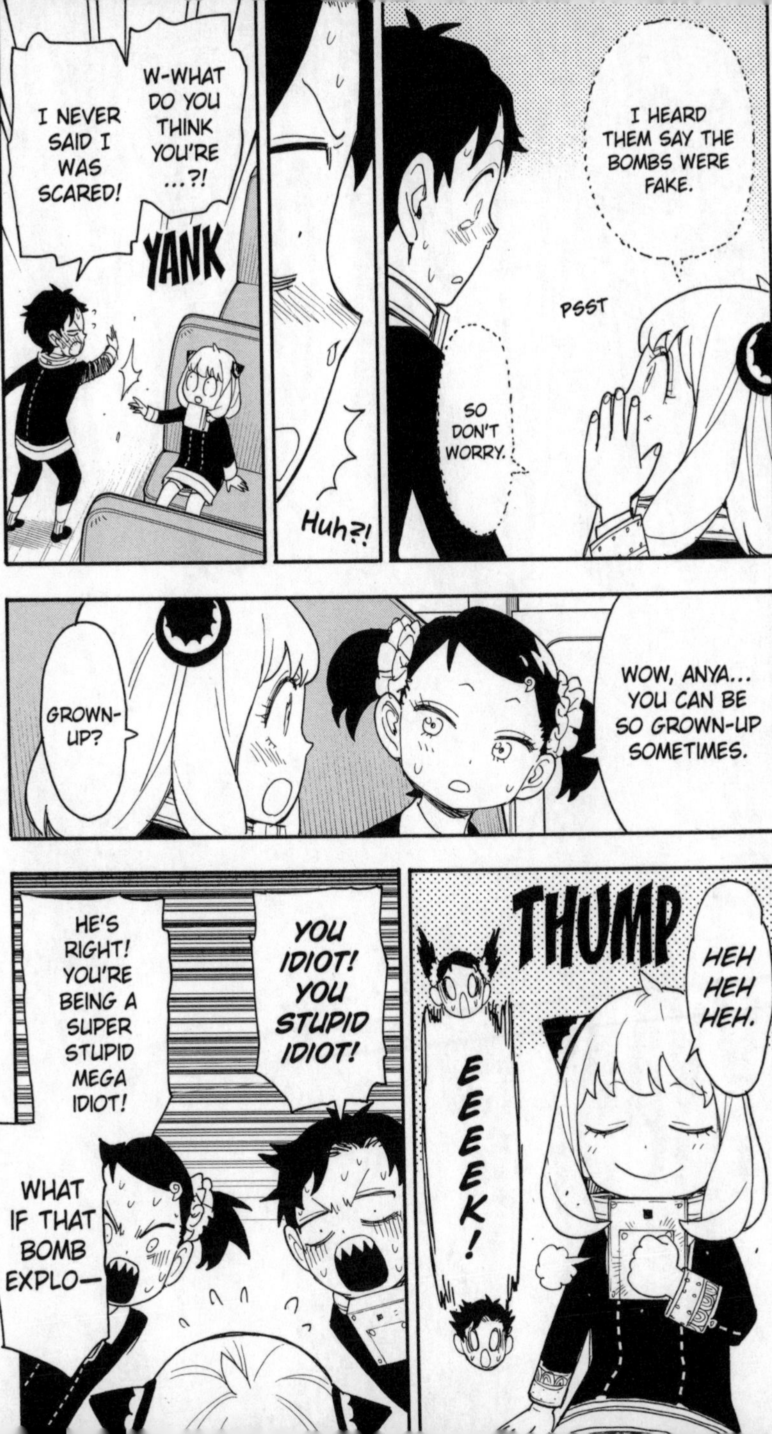
I HEARD THEM SAY THE BOMBS WERE FAKE.
PSST
SO DON'T WORRY.
Huh?!
W-WHAT DO YOU THINK YOU'RE ...?!
I NEVER SAID I WAS SCARED!
YANK
WOW, ANYA... YOU CAN BE SO GROWN-UP SOMETIMES.
GROWN-UP?
THUMP
HEH HEH HEH.
EEEEK!
YOU IDIOT! YOU STUPID IDIOT!
HE'S RIGHT! YOU'RE BEING A SUPER STUPID MEGA IDIOT!
WHAT IF THAT BOMB EXPLO—

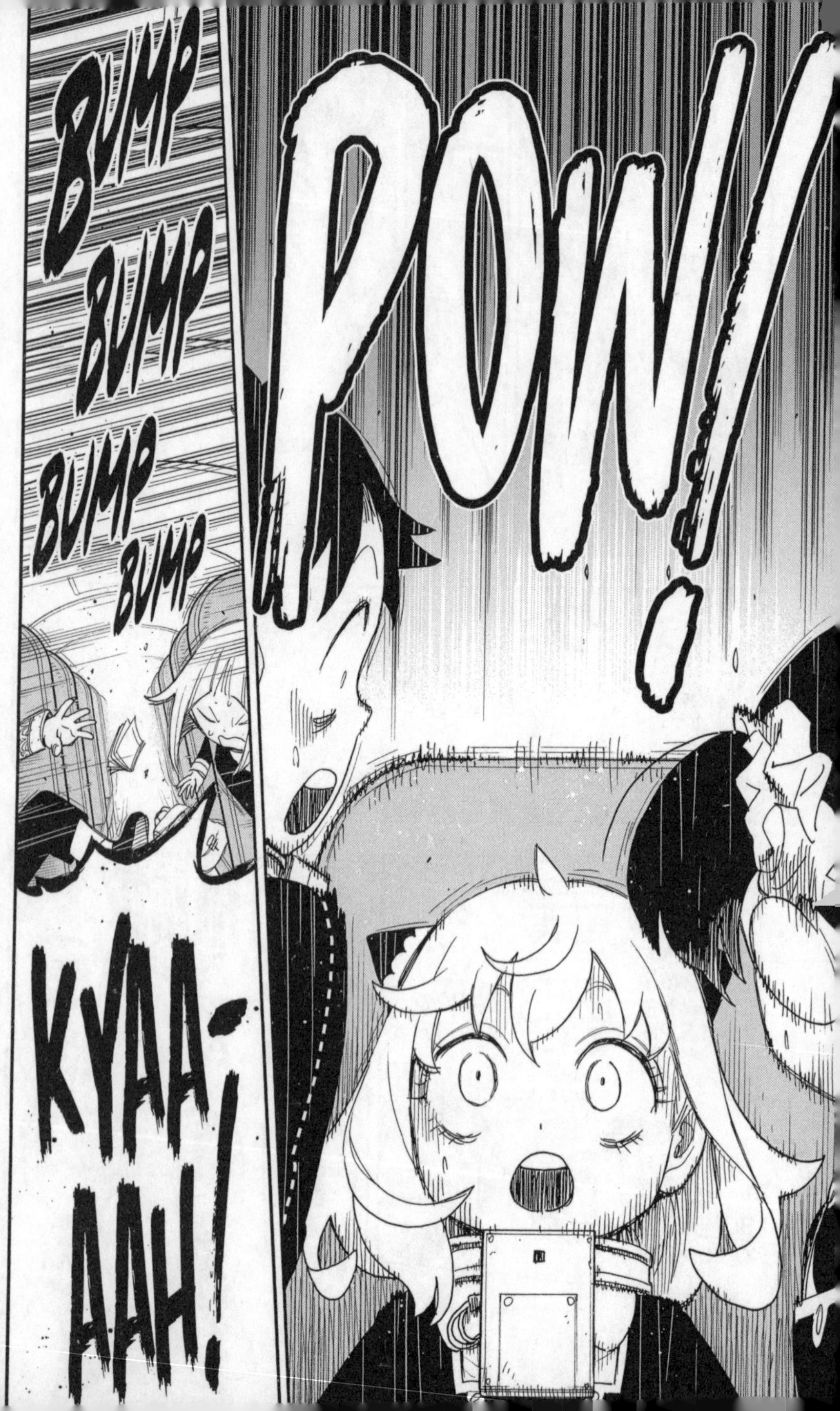
POW!
BUMP
BUMP
BUMP
BUMP
KYAA-AAH!

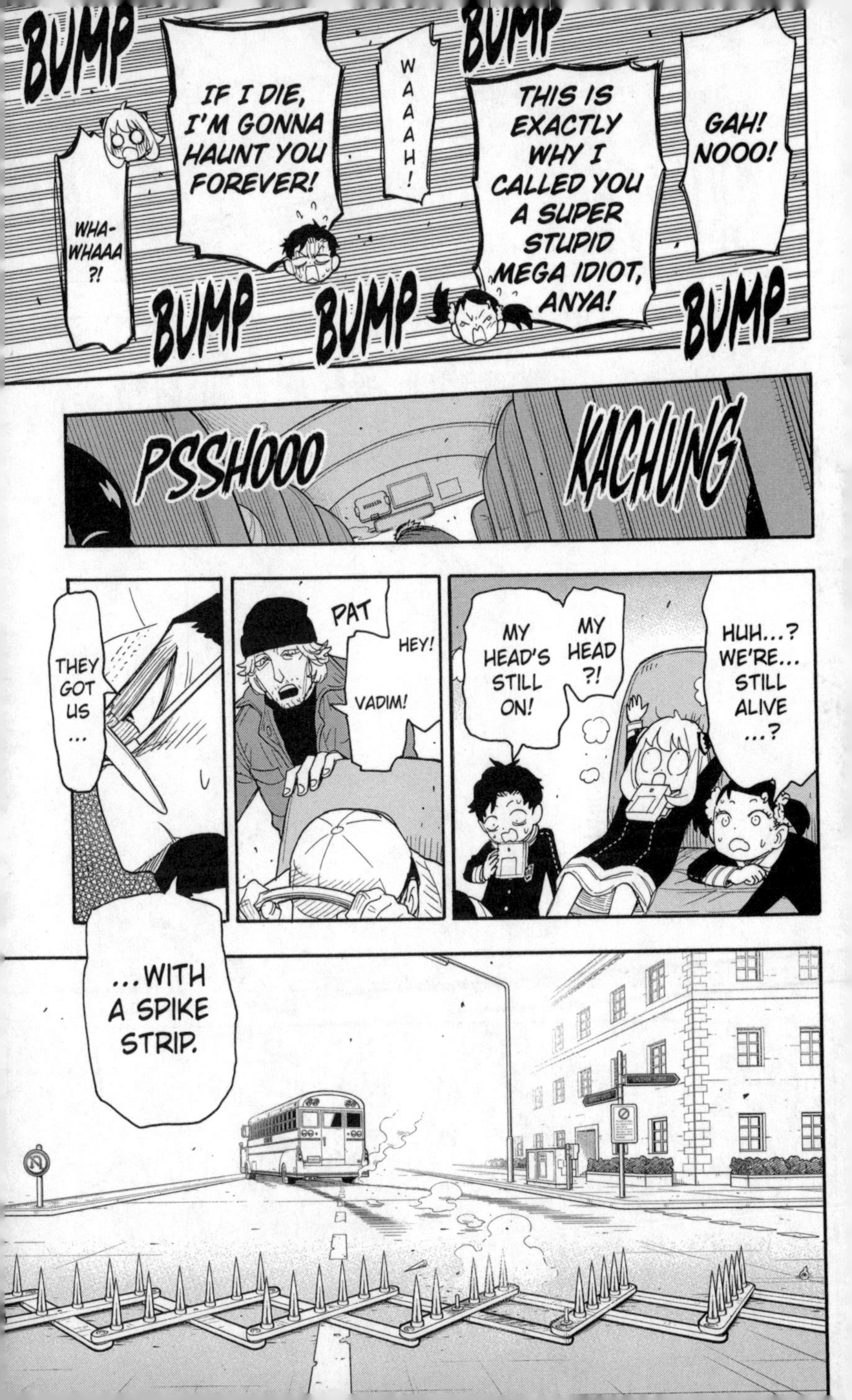
GAH! NOOO!
BUMP
BUMP
THIS IS EXACTLY WHY I CALLED YOU A SUPER STUPID MEGA IDIOT, ANYA!
BUMP
WAAAAH!
IF I DIE, I'M GONNA HAUNT YOU FOREVER!
BUMP
BUMP
WHA-WHAAA?!
KACHUNG
PSSHOOO
HUH...? WE'RE... STILL ALIVE...?
MY HEAD?!
MY HEAD'S STILL ON!
HEY! VADIM!
PAT
THEY GOT US...
...WITH A SPIKE STRIP.

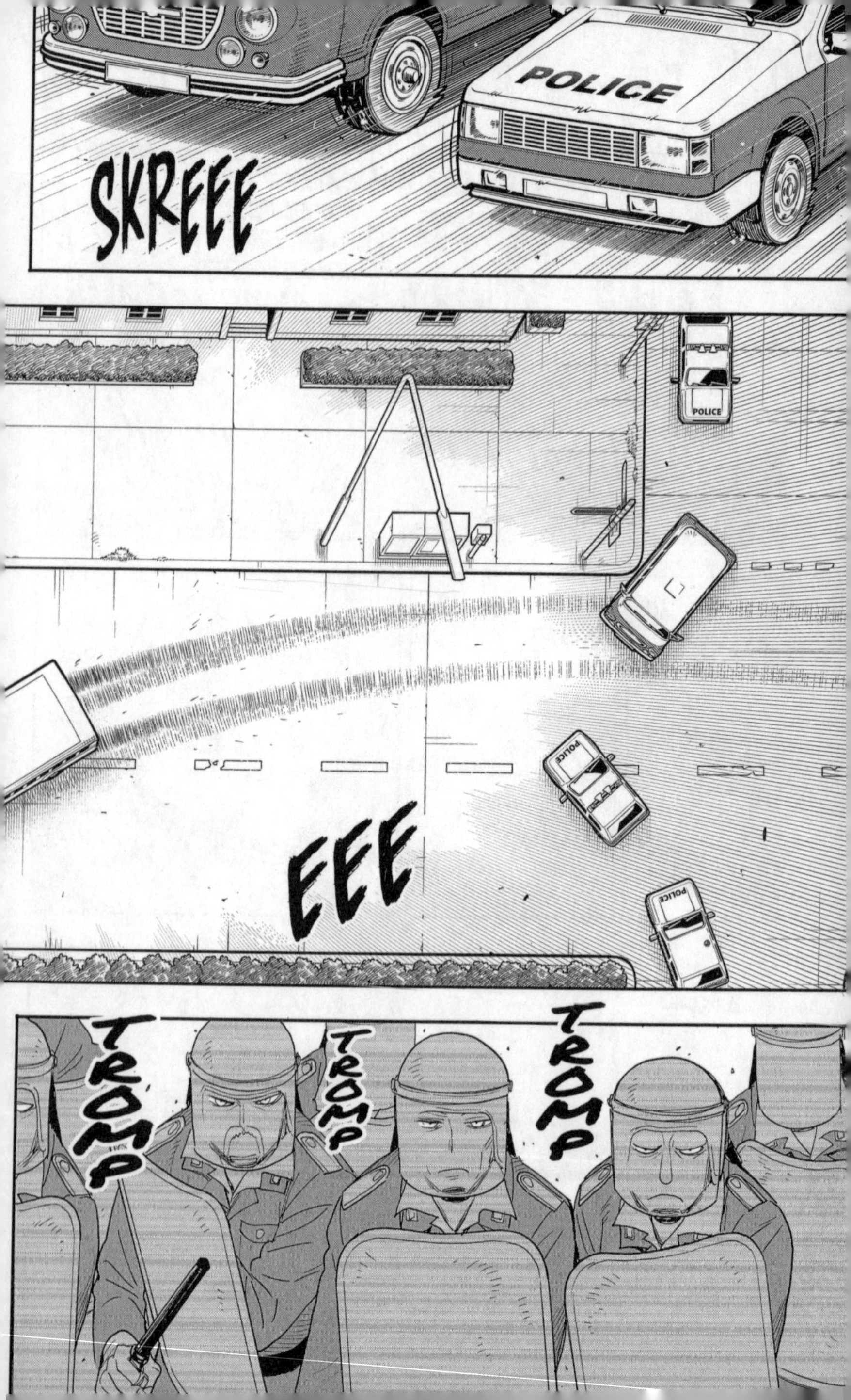
POLICE
SKREEE
POLICE
POLICE
POLICE
EEE
TROMP
TROMP
TROMP

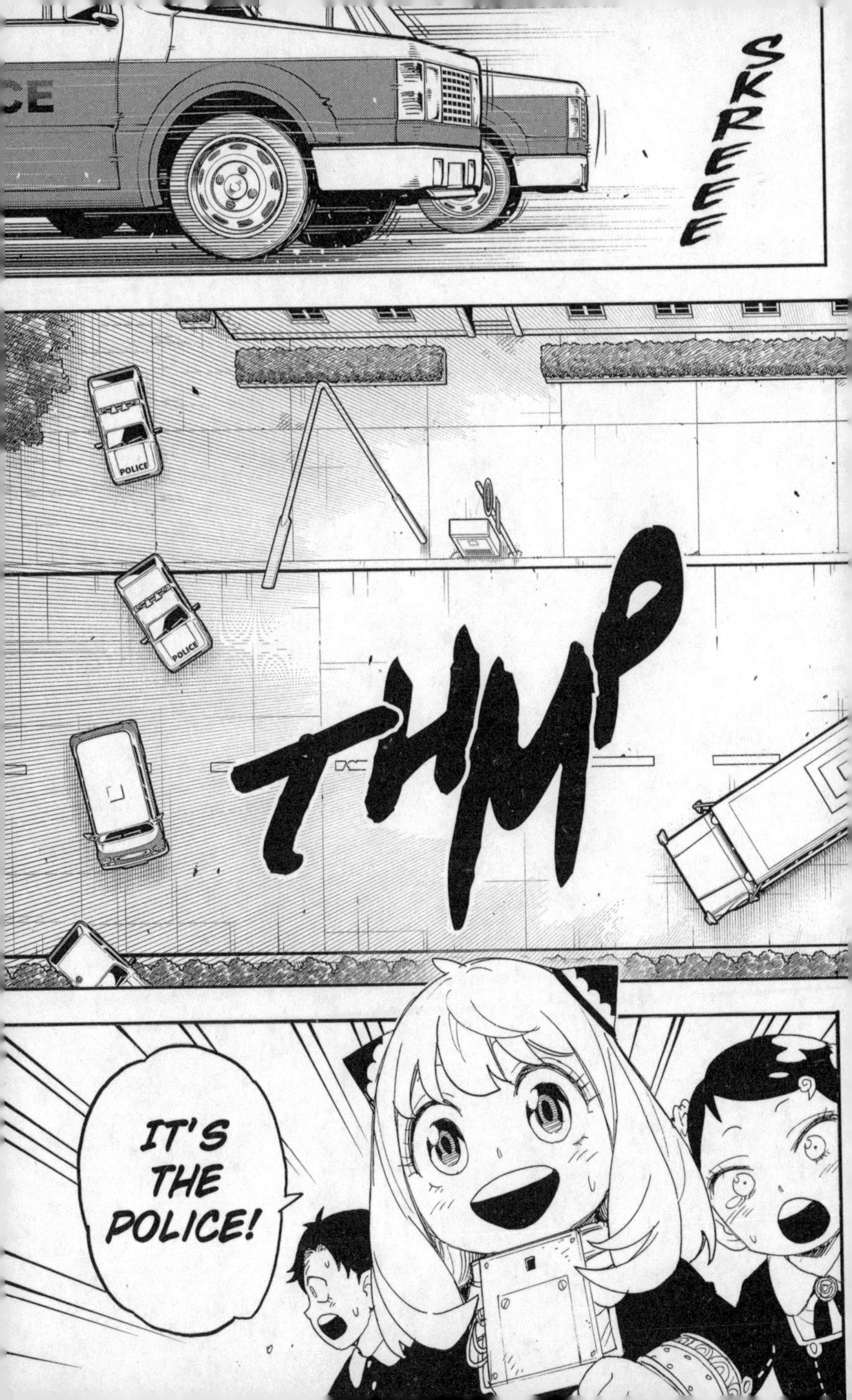
SKREEE
THMP
IT'S THE POLICE!

SPY×FAMILY

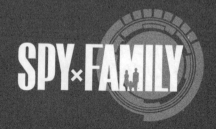

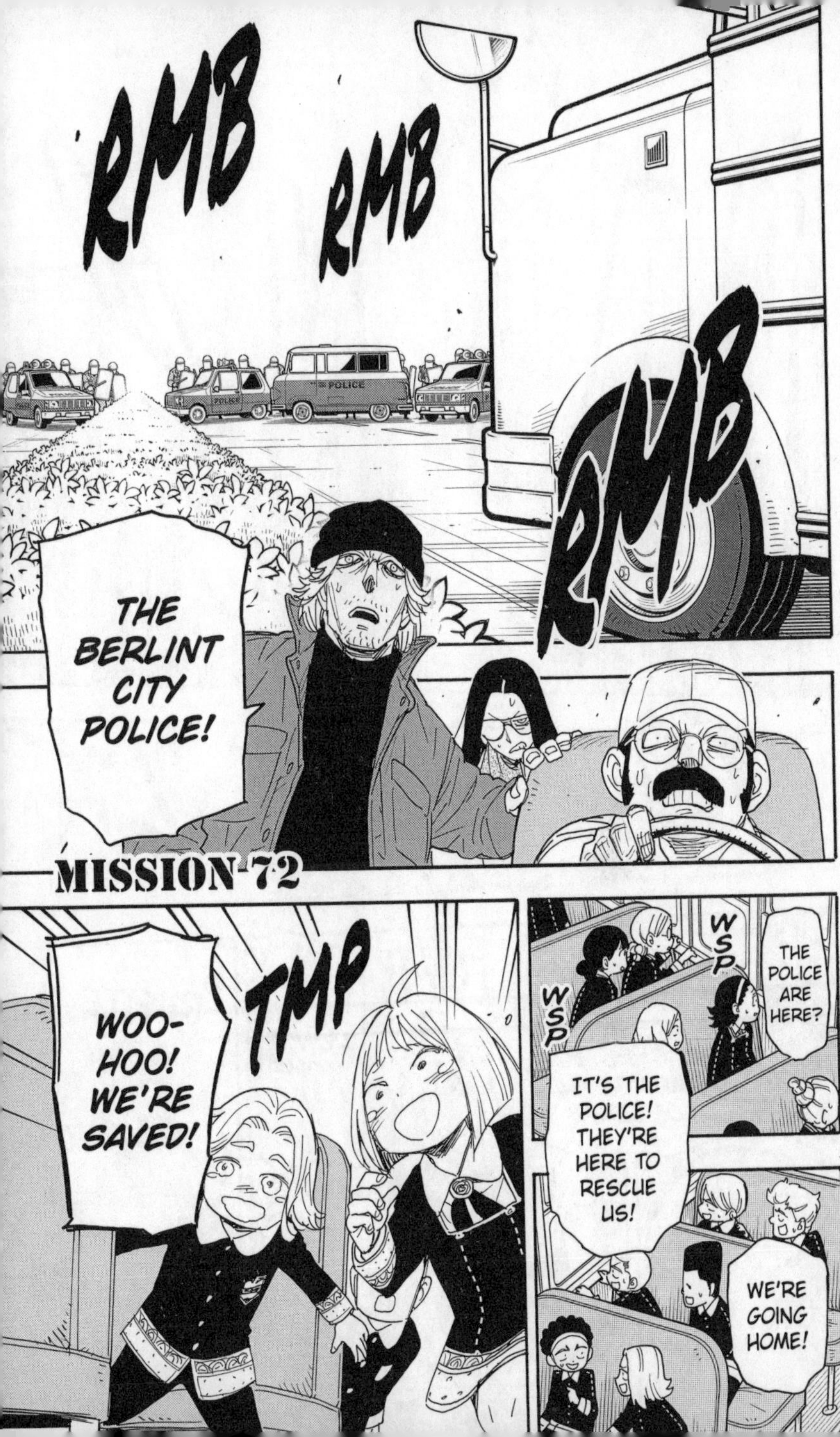
RMB RMB
RMB
THE BERLINT CITY POLICE!
MISSION 72
WSP
WSP
THE POLICE ARE HERE?
IT'S THE POLICE! THEY'RE HERE TO RESCUE US!
WE'RE GOING HOME!
TMP
WOO-HOO! WE'RE SAVED!

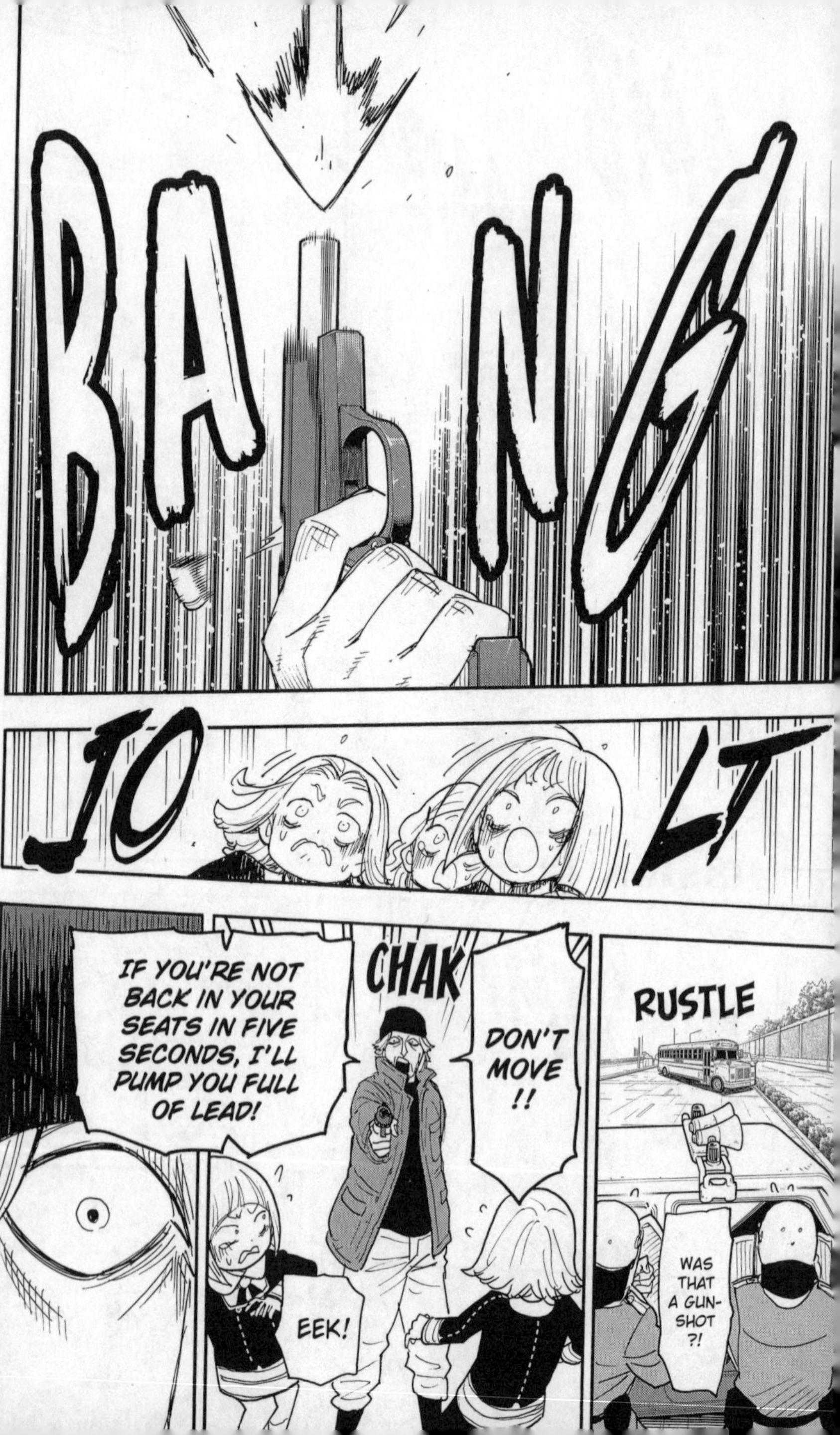
BANG
JOLT
RUSTLE
WAS THAT A GUN-SHOT ?!
CHAK
DON'T MOVE !!
IF YOU'RE NOT BACK IN YOUR SEATS IN FIVE SECONDS, I'LL PUMP YOU FULL OF LEAD!
EEK!

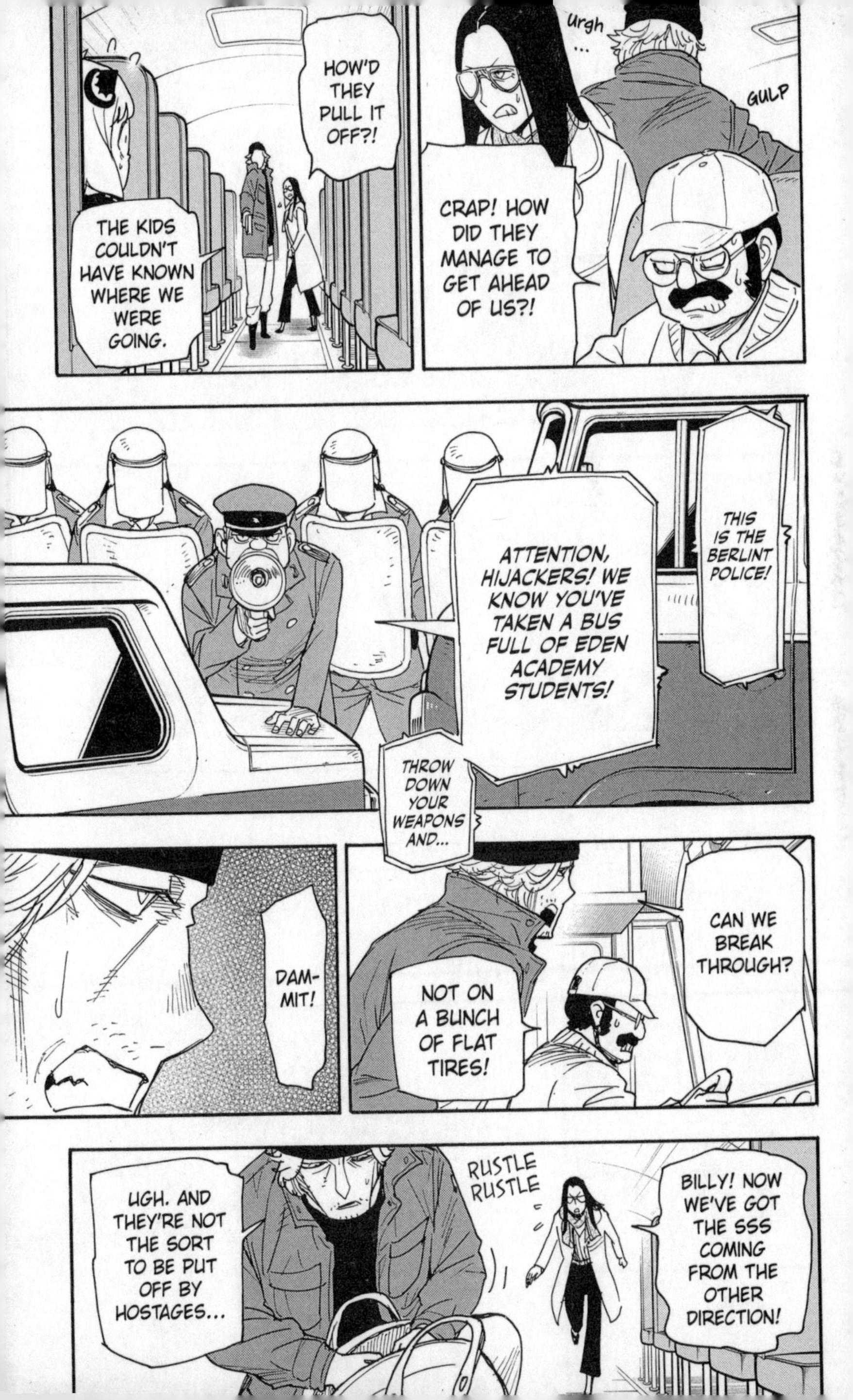
Urgh ...
GULP
CRAP! HOW DID THEY MANAGE TO GET AHEAD OF US?!
HOW'D THEY PULL IT OFF?!
THE KIDS COULDN'T HAVE KNOWN WHERE WE WERE GOING.
THIS IS THE BERLINT POLICE!
ATTENTION, HIJACKERS! WE KNOW YOU'VE TAKEN A BUS FULL OF EDEN ACADEMY STUDENTS!
THROW DOWN YOUR WEAPONS AND...
CAN WE BREAK THROUGH?
NOT ON A BUNCH OF FLAT TIRES!
DAM-MIT!
BILLY! NOW WE'VE GOT THE SSS COMING FROM THE OTHER DIRECTION!
RUSTLE RUSTLE
UGH. AND THEY'RE NOT THE SORT TO BE PUT OFF BY HOSTAGES...

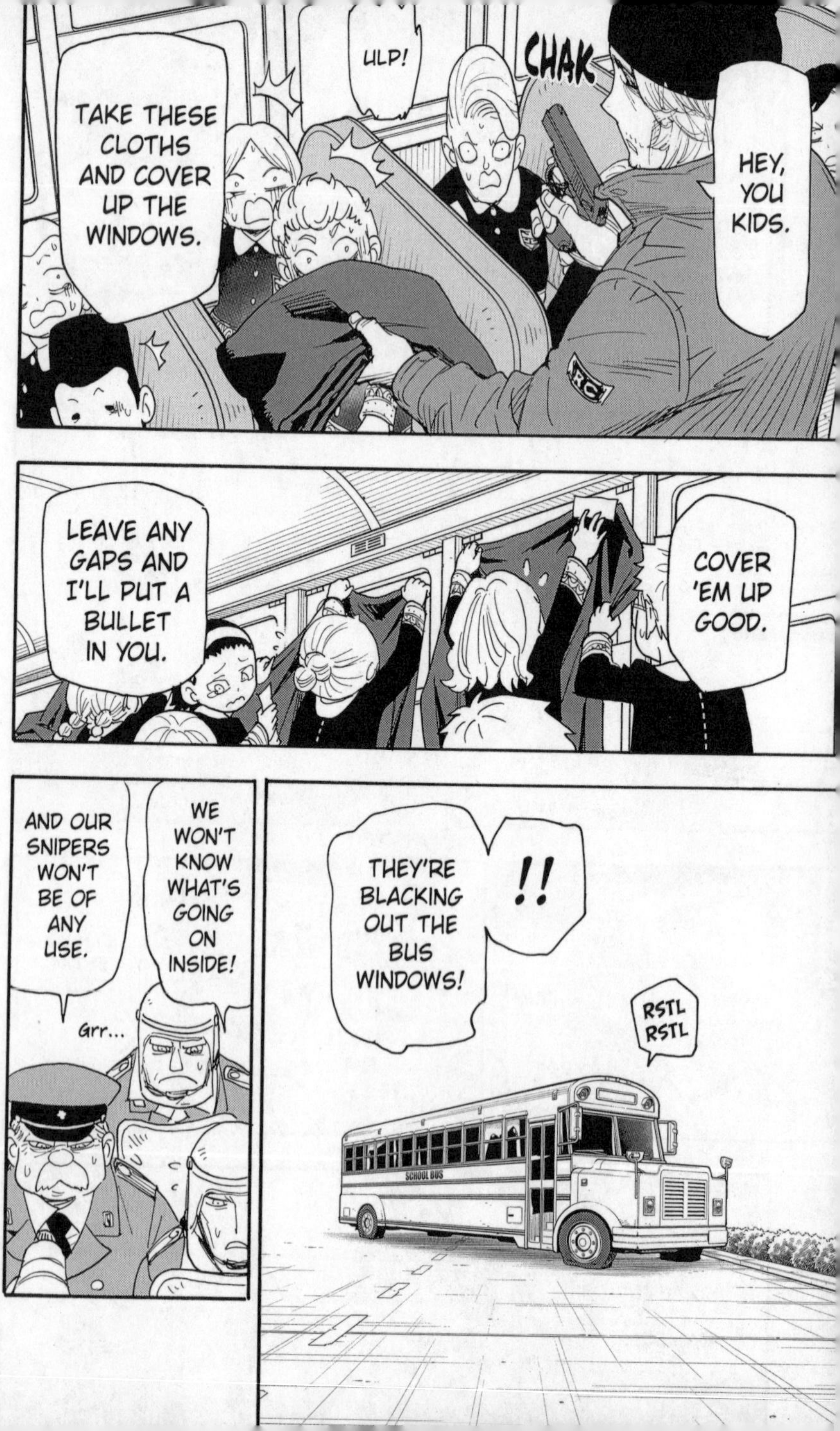
HEY, YOU KIDS.
CHAK
ULP!
TAKE THESE CLOTHS AND COVER UP THE WINDOWS.
COVER 'EM UP GOOD.
LEAVE ANY GAPS AND I'LL PUT A BULLET IN YOU.
!!
THEY'RE BLACKING OUT THE BUS WINDOWS!
RSTL RSTL
SCHOOL BUS
WE WON'T KNOW WHAT'S GOING ON INSIDE!
AND OUR SNIPERS WON'T BE OF ANY USE.
Grr...

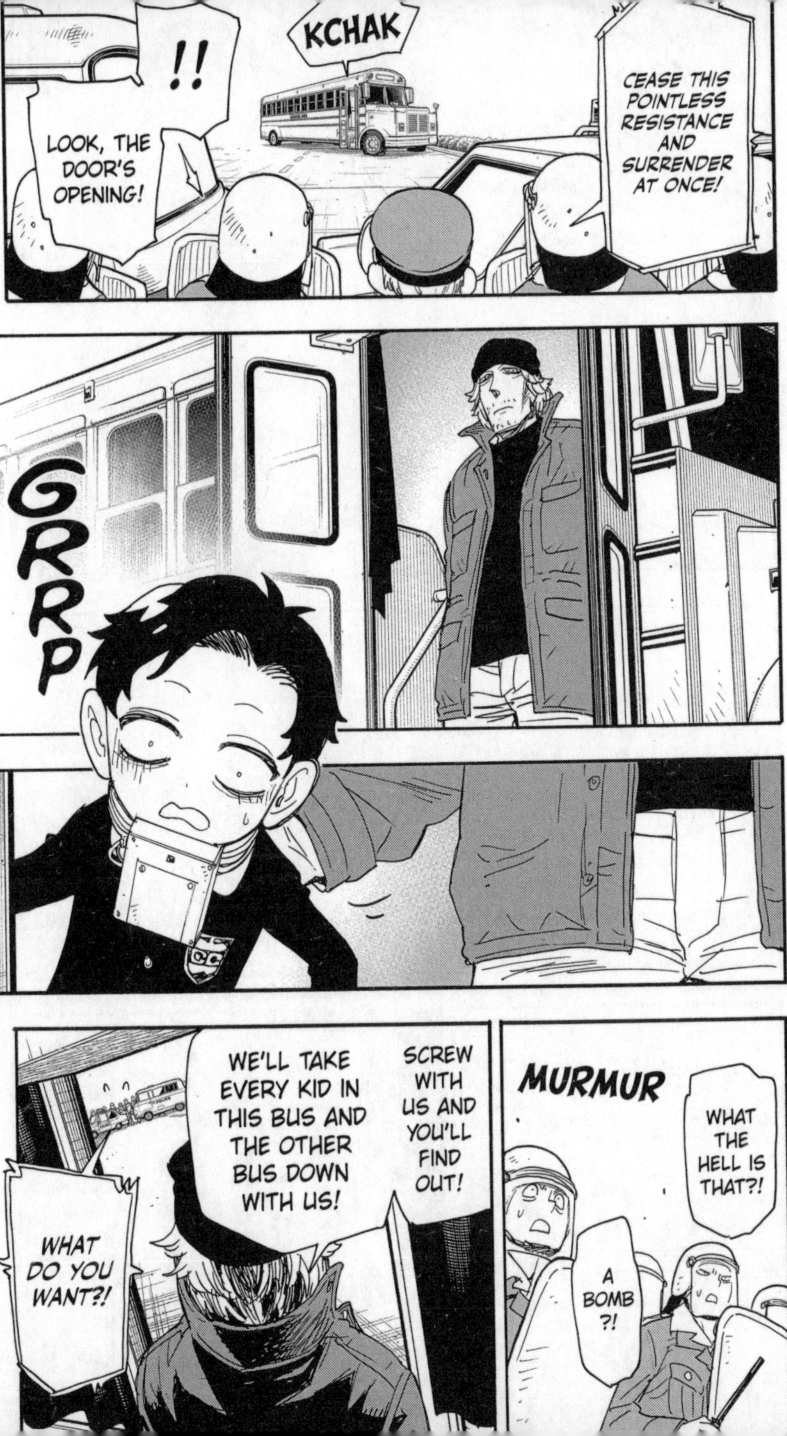
CEASE THIS POINTLESS RESISTANCE AND SURRENDER AT ONCE!
KCHAK
!!
LOOK, THE DOOR'S OPENING!
GRRP
MURMUR
WHAT THE HELL IS THAT?!
A BOMB ?!
SCREW WITH US AND YOU'LL FIND OUT!
WE'LL TAKE EVERY KID IN THIS BUS AND THE OTHER BUS DOWN WITH US!
WHAT DO YOU WANT?!

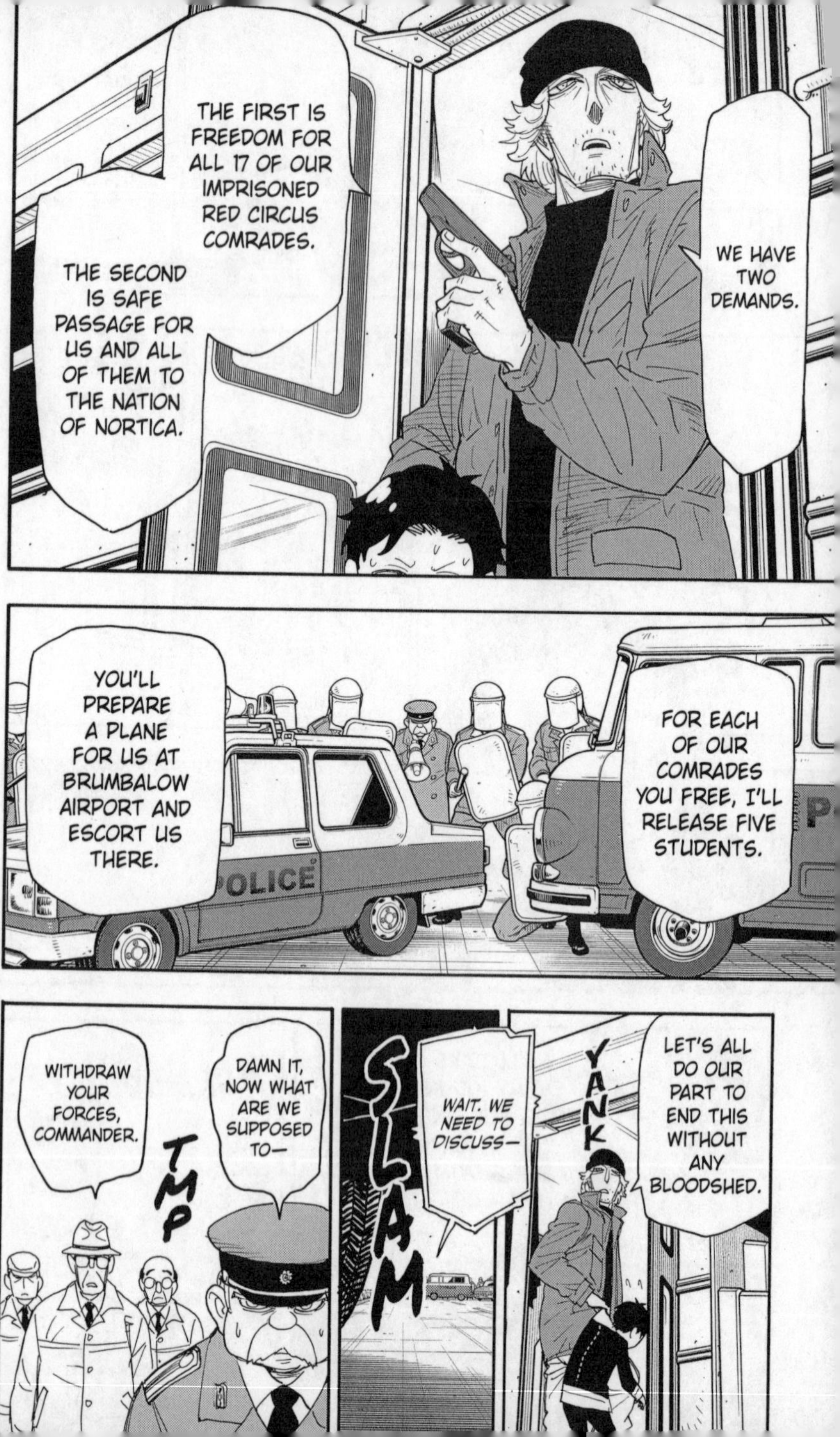
WE HAVE TWO DEMANDS.
THE FIRST IS FREEDOM FOR ALL 17 OF OUR IMPRISONED RED CIRCUS COMRADES.
THE SECOND IS SAFE PASSAGE FOR US AND ALL OF THEM TO THE NATION OF NORTICA.
FOR EACH OF OUR COMRADES YOU FREE, I'LL RELEASE FIVE STUDENTS.
YOU'LL PREPARE A PLANE FOR US AT BRUMBALOW AIRPORT AND ESCORT US THERE.
POLICE
LET'S ALL DO OUR PART TO END THIS WITHOUT ANY BLOODSHED.
YANK
WAIT. WE NEED TO DISCUSS—
SLAM
DAMN IT, NOW WHAT ARE WE SUPPOSED TO—
TMP
WITHDRAW YOUR FORCES, COMMANDER.

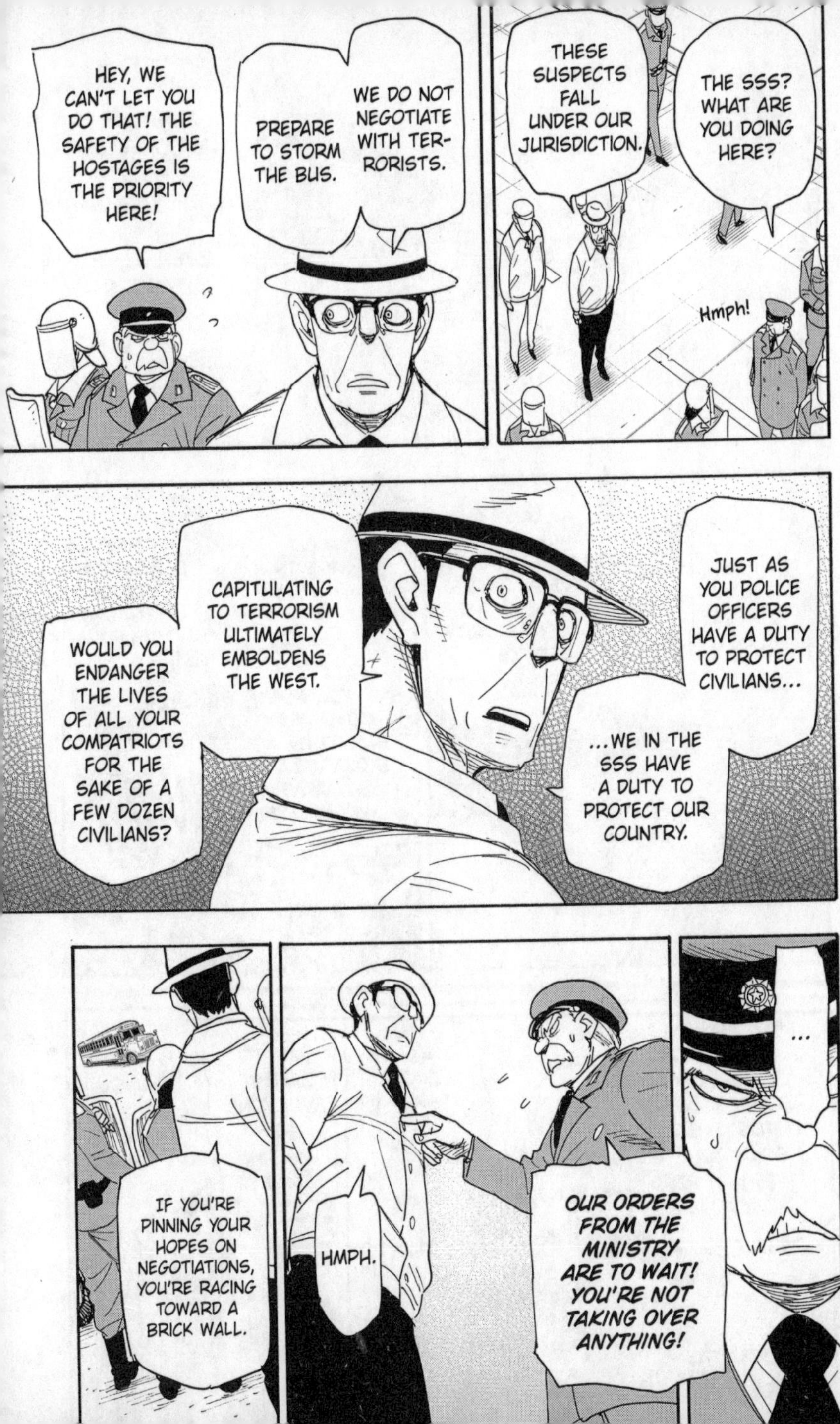
THE SSS? WHAT ARE YOU DOING HERE?
THESE SUSPECTS FALL UNDER OUR JURISDICTION.
Hmph!
WE DO NOT NEGOTIATE WITH TERRORISTS.
PREPARE TO STORM THE BUS.
HEY, WE CAN'T LET YOU DO THAT! THE SAFETY OF THE HOSTAGES IS THE PRIORITY HERE!
JUST AS YOU POLICE OFFICERS HAVE A DUTY TO PROTECT CIVILIANS...
...WE IN THE SSS HAVE A DUTY TO PROTECT OUR COUNTRY.
CAPITULATING TO TERRORISM ULTIMATELY EMBOLDENS THE WEST.
WOULD YOU ENDANGER THE LIVES OF ALL YOUR COMPATRIOTS FOR THE SAKE OF A FEW DOZEN CIVILIANS?
...
OUR ORDERS FROM THE MINISTRY ARE TO WAIT! YOU'RE NOT TAKING OVER ANYTHING!
HMPH.
IF YOU'RE PINNING YOUR HOPES ON NEGOTIATIONS, YOU'RE RACING TOWARD A BRICK WALL.

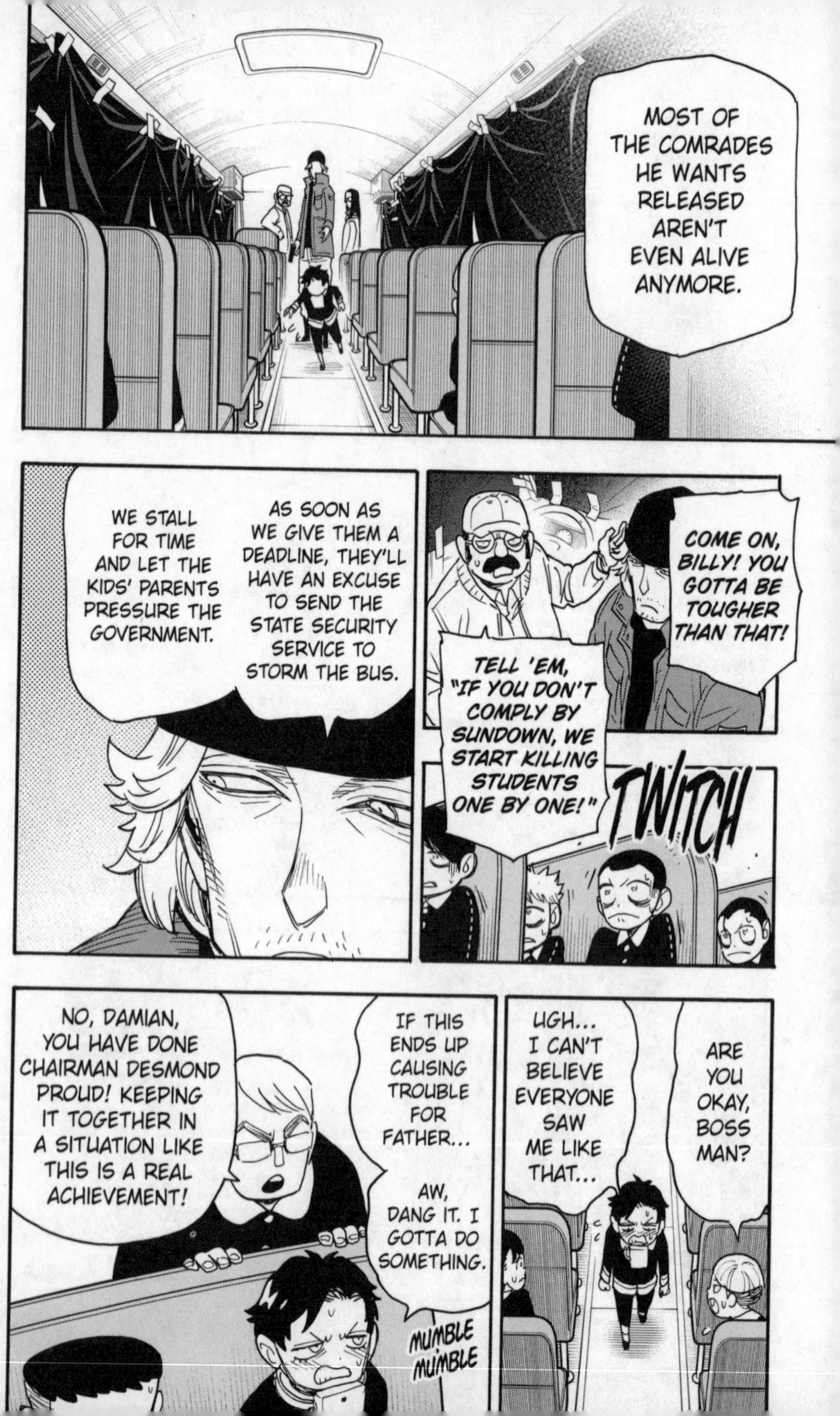
MOST OF THE COMRADES HE WANTS RELEASED AREN'T EVEN ALIVE ANYMORE.
COME ON, BILLY! YOU GOTTA BE TOUGHER THAN THAT!
TELL 'EM, "IF YOU DON'T COMPLY BY SUNDOWN, WE START KILLING STUDENTS ONE BY ONE!"
TWITCH
AS SOON AS WE GIVE THEM A DEADLINE, THEY'LL HAVE AN EXCUSE TO SEND THE STATE SECURITY SERVICE TO STORM THE BUS.
WE STALL FOR TIME AND LET THE KIDS' PARENTS PRESSURE THE GOVERNMENT.
ARE YOU OKAY, BOSS MAN?
UGH... I CAN'T BELIEVE EVERYONE SAW ME LIKE THAT...
IF THIS ENDS UP CAUSING TROUBLE FOR FATHER...
AW, DANG IT. I GOTTA DO SOMETHING.
MUMBLE MUMBLE
NO, DAMIAN, YOU HAVE DONE CHAIRMAN DESMOND PROUD! KEEPING IT TOGETHER IN A SITUATION LIKE THIS IS A REAL ACHIEVEMENT!

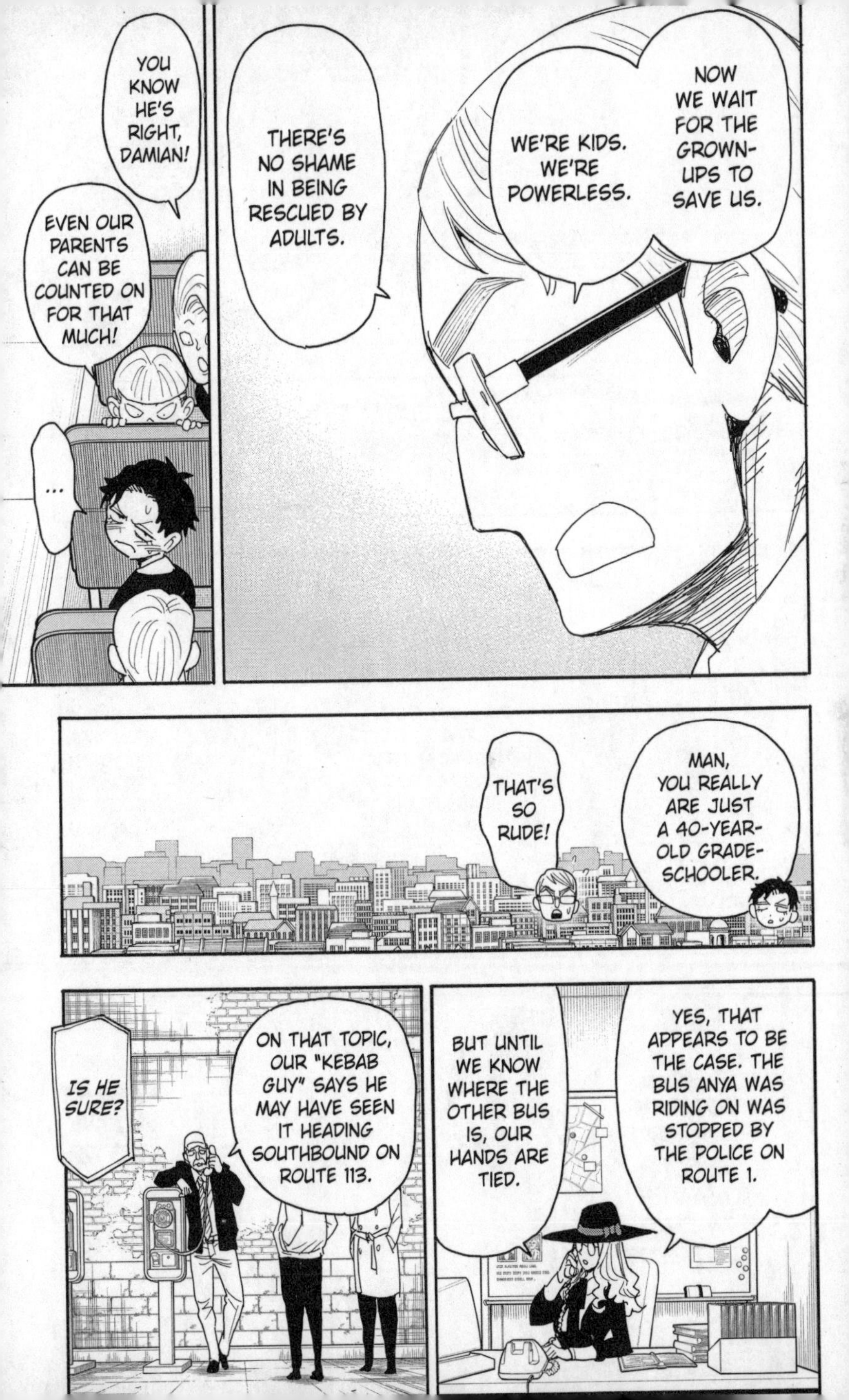
NOW WE WAIT FOR THE GROWN-UPS TO SAVE US.
WE'RE KIDS. WE'RE POWERLESS.
THERE'S NO SHAME IN BEING RESCUED BY ADULTS.
YOU KNOW HE'S RIGHT, DAMIAN!
EVEN OUR PARENTS CAN BE COUNTED ON FOR THAT MUCH!
...
MAN, YOU REALLY ARE JUST A 40-YEAR-OLD GRADE-SCHOOLER.
THAT'S SO RUDE!
YES, THAT APPEARS TO BE THE CASE. THE BUS ANYA WAS RIDING ON WAS STOPPED BY THE POLICE ON ROUTE 1.
BUT UNTIL WE KNOW WHERE THE OTHER BUS IS, OUR HANDS ARE TIED.
ON THAT TOPIC, OUR "KEBAB GUY" SAYS HE MAY HAVE SEEN IT HEADING SOUTHBOUND ON ROUTE 113.
IS HE SURE?

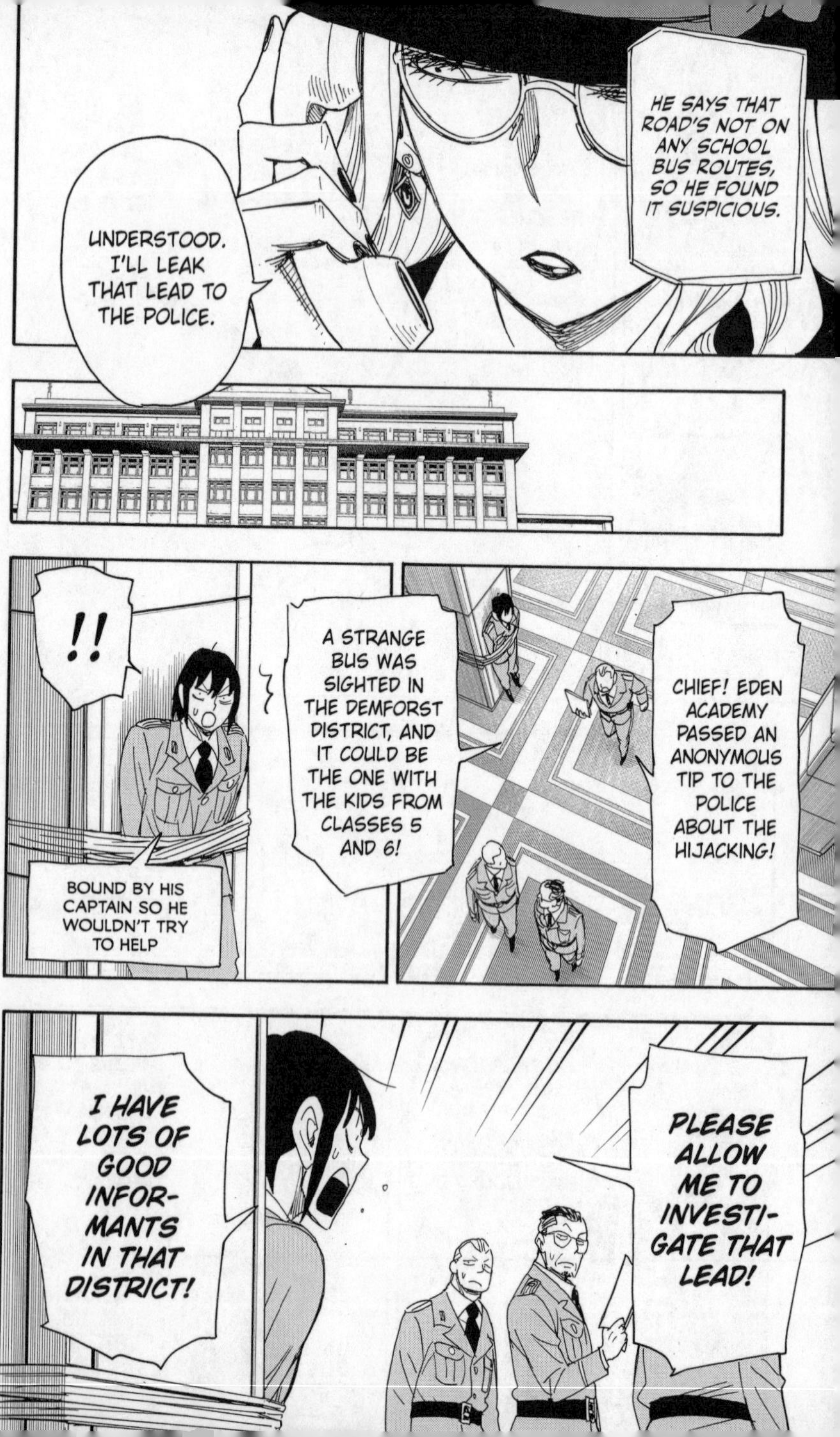

HE SAYS THAT ROAD'S NOT ON ANY SCHOOL BUS ROUTES, SO HE FOUND IT SUSPICIOUS.
UNDERSTOOD. I'LL LEAK THAT LEAD TO THE POLICE.
CHIEF! EDEN ACADEMY PASSED AN ANONYMOUS TIP TO THE POLICE ABOUT THE HIJACKING!
A STRANGE BUS WAS SIGHTED IN THE DEMFORST DISTRICT, AND IT COULD BE THE ONE WITH THE KIDS FROM CLASSES 5 AND 6!
!!
BOUND BY HIS CAPTAIN SO HE WOULDN'T TRY TO HELP
PLEASE ALLOW ME TO INVESTI-GATE THAT LEAD!
I HAVE LOTS OF GOOD INFOR-MANTS IN THAT DISTRICT!

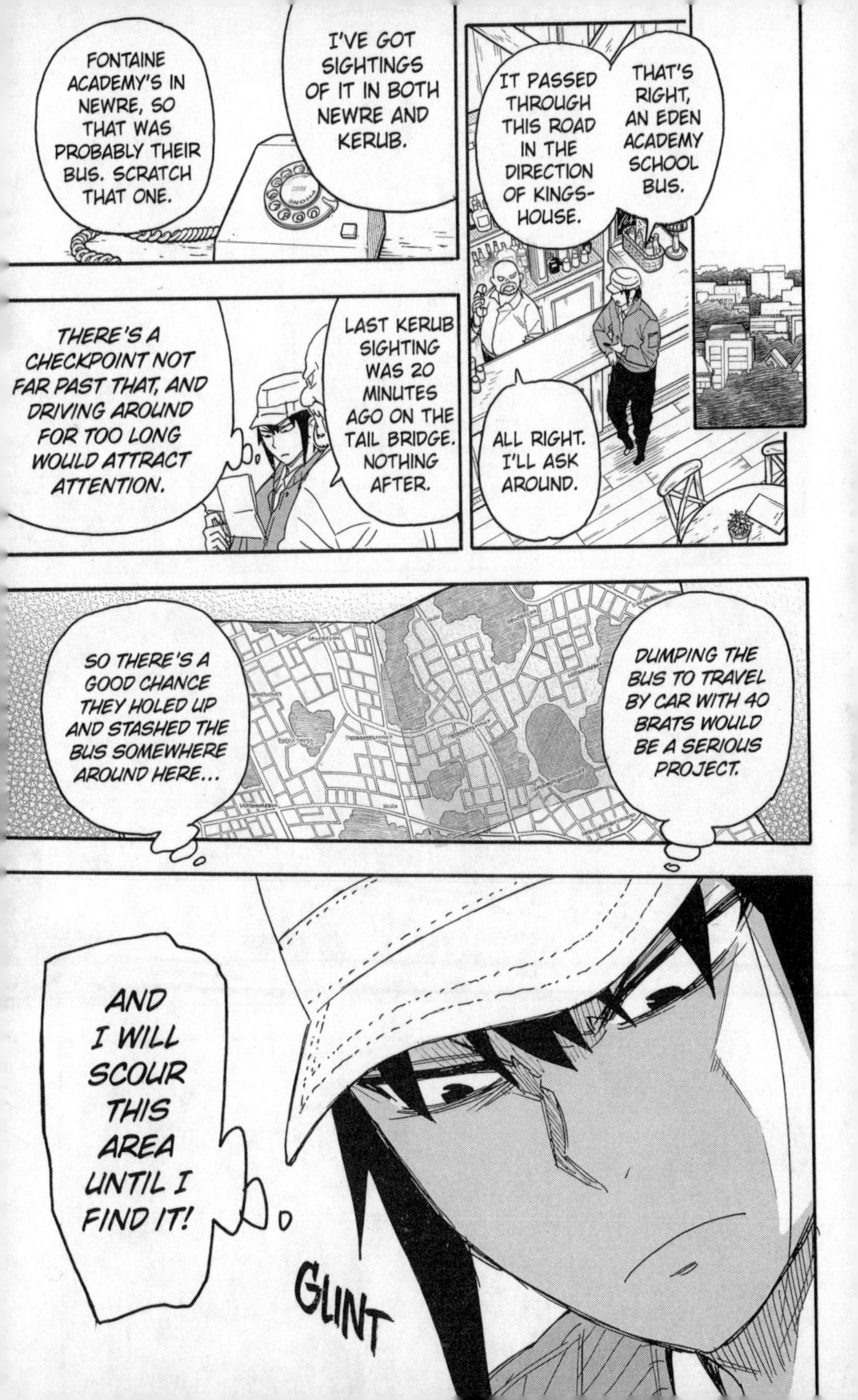
THAT'S RIGHT, AN EDEN ACADEMY SCHOOL BUS.
IT PASSED THROUGH THIS ROAD IN THE DIRECTION OF KINGS-HOUSE.
ALL RIGHT. I'LL ASK AROUND.
I'VE GOT SIGHTINGS OF IT IN BOTH NEWRE AND KERUB.
FONTAINE ACADEMY'S IN NEWRE, SO THAT WAS PROBABLY THEIR BUS. SCRATCH THAT ONE.
LAST KERUB SIGHTING WAS 20 MINUTES AGO ON THE TAIL BRIDGE. NOTHING AFTER.
THERE'S A CHECKPOINT NOT FAR PAST THAT, AND DRIVING AROUND FOR TOO LONG WOULD ATTRACT ATTENTION.
DUMPING THE BUS TO TRAVEL BY CAR WITH 40 BRATS WOULD BE A SERIOUS PROJECT.
SO THERE'S A GOOD CHANCE THEY HOLED UP AND STASHED THE BUS SOMEWHERE AROUND HERE...
AND I WILL SCOUR THIS AREA UNTIL I FIND IT!
GLINT

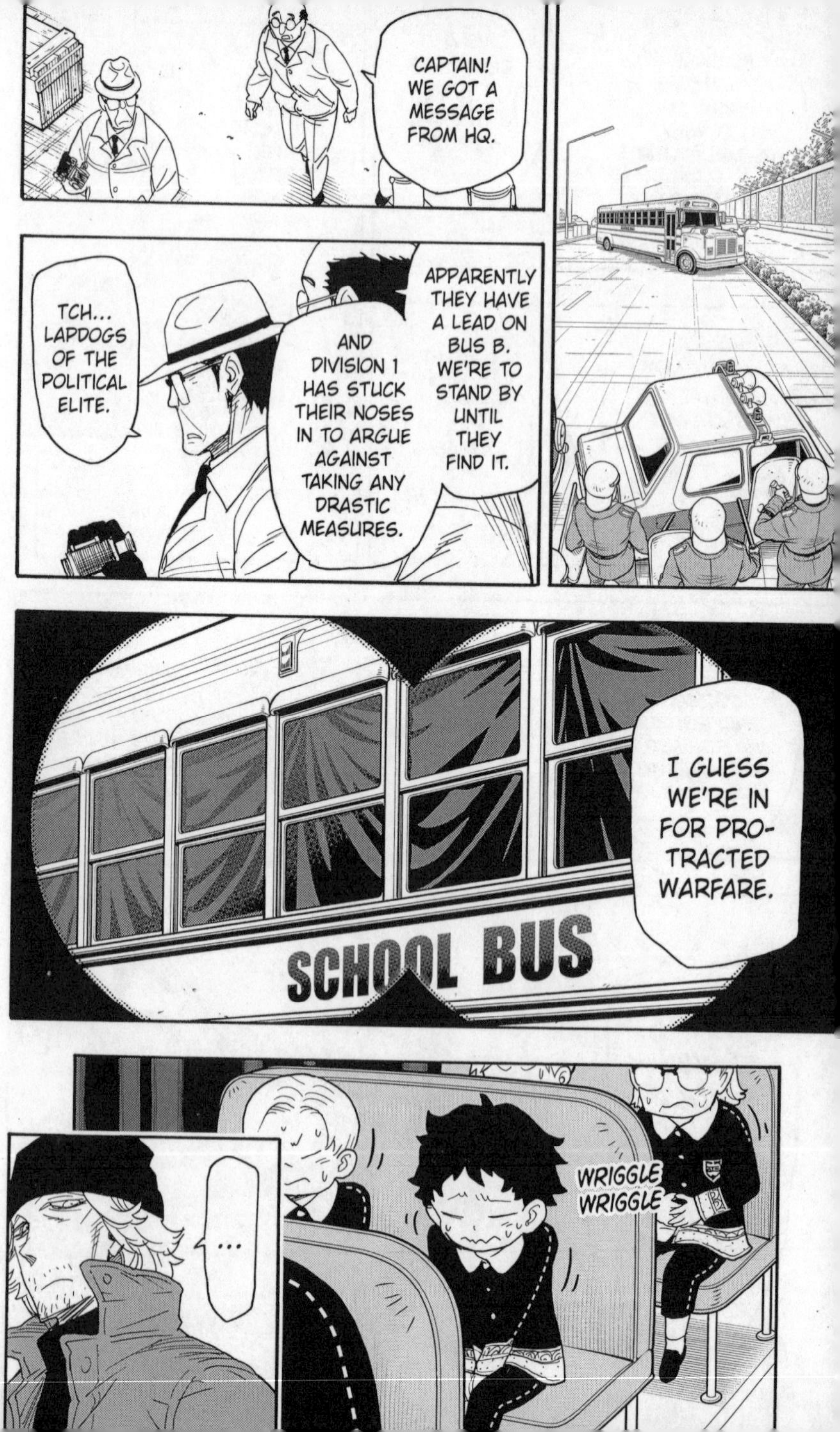
CAPTAIN! WE GOT A MESSAGE FROM HQ.
APPARENTLY THEY HAVE A LEAD ON BUS B. WE'RE TO STAND BY UNTIL THEY FIND IT.
AND DIVISION 1 HAS STUCK THEIR NOSES IN TO ARGUE AGAINST TAKING ANY DRASTIC MEASURES.
TCH... LAPDOGS OF THE POLITICAL ELITE.
SCHOOL BUS
I GUESS WE'RE IN FOR PRO-TRACTED WARFARE.
WRIGGLE WRIGGLE
...

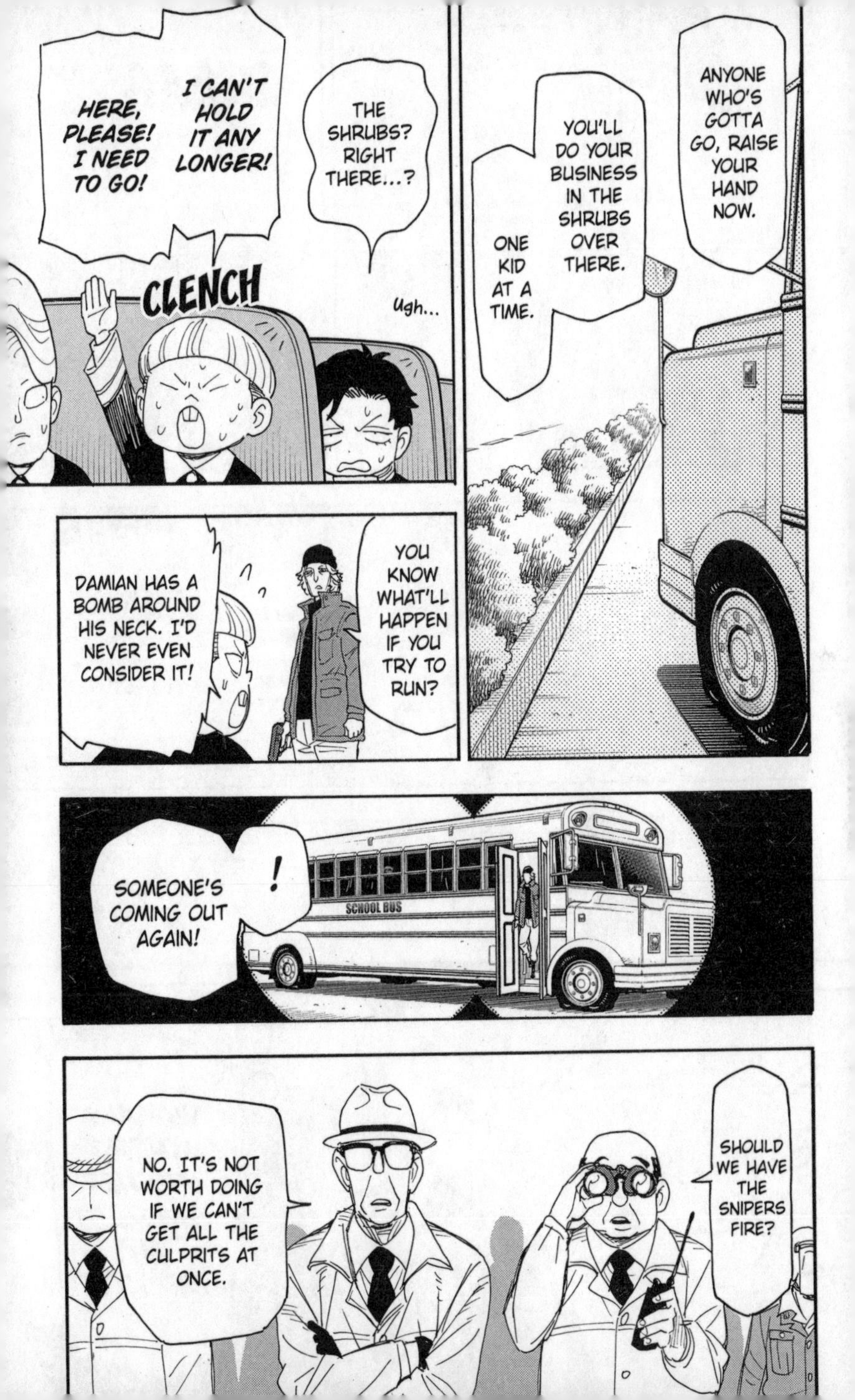
ANYONE WHO'S GOTTA GO, RAISE YOUR HAND NOW.
YOU'LL DO YOUR BUSINESS IN THE SHRUBS OVER THERE.
ONE KID AT A TIME.
THE SHRUBS? RIGHT THERE...?
I CAN'T HOLD IT ANY LONGER!
HERE, PLEASE! I NEED TO GO!
Ugh...
CLENCH
YOU KNOW WHAT'LL HAPPEN IF YOU TRY TO RUN?
DAMIAN HAS A BOMB AROUND HIS NECK. I'D NEVER EVEN CONSIDER IT!
!
SOMEONE'S COMING OUT AGAIN!
SCHOOL BUS
SHOULD WE HAVE THE SNIPERS FIRE?
NO. IT'S NOT WORTH DOING IF WE CAN'T GET ALL THE CULPRITS AT ONCE.

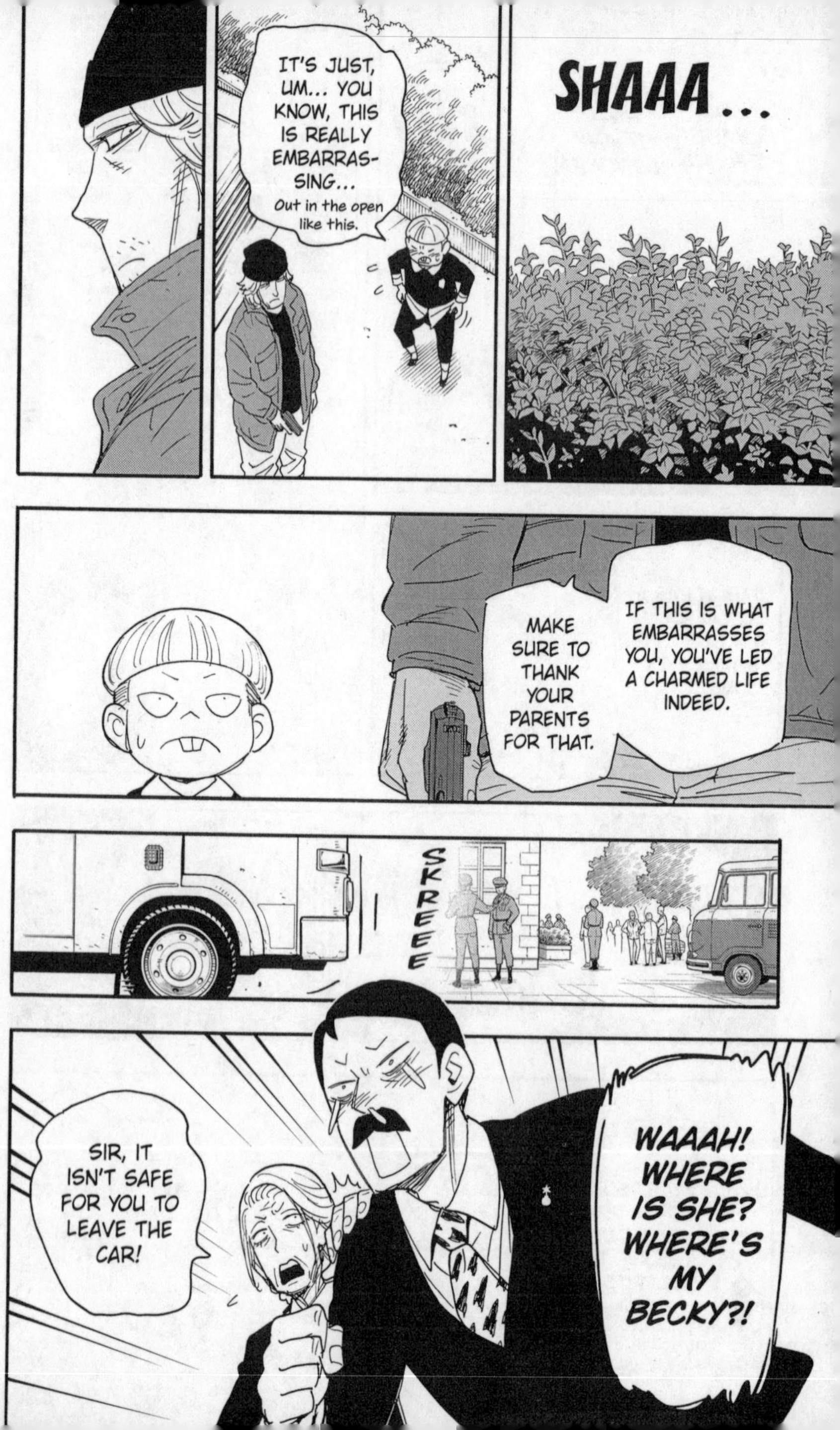
SHAAA...
IT'S JUST, UM... YOU KNOW, THIS IS REALLY EMBARRAS-SING...
Out in the open like this.
IF THIS IS WHAT EMBARRASSES YOU, YOU'VE LED A CHARMED LIFE INDEED.
MAKE SURE TO THANK YOUR PARENTS FOR THAT.
SKREEE
WAAAH! WHERE IS SHE? WHERE'S MY BECKY?!
SIR, IT ISN'T SAFE FOR YOU TO LEAVE THE CAR!

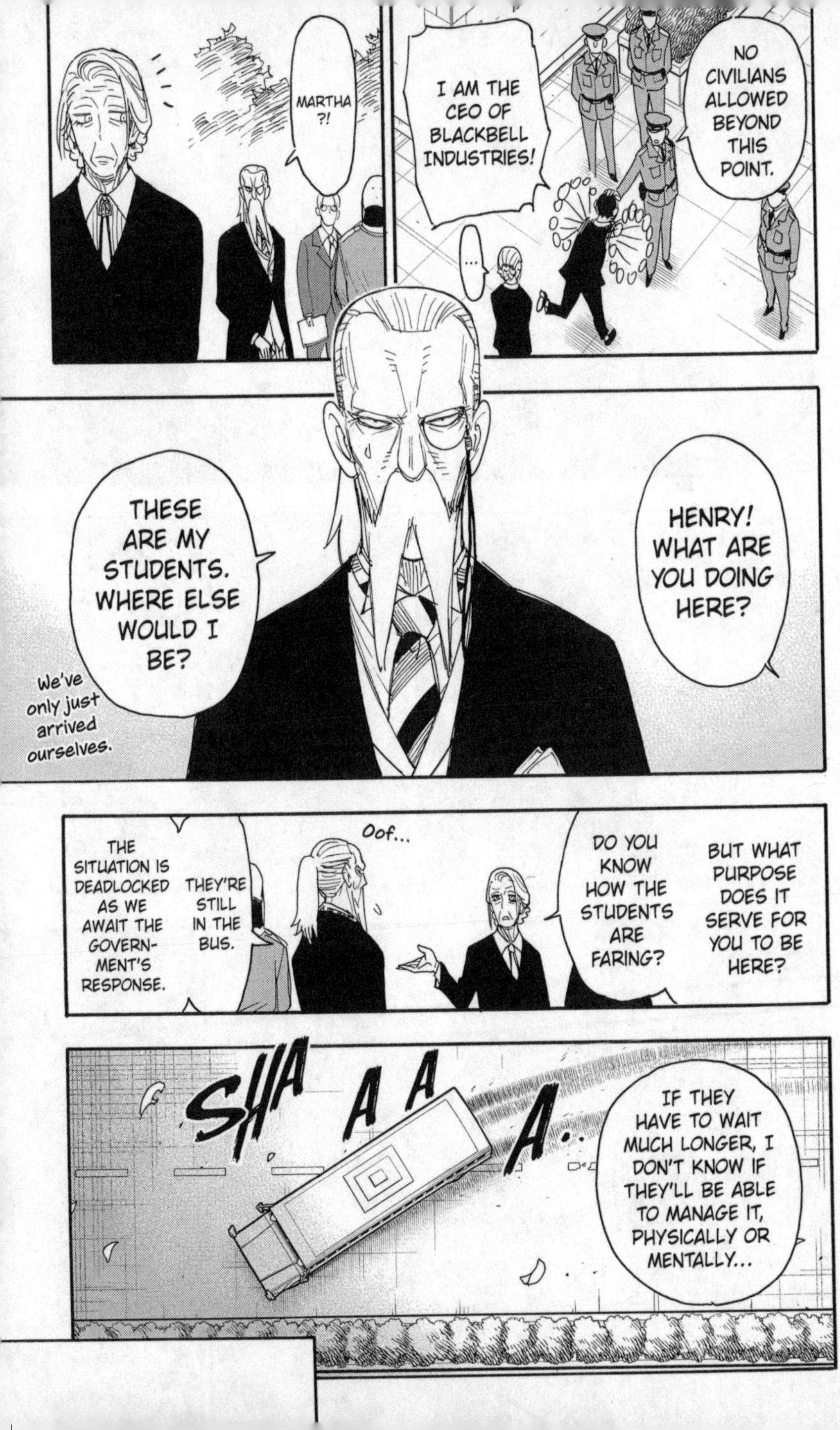
NO CIVILIANS ALLOWED BEYOND THIS POINT.
I AM THE CEO OF BLACKBELL INDUSTRIES!
...
MARTHA ?!
HENRY! WHAT ARE YOU DOING HERE?
THESE ARE MY STUDENTS. WHERE ELSE WOULD I BE?
We've only just arrived ourselves.
BUT WHAT PURPOSE DOES IT SERVE FOR YOU TO BE HERE?
DO YOU KNOW HOW THE STUDENTS ARE FARING?
Oof...
THEY'RE STILL IN THE BUS.
THE SITUATION IS DEADLOCKED AS WE AWAIT THE GOVERNMENT'S RESPONSE.
IF THEY HAVE TO WAIT MUCH LONGER, I DON'T KNOW IF THEY'LL BE ABLE TO MANAGE IT, PHYSICALLY OR MENTALLY...
SHAAAA

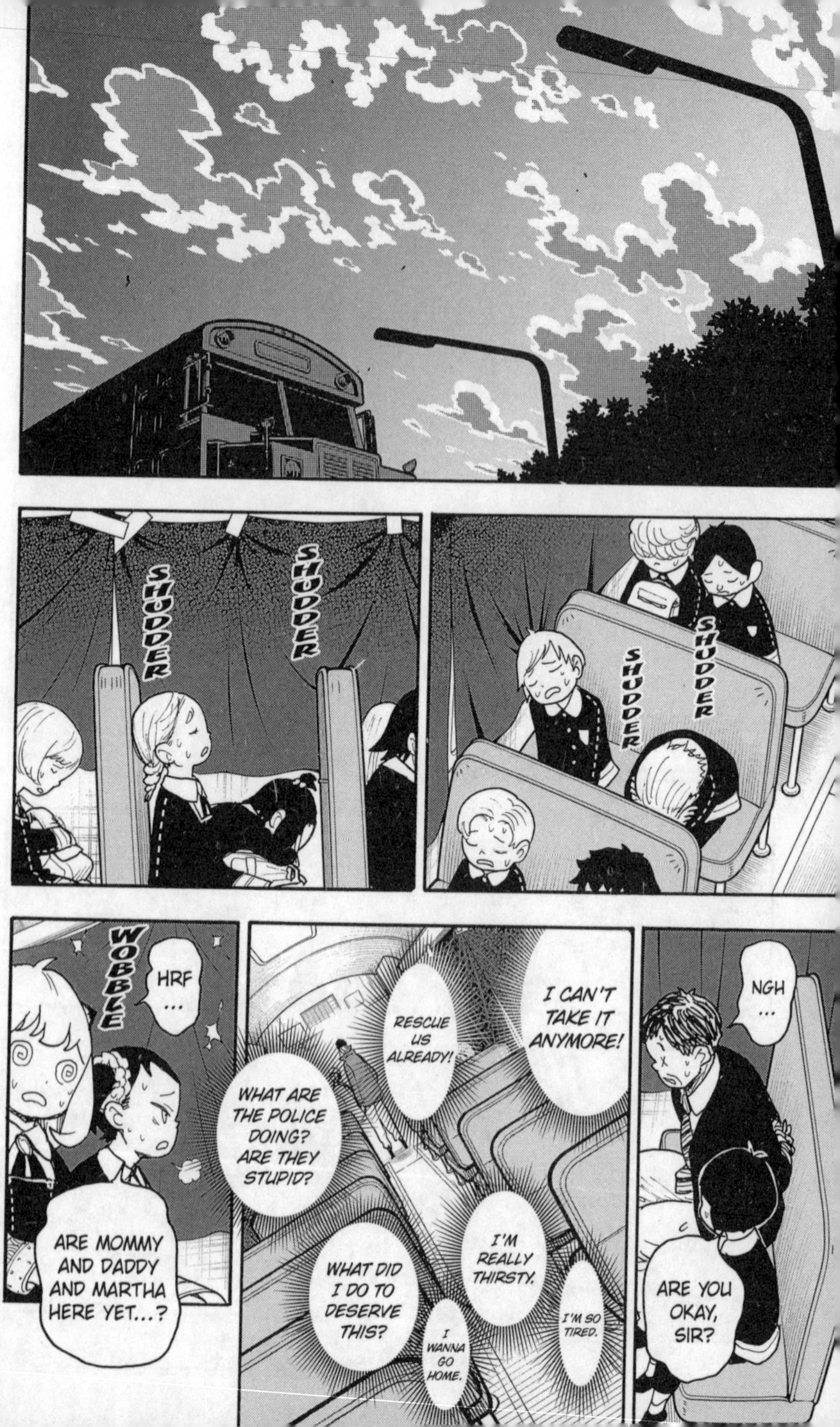
SHUDDER
SHUDDER
SHUDDER
SHUDDER
NGH...
ARE YOU OKAY, SIR?
I CAN'T TAKE IT ANYMORE!
RESCUE US ALREADY!
WHAT ARE THE POLICE DOING? ARE THEY STUPID?
I'M REALLY THIRSTY.
WHAT DID I DO TO DESERVE THIS?
I'M SO TIRED.
I WANNA GO HOME.
WOBBLE
HRF...
ARE MOMMY AND DADDY AND MARTHA HERE YET...?

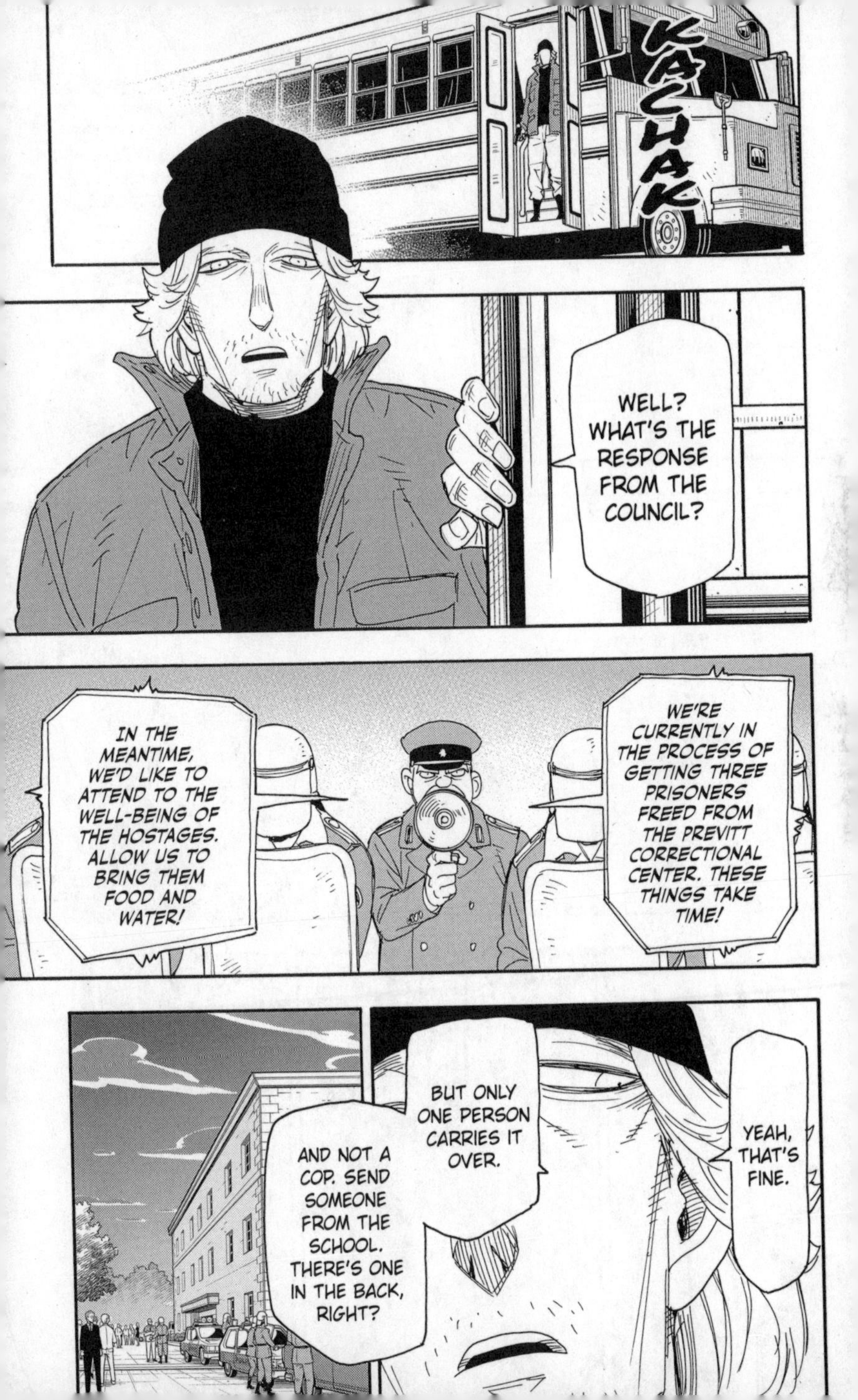
KACHAK
WELL? WHAT'S THE RESPONSE FROM THE COUNCIL?
WE'RE CURRENTLY IN THE PROCESS OF GETTING THREE PRISONERS FREED FROM THE PREVITT CORRECTIONAL CENTER. THESE THINGS TAKE TIME!
IN THE MEANTIME, WE'D LIKE TO ATTEND TO THE WELL-BEING OF THE HOSTAGES. ALLOW US TO BRING THEM FOOD AND WATER!
YEAH, THAT'S FINE.
BUT ONLY ONE PERSON CARRIES IT OVER.
AND NOT A COP. SEND SOMEONE FROM THE SCHOOL. THERE'S ONE IN THE BACK, RIGHT?

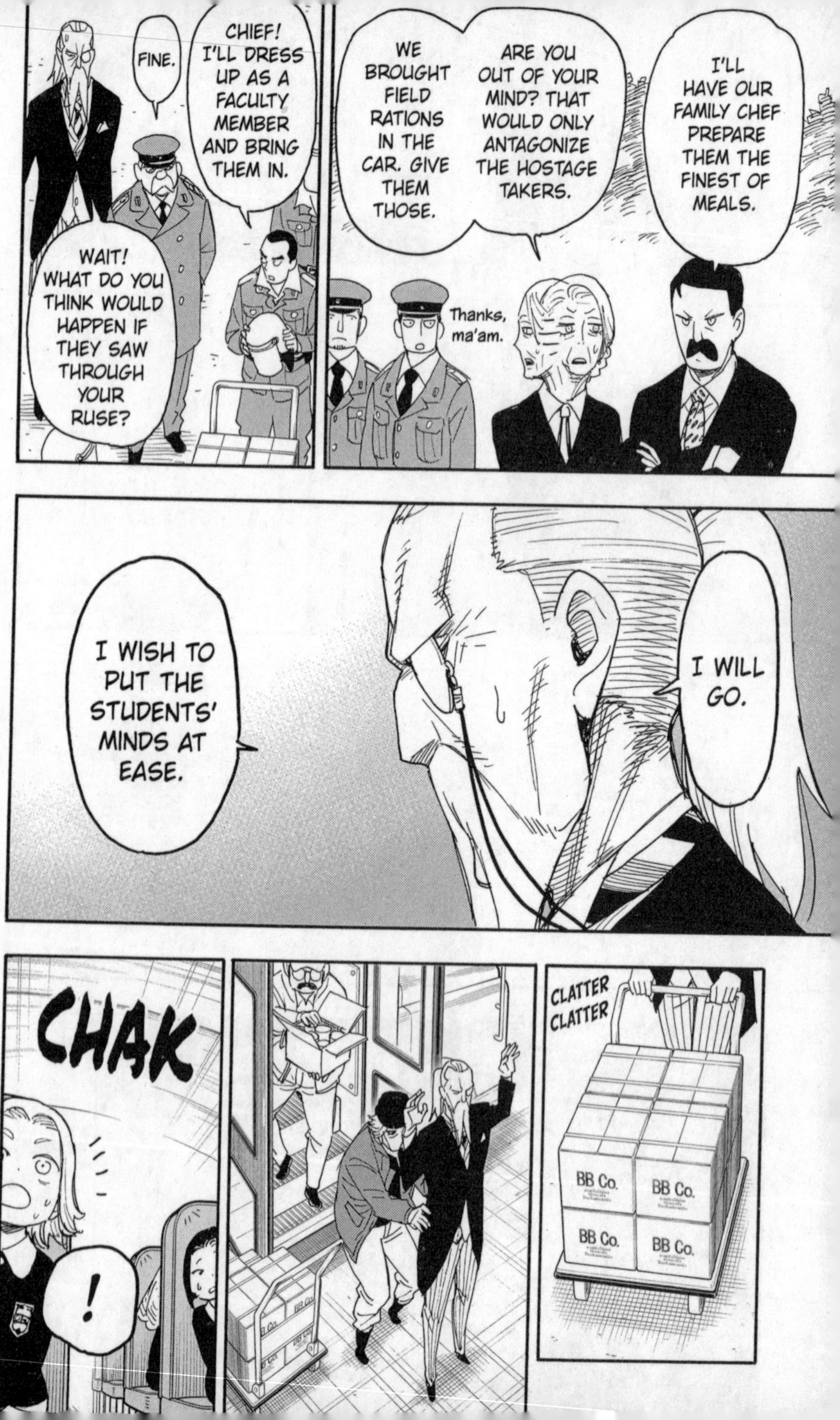
I'LL HAVE OUR FAMILY CHEF PREPARE THEM THE FINEST OF MEALS.
ARE YOU OUT OF YOUR MIND? THAT WOULD ONLY ANTAGONIZE THE HOSTAGE TAKERS.
WE BROUGHT FIELD RATIONS IN THE CAR. GIVE THEM THOSE.
Thanks, ma'am.
CHIEF! I'LL DRESS UP AS A FACULTY MEMBER AND BRING THEM IN.
FINE.
WAIT! WHAT DO YOU THINK WOULD HAPPEN IF THEY SAW THROUGH YOUR RUSE?
I WILL GO.
I WISH TO PUT THE STUDENTS' MINDS AT EASE.
CLATTER CLATTER
BB Co.
BB Co.
BB Co.
BB Co.
CHAK
!

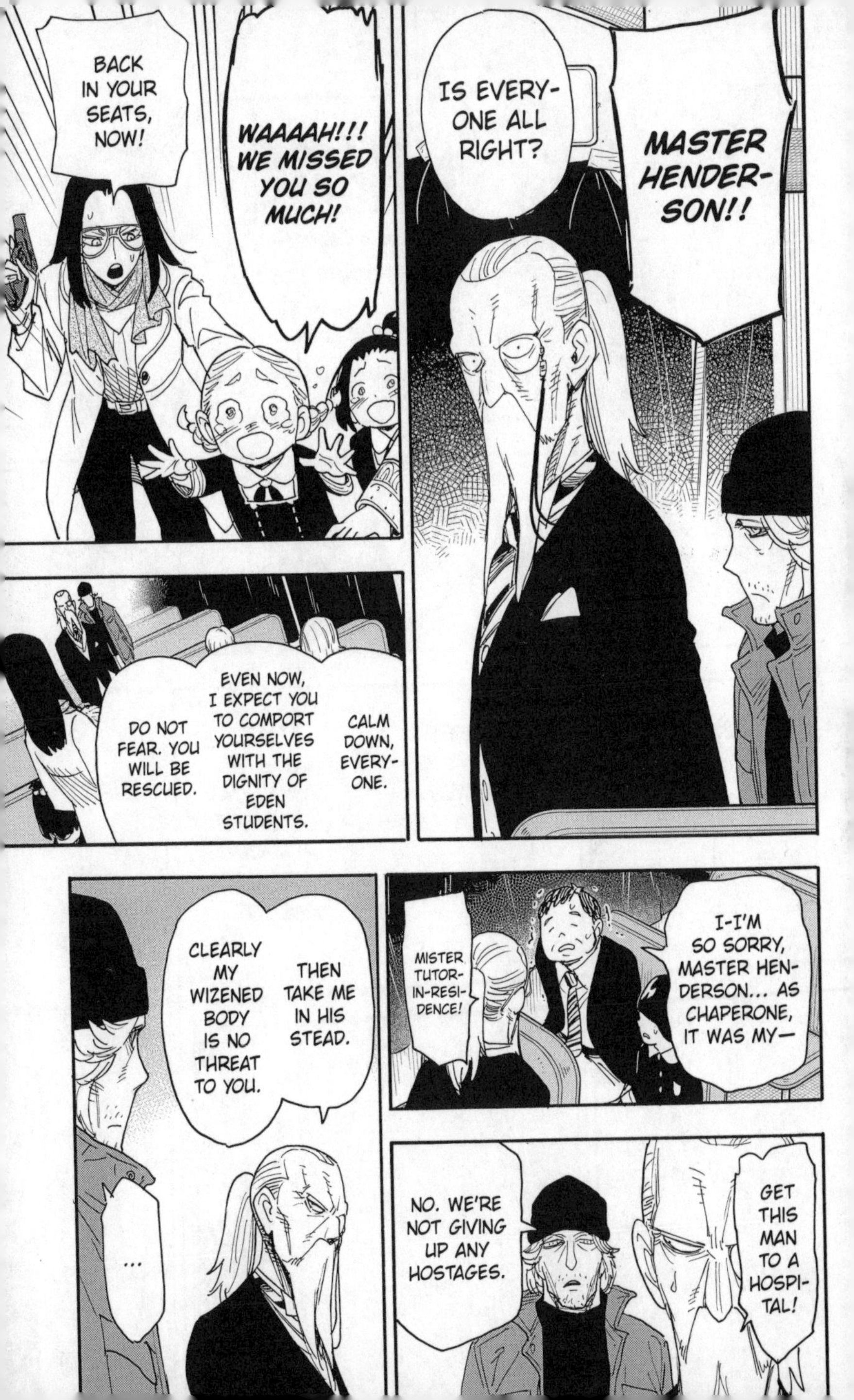
IS EVERY-ONE ALL RIGHT?
MASTER HENDER-SON!!
WAAAAH!!! WE MISSED YOU SO MUCH!
BACK IN YOUR SEATS, NOW!
CALM DOWN, EVERY-ONE.
EVEN NOW, I EXPECT YOU TO COMPORT YOURSELVES WITH THE DIGNITY OF EDEN STUDENTS.
DO NOT FEAR. YOU WILL BE RESCUED.
I-I'M SO SORRY, MASTER HEN-DERSON... AS CHAPERONE, IT WAS MY—
MISTER TUTOR-IN-RESI-DENCE!
GET THIS MAN TO A HOSPI-TAL!
NO. WE'RE NOT GIVING UP ANY HOSTAGES.
THEN TAKE ME IN HIS STEAD.
CLEARLY MY WIZENED BODY IS NO THREAT TO YOU.
...

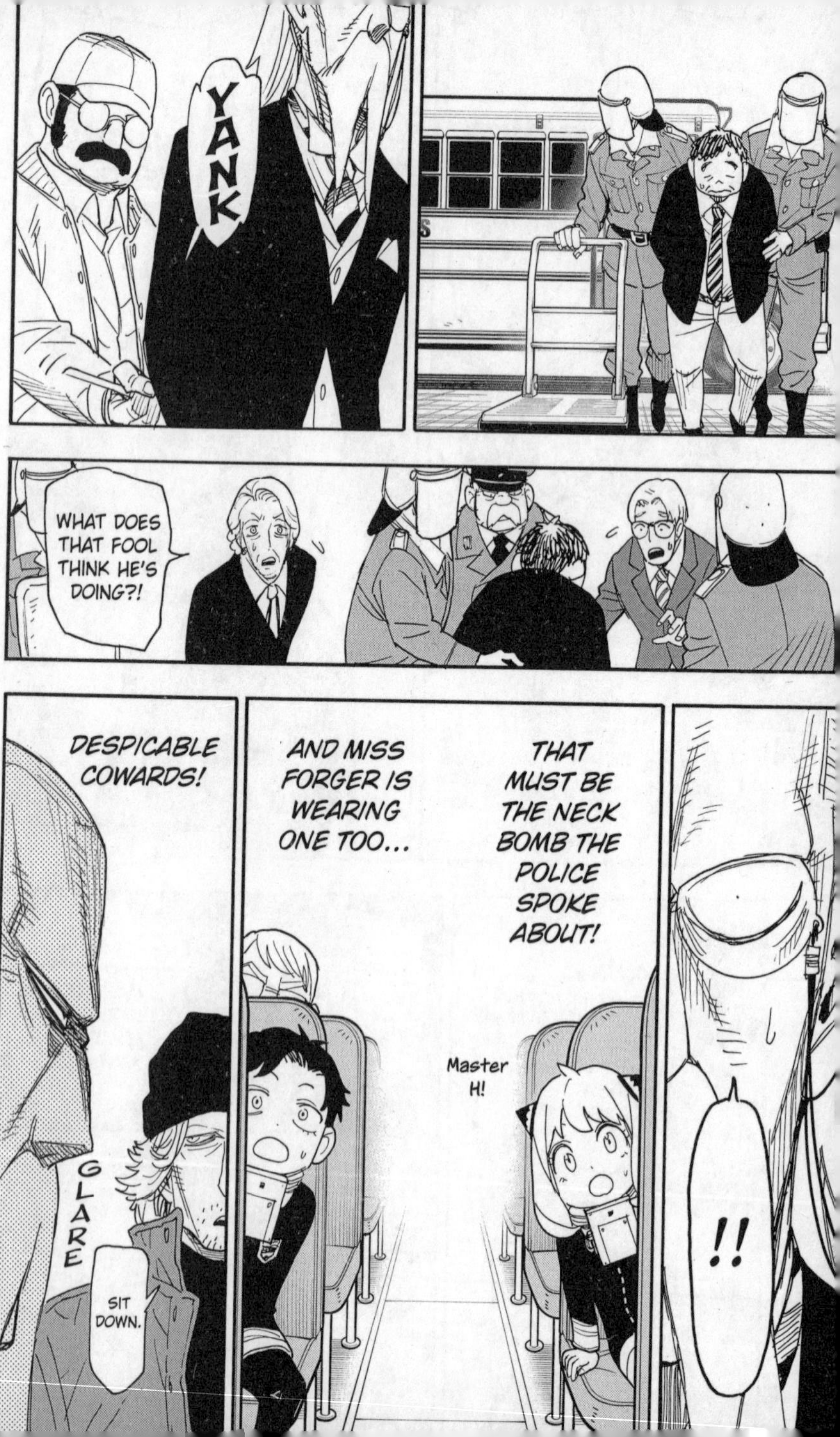
YANK
WHAT DOES THAT FOOL THINK HE'S DOING?!
!!
THAT MUST BE THE NECK BOMB THE POLICE SPOKE ABOUT!
AND MISS FORGER IS WEARING ONE TOO...
Master H!
DESPICABLE COWARDS!
GLARE
SIT DOWN.

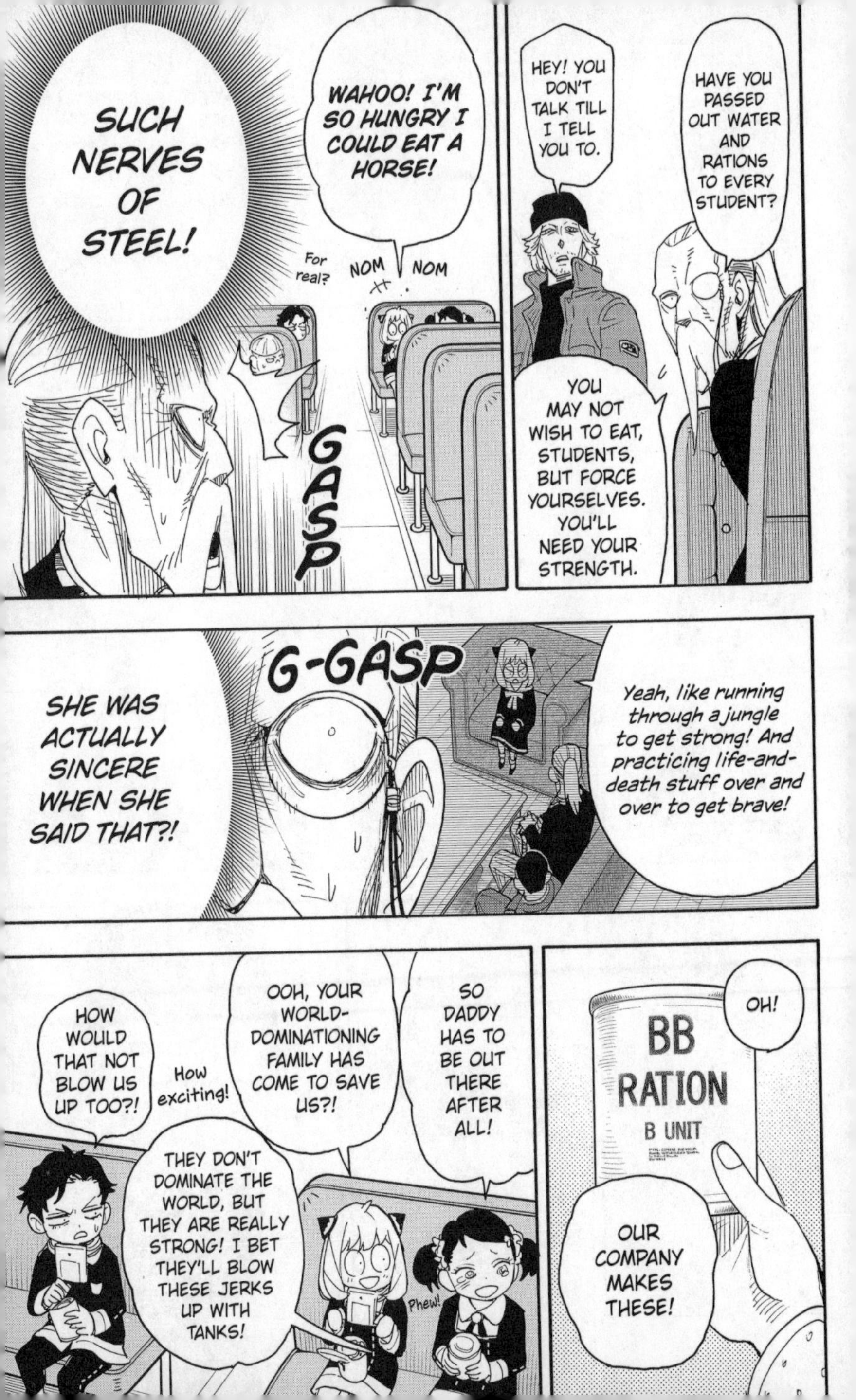
HAVE YOU PASSED OUT WATER AND RATIONS TO EVERY STUDENT?
HEY! YOU DON'T TALK TILL I TELL YOU TO.
YOU MAY NOT WISH TO EAT, STUDENTS, BUT FORCE YOURSELVES. YOU'LL NEED YOUR STRENGTH.
WAHOO! I'M SO HUNGRY I COULD EAT A HORSE!
SUCH NERVES OF STEEL!
For real?
NOM NOM
GASP
Yeah, like running through a jungle to get strong! And practicing life-and-death stuff over and over to get brave!
G-GASP
SHE WAS ACTUALLY SINCERE WHEN SHE SAID THAT?!
OH!
BB RATION
B UNIT
OUR COMPANY MAKES THESE!
SO DADDY HAS TO BE OUT THERE AFTER ALL!
OOH, YOUR WORLD-DOMINATIONING FAMILY HAS COME TO SAVE US?!
How exciting!
HOW WOULD THAT NOT BLOW US UP TOO?!
THEY DON'T DOMINATE THE WORLD, BUT THEY ARE REALLY STRONG! I BET THEY'LL BLOW THESE JERKS UP WITH TANKS!
Phew!

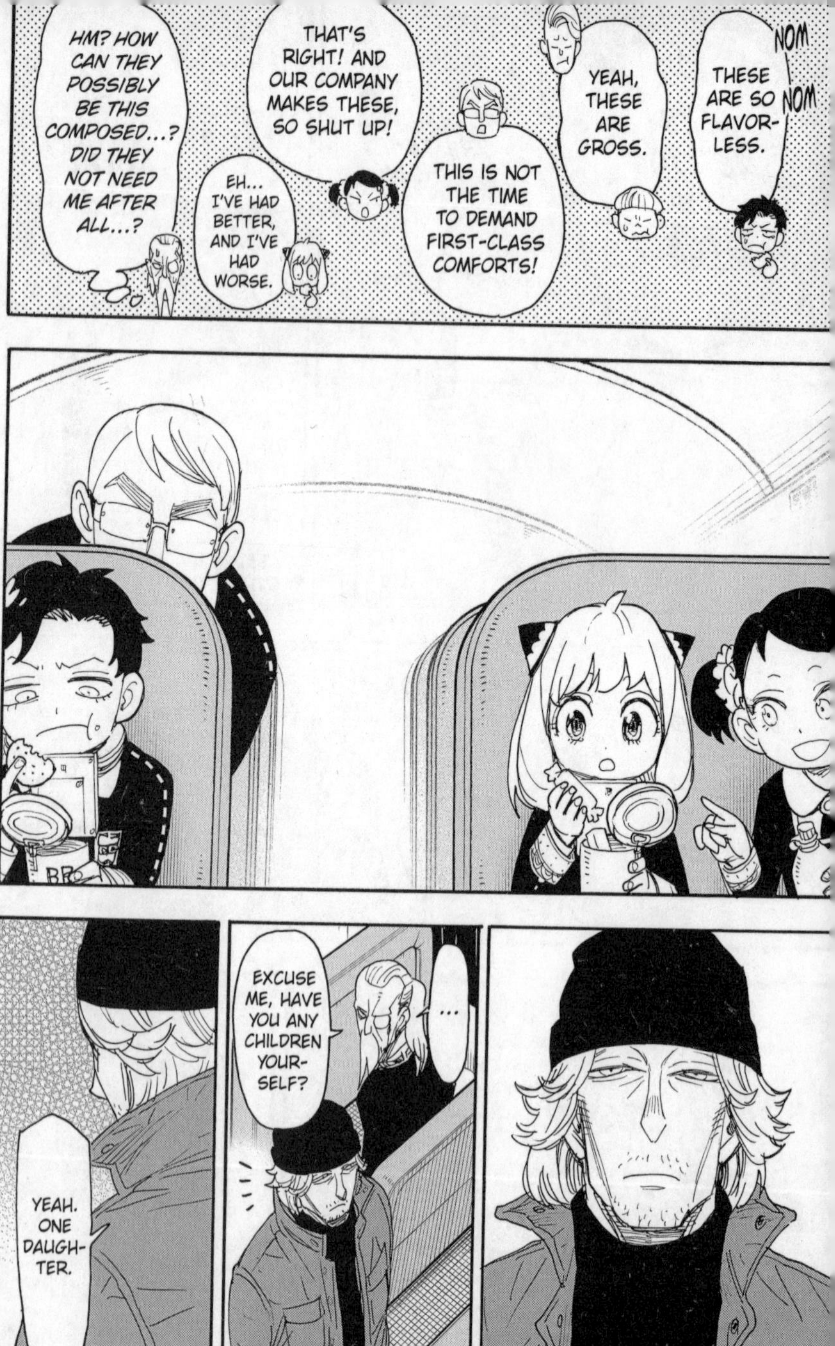
NOM NOM
THESE ARE SO FLAVORLESS.
YEAH, THESE ARE GROSS.
THIS IS NOT THE TIME TO DEMAND FIRST-CLASS COMFORTS!
THAT'S RIGHT! AND OUR COMPANY MAKES THESE, SO SHUT UP!
EH... I'VE HAD BETTER, AND I'VE HAD WORSE.
HM? HOW CAN THEY POSSIBLY BE THIS COMPOSED...? DID THEY NOT NEED ME AFTER ALL...?
...
EXCUSE ME, HAVE YOU ANY CHILDREN YOURSELF?
YEAH. ONE DAUGHTER.

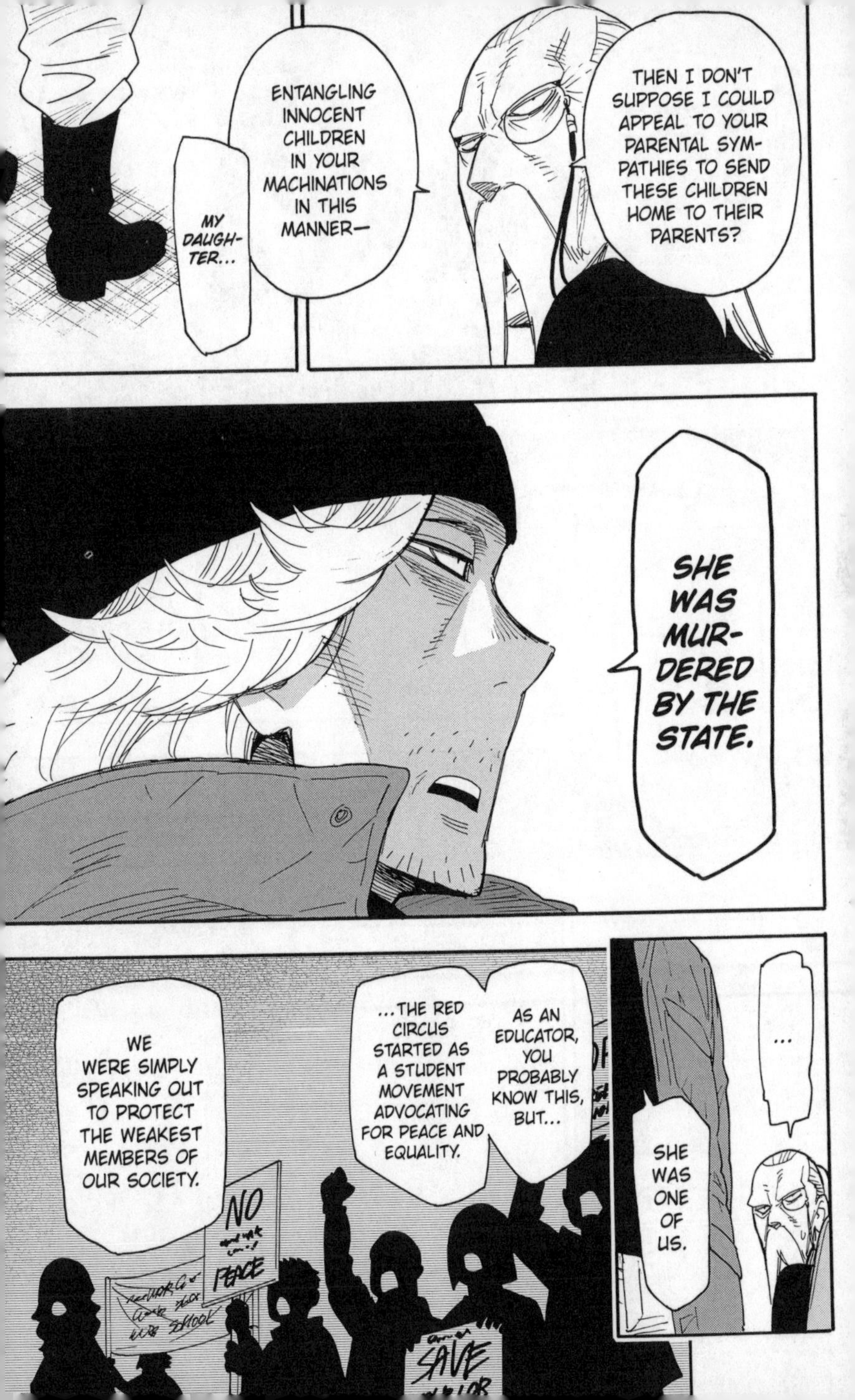
THEN I DON'T SUPPOSE I COULD APPEAL TO YOUR PARENTAL SYMPATHIES TO SEND THESE CHILDREN HOME TO THEIR PARENTS?
ENTANGLING INNOCENT CHILDREN IN YOUR MACHINATIONS IN THIS MANNER—
MY DAUGHTER...
SHE WAS MURDERED BY THE STATE.
...
SHE WAS ONE OF US.
AS AN EDUCATOR, YOU PROBABLY KNOW THIS, BUT...
...THE RED CIRCUS STARTED AS A STUDENT MOVEMENT ADVOCATING FOR PEACE AND EQUALITY.
WE WERE SIMPLY SPEAKING OUT TO PROTECT THE WEAKEST MEMBERS OF OUR SOCIETY.
NO
PEACE
SAVE

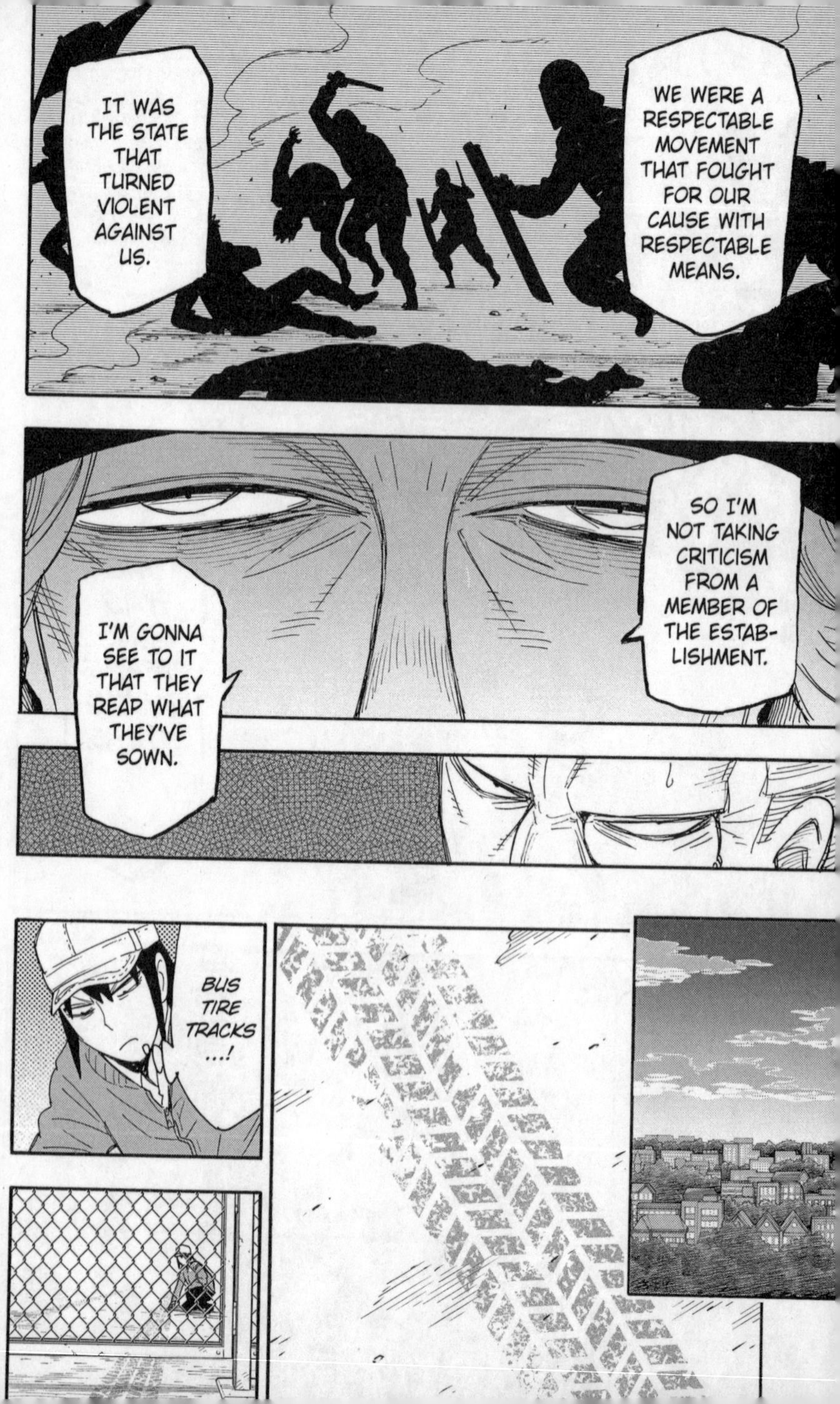
WE WERE A RESPECTABLE MOVEMENT THAT FOUGHT FOR OUR CAUSE WITH RESPECTABLE MEANS.
IT WAS THE STATE THAT TURNED VIOLENT AGAINST US.
SO I'M NOT TAKING CRITICISM FROM A MEMBER OF THE ESTAB-LISHMENT.
I'M GONNA SEE TO IT THAT THEY REAP WHAT THEY'VE SOWN.
BUS TIRE TRACKS ...!

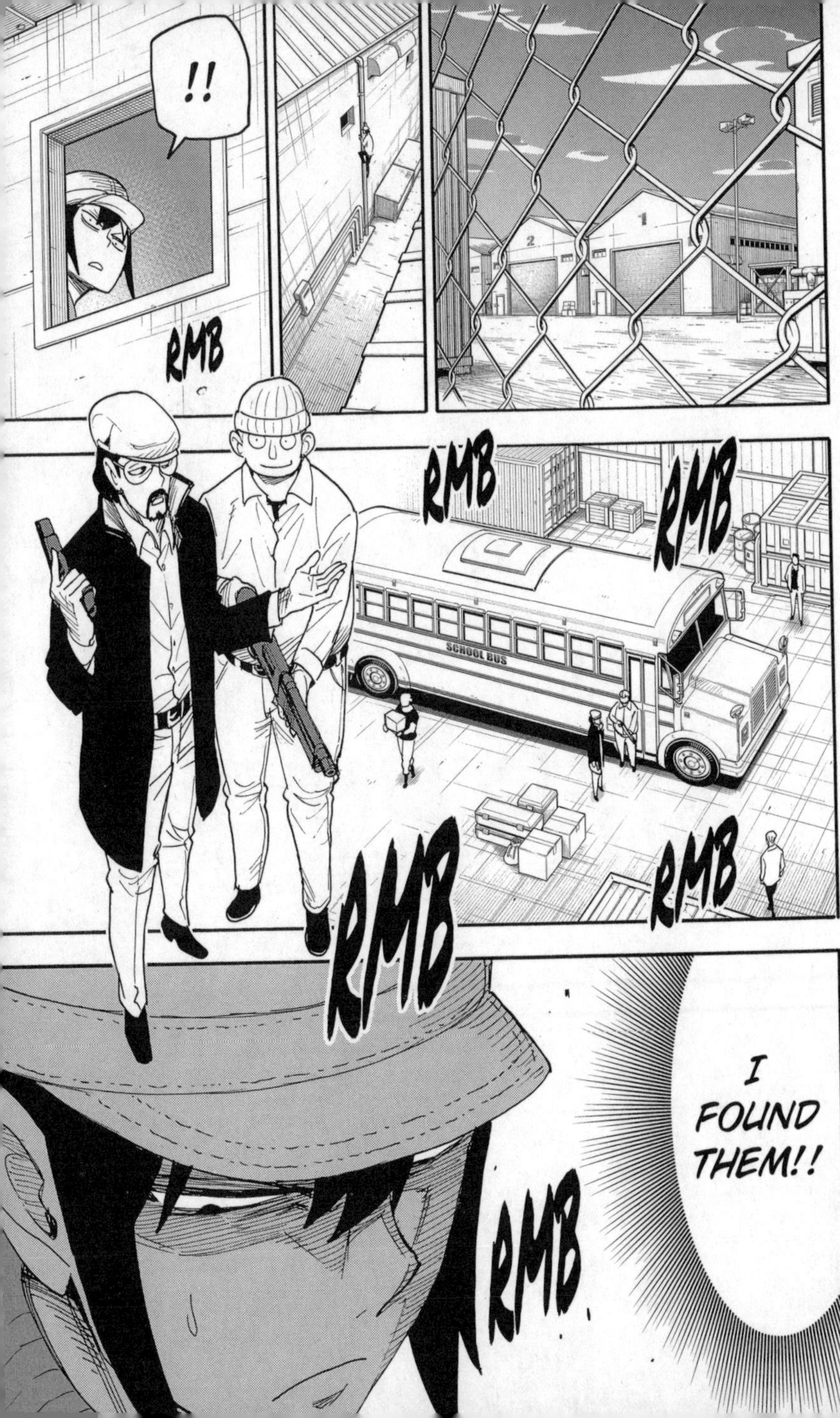
!!
RMB
RMB
RMB
RMB
RMB
I FOUND THEM!!
RMB

SPY×FAMILY

MISSION 73

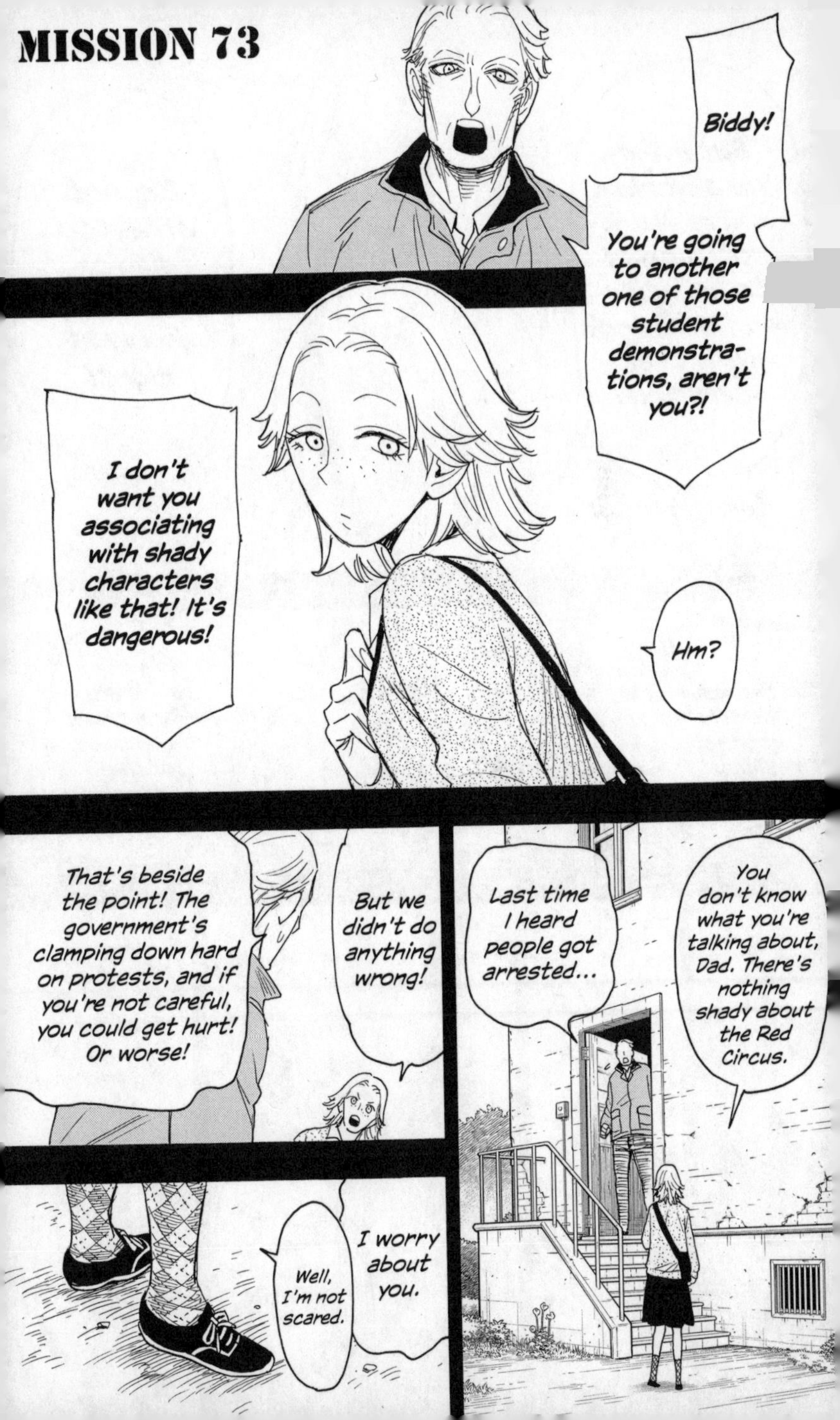
Biddy!
You're going to another one of those student demonstra-tions, aren't you?!
Hm?
I don't want you associating with shady characters like that! It's dangerous!
You don't know what you're talking about, Dad. There's nothing shady about the Red Circus.
Last time I heard people got arrested...
But we didn't do anything wrong!
That's beside the point! The government's clamping down hard on protests, and if you're not careful, you could get hurt! Or worse!
I worry about you.
Well, I'm not scared.

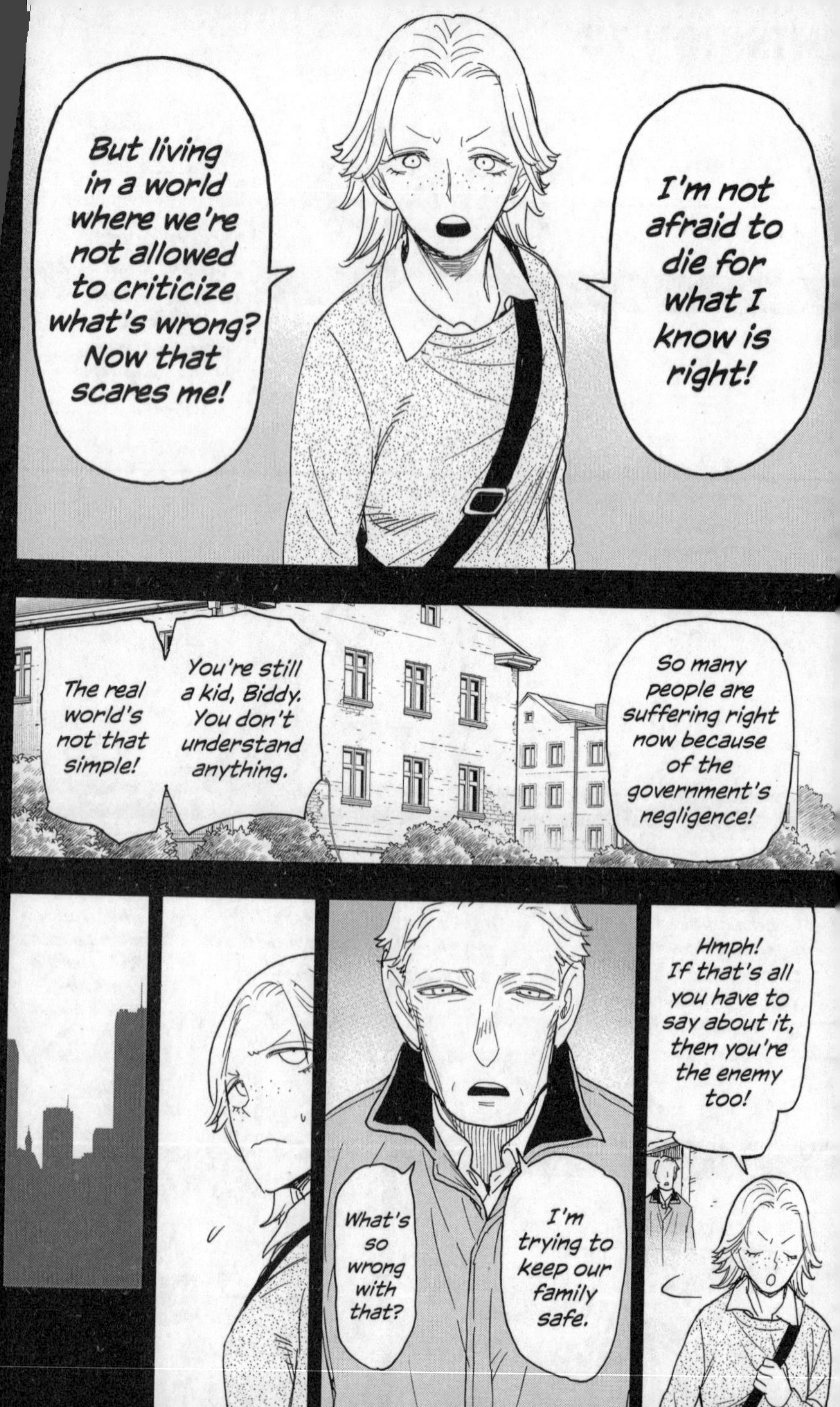
I'm not afraid to die for what I know is right!
But living in a world where we're not allowed to criticize what's wrong? Now that scares me!
So many people are suffering right now because of the government's negligence!
You're still a kid, Biddy. You don't understand anything.
The real world's not that simple!
Hmph! If that's all you have to say about it, then you're the enemy too!
I'm trying to keep our family safe.
What's so wrong with that?

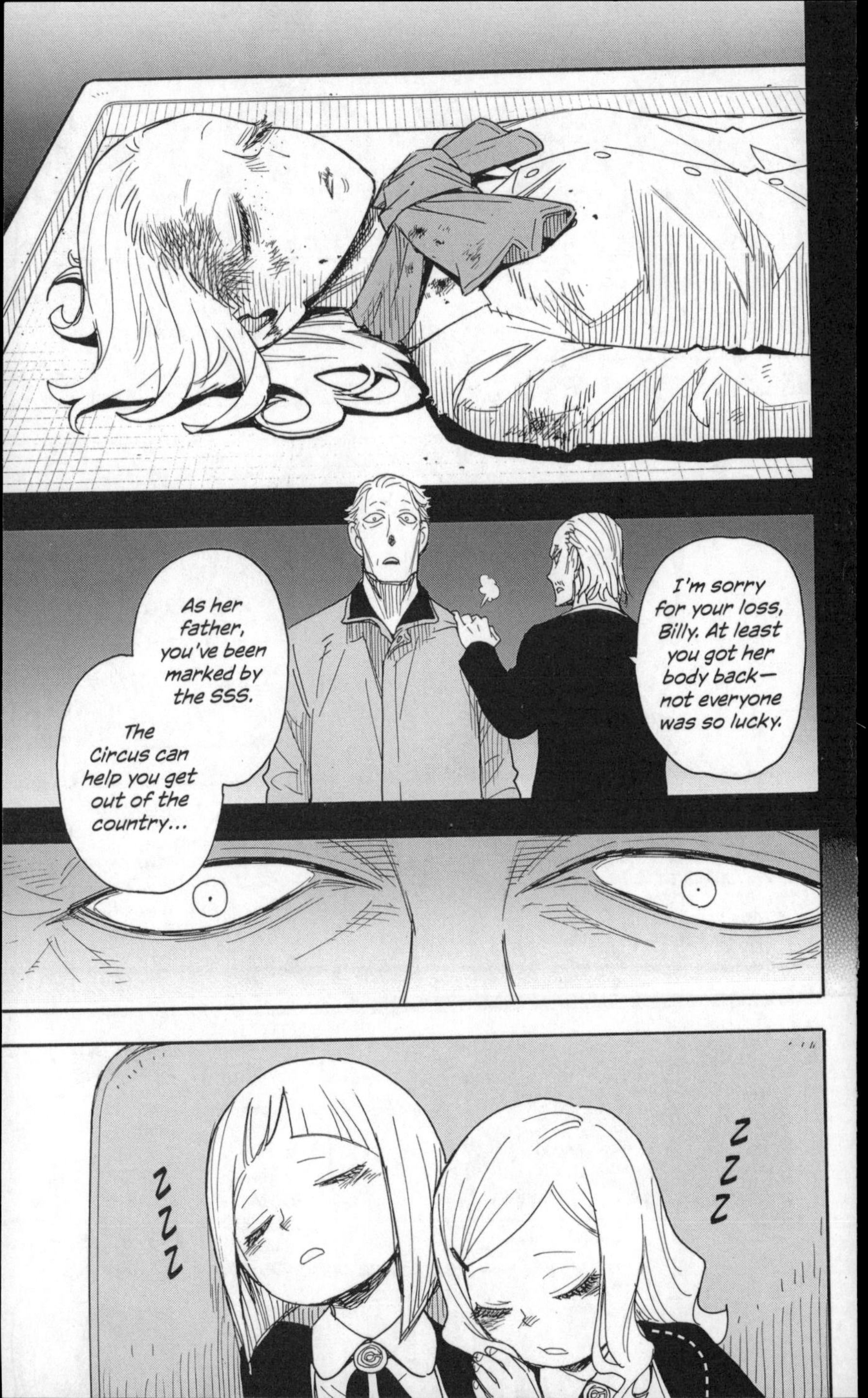
I'm sorry for your loss, Billy. At least you got her body back—not everyone was so lucky.
As her father, you've been marked by the SSS.
The Circus can help you get out of the country...
ZZZ
ZZZ

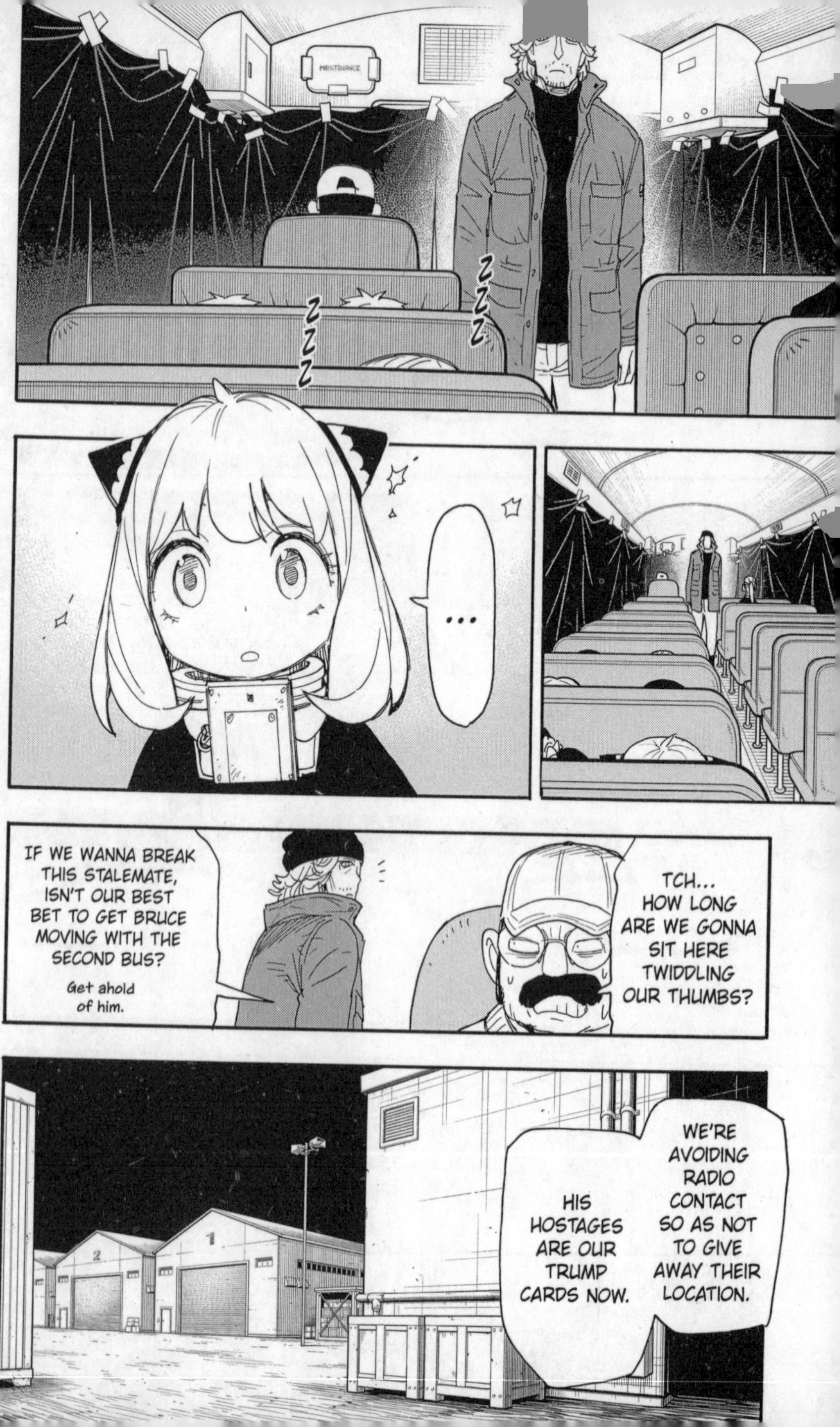
ZZZ
ZZZ
...
TCH... HOW LONG ARE WE GONNA SIT HERE TWIDDLING OUR THUMBS?
IF WE WANNA BREAK THIS STALEMATE, ISN'T OUR BEST BET TO GET BRUCE MOVING WITH THE SECOND BUS?
Get ahold of him.
WE'RE AVOIDING RADIO CONTACT SO AS NOT TO GIVE AWAY THEIR LOCATION.
HIS HOSTAGES ARE OUR TRUMP CARDS NOW.

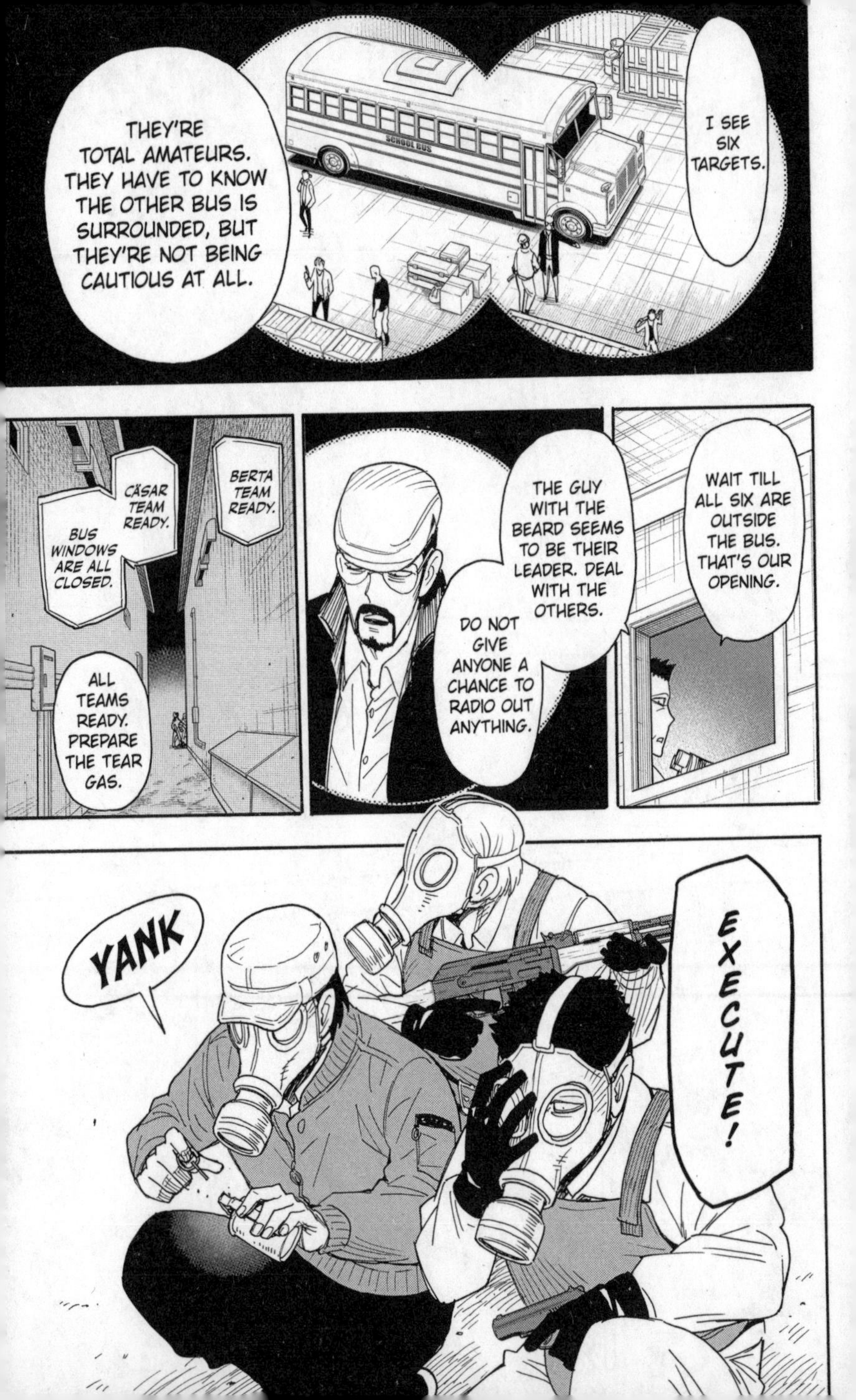
I SEE SIX TARGETS.
THEY'RE TOTAL AMATEURS. THEY HAVE TO KNOW THE OTHER BUS IS SURROUNDED, BUT THEY'RE NOT BEING CAUTIOUS AT ALL.
WAIT TILL ALL SIX ARE OUTSIDE THE BUS. THAT'S OUR OPENING.
THE GUY WITH THE BEARD SEEMS TO BE THEIR LEADER. DEAL WITH THE OTHERS.
DO NOT GIVE ANYONE A CHANCE TO RADIO OUT ANYTHING.
BERTA TEAM READY.
CÄSAR TEAM READY.
BUS WINDOWS ARE ALL CLOSED.
ALL TEAMS READY. PREPARE THE TEAR GAS.
EXECUTE!
YANK

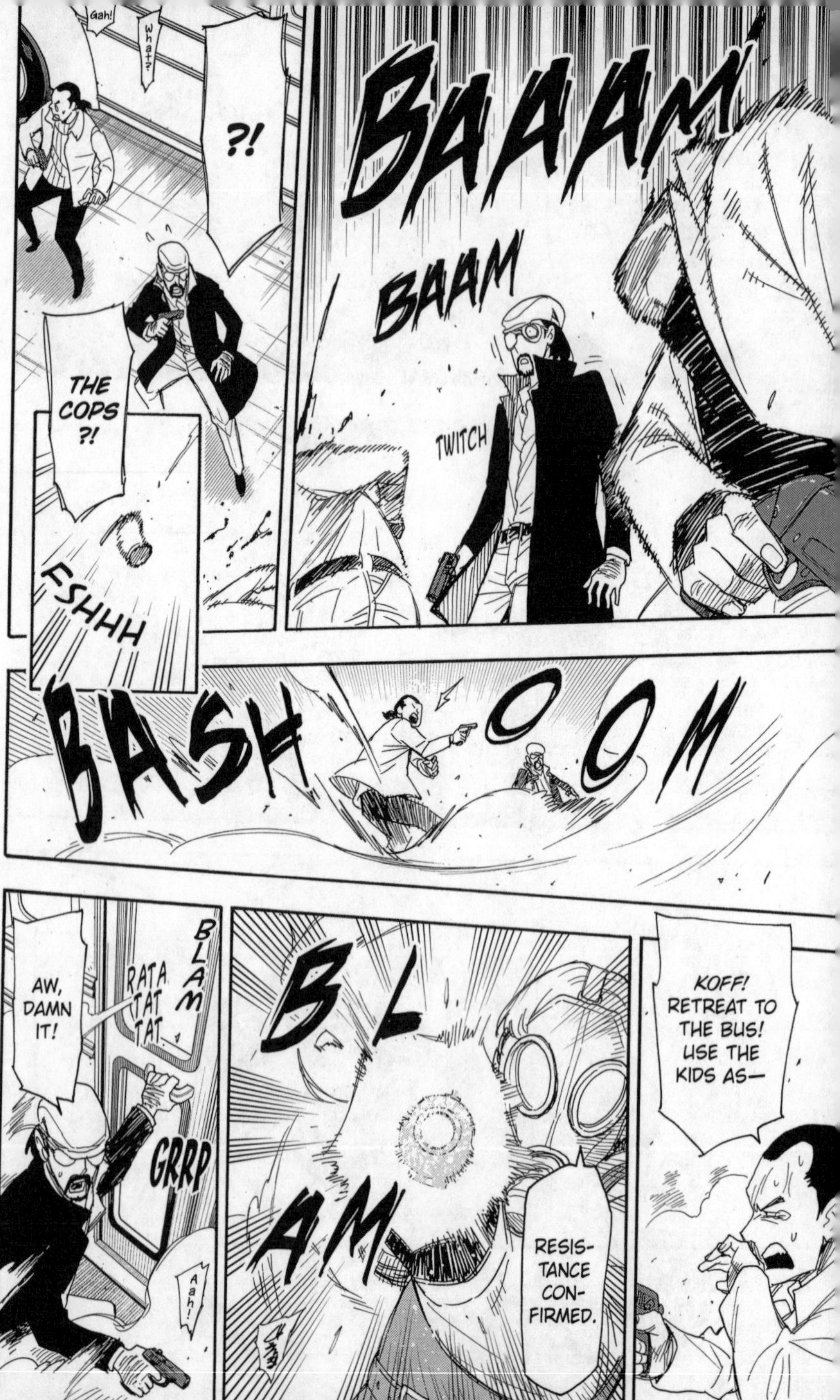
BAAAM
BAAM
TWITCH
Gah!
What?
?!
THE COPS?!
FSHHH
BASH
OOM
KOFF! RETREAT TO THE BUS! USE THE KIDS AS—
BLAM
RESISTANCE CONFIRMED.
BLAM
RATA TAT TAT
AW, DAMN IT!
GRRP
Aah!

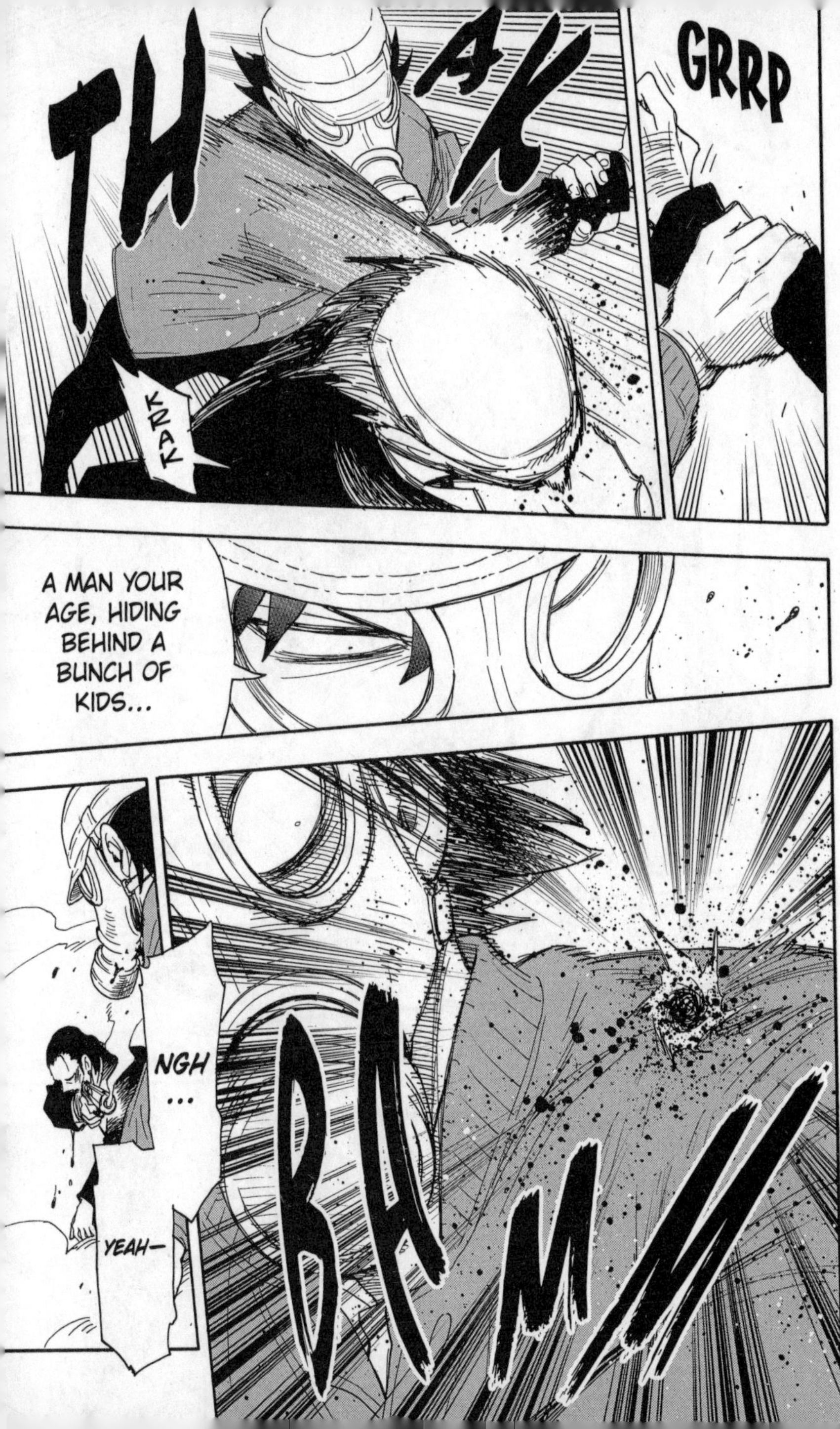
GRRP
THWAK
KRAK
A MAN YOUR AGE, HIDING BEHIND A BUNCH OF KIDS...
BAMM
NGH ...
YEAH—

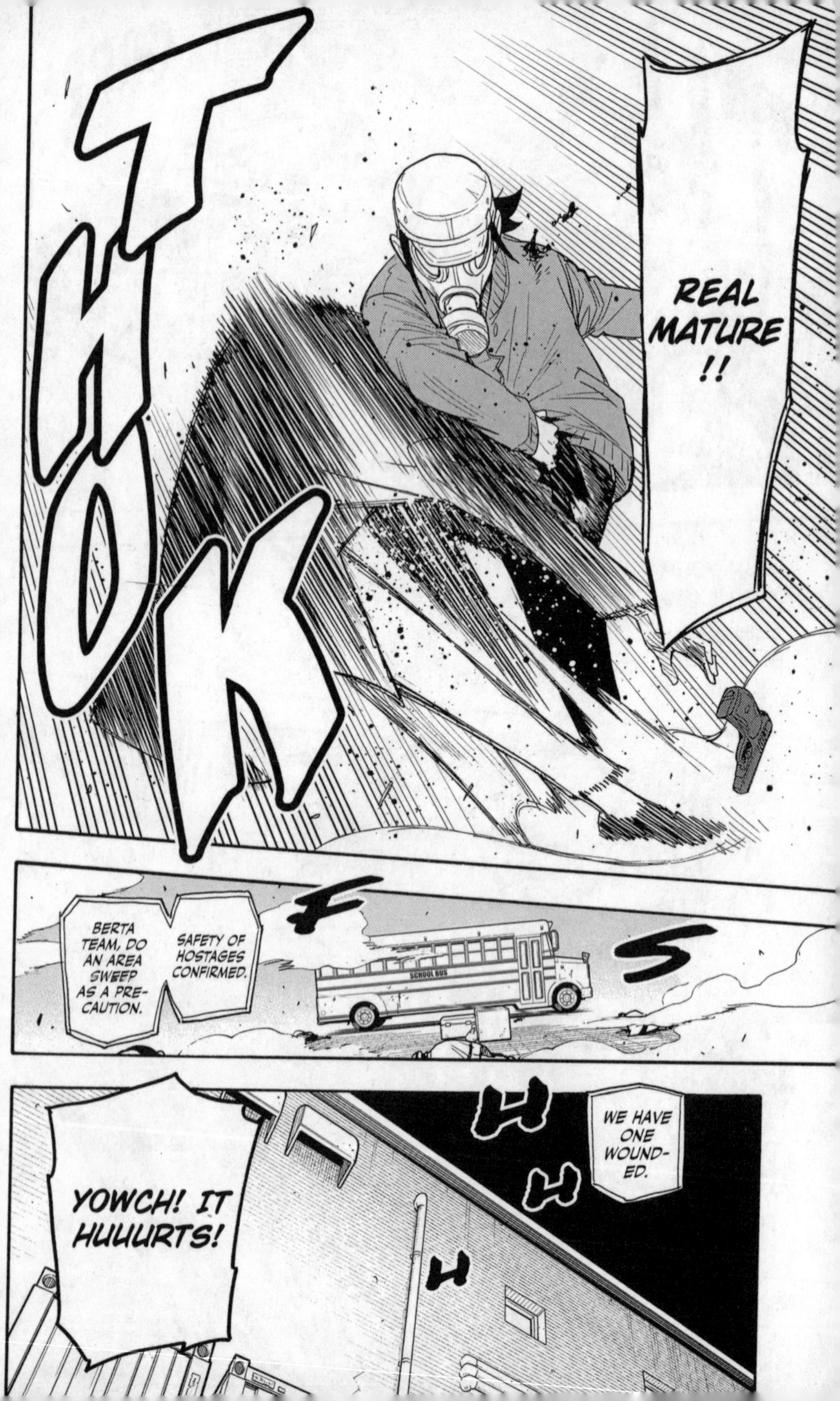
REAL MATURE !!
SAFETY OF HOSTAGES CONFIRMED.
BERTA TEAM, DO AN AREA SWEEP AS A PRE-CAUTION.
SCHOOL BUS
WE HAVE ONE WOUND-ED.
YOWCH! IT HUUURTS!

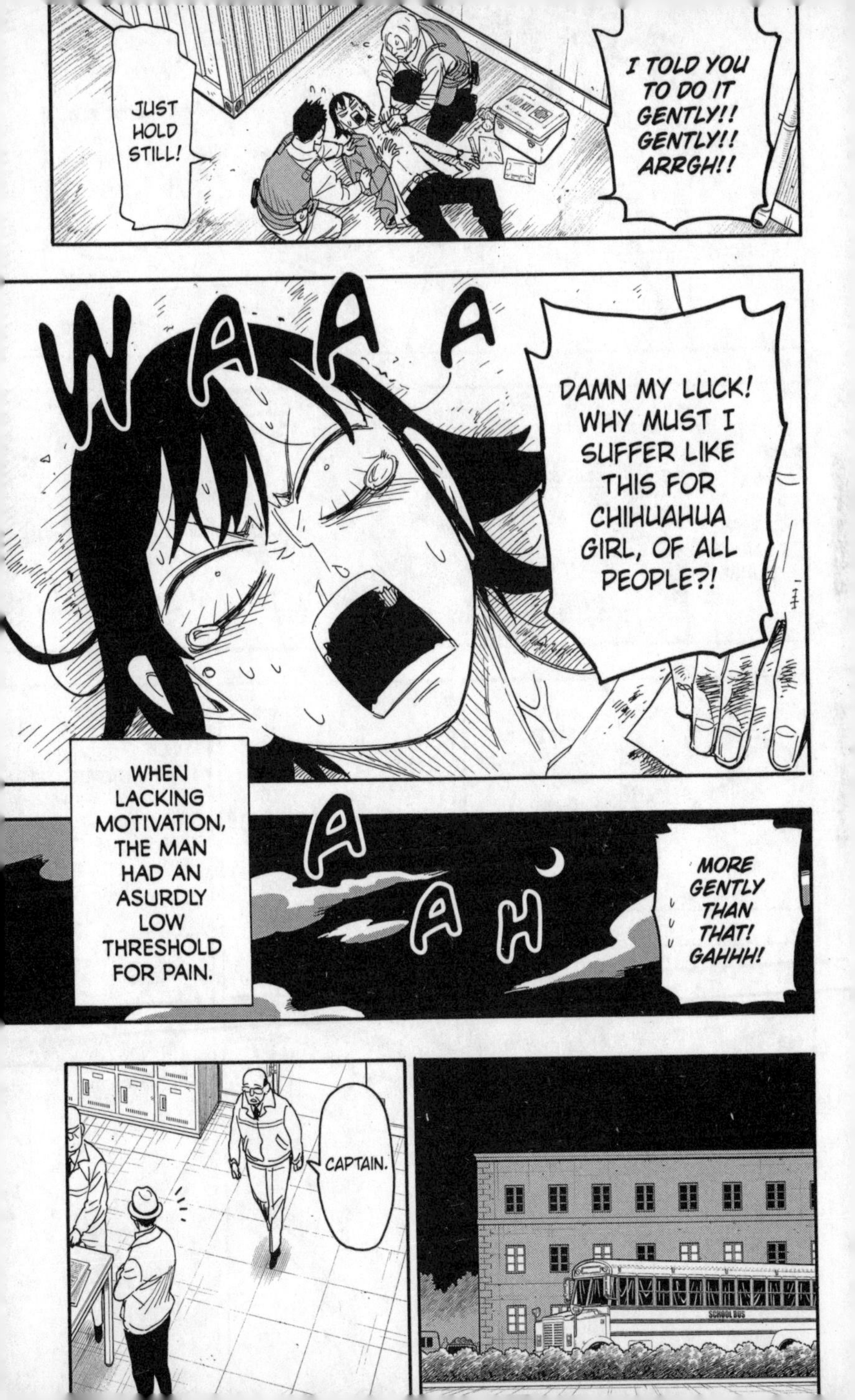
I TOLD YOU TO DO IT GENTLY!! GENTLY!! ARRGH!!
JUST HOLD STILL!
DAMN MY LUCK! WHY MUST I SUFFER LIKE THIS FOR CHIHUAHUA GIRL, OF ALL PEOPLE?!
WAAA
MORE GENTLY THAN THAT! GAHHH!
AAAH
WHEN LACKING MOTIVATION, THE MAN HAD AN ASURDLY LOW THRESHOLD FOR PAIN.
SCHOOL BUS
CAPTAIN.

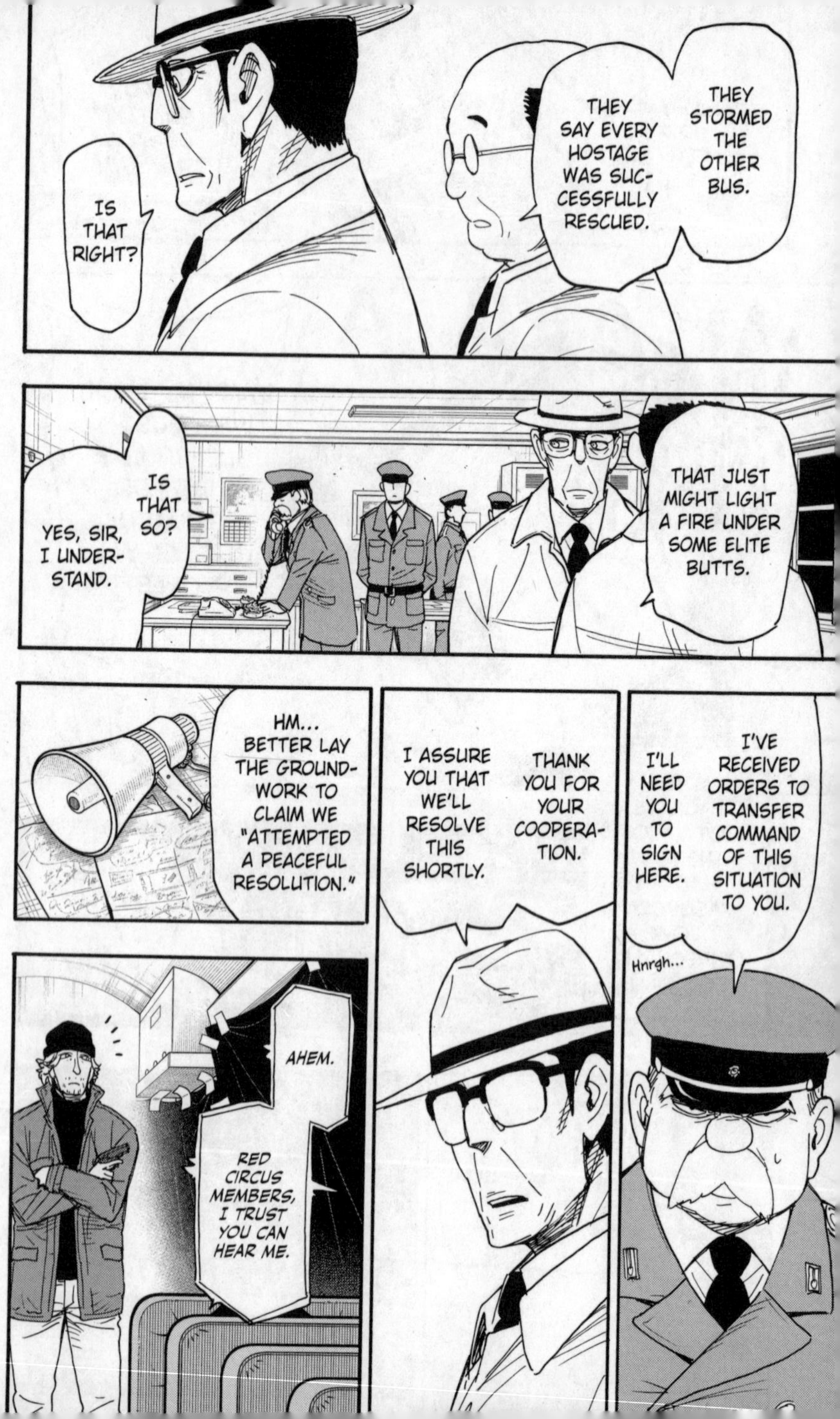
THEY STORMED THE OTHER BUS.
THEY SAY EVERY HOSTAGE WAS SUC-CESSFULLY RESCUED.
IS THAT RIGHT?
THAT JUST MIGHT LIGHT A FIRE UNDER SOME ELITE BUTTS.
IS THAT SO?
YES, SIR, I UNDER-STAND.
I'VE RECEIVED ORDERS TO TRANSFER COMMAND OF THIS SITUATION TO YOU.
I'LL NEED YOU TO SIGN HERE.
Hnrgh...
THANK YOU FOR YOUR COOPERA-TION.
I ASSURE YOU THAT WE'LL RESOLVE THIS SHORTLY.
HM... BETTER LAY THE GROUND-WORK TO CLAIM WE "ATTEMPTED A PEACEFUL RESOLUTION."
AHEM.
RED CIRCUS MEMBERS, I TRUST YOU CAN HEAR ME.

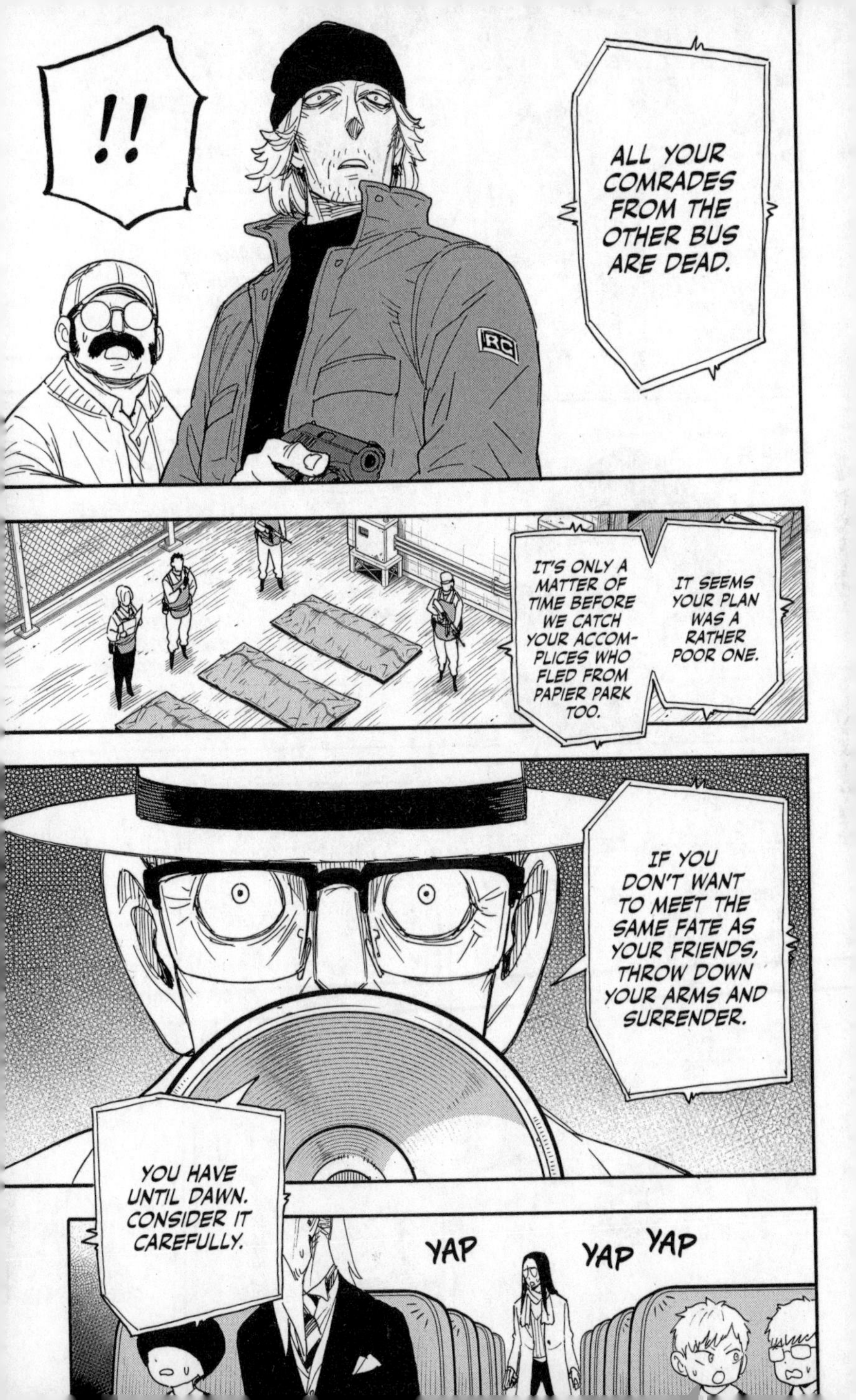
ALL YOUR COMRADES FROM THE OTHER BUS ARE DEAD.
!!
IT SEEMS YOUR PLAN WAS A RATHER POOR ONE.
IT'S ONLY A MATTER OF TIME BEFORE WE CATCH YOUR ACCOMPLICES WHO FLED FROM PAPIER PARK TOO.
IF YOU DON'T WANT TO MEET THE SAME FATE AS YOUR FRIENDS, THROW DOWN YOUR ARMS AND SURRENDER.
YOU HAVE UNTIL DAWN. CONSIDER IT CAREFULLY.
YAP YAP
YAP

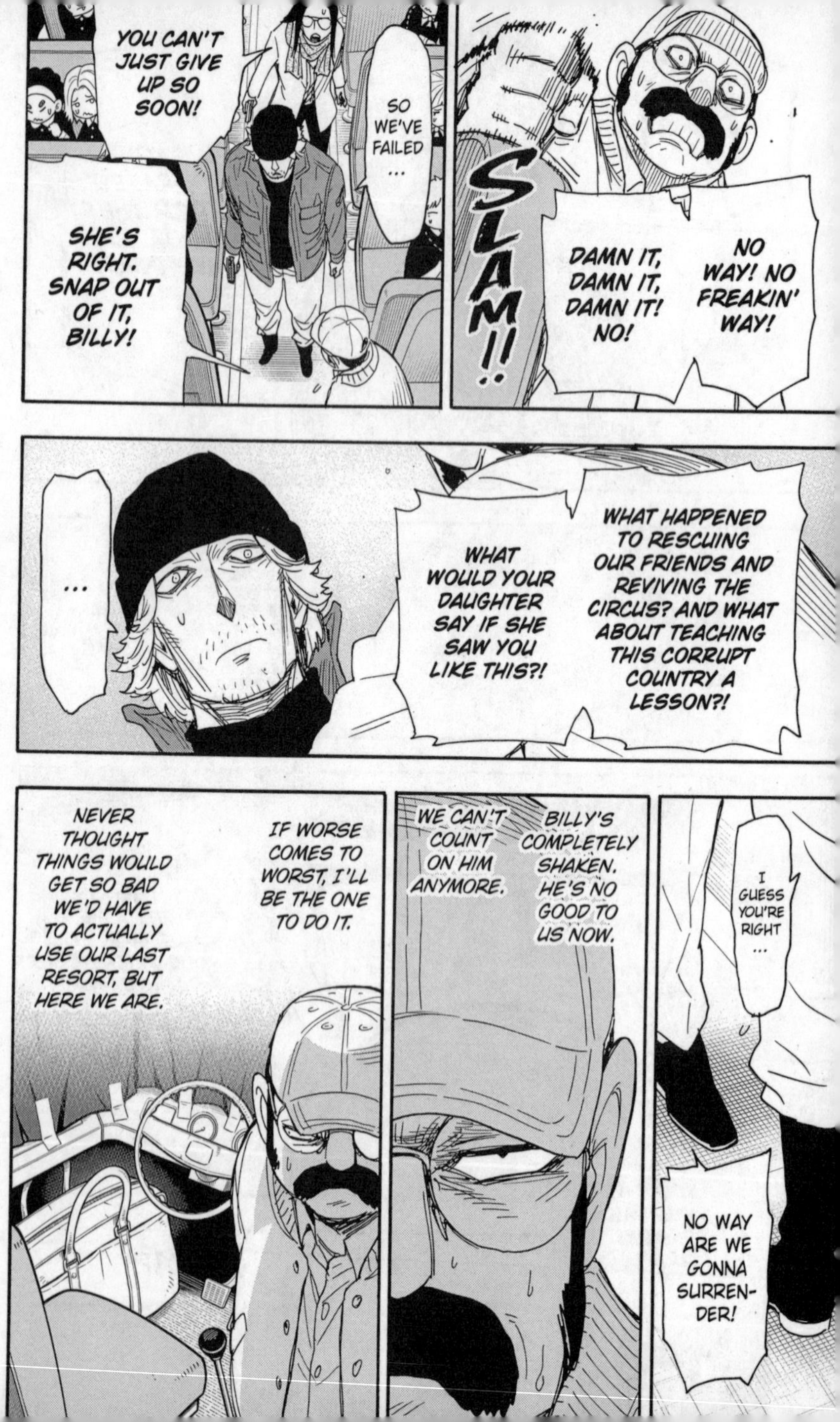
NO WAY! NO FREAKIN' WAY!
DAMN IT, DAMN IT, DAMN IT! NO!
SLAM!!
SO WE'VE FAILED ...
YOU CAN'T JUST GIVE UP SO SOON!
SHE'S RIGHT. SNAP OUT OF IT, BILLY!
WHAT HAPPENED TO RESCUING OUR FRIENDS AND REVIVING THE CIRCUS? AND WHAT ABOUT TEACHING THIS CORRUPT COUNTRY A LESSON?!
WHAT WOULD YOUR DAUGHTER SAY IF SHE SAW YOU LIKE THIS?!
...
I GUESS YOU'RE RIGHT ...
NO WAY ARE WE GONNA SURREN-DER!
BILLY'S COMPLETELY SHAKEN. HE'S NO GOOD TO US NOW.
WE CAN'T COUNT ON HIM ANYMORE.
IF WORSE COMES TO WORST, I'LL BE THE ONE TO DO IT.
NEVER THOUGHT THINGS WOULD GET SO BAD WE'D HAVE TO ACTUALLY USE OUR LAST RESORT, BUT HERE WE ARE.

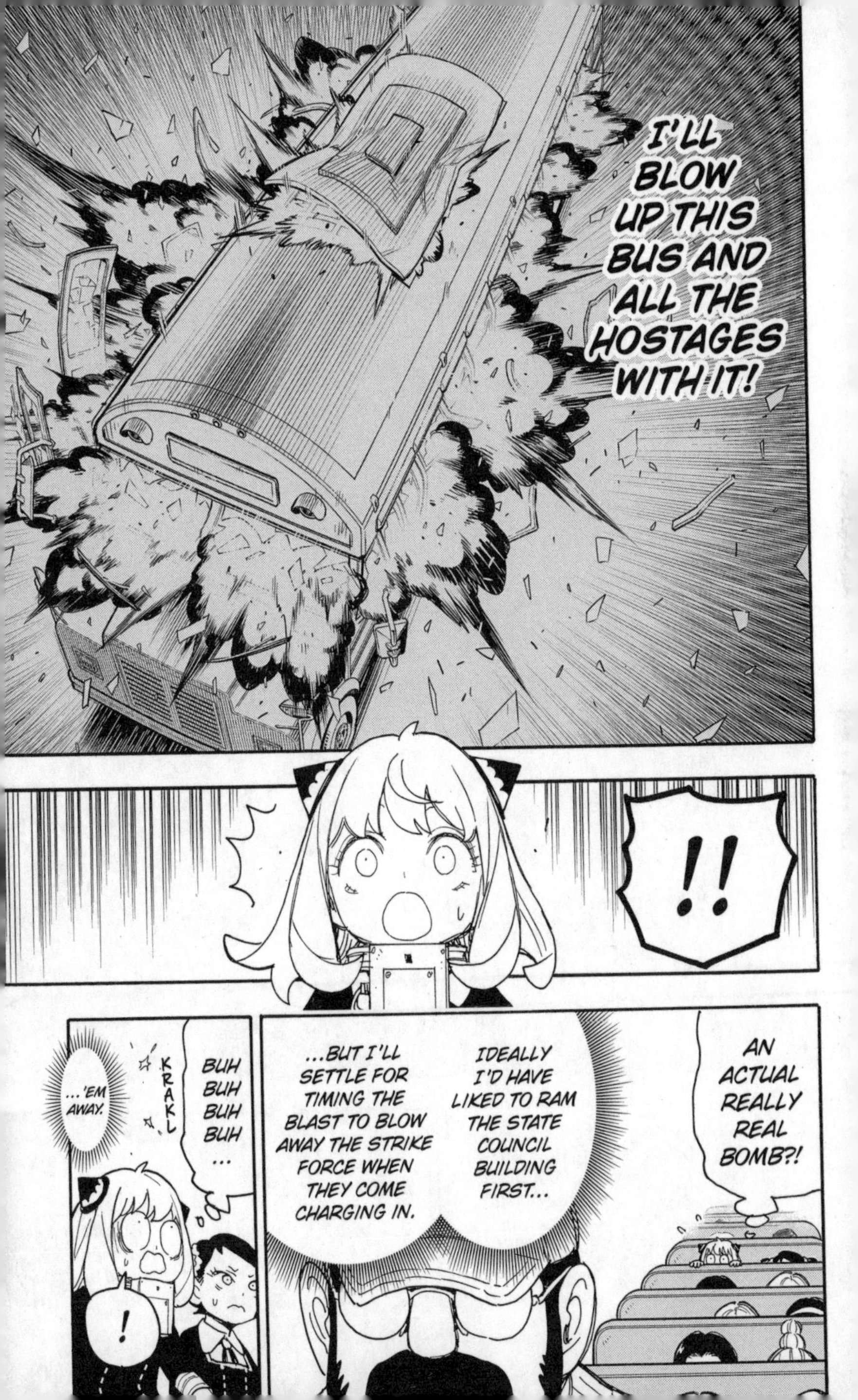
I'LL BLOW UP THIS BUS AND ALL THE HOSTAGES WITH IT!
!!
AN ACTUAL REALLY REAL BOMB?!
IDEALLY I'D HAVE LIKED TO RAM THE STATE COUNCIL BUILDING FIRST...
...BUT I'LL SETTLE FOR TIMING THE BLAST TO BLOW AWAY THE STRIKE FORCE WHEN THEY COME CHARGING IN.
BUH BUH BUH BUH ...
KRAKL
...'EM AWAY.
!

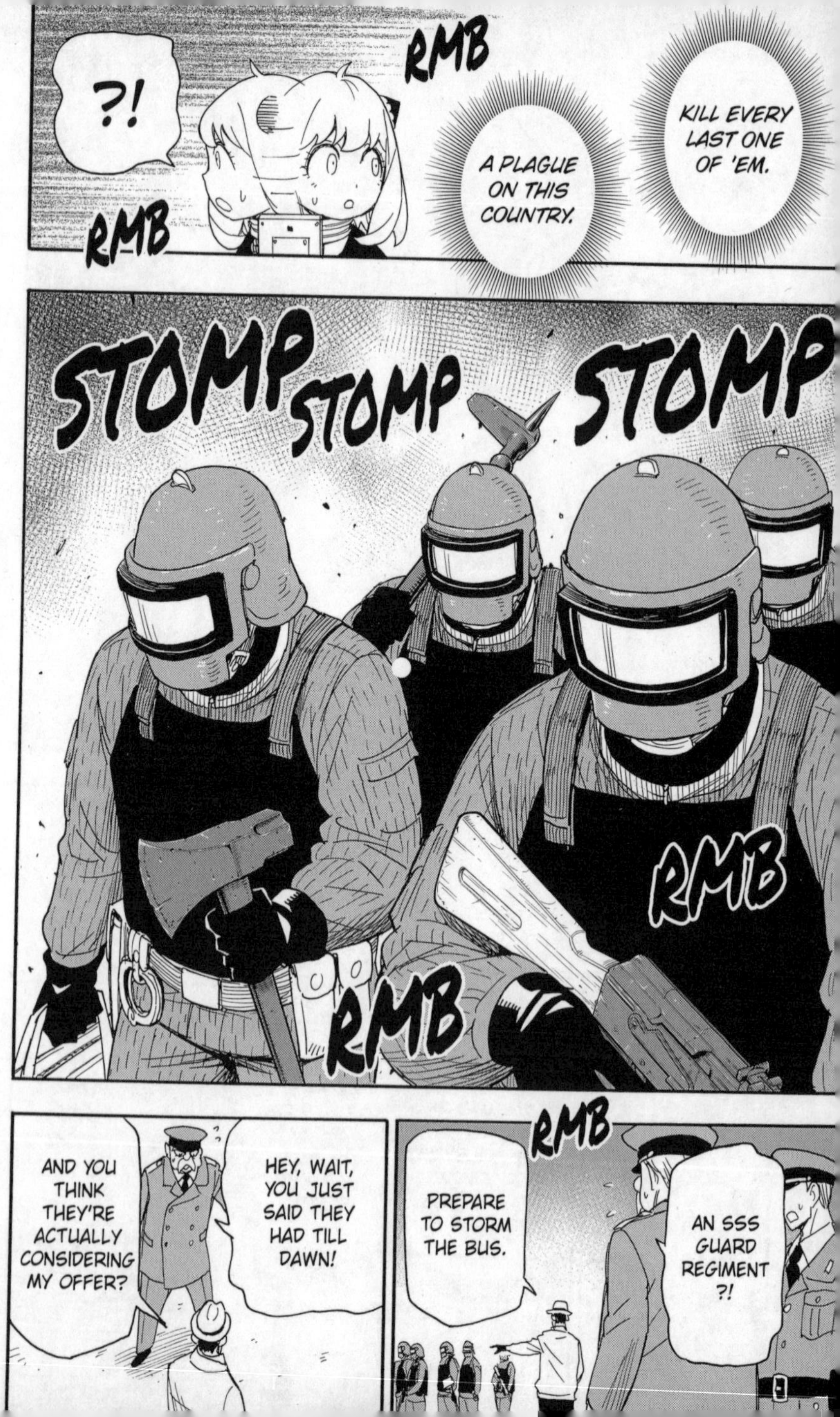
KILL EVERY LAST ONE OF 'EM.
A PLAGUE ON THIS COUNTRY.
RMB
?!
RMB
STOMP
STOMP
STOMP
RMB
RMB
RMB
AN SSS GUARD REGIMENT ?!
PREPARE TO STORM THE BUS.
HEY, WAIT, YOU JUST SAID THEY HAD TILL DAWN!
AND YOU THINK THEY'RE ACTUALLY CONSIDERING MY OFFER?

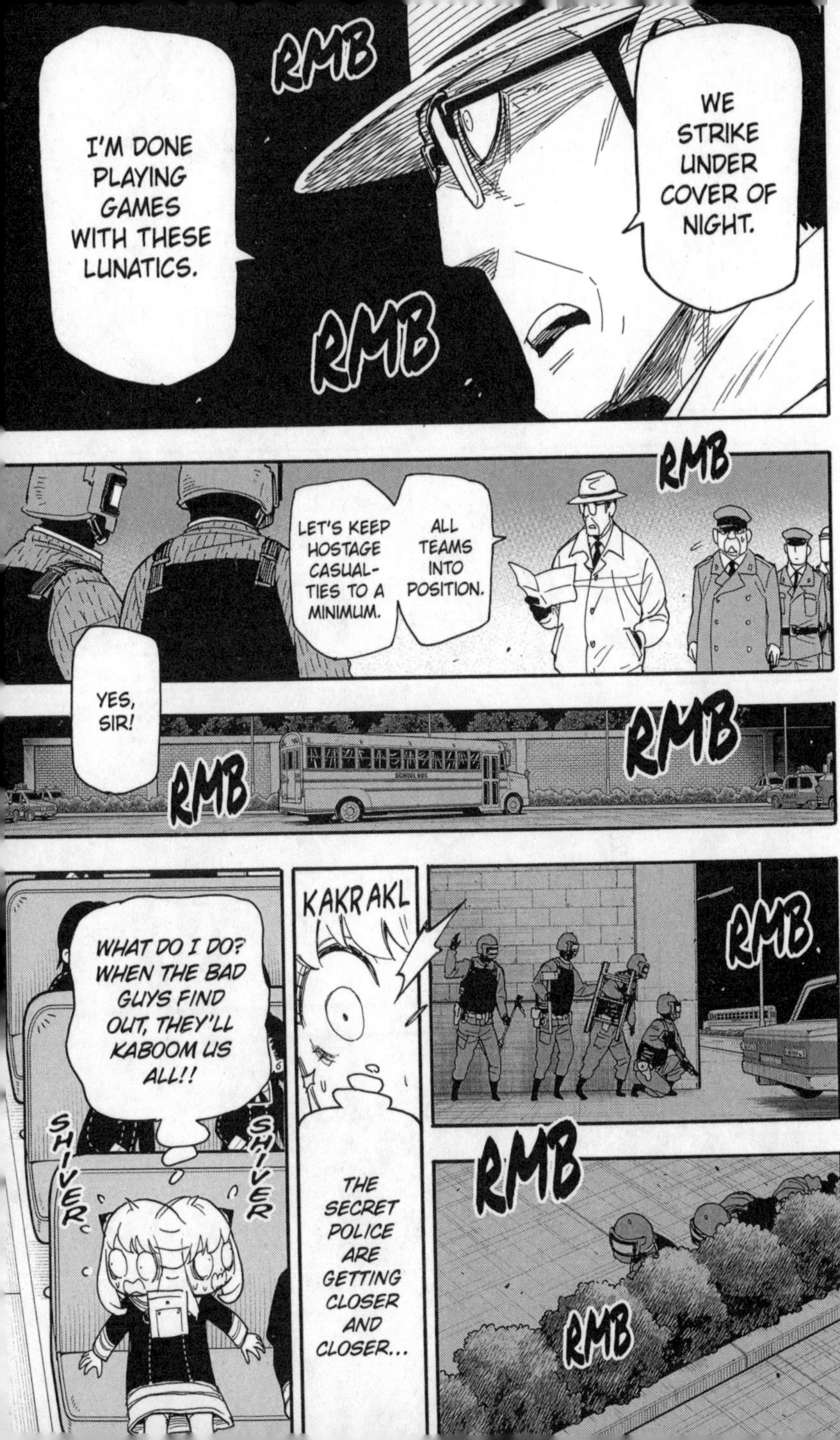
WE STRIKE UNDER COVER OF NIGHT.
RMB
I'M DONE PLAYING GAMES WITH THESE LUNATICS.
RMB
RMB
ALL TEAMS INTO POSITION.
LET'S KEEP HOSTAGE CASUAL-TIES TO A MINIMUM.
YES, SIR!
RMB
RMB
RMB
RMB
RMB
KAKRAKL
THE SECRET POLICE ARE GETTING CLOSER AND CLOSER...
WHAT DO I DO? WHEN THE BAD GUYS FIND OUT, THEY'LL KABOOM US ALL!!
SHIVER
SHIVER

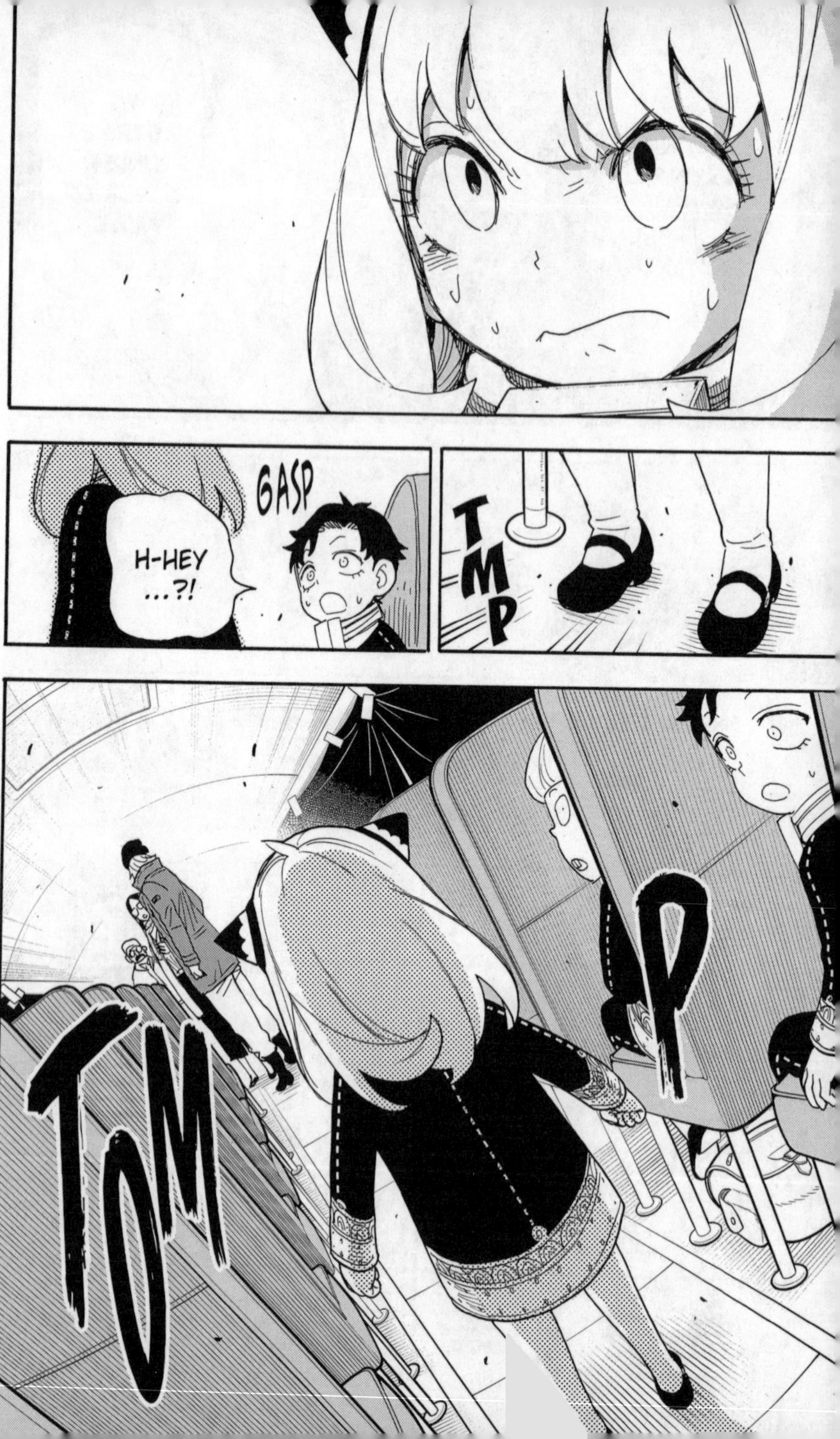
TMP
GASP
H-HEY ...?!
TOMP

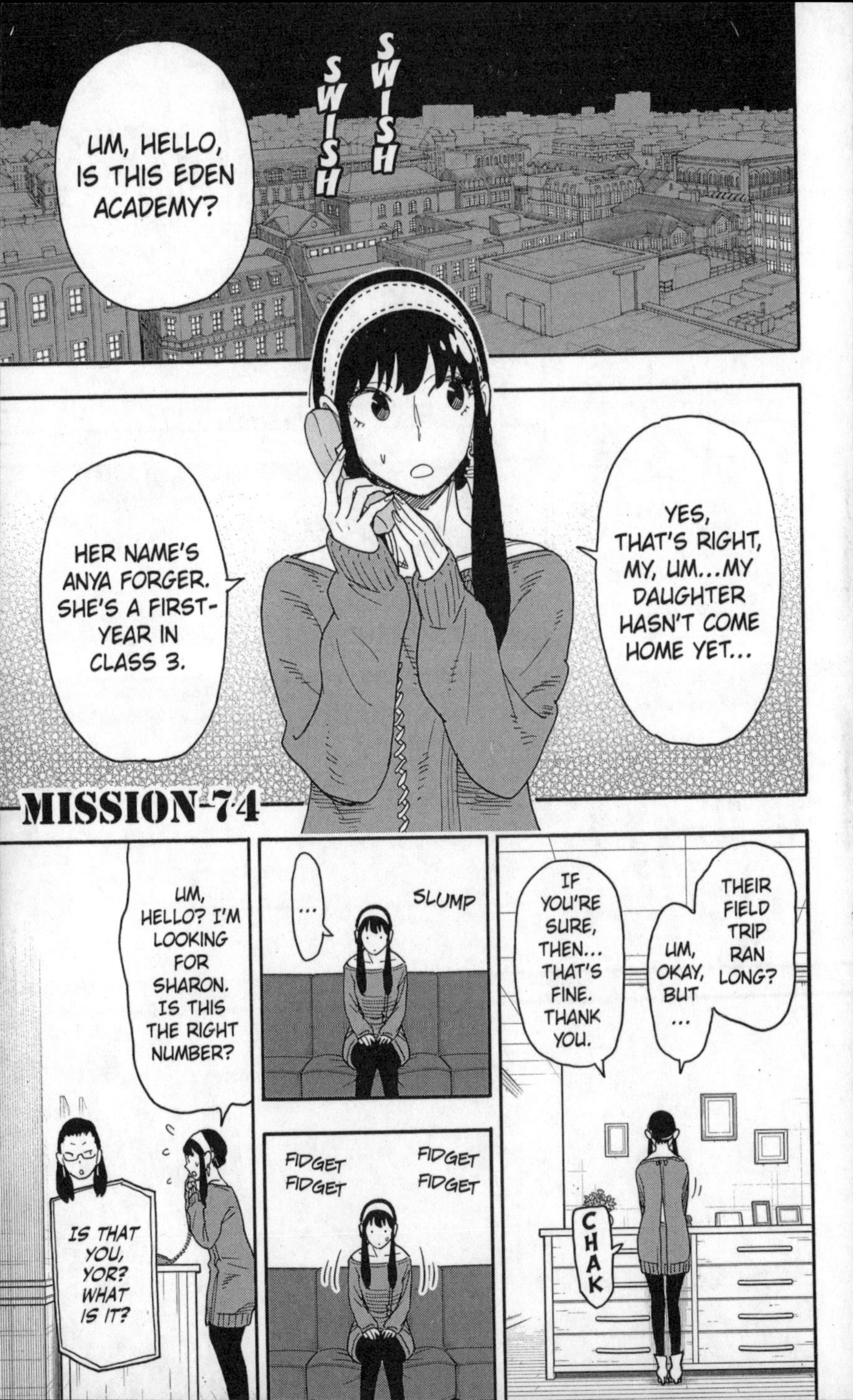
SWISH
SWISH
UM, HELLO, IS THIS EDEN ACADEMY?
YES, THAT'S RIGHT, MY, UM...MY DAUGHTER HASN'T COME HOME YET...
HER NAME'S ANYA FORGER. SHE'S A FIRST-YEAR IN CLASS 3.
MISSION 74
THEIR FIELD TRIP RAN LONG?
UM, OKAY, BUT ...
IF YOU'RE SURE, THEN... THAT'S FINE. THANK YOU.
CHAK
...
SLUMP
FIDGET FIDGET
FIDGET FIDGET
UM, HELLO? I'M LOOKING FOR SHARON. IS THIS THE RIGHT NUMBER?
IS THAT YOU, YOR? WHAT IS IT?

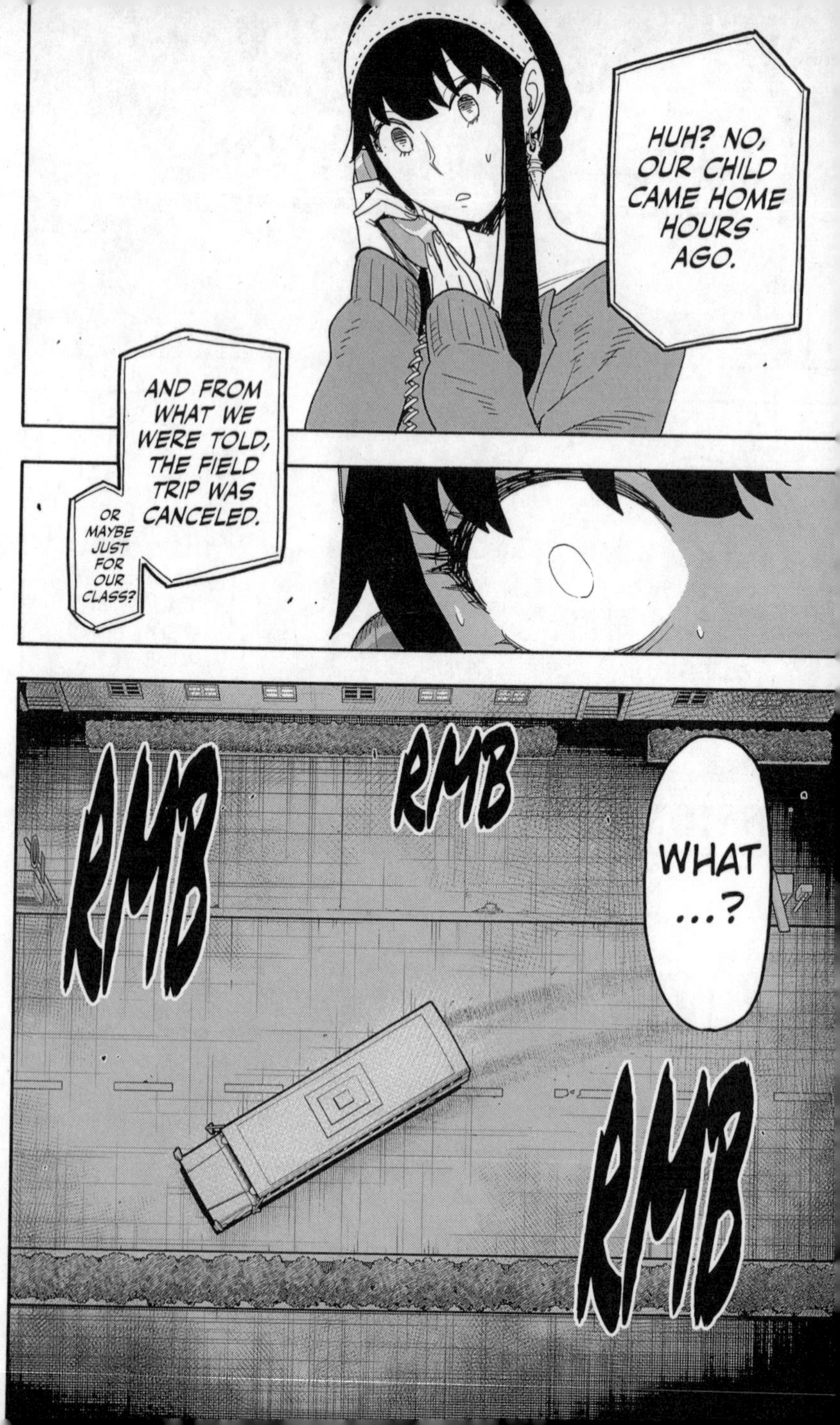
HUH? NO, OUR CHILD CAME HOME HOURS AGO.
AND FROM WHAT WE WERE TOLD, THE FIELD TRIP WAS CANCELED.
OR MAYBE JUST FOR OUR CLASS?
WHAT ...?
RMB
RMB
RMB

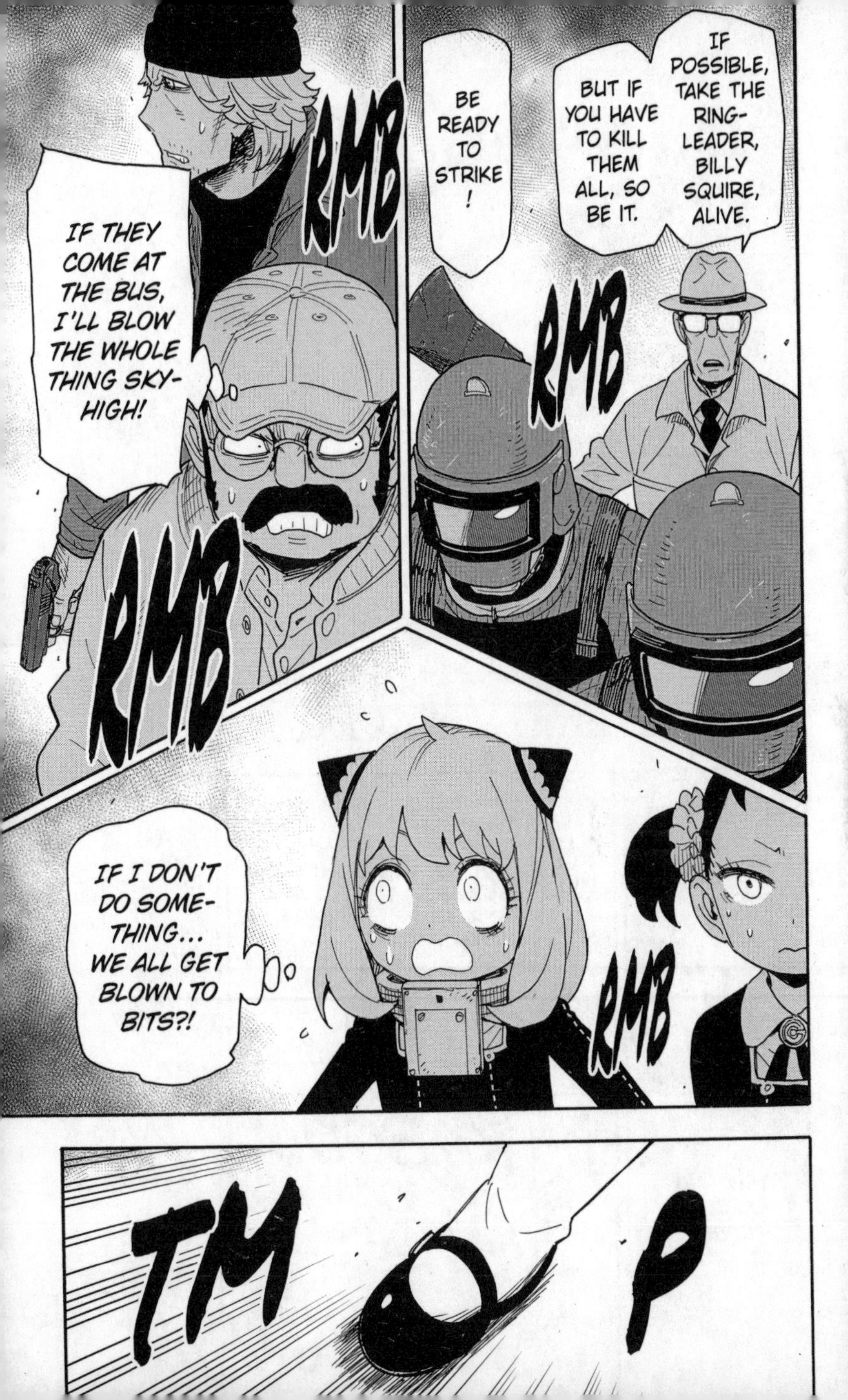
IF POSSIBLE, TAKE THE RING-LEADER, BILLY SQUIRE, ALIVE.
BUT IF YOU HAVE TO KILL THEM ALL, SO BE IT.
BE READY TO STRIKE!
RMB
RMB
IF THEY COME AT THE BUS, I'LL BLOW THE WHOLE THING SKY-HIGH!
RMB
RMB
IF I DON'T DO SOME-THING... WE ALL GET BLOWN TO BITS?!
TMP

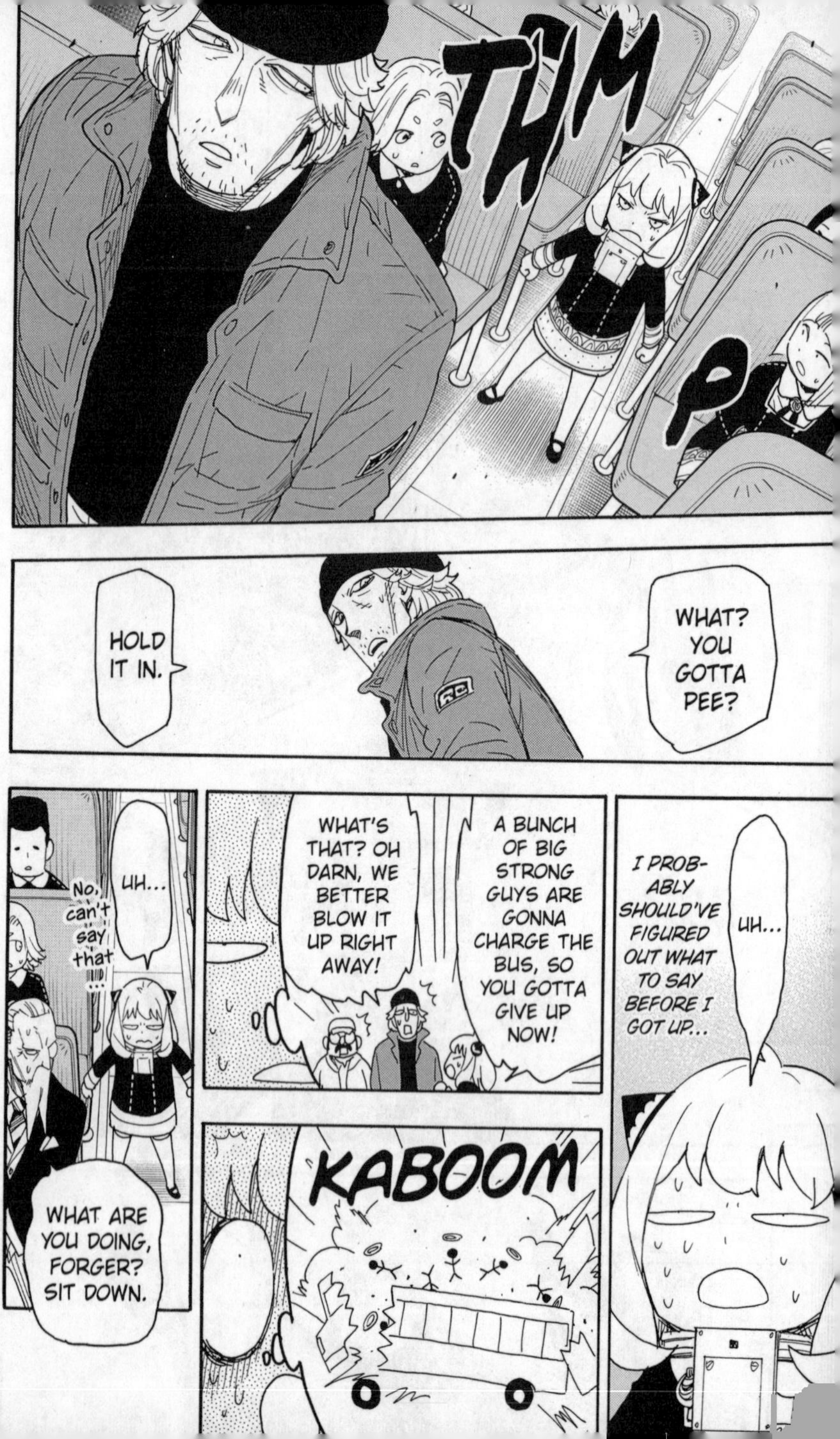

THM
P
WHAT? YOU GOTTA PEE?
HOLD IT IN.
UH...
I PROBABLY SHOULD'VE FIGURED OUT WHAT TO SAY BEFORE I GOT UP...
A BUNCH OF BIG STRONG GUYS ARE GONNA CHARGE THE BUS, SO YOU GOTTA GIVE UP NOW!
WHAT'S THAT? OH DARN, WE BETTER BLOW IT UP RIGHT AWAY!
KABOOM
UH...
No, can't say that...
WHAT ARE YOU DOING, FORGER? SIT DOWN.

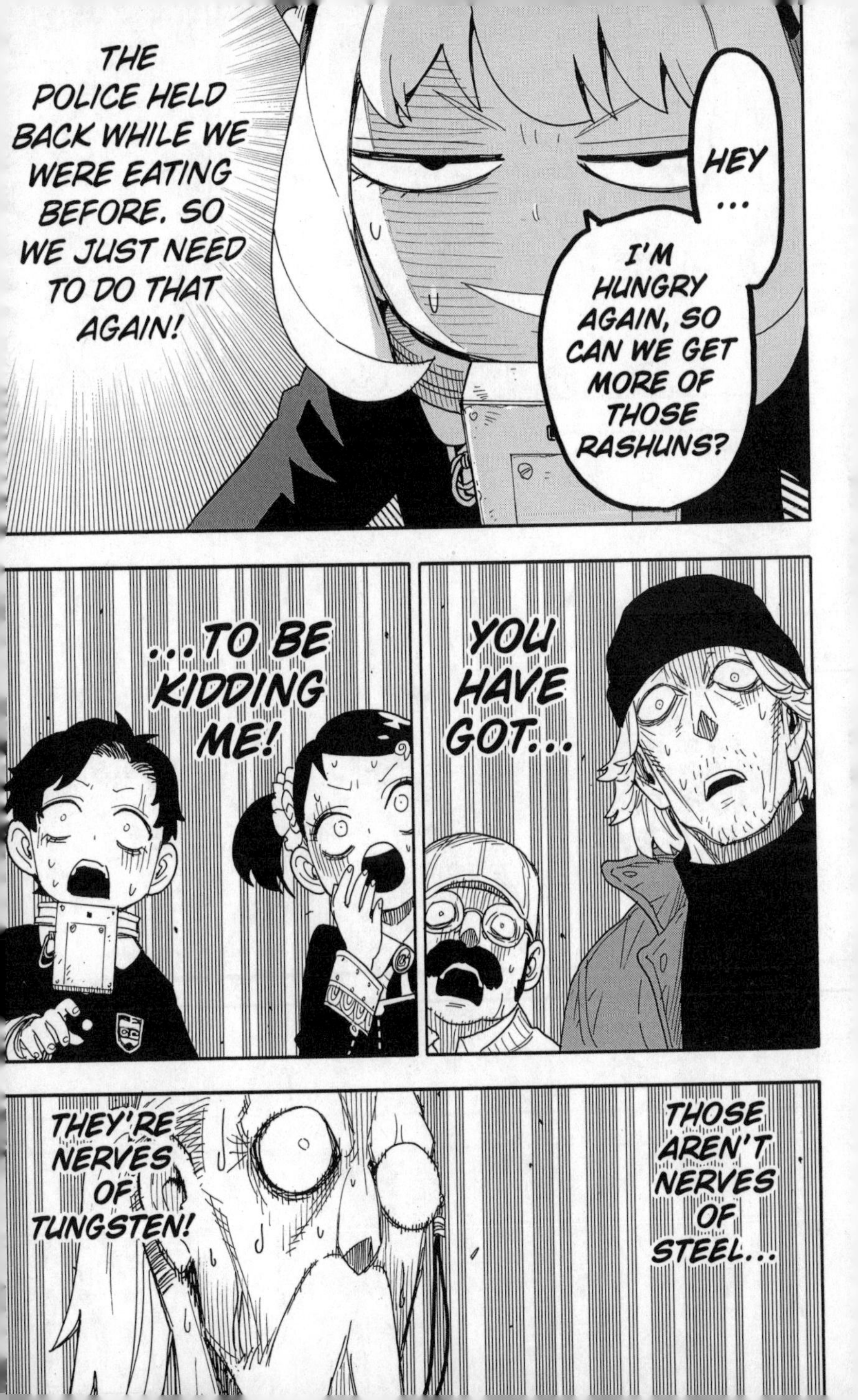
HEY...
I'M HUNGRY AGAIN, SO CAN WE GET MORE OF THOSE RASHUNS?
THE POLICE HELD BACK WHILE WE WERE EATING BEFORE. SO WE JUST NEED TO DO THAT AGAIN!
YOU HAVE GOT...
...TO BE KIDDING ME!
THOSE AREN'T NERVES OF STEEL...
THEY'RE NERVES OF TUNGSTEN!

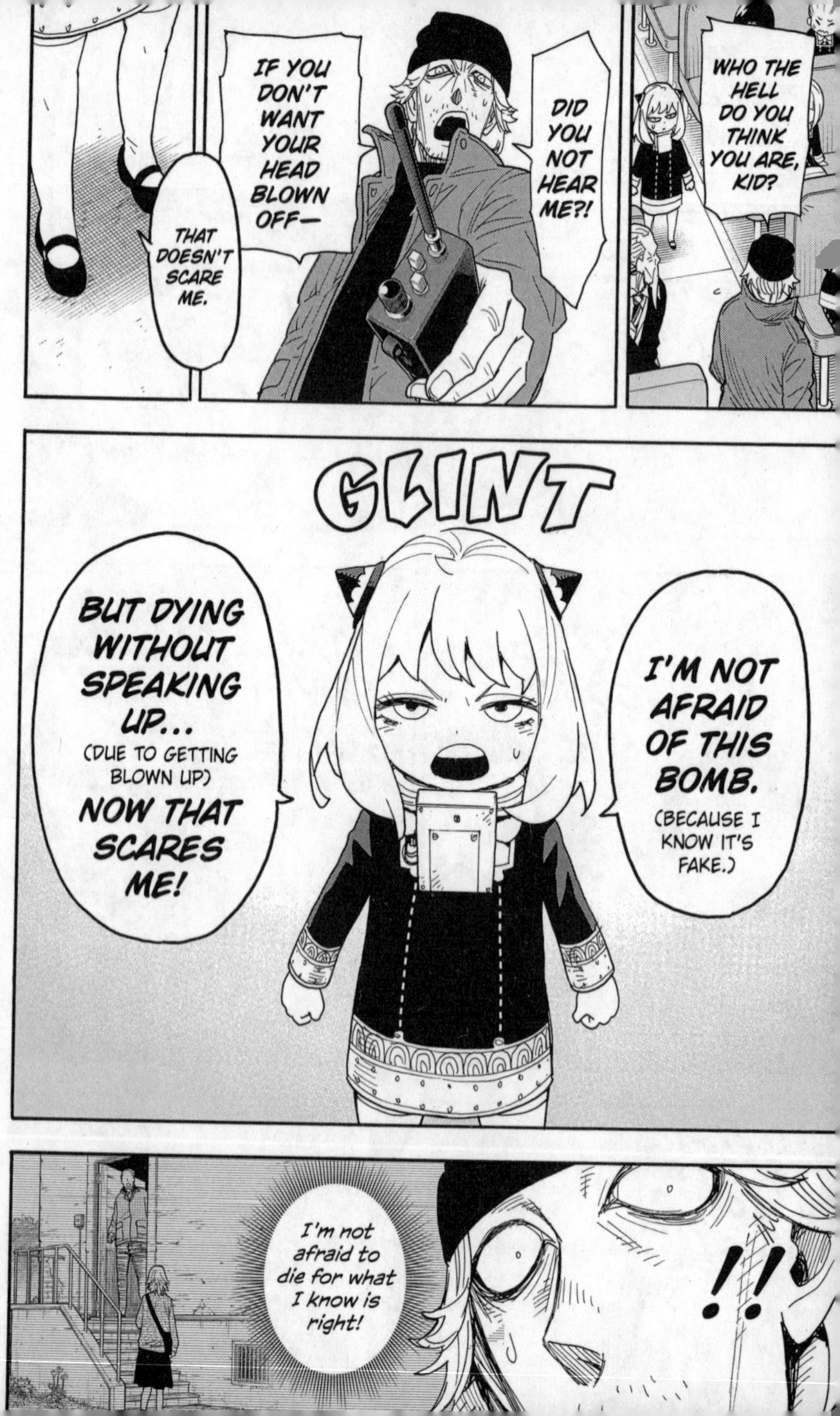
WHO THE HELL DO YOU THINK YOU ARE, KID?
DID YOU NOT HEAR ME?!
IF YOU DON'T WANT YOUR HEAD BLOWN OFF—
THAT DOESN'T SCARE ME.
GLINT
I'M NOT AFRAID OF THIS BOMB.
(BECAUSE I KNOW IT'S FAKE.)
BUT DYING WITHOUT SPEAKING UP...
(DUE TO GETTING BLOWN UP)
NOW THAT SCARES ME!
!!
I'm not afraid to die for what I know is right!

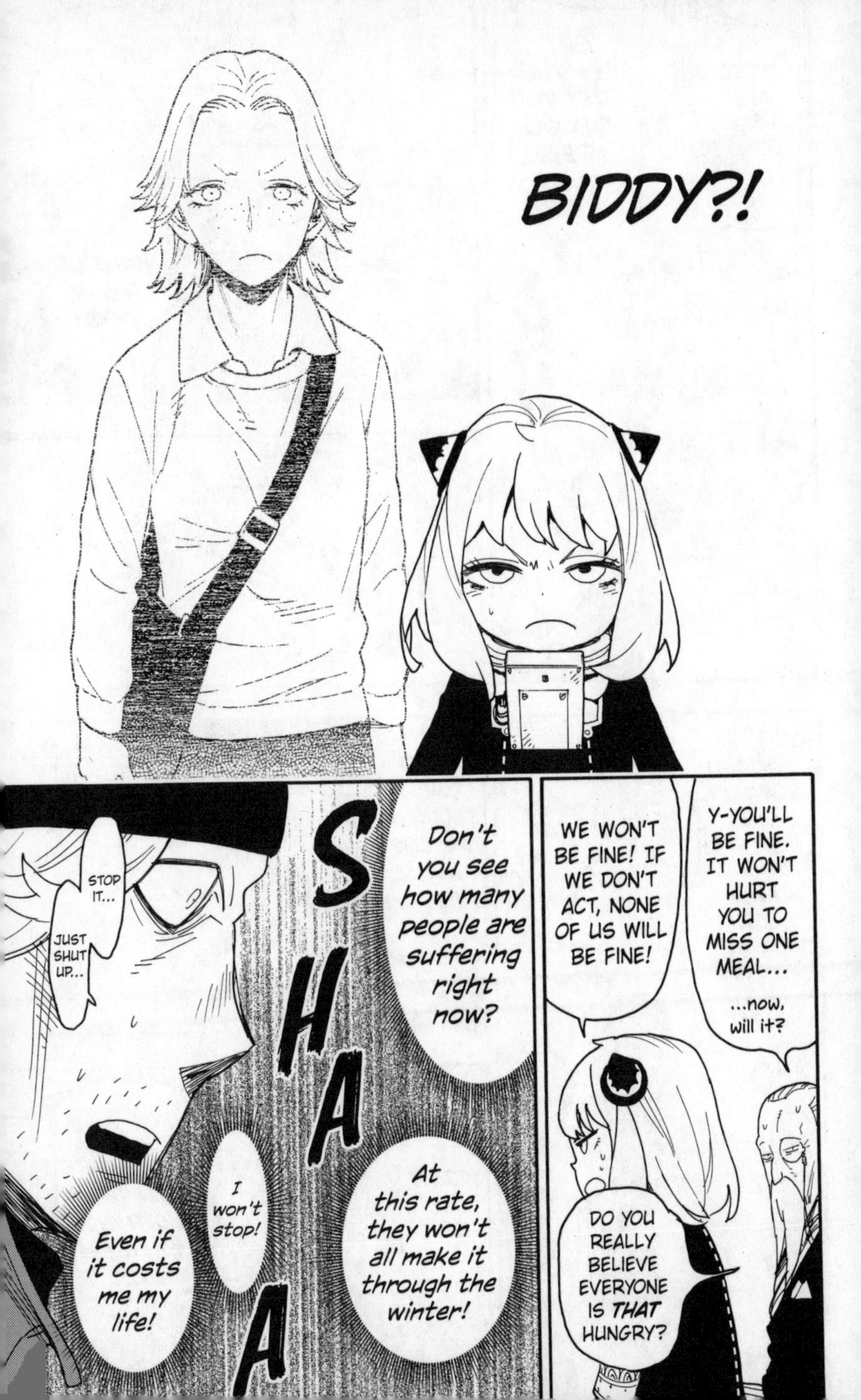
BIDDY?!
Y-YOU'LL BE FINE. IT WON'T HURT YOU TO MISS ONE MEAL...
...now, will it?
WE WON'T BE FINE! IF WE DON'T ACT, NONE OF US WILL BE FINE!
DO YOU REALLY BELIEVE EVERYONE IS THAT HUNGRY?
Don't you see how many people are suffering right now?
At this rate, they won't all make it through the winter!
SHAA
I won't stop!
Even if it costs me my life!
STOP IT...
JUST SHUT UP...

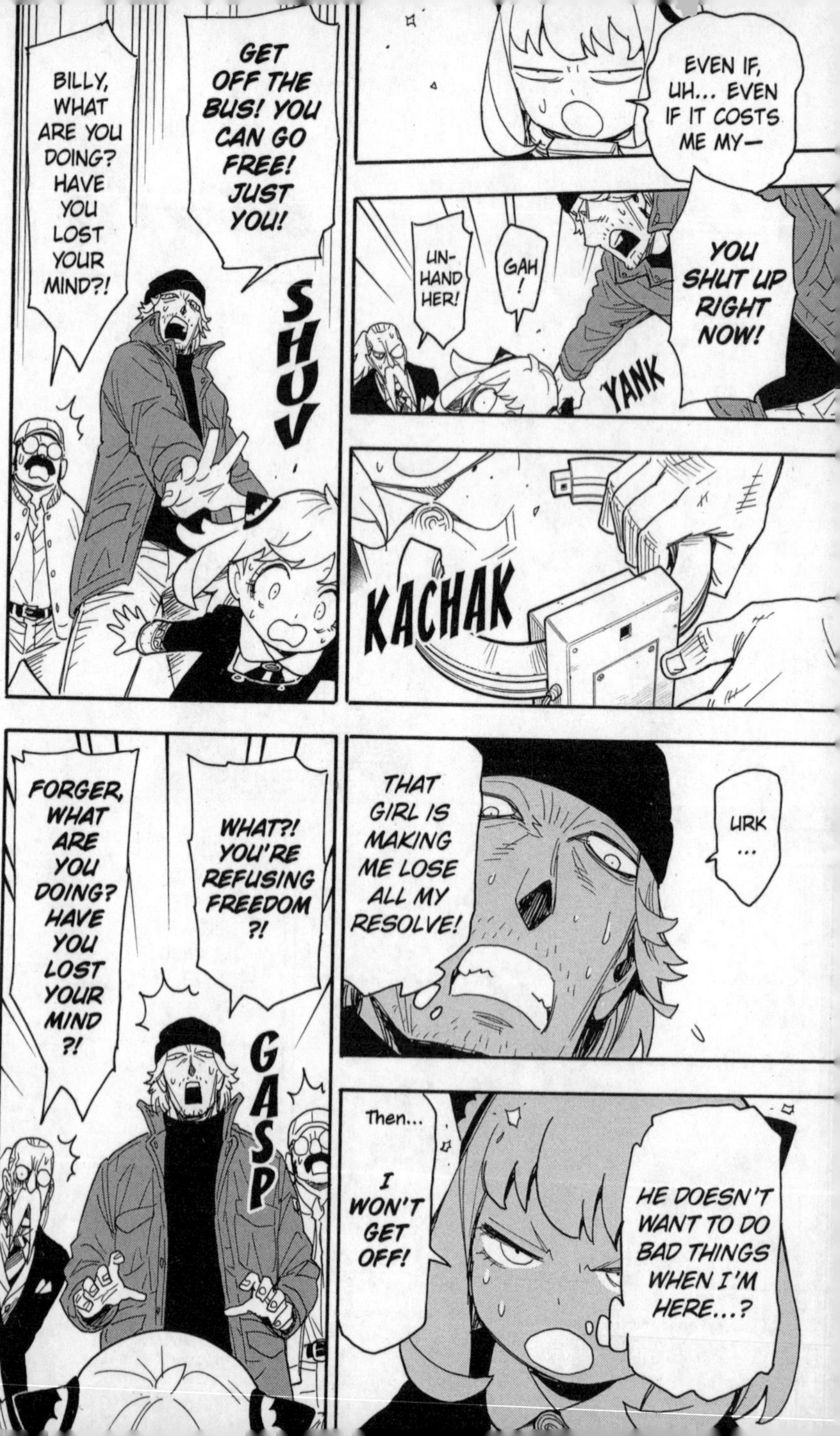
EVEN IF, UH... EVEN IF IT COSTS ME MY—
YOU SHUT UP RIGHT NOW!
GAH!
UN-HAND HER!
YANK
KACHAK
GET OFF THE BUS! YOU CAN GO FREE! JUST YOU!
BILLY, WHAT ARE YOU DOING? HAVE YOU LOST YOUR MIND?!
SHUV
URK...
THAT GIRL IS MAKING ME LOSE ALL MY RESOLVE!
HE DOESN'T WANT TO DO BAD THINGS WHEN I'M HERE...?
Then...
I WON'T GET OFF!
WHAT?! YOU'RE REFUSING FREEDOM?!
FORGER, WHAT ARE YOU DOING? HAVE YOU LOST YOUR MIND?!
GASP

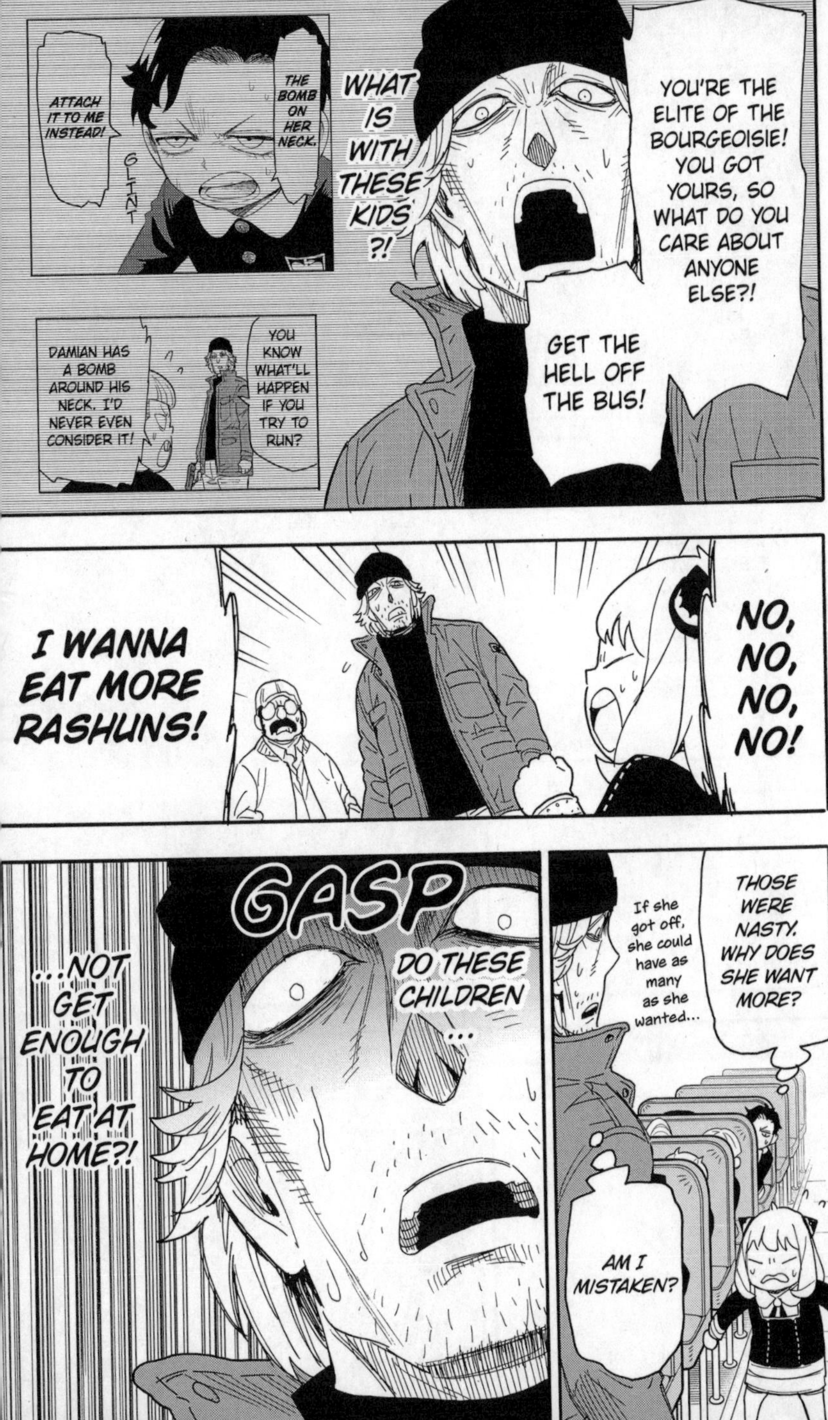
YOU'RE THE ELITE OF THE BOURGEOISIE! YOU GOT YOURS, SO WHAT DO YOU CARE ABOUT ANYONE ELSE?!
WHAT IS WITH THESE KIDS?!
GET THE HELL OFF THE BUS!
THE BOMB ON HER NECK.
ATTACH IT TO ME INSTEAD!
GLINT
YOU KNOW WHAT'LL HAPPEN IF YOU TRY TO RUN?
DAMIAN HAS A BOMB AROUND HIS NECK. I'D NEVER EVEN CONSIDER IT!
NO, NO, NO, NO!
I WANNA EAT MORE RASHUNS!
THOSE WERE NASTY. WHY DOES SHE WANT MORE?
If she got off, she could have as many as she wanted...
AM I MISTAKEN?
GASP
DO THESE CHILDREN...
...NOT GET ENOUGH TO EAT AT HOME?!

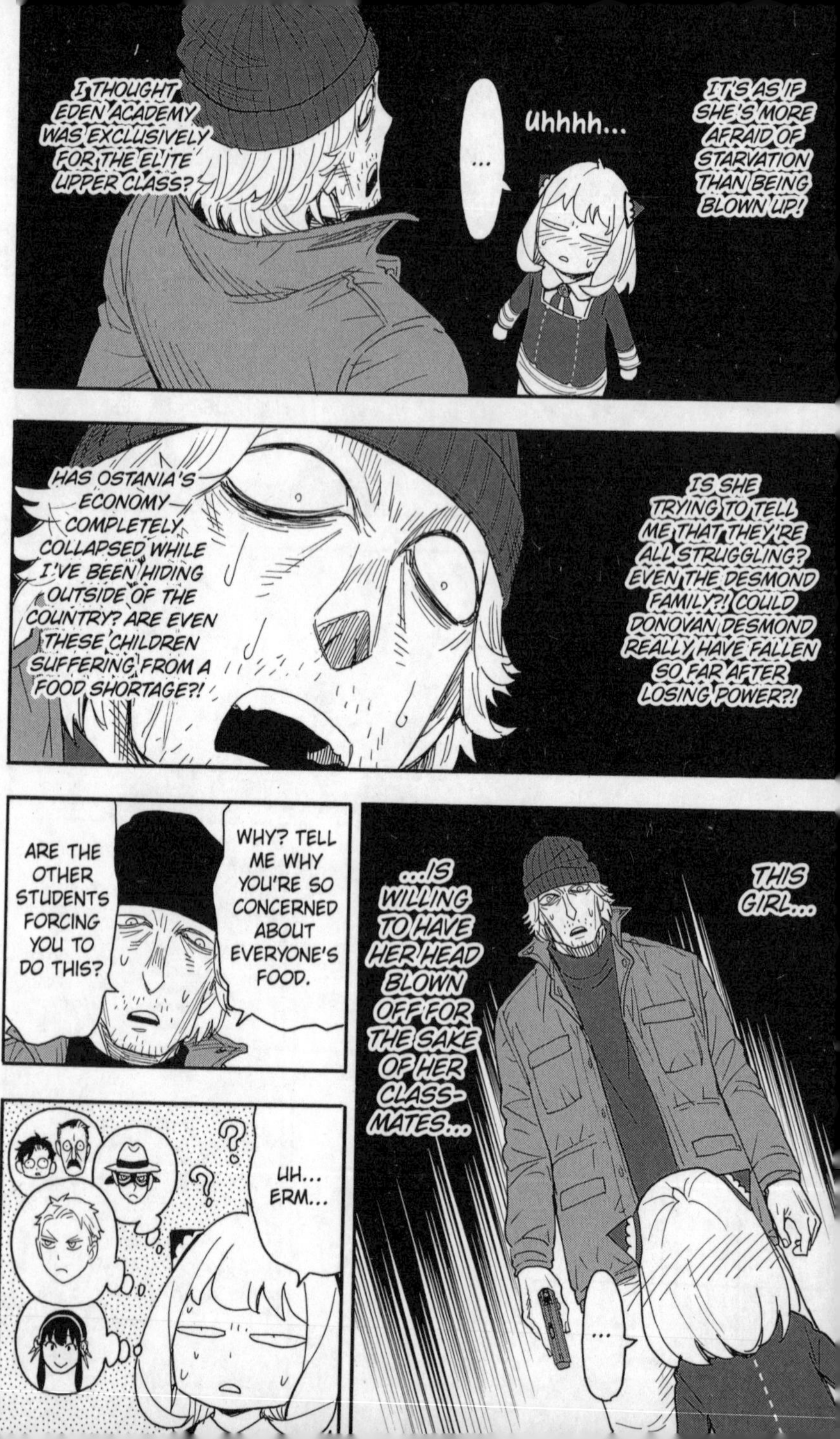
IT'S AS IF SHE'S MORE AFRAID OF STARVATION THAN BEING BLOWN UP!
Uhhhh...
...
I THOUGHT EDEN ACADEMY WAS EXCLUSIVELY FOR THE ELITE UPPER CLASS?
IS SHE TRYING TO TELL ME THAT THEY'RE ALL STRUGGLING? EVEN THE DESMOND FAMILY?! COULD DONOVAN DESMOND REALLY HAVE FALLEN SO FAR AFTER LOSING POWER?!
HAS OSTANIA'S ECONOMY COMPLETELY COLLAPSED WHILE I'VE BEEN HIDING OUTSIDE OF THE COUNTRY? ARE EVEN THESE CHILDREN SUFFERING FROM A FOOD SHORTAGE?!
THIS GIRL...
...IS WILLING TO HAVE HER HEAD BLOWN OFF FOR THE SAKE OF HER CLASS-MATES...
...
WHY? TELL ME WHY YOU'RE SO CONCERNED ABOUT EVERYONE'S FOOD.
ARE THE OTHER STUDENTS FORCING YOU TO DO THIS?
UH... ERM...

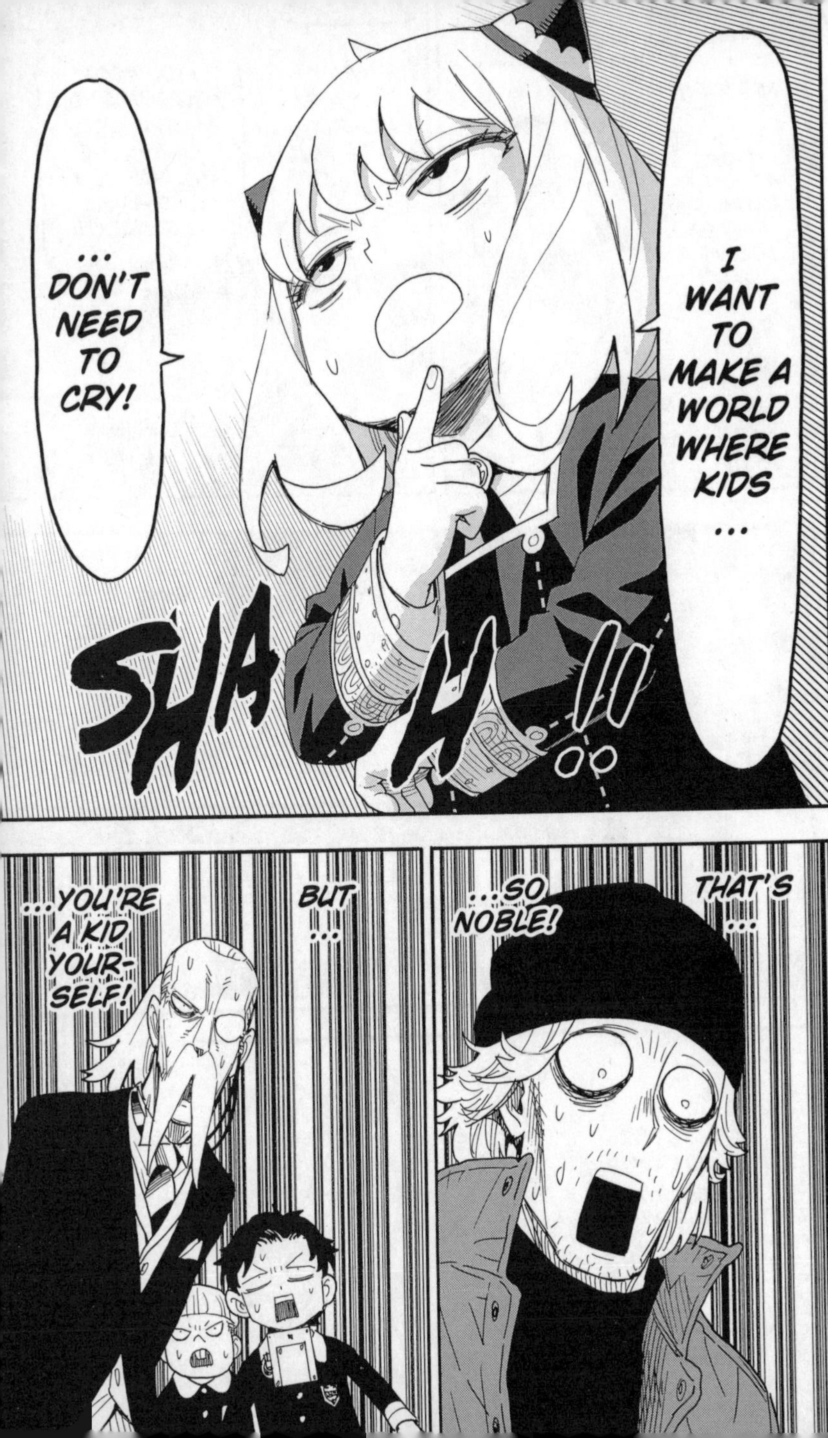
I WANT TO MAKE A WORLD WHERE KIDS...
...DON'T NEED TO CRY!
SHAH!!
THAT'S...
...SO NOBLE!
BUT...
...YOU'RE A KID YOURSELF!

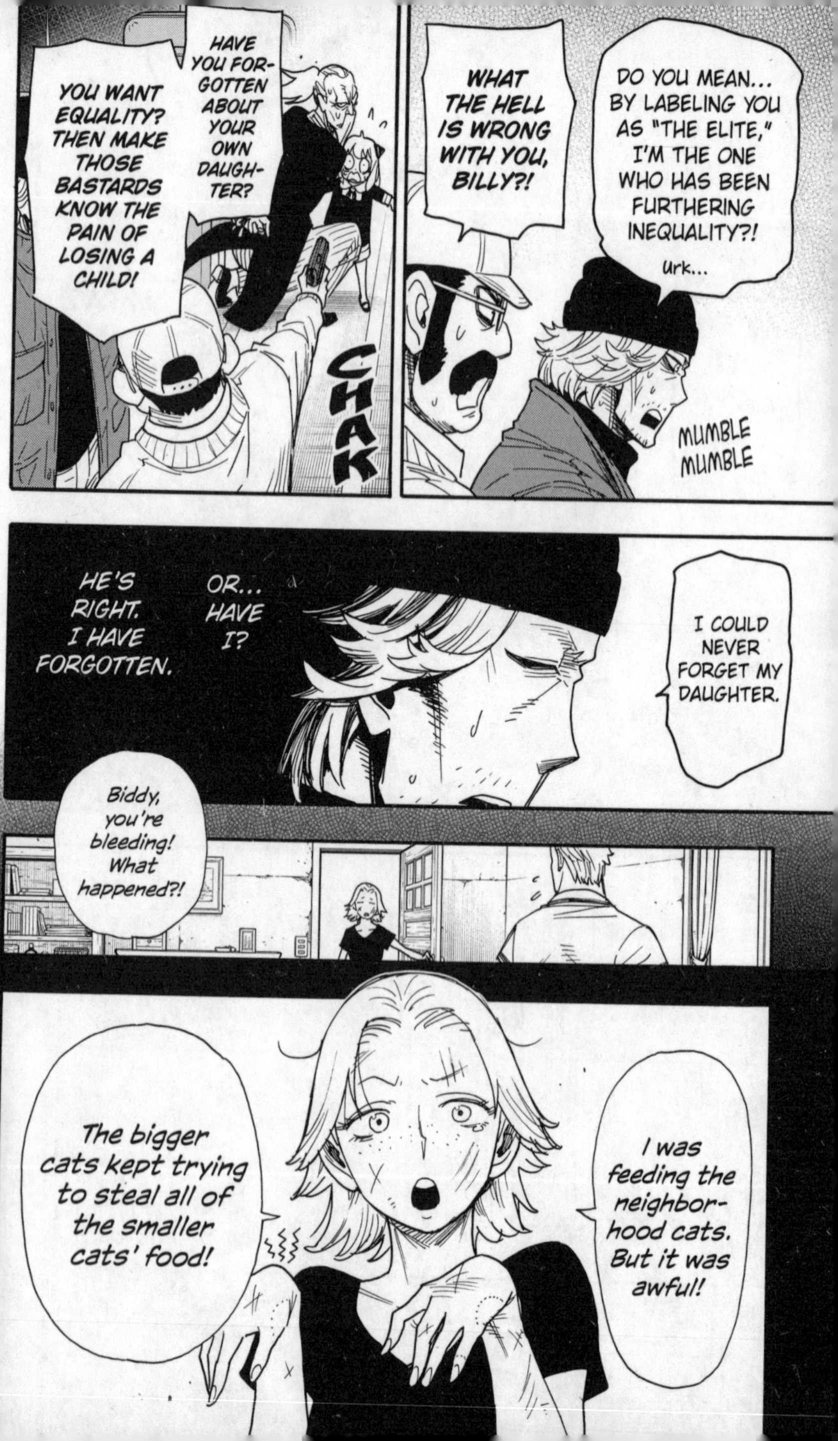
DO YOU MEAN... BY LABELING YOU AS "THE ELITE," I'M THE ONE WHO HAS BEEN FURTHERING INEQUALITY?!
Urk...
MUMBLE MUMBLE
WHAT THE HELL IS WRONG WITH YOU, BILLY?!
HAVE YOU FORGOTTEN ABOUT YOUR OWN DAUGHTER?
YOU WANT EQUALITY? THEN MAKE THOSE BASTARDS KNOW THE PAIN OF LOSING A CHILD!
CHAK
I COULD NEVER FORGET MY DAUGHTER.
OR... HAVE I?
HE'S RIGHT. I HAVE FORGOTTEN.
Biddy, you're bleeding! What happened?!
I was feeding the neighborhood cats. But it was awful!
The bigger cats kept trying to steal all of the smaller cats' food!

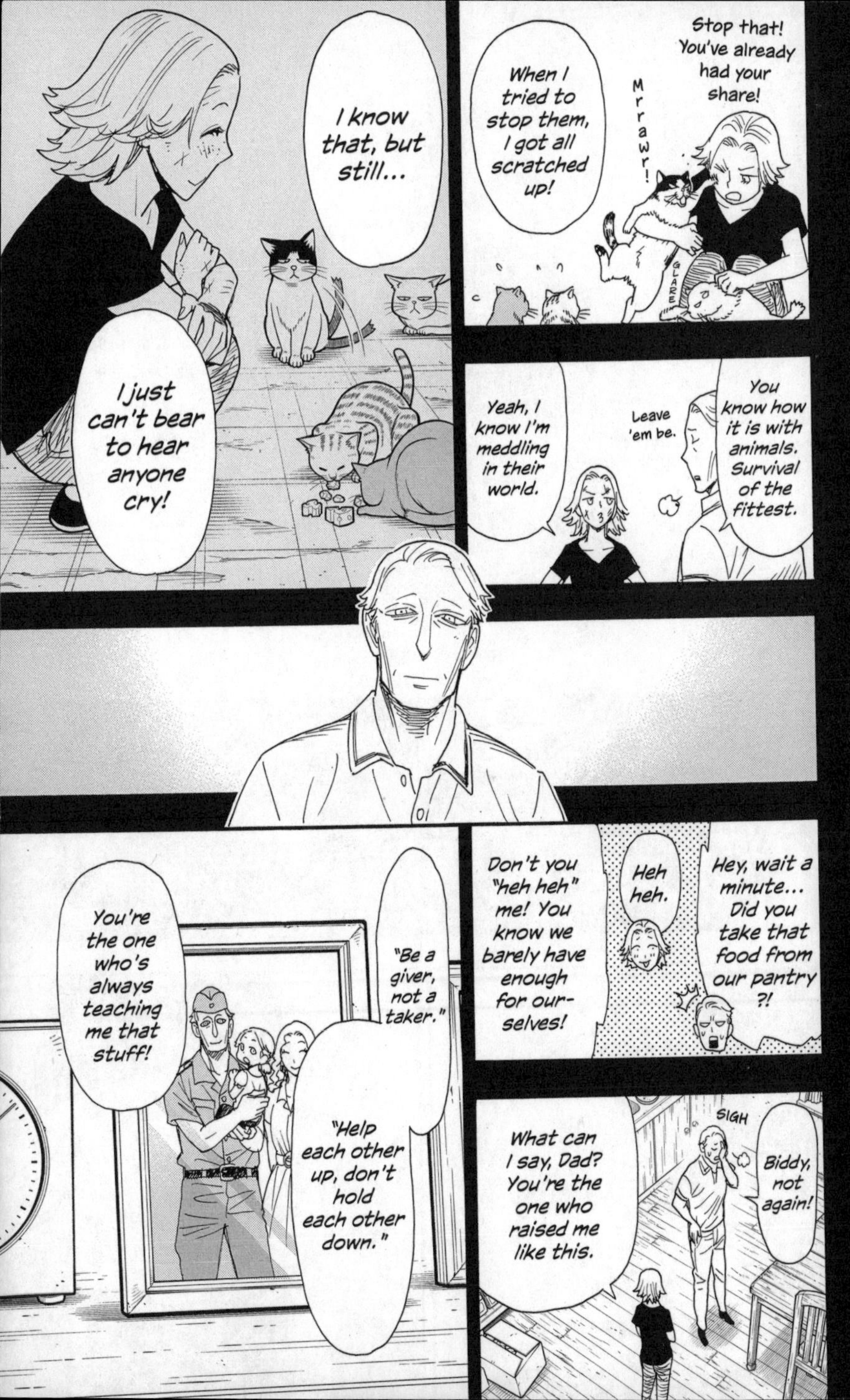
Stop that! You've already had your share!
Mrrawr!
GLARE
When I tried to stop them, I got all scratched up!
You know how it is with animals. Survival of the fittest.
Leave 'em be.
Yeah, I know I'm meddling in their world.
I know that, but still...
I just can't bear to hear anyone cry!
Hey, wait a minute... Did you take that food from our pantry?!
Heh heh.
Don't you "heh heh" me! You know we barely have enough for ourselves!
Biddy, not again!
SIGH
What can I say, Dad? You're the one who raised me like this.
"Be a giver, not a taker."
"Help each other up, don't hold each other down."
You're the one who's always teaching me that stuff!

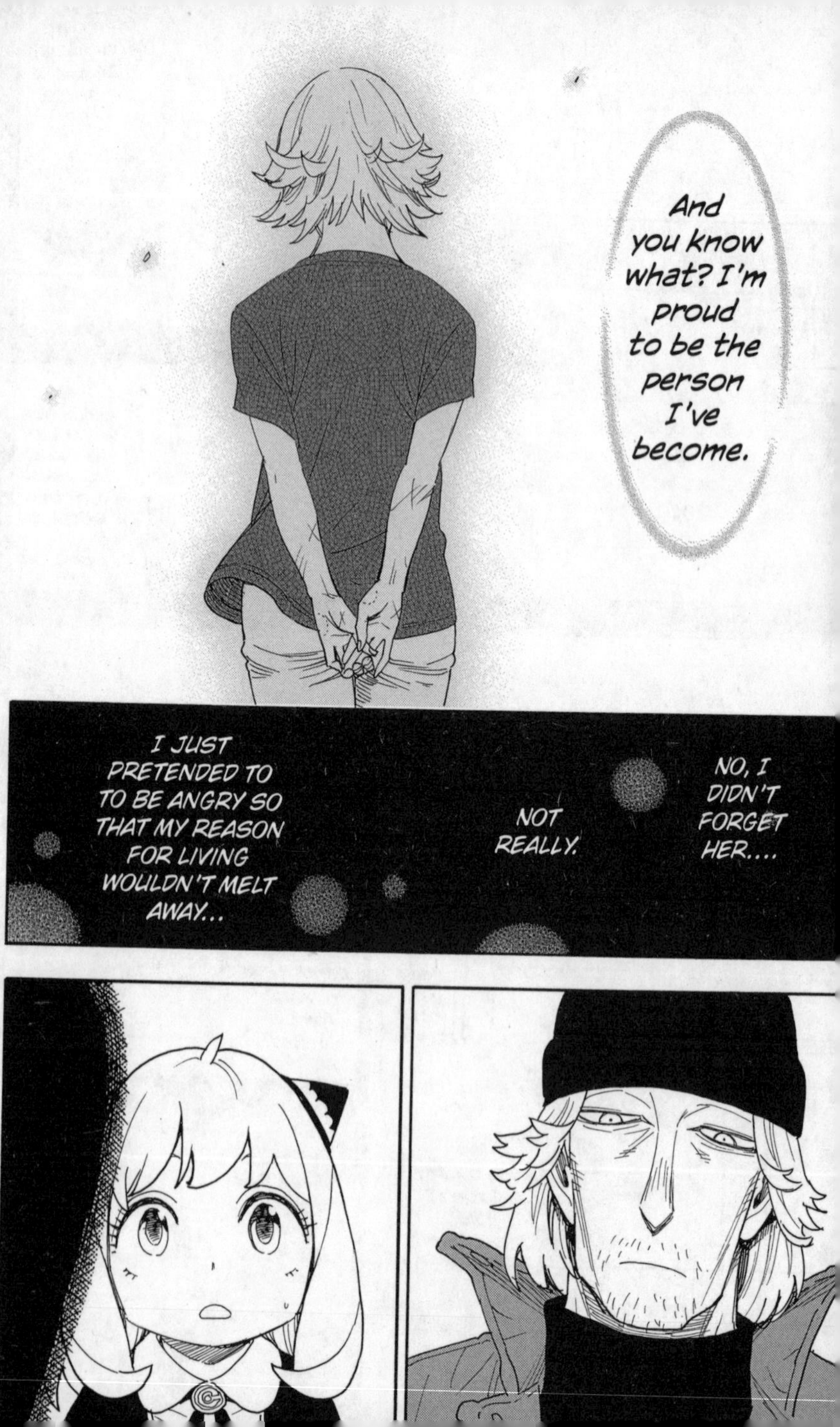
And you know what? I'm proud to be the person I've become.
NO, I DIDN'T FORGET HER....
NOT REALLY.
I JUST PRETENDED TO TO BE ANGRY SO THAT MY REASON FOR LIVING WOULDN'T MELT AWAY...

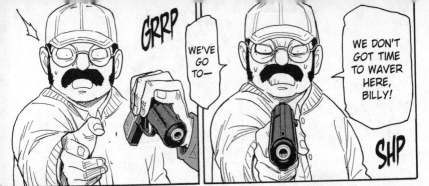

WE DON'T GOT TIME TO WAVER HERE, BILLY!
SHP
GRRP
WE'VE GO TO—
P
SHM
TMP
BILLY ?!
!!
SHNK
CLATTER
ALL FORCES HOLD. X-1 HAS LEFT THE BUS.
THE RED CIRCUS'S METHODS ARE WRONG. I'VE NEVER HAD ANY ILLUSIONS ABOUT THAT.
TMP
AND YET I NEVER DID A THING TO STOP THEM.
TMP

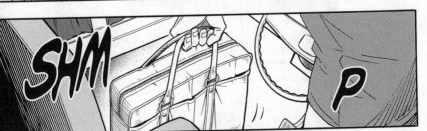

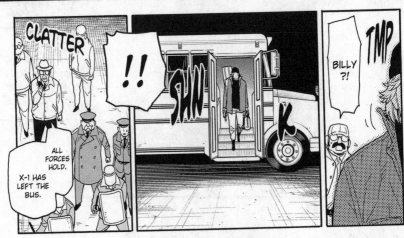

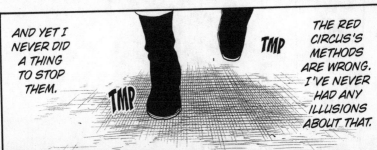

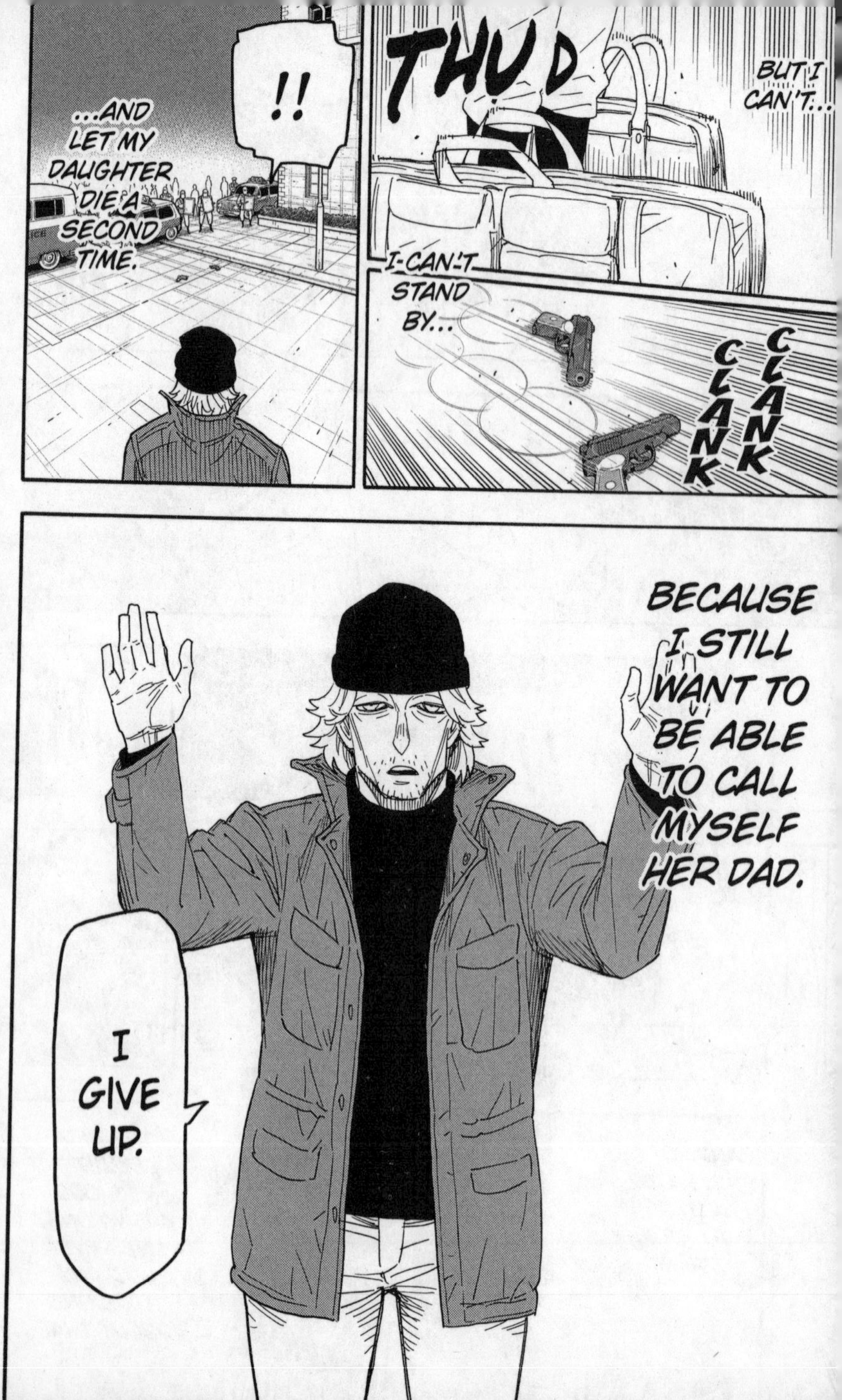
THUD
BUT I CAN'T...
I-CAN'T STAND BY...
CLANK CLANK
!!
...AND LET MY DAUGHTER DIE A SECOND TIME.
BECAUSE I STILL WANT TO BE ABLE TO CALL MYSELF HER DAD.
I GIVE UP.

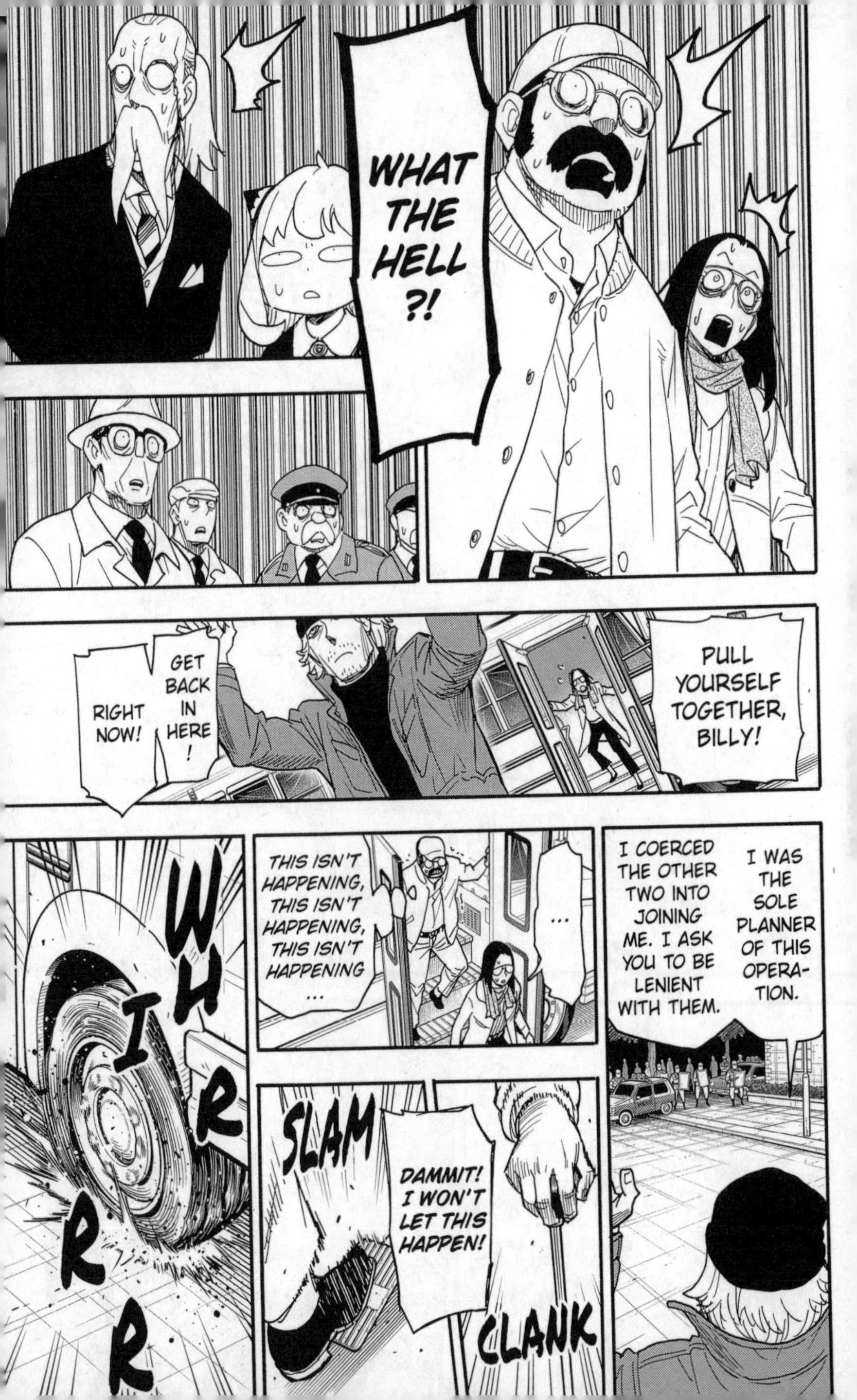
WHAT THE HELL ?!
PULL YOURSELF TOGETHER, BILLY!
GET BACK IN HERE!
RIGHT NOW!
I WAS THE SOLE PLANNER OF THIS OPERATION.
I COERCED THE OTHER TWO INTO JOINING ME. I ASK YOU TO BE LENIENT WITH THEM.
...
THIS ISN'T HAPPENING, THIS ISN'T HAPPENING, THIS ISN'T HAPPENING ...
CLANK
DAMMIT! I WON'T LET THIS HAPPEN!
SLAM
WHIRRR

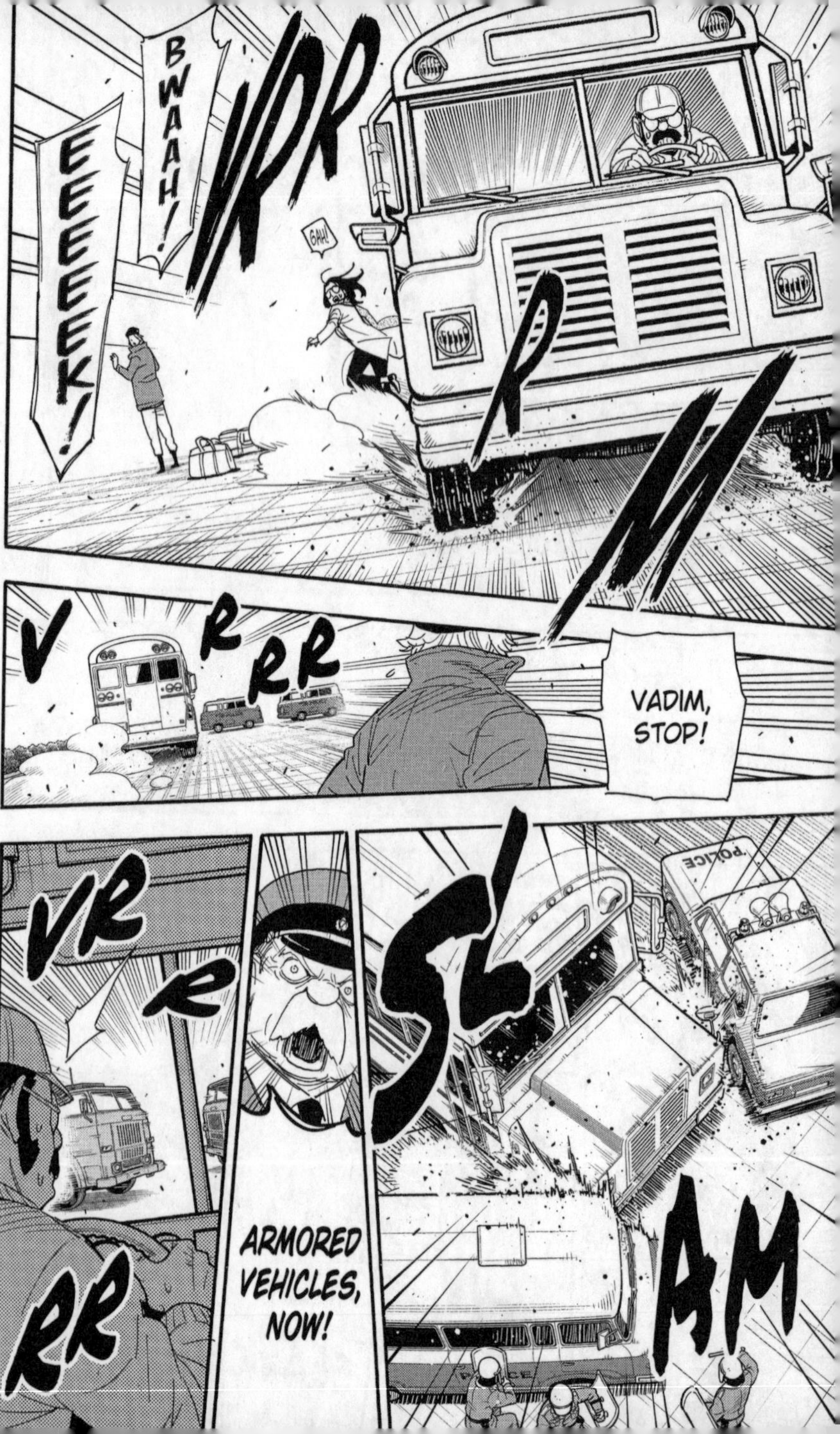
VRR
GAH!
BWAAAH!
EEEEEEEK!
RRM
VADIM, STOP!
V R RR
POLICE
SL
AM
ARMORED VEHICLES, NOW!
VR R RR

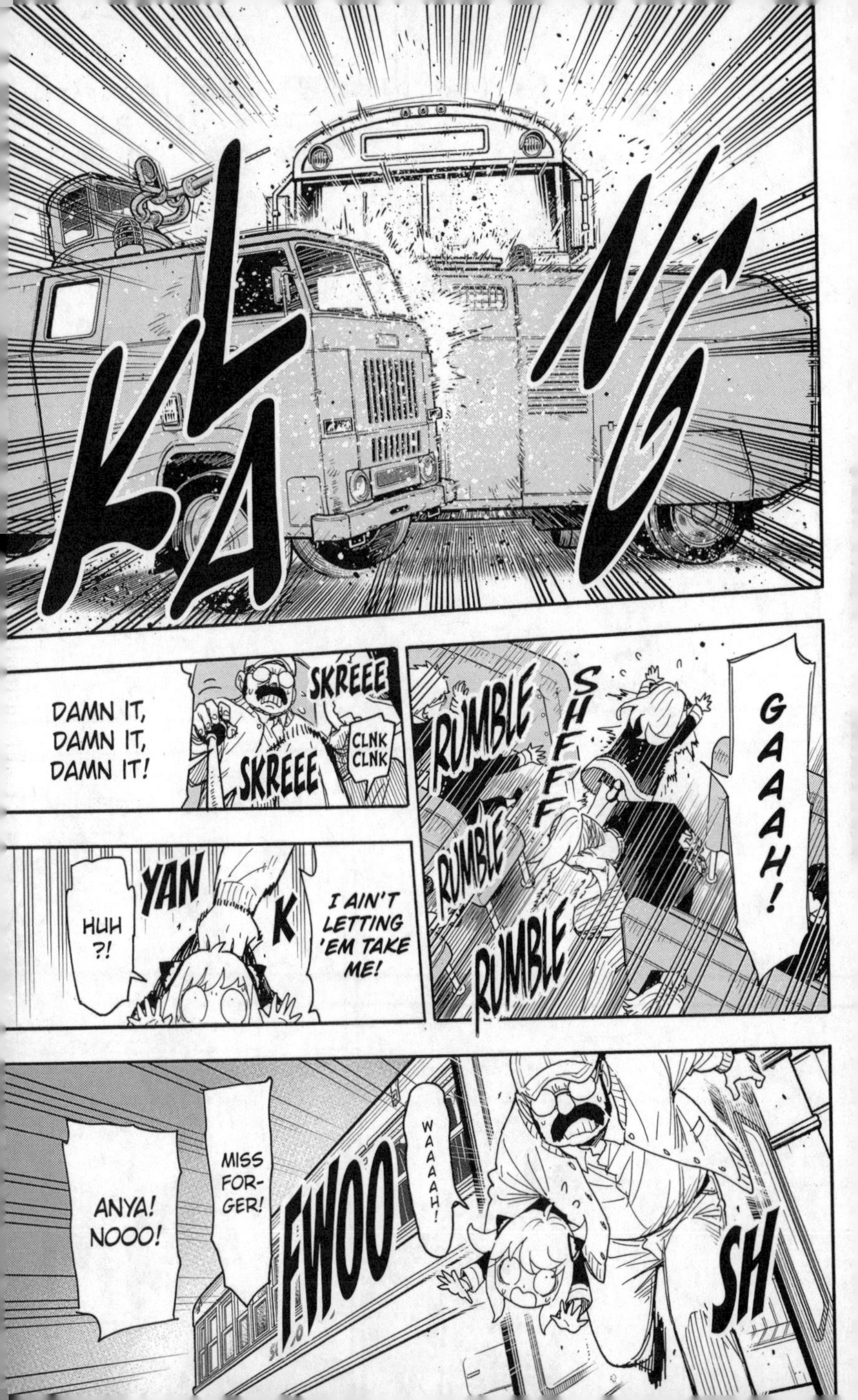
KLANG
GAAAH!
SHFFFF
RUMBLE
RUMBLE
RUMBLE
SKREEE
CLNK CLNK
SKREEE
DAMN IT, DAMN IT, DAMN IT!
I AIN'T LETTING 'EM TAKE ME!
YANK
HUH?!
WAAAAH!
FWOOSH
MISS FORGER!
ANYA! NOOO!

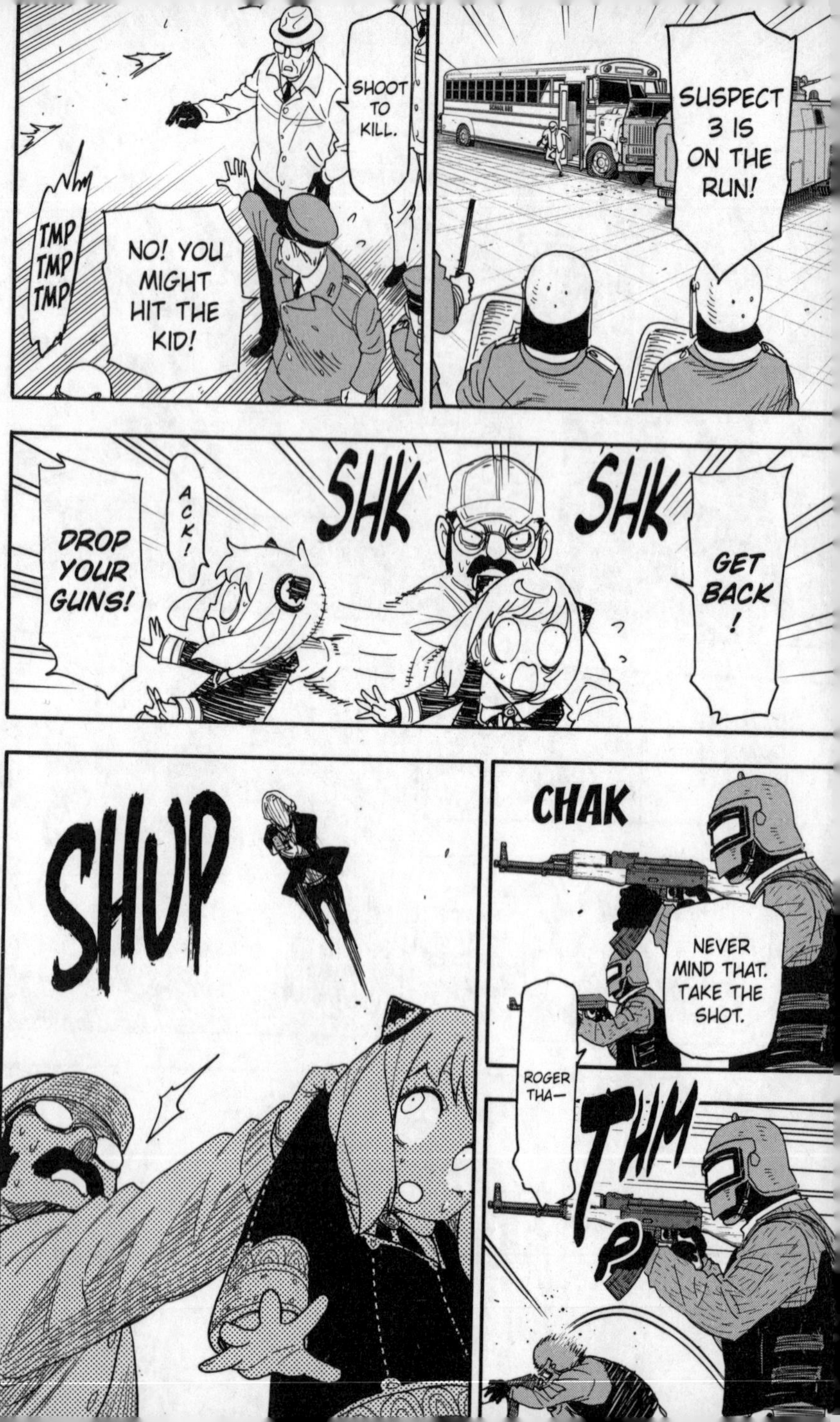
SUSPECT 3 IS ON THE RUN!
SHOOT TO KILL.
NO! YOU MIGHT HIT THE KID!
TMP TMP TMP
GET BACK!
SHK
SHK
ACK!
DROP YOUR GUNS!
CHAK
NEVER MIND THAT. TAKE THE SHOT.
THM
ROGER THA—
SHUP

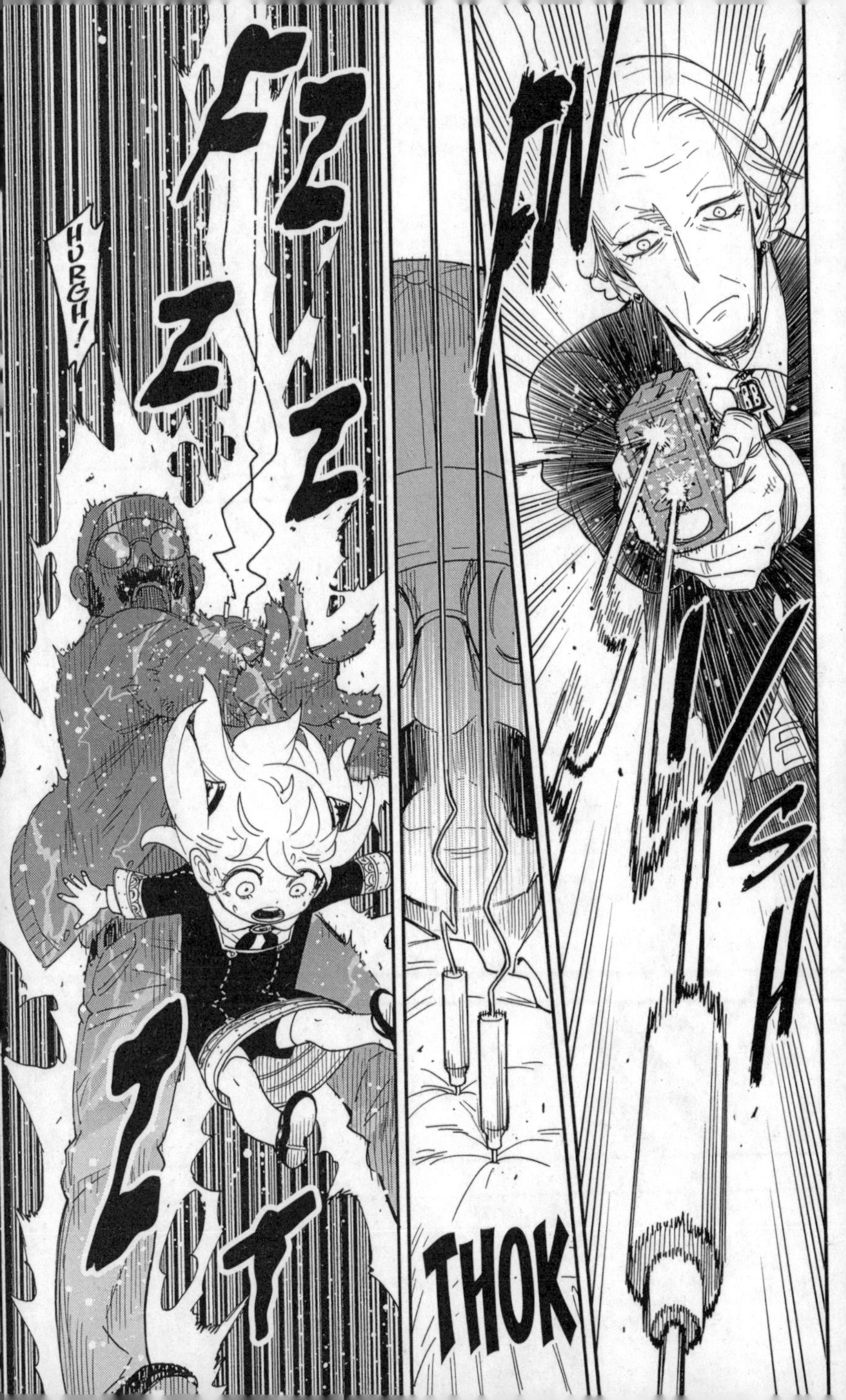
THOK
HURGH!

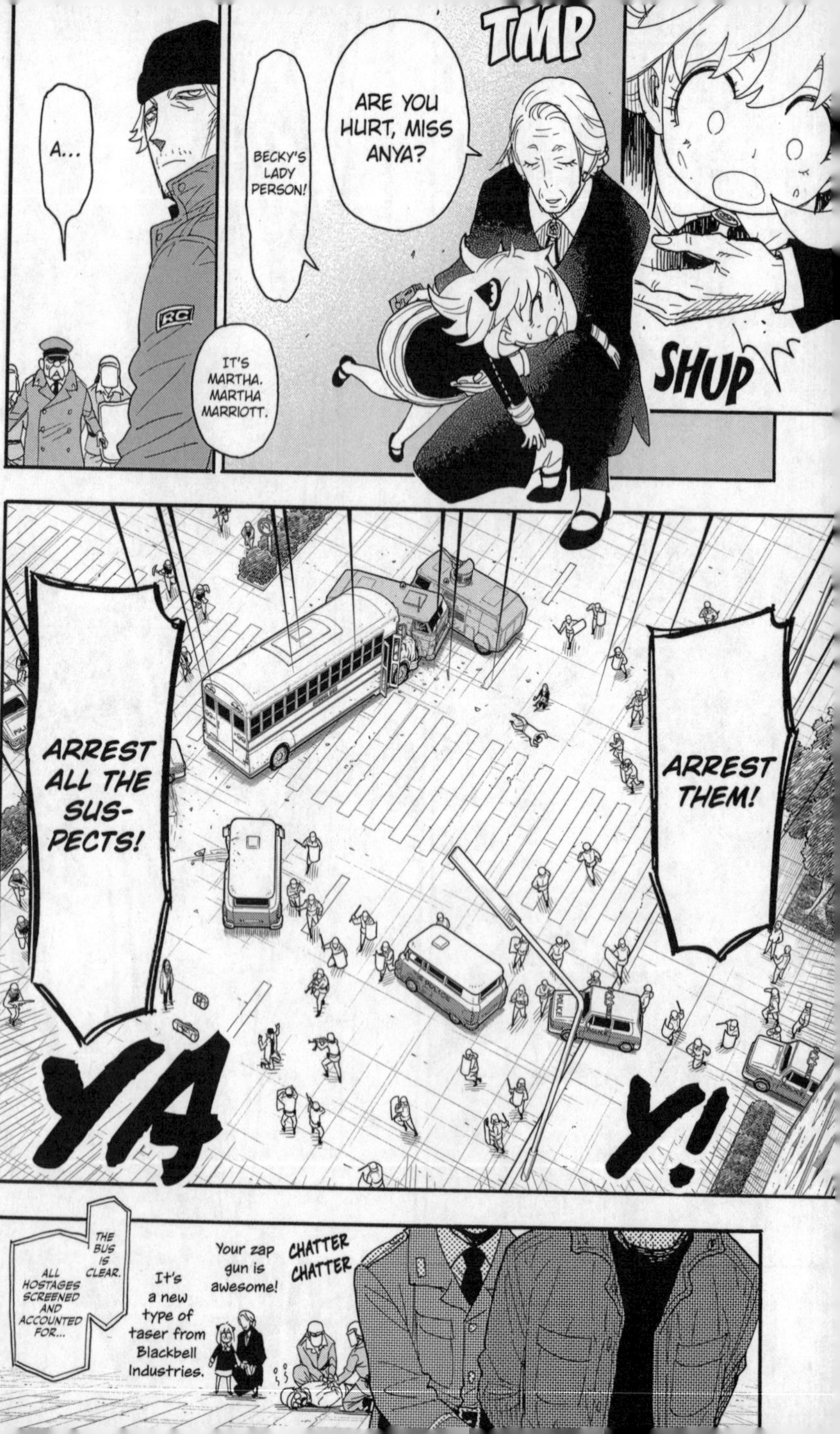
SHUP
TMP
ARE YOU HURT, MISS ANYA?
BECKY'S LADY PERSON!
IT'S MARTHA. MARTHA MARRIOTT.
A...
ARREST THEM!
ARREST ALL THE SUS-PECTS!
YA
Y!
THE BUS IS CLEAR.
ALL HOSTAGES SCREENED AND ACCOUNTED FOR...
CHATTER CHATTER
Your zap gun is awesome!
It's a new type of taser from Blackbell Industries.

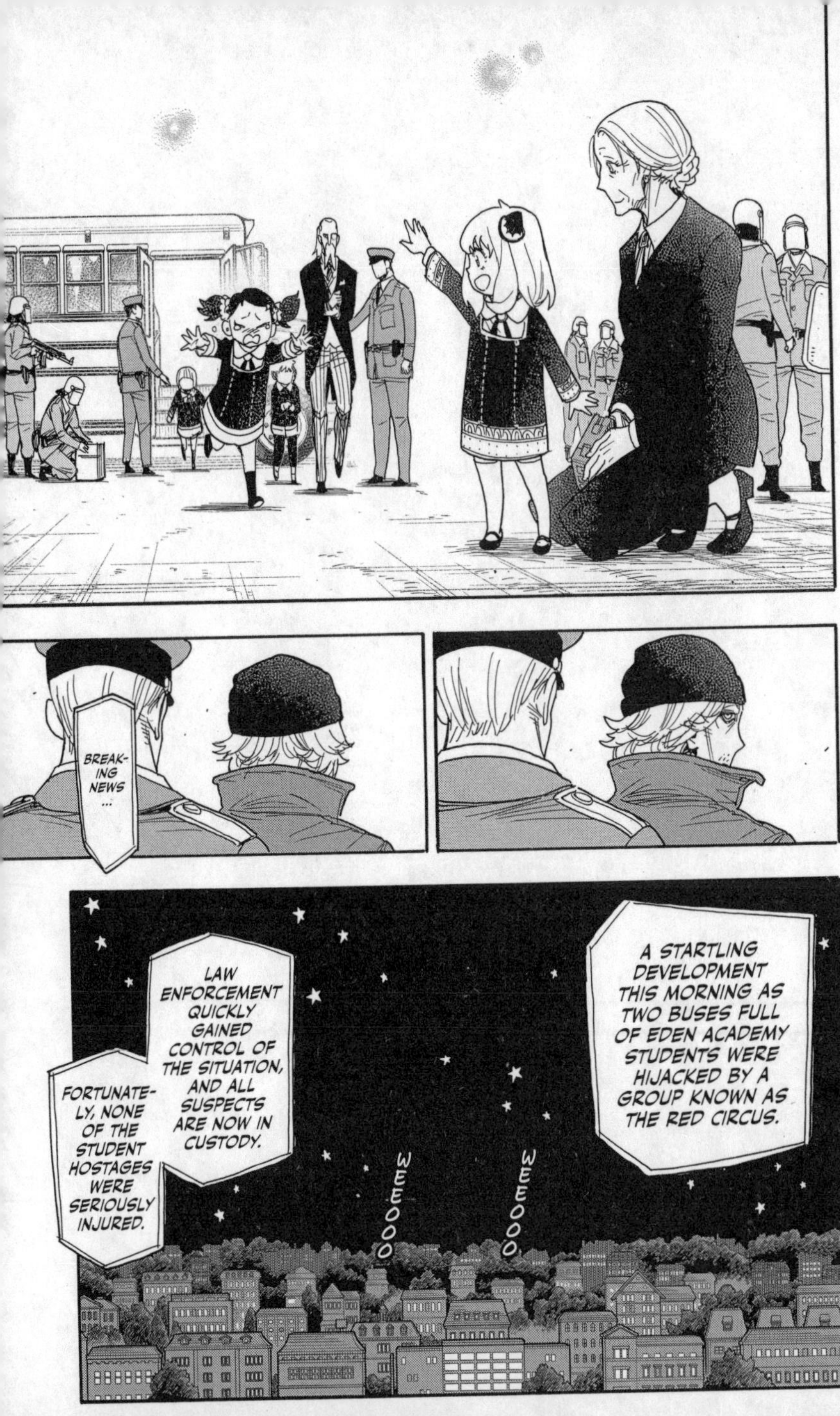
BREAKING-NEWS ...
A STARTLING DEVELOPMENT THIS MORNING AS TWO BUSES FULL OF EDEN ACADEMY STUDENTS WERE HIJACKED BY A GROUP KNOWN AS THE RED CIRCUS.
LAW ENFORCEMENT QUICKLY GAINED CONTROL OF THE SITUATION, AND ALL SUSPECTS ARE NOW IN CUSTODY.
WEEOOO
WEEOOO
FORTUNATE-LY, NONE OF THE STUDENT HOSTAGES WERE SERIOUSLY INJURED.

SPY×FAMILY

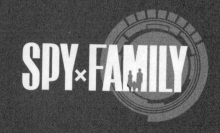

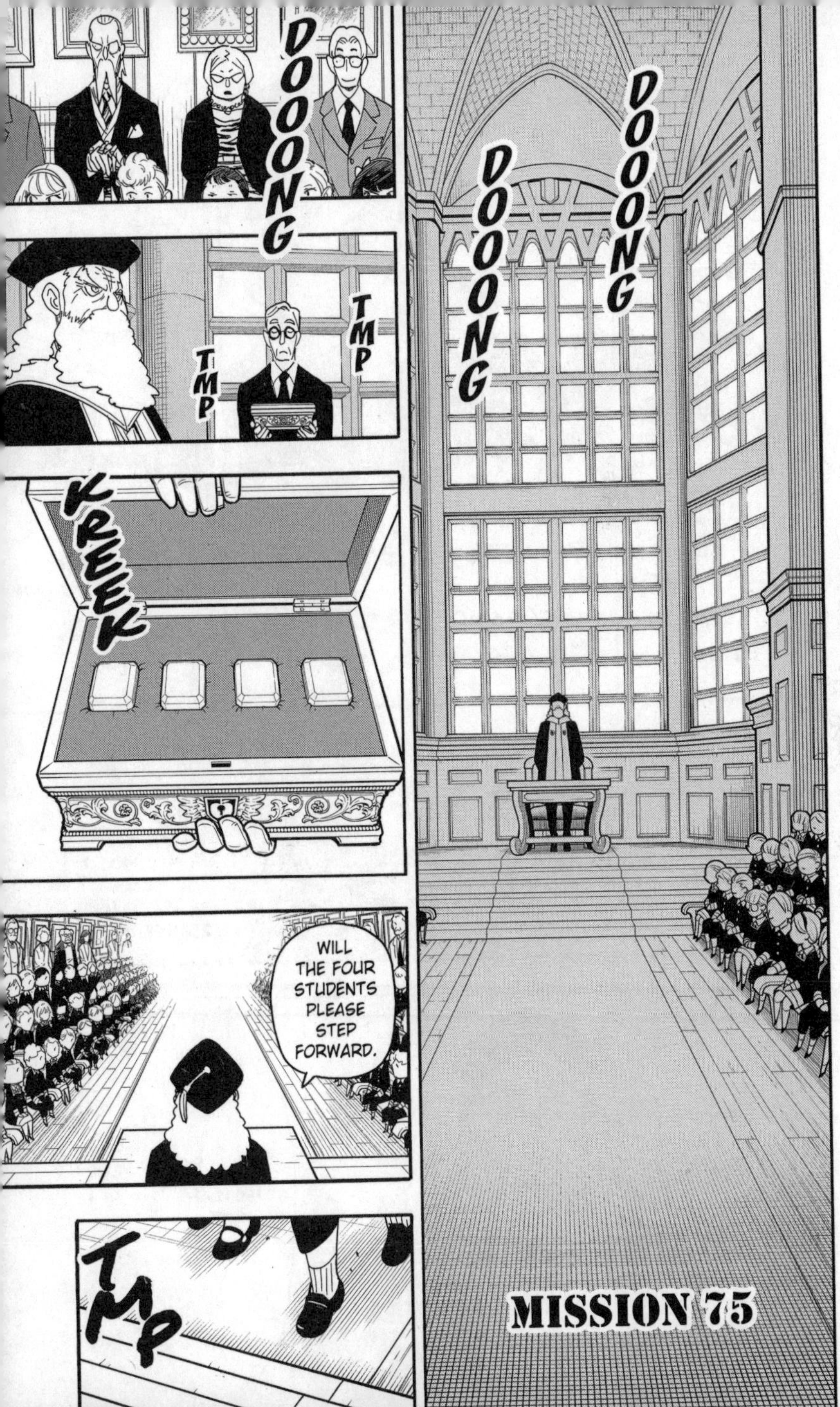
DOOOONG
DOOOONG
MISSION 75
DOOOONG
TMP
TMP
KREEK
WILL THE FOUR STUDENTS PLEASE STEP FORWARD.
TMP

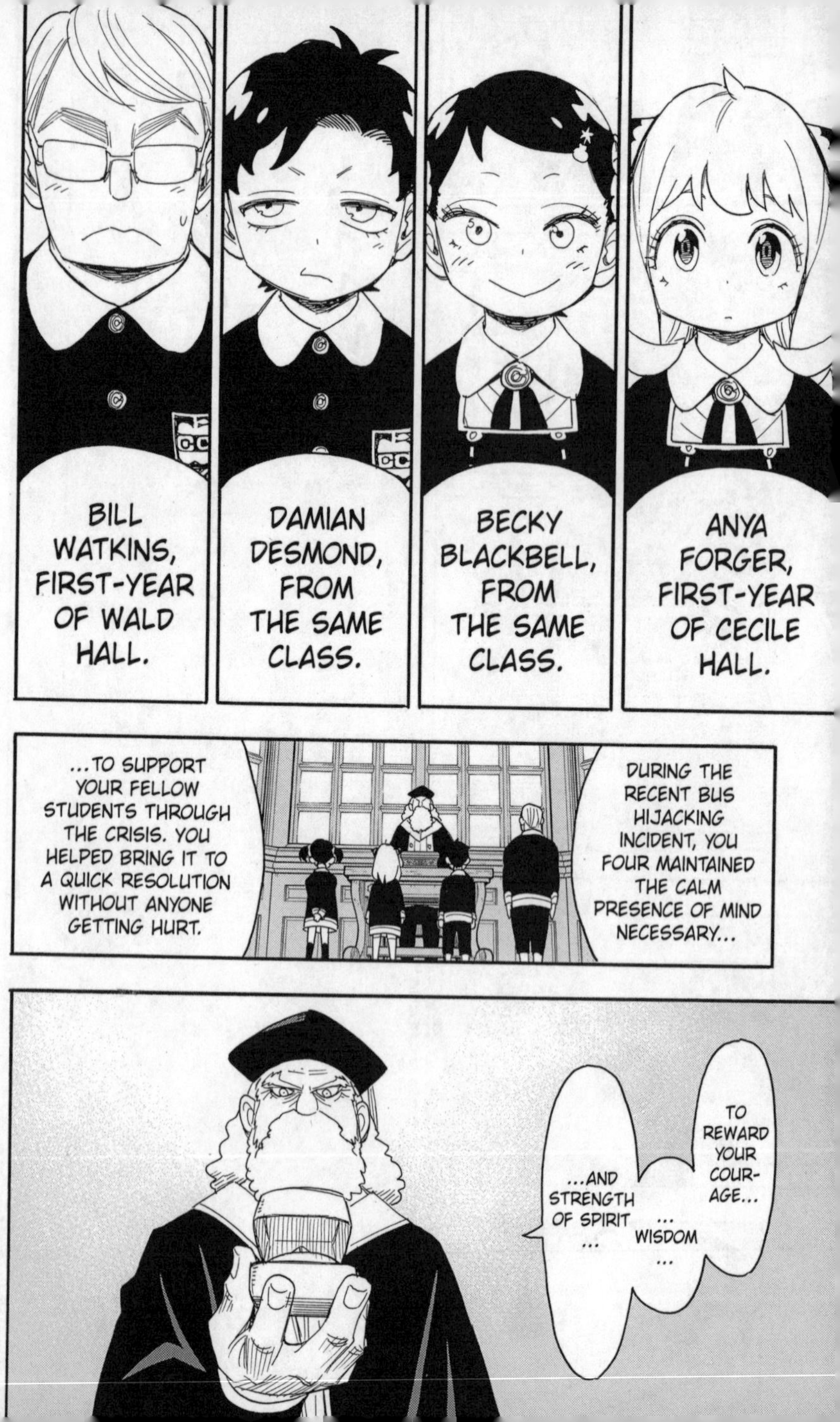
ANYA FORGER, FIRST-YEAR OF CECILE HALL.
BECKY BLACKBELL, FROM THE SAME CLASS.
DAMIAN DESMOND, FROM THE SAME CLASS.
BILL WATKINS, FIRST-YEAR OF WALD HALL.
DURING THE RECENT BUS HIJACKING INCIDENT, YOU FOUR MAINTAINED THE CALM PRESENCE OF MIND NECESSARY...
...TO SUPPORT YOUR FELLOW STUDENTS THROUGH THE CRISIS. YOU HELPED BRING IT TO A QUICK RESOLUTION WITHOUT ANYONE GETTING HURT.
TO REWARD YOUR COURAGE...
...WISDOM...
...AND STRENGTH OF SPIRIT...

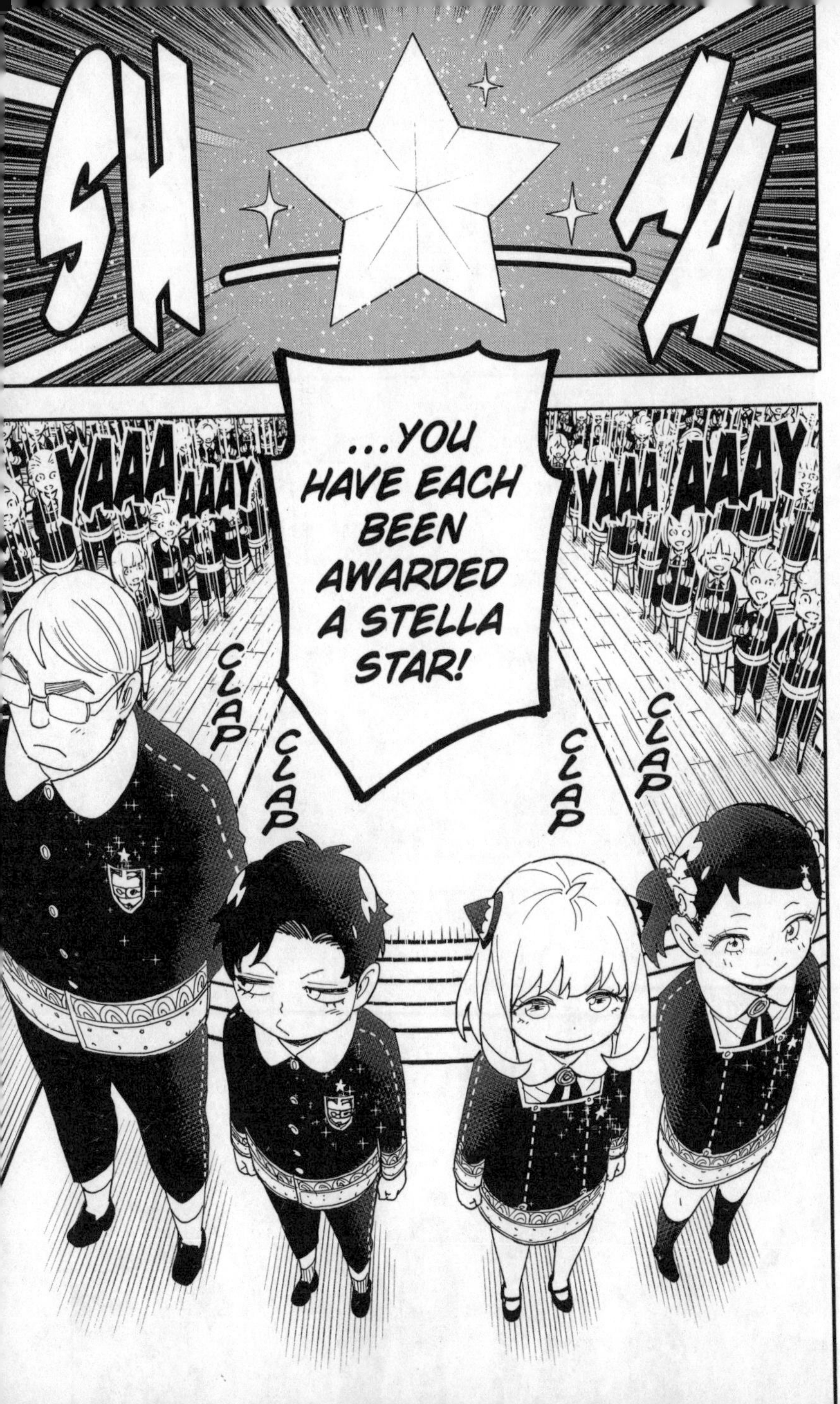
SHAA
...YOU HAVE EACH BEEN AWARDED A STELLA STAR!
YAAAAAAY
YAAAAAAY
CLAP
CLAP
CLAP
CLAP

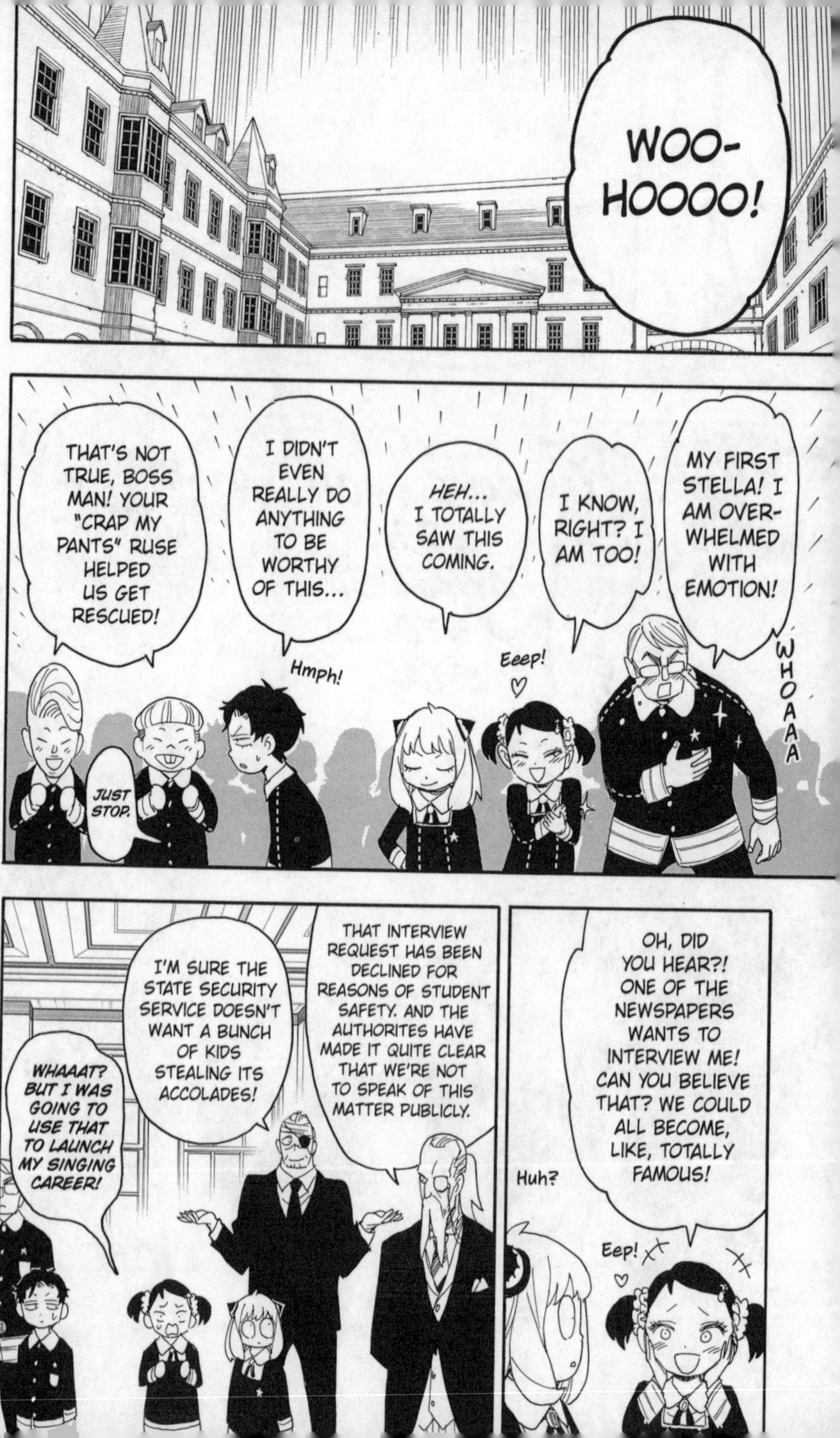
WOO-HOOOO!
MY FIRST STELLA! I AM OVERWHELMED WITH EMOTION!
WHOAAA
I KNOW, RIGHT? I AM TOO!
Eeep!
HEH... I TOTALLY SAW THIS COMING.
I DIDN'T EVEN REALLY DO ANYTHING TO BE WORTHY OF THIS...
Hmph!
THAT'S NOT TRUE, BOSS MAN! YOUR "CRAP MY PANTS" RUSE HELPED US GET RESCUED!
JUST STOP.
OH, DID YOU HEAR?! ONE OF THE NEWSPAPERS WANTS TO INTERVIEW ME! CAN YOU BELIEVE THAT? WE COULD ALL BECOME, LIKE, TOTALLY FAMOUS!
Eep!
Huh?
THAT INTERVIEW REQUEST HAS BEEN DECLINED FOR REASONS OF STUDENT SAFETY. AND THE AUTHORITES HAVE MADE IT QUITE CLEAR THAT WE'RE NOT TO SPEAK OF THIS MATTER PUBLICLY.
I'M SURE THE STATE SECURITY SERVICE DOESN'T WANT A BUNCH OF KIDS STEALING ITS ACCOLADES!
WHAAAT? BUT I WAS GOING TO USE THAT TO LAUNCH MY SINGING CAREER!

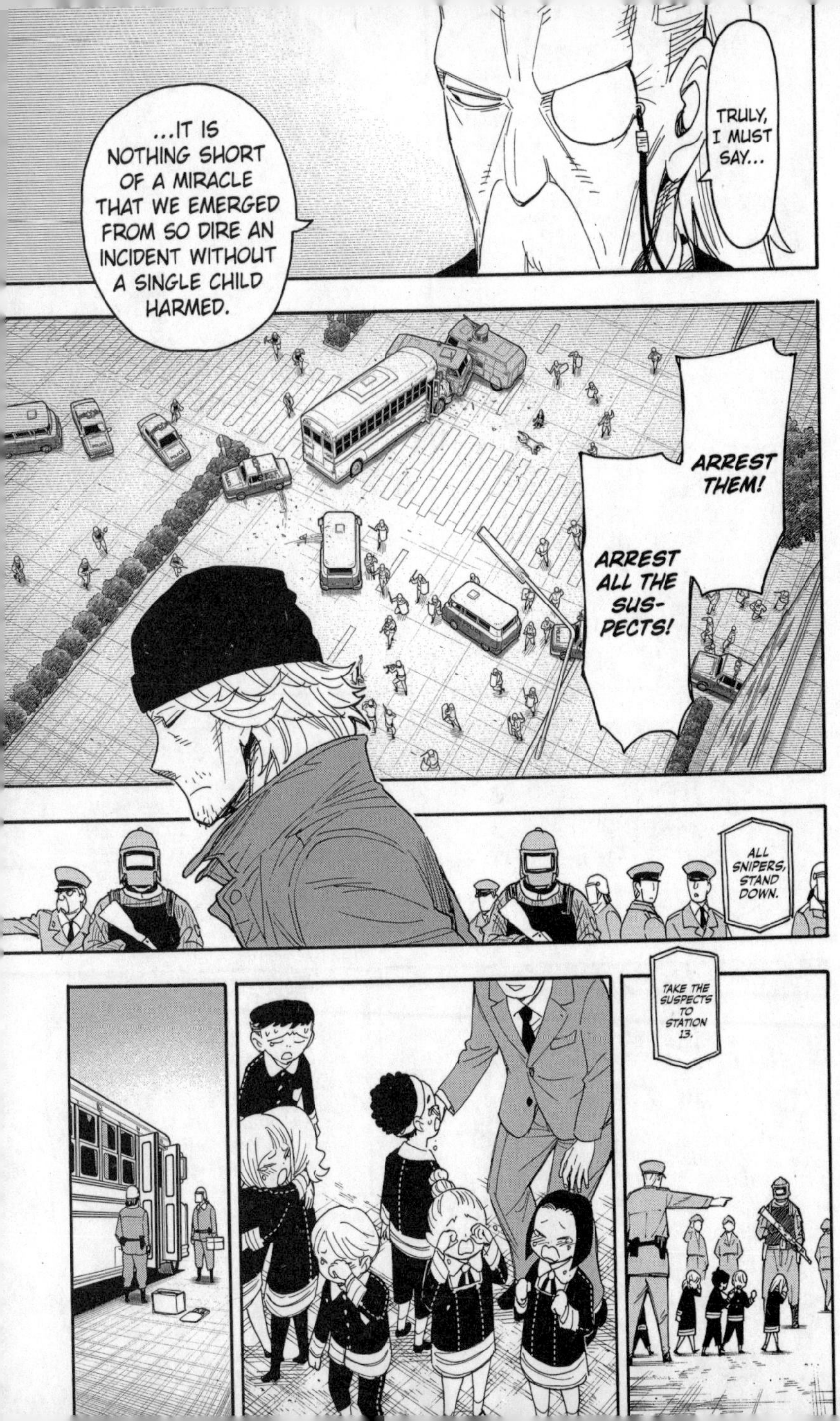

TRULY, I MUST SAY...
...IT IS NOTHING SHORT OF A MIRACLE THAT WE EMERGED FROM SO DIRE AN INCIDENT WITHOUT A SINGLE CHILD HARMED.
ARREST THEM!
ARREST ALL THE SUS-PECTS!
ALL SNIPERS, STAND DOWN.
TAKE THE SUSPECTS TO STATION 13.

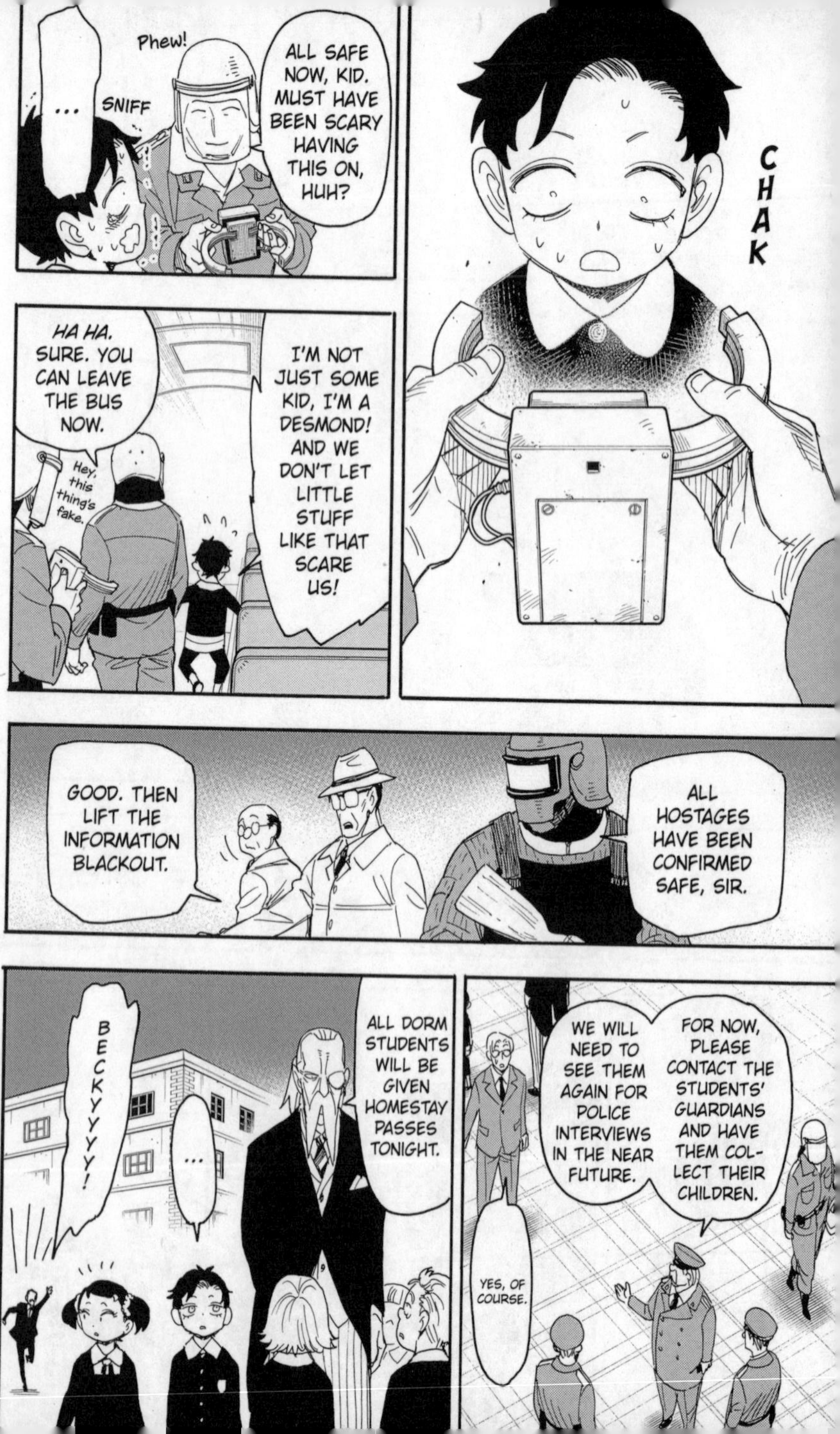
CHAK
ALL SAFE NOW, KID. MUST HAVE BEEN SCARY HAVING THIS ON, HUH?
Phew!
SNIFF
...
I'M NOT JUST SOME KID, I'M A DESMOND! AND WE DON'T LET LITTLE STUFF LIKE THAT SCARE US!
HA HA. SURE. YOU CAN LEAVE THE BUS NOW.
Hey, this thing's fake.
ALL HOSTAGES HAVE BEEN CONFIRMED SAFE, SIR.
GOOD. THEN LIFT THE INFORMATION BLACKOUT.
FOR NOW, PLEASE CONTACT THE STUDENTS' GUARDIANS AND HAVE THEM COL-LECT THEIR CHILDREN.
WE WILL NEED TO SEE THEM AGAIN FOR POLICE INTERVIEWS IN THE NEAR FUTURE.
YES, OF COURSE.
ALL DORM STUDENTS WILL BE GIVEN HOMESTAY PASSES TONIGHT.
...
BECKYYYY!

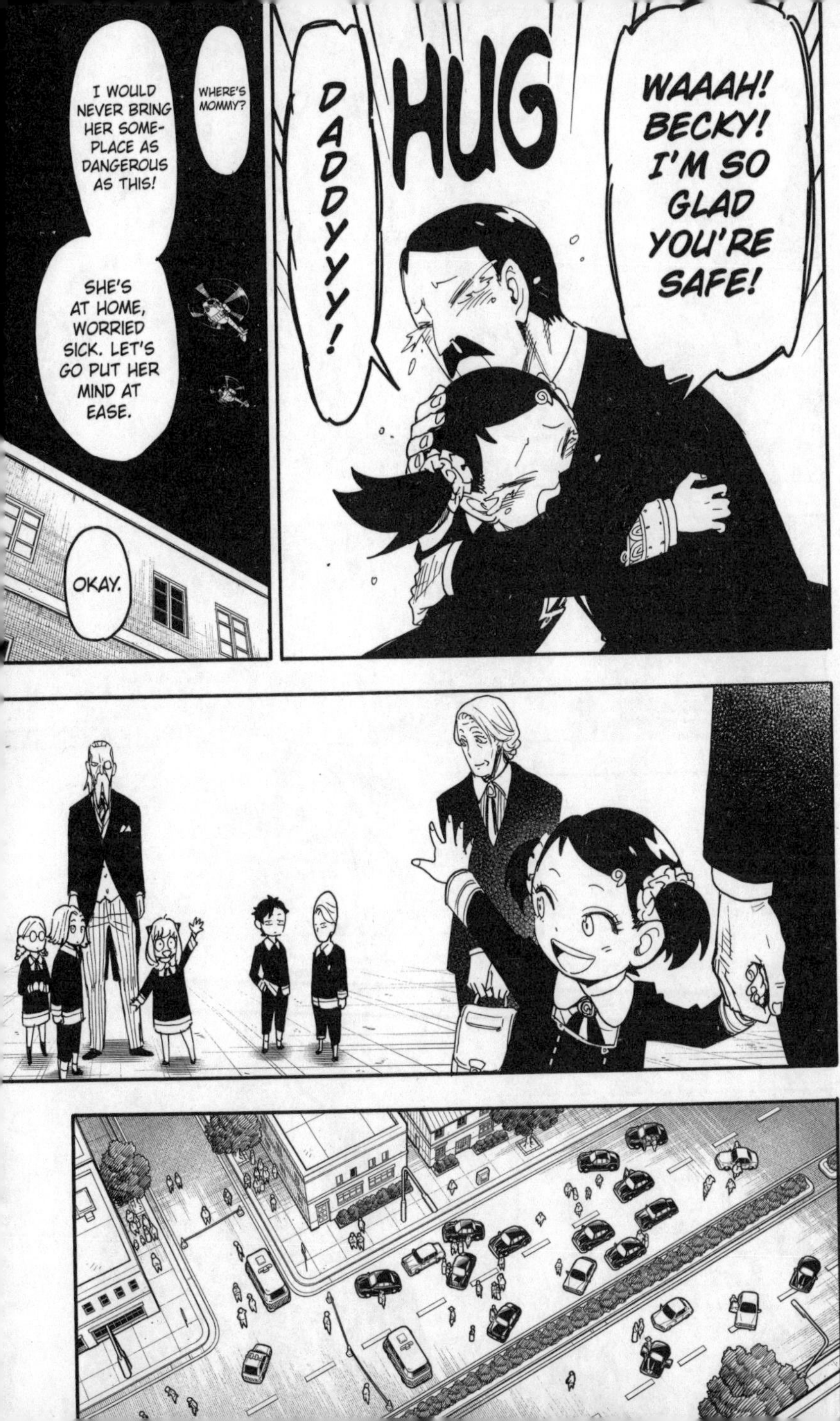
WAAAH! BECKY! I'M SO GLAD YOU'RE SAFE!
HUG
DADDYYY!
WHERE'S MOMMY?
I WOULD NEVER BRING HER SOME-PLACE AS DANGEROUS AS THIS!
SHE'S AT HOME, WORRIED SICK. LET'S GO PUT HER MIND AT EASE.
OKAY.

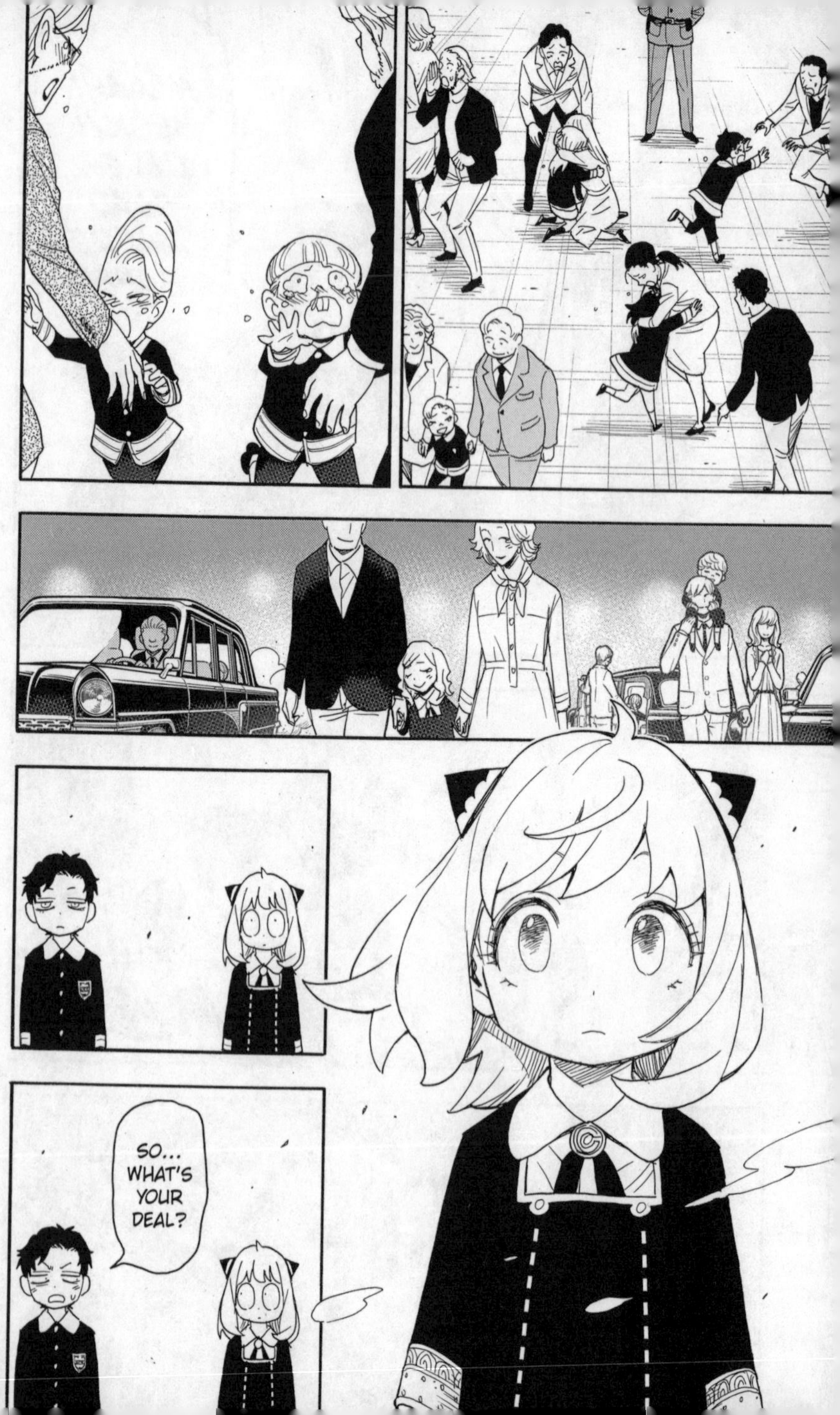
SO... WHAT'S YOUR DEAL?

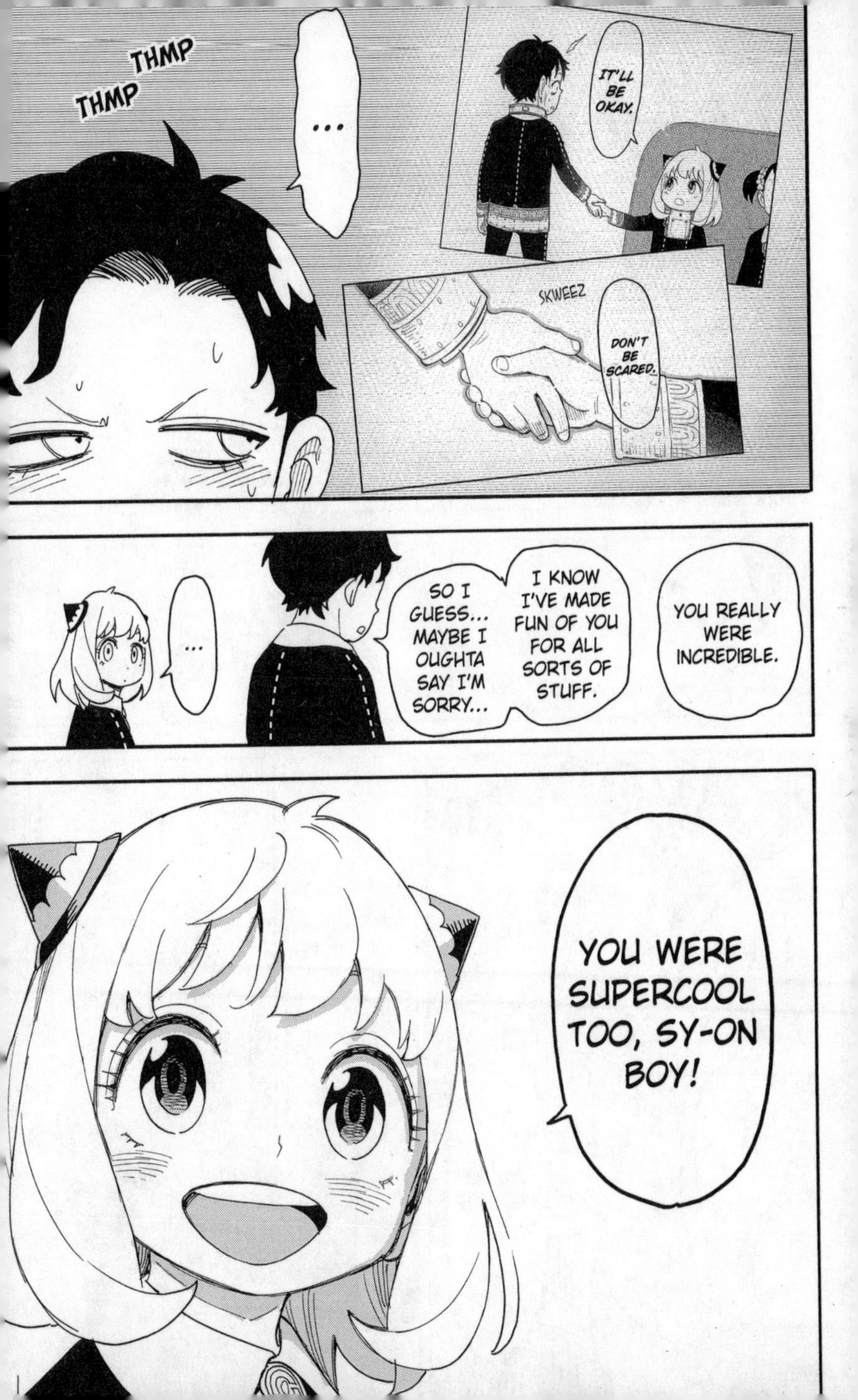
IT'LL BE OKAY.
SKWEEZ
DON'T BE SCARED.
...
THMP THMP
YOU REALLY WERE INCREDIBLE.
I KNOW I'VE MADE FUN OF YOU FOR ALL SORTS OF STUFF.
SO I GUESS... MAYBE I OUGHTA SAY I'M SORRY...
...
YOU WERE SUPERCOOL TOO, SY-ON BOY!

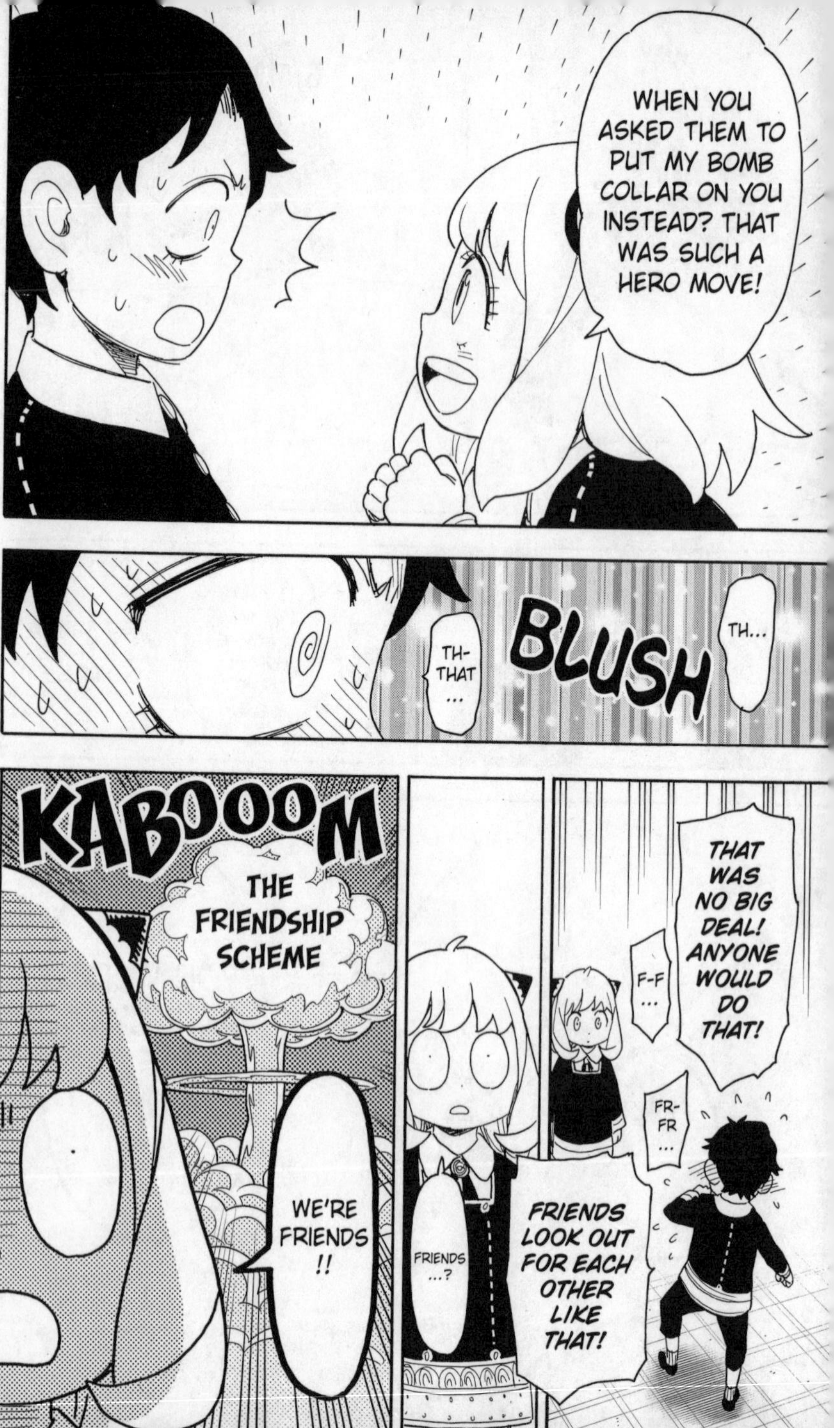
WHEN YOU ASKED THEM TO PUT MY BOMB COLLAR ON YOU INSTEAD? THAT WAS SUCH A HERO MOVE!
TH...
BLUSH
TH-THAT ...
THAT WAS NO BIG DEAL! ANYONE WOULD DO THAT!
F-F ...
FR-FR ...
FRIENDS LOOK OUT FOR EACH OTHER LIKE THAT!
FRIENDS ...?
KABOOOM
THE FRIENDSHIP SCHEME
WE'RE FRIENDS !!

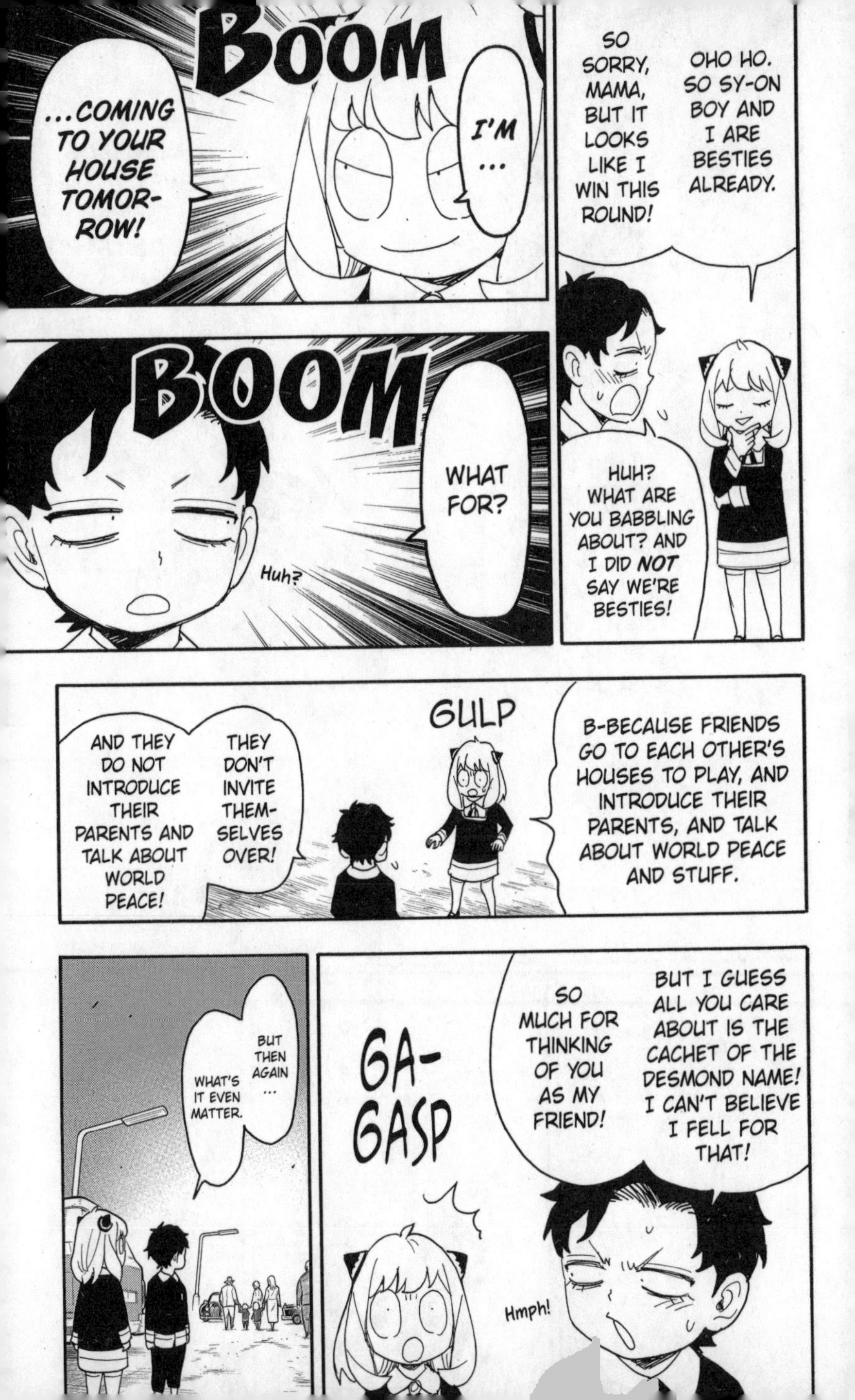
OHO HO. SO SY-ON BOY AND I ARE BESTIES ALREADY.
SO SORRY, MAMA, BUT IT LOOKS LIKE I WIN THIS ROUND!
HUH? WHAT ARE YOU BABBLING ABOUT? AND I DID **NOT** SAY WE'RE BESTIES!
BOOM
I'M ...
...COMING TO YOUR HOUSE TOMORROW!
WHAT FOR?
BOOM
Huh?
B-BECAUSE FRIENDS GO TO EACH OTHER'S HOUSES TO PLAY, AND INTRODUCE THEIR PARENTS, AND TALK ABOUT WORLD PEACE AND STUFF.
GULP
THEY DON'T INVITE THEMSELVES OVER!
AND THEY DO NOT INTRODUCE THEIR PARENTS AND TALK ABOUT WORLD PEACE!
BUT I GUESS ALL YOU CARE ABOUT IS THE CACHET OF THE DESMOND NAME! I CAN'T BELIEVE I FELL FOR THAT!
SO MUCH FOR THINKING OF YOU AS MY FRIEND!
GA-GASP
Hmph!
BUT THEN AGAIN ...
WHAT'S IT EVEN MATTER.

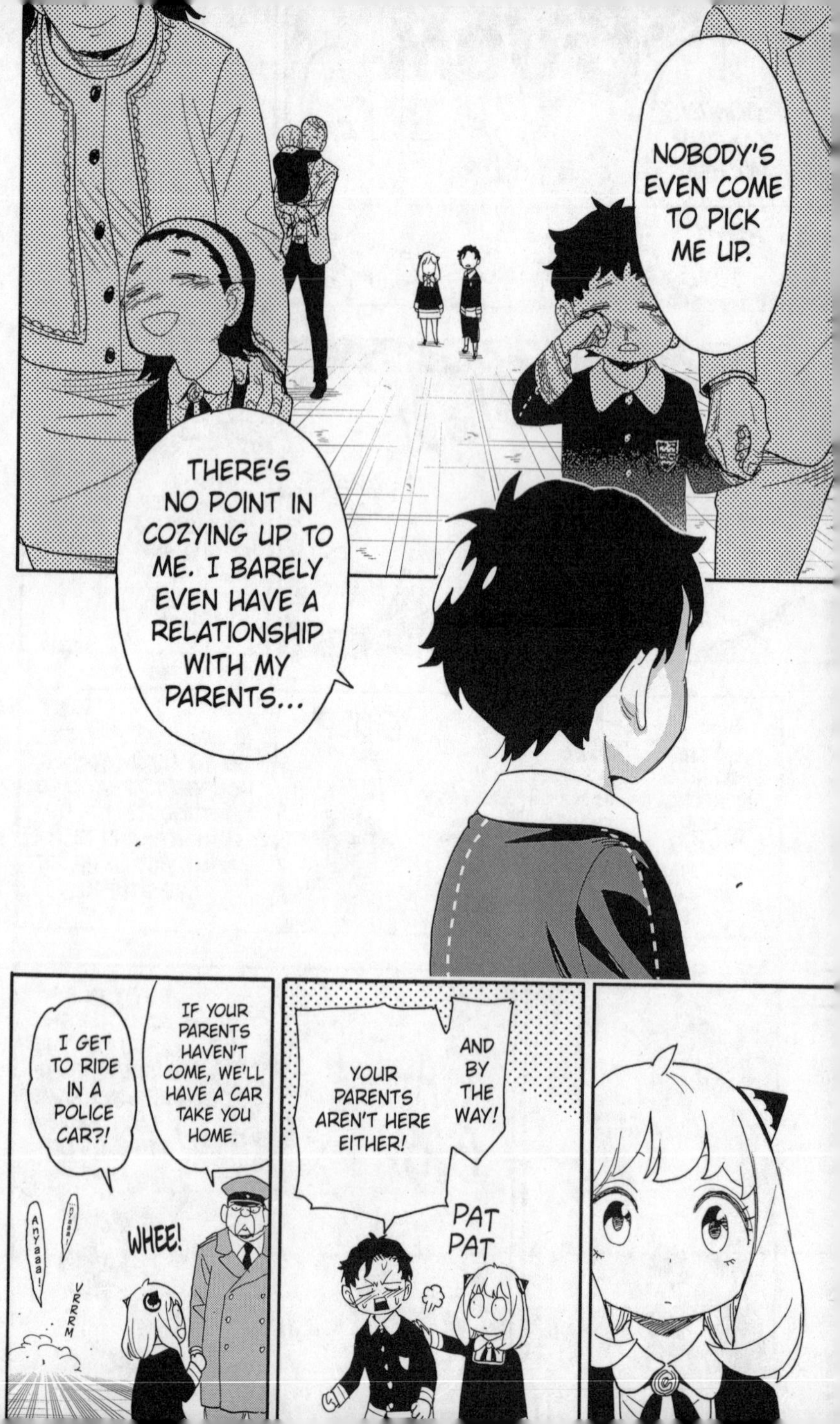
NOBODY'S EVEN COME TO PICK ME UP.
THERE'S NO POINT IN COZYING UP TO ME. I BARELY EVEN HAVE A RELATIONSHIP WITH MY PARENTS...
AND BY THE WAY!
YOUR PARENTS AREN'T HERE EITHER!
PAT PAT
IF YOUR PARENTS HAVEN'T COME, WE'LL HAVE A CAR TAKE YOU HOME.
I GET TO RIDE IN A POLICE CAR?!
WHEE!
...nyaaa!
Anyaaa!
VRRRM

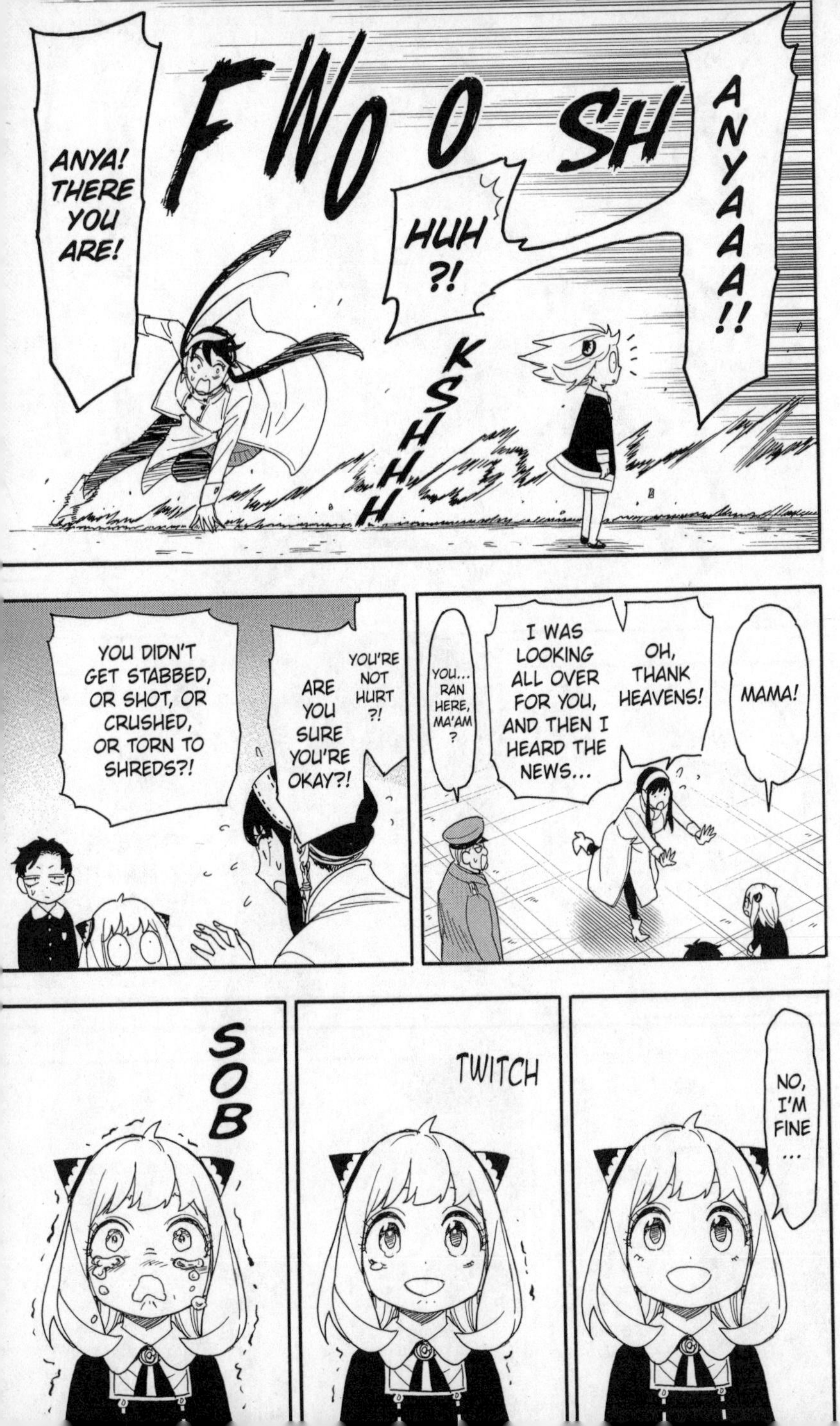
ANYAAAA!!
HUH ?!
FWOOSH
KSHHHH
ANYA! THERE YOU ARE!
MAMA!
OH, THANK HEAVENS!
I WAS LOOKING ALL OVER FOR YOU, AND THEN I HEARD THE NEWS...
YOU... RAN HERE, MA'AM ?
YOU'RE NOT HURT ?!
ARE YOU SURE YOU'RE OKAY?!
YOU DIDN'T GET STABBED, OR SHOT, OR CRUSHED, OR TORN TO SHREDS?!
NO, I'M FINE ...
TWITCH
SOB

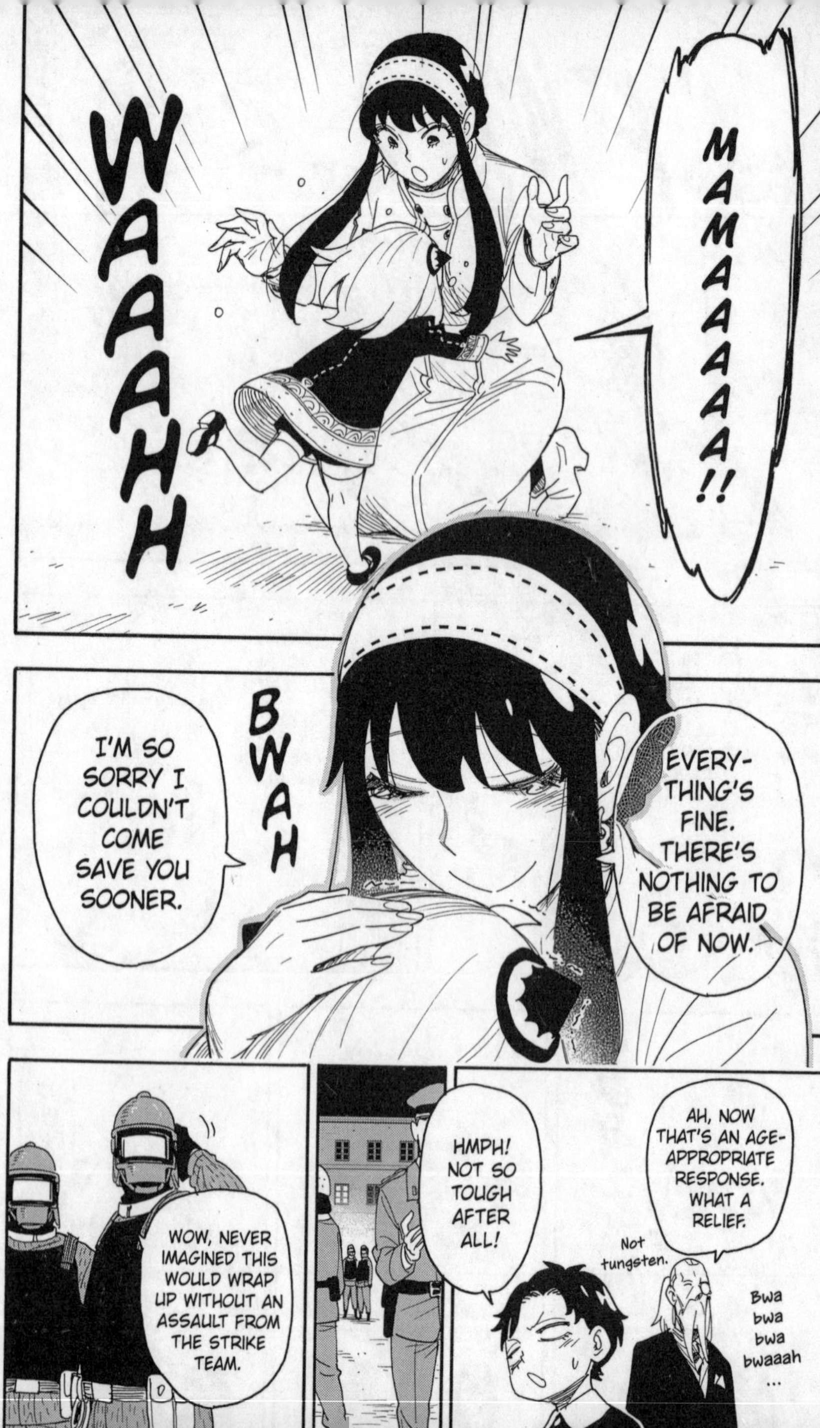
MAMAAAAAA!!
WAAAAHH
EVERY-THING'S FINE. THERE'S NOTHING TO BE AFRAID OF NOW.
BWAH
I'M SO SORRY I COULDN'T COME SAVE YOU SOONER.
AH, NOW THAT'S AN AGE-APPROPRIATE RESPONSE. WHAT A RELIEF.
Not tungsten.
Bwa bwa bwa bwaaah ...
HMPH! NOT SO TOUGH AFTER ALL!
WOW, NEVER IMAGINED THIS WOULD WRAP UP WITHOUT AN ASSAULT FROM THE STRIKE TEAM.

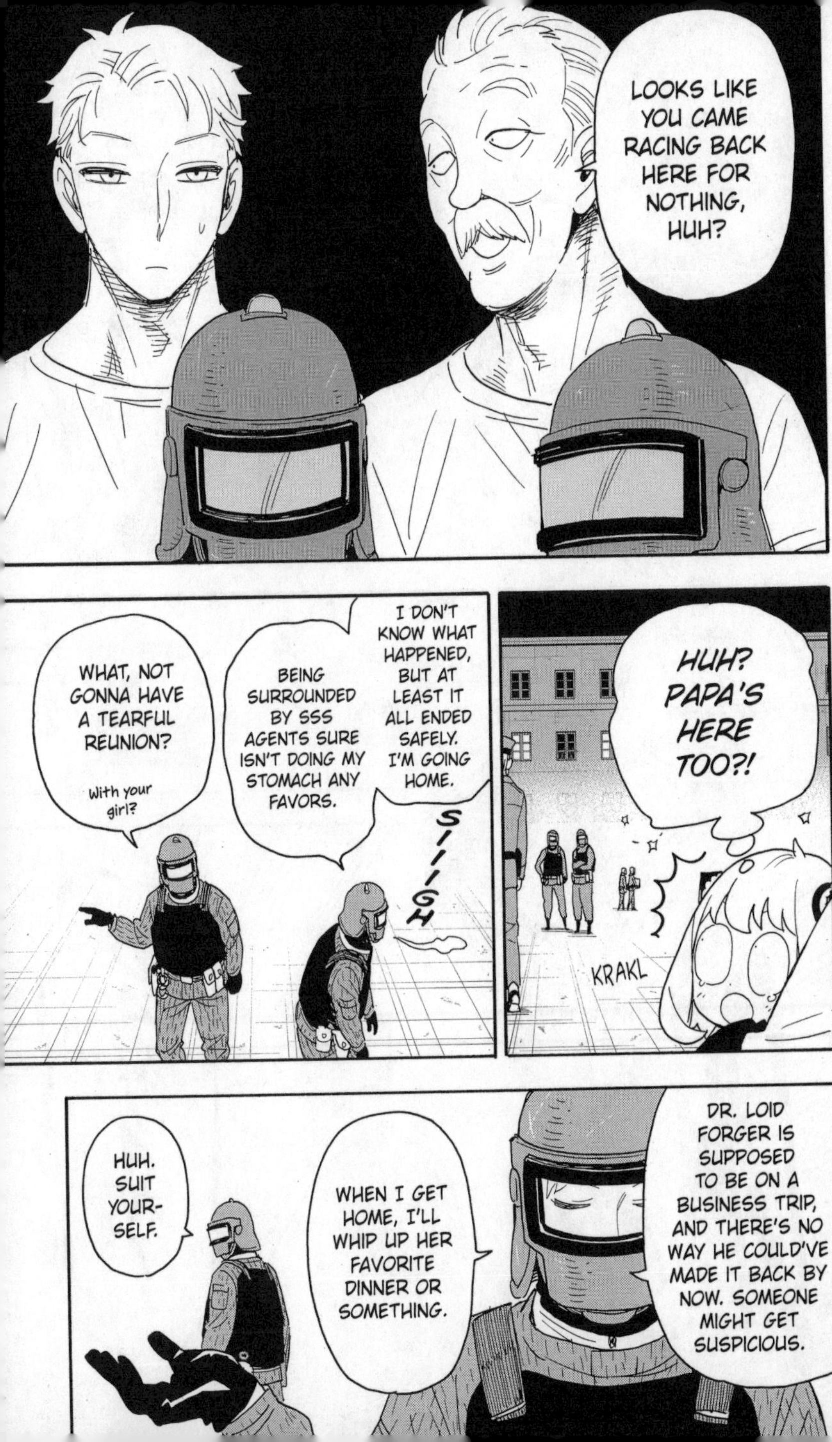
LOOKS LIKE YOU CAME RACING BACK HERE FOR NOTHING, HUH?
HUH? PAPA'S HERE TOO?!
KRAKL
I DON'T KNOW WHAT HAPPENED, BUT AT LEAST IT ALL ENDED SAFELY. I'M GOING HOME.
BEING SURROUNDED BY SSS AGENTS SURE ISN'T DOING MY STOMACH ANY FAVORS.
SIIIGH
WHAT, NOT GONNA HAVE A TEARFUL REUNION?
With your girl?
DR. LOID FORGER IS SUPPOSED TO BE ON A BUSINESS TRIP, AND THERE'S NO WAY HE COULD'VE MADE IT BACK BY NOW. SOMEONE MIGHT GET SUSPICIOUS.
WHEN I GET HOME, I'LL WHIP UP HER FAVORITE DINNER OR SOMETHING.
HUH. SUIT YOURSELF.

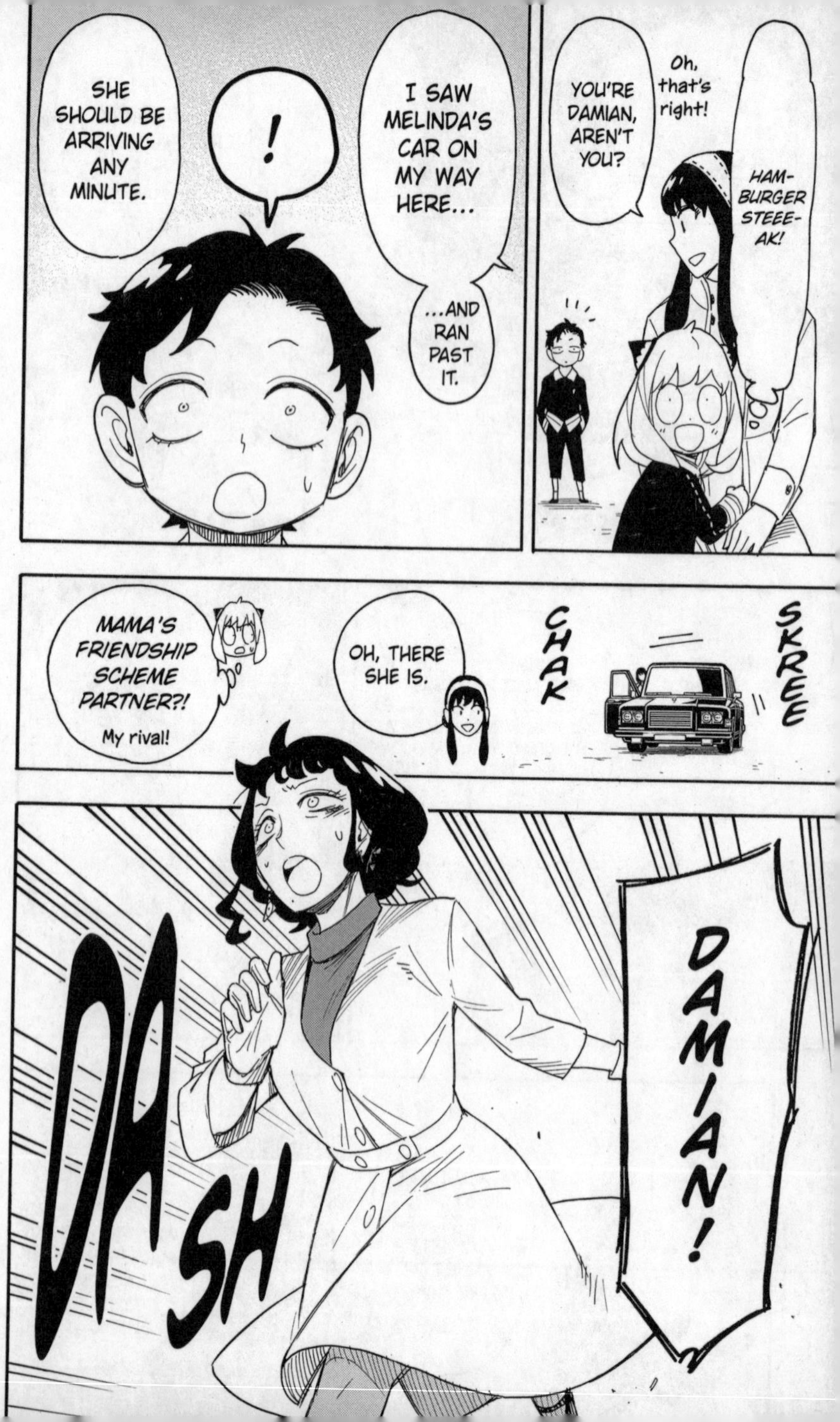
HAM-BURGER STEEE-AK!
Oh, that's right!
YOU'RE DAMIAN, AREN'T YOU?
I SAW MELINDA'S CAR ON MY WAY HERE...
...AND RAN PAST IT.
!
SHE SHOULD BE ARRIVING ANY MINUTE.
SKREE
CHAK
OH, THERE SHE IS.
MAMA'S FRIENDSHIP SCHEME PARTNER?!
My rival!
DAMIAN!
DASH

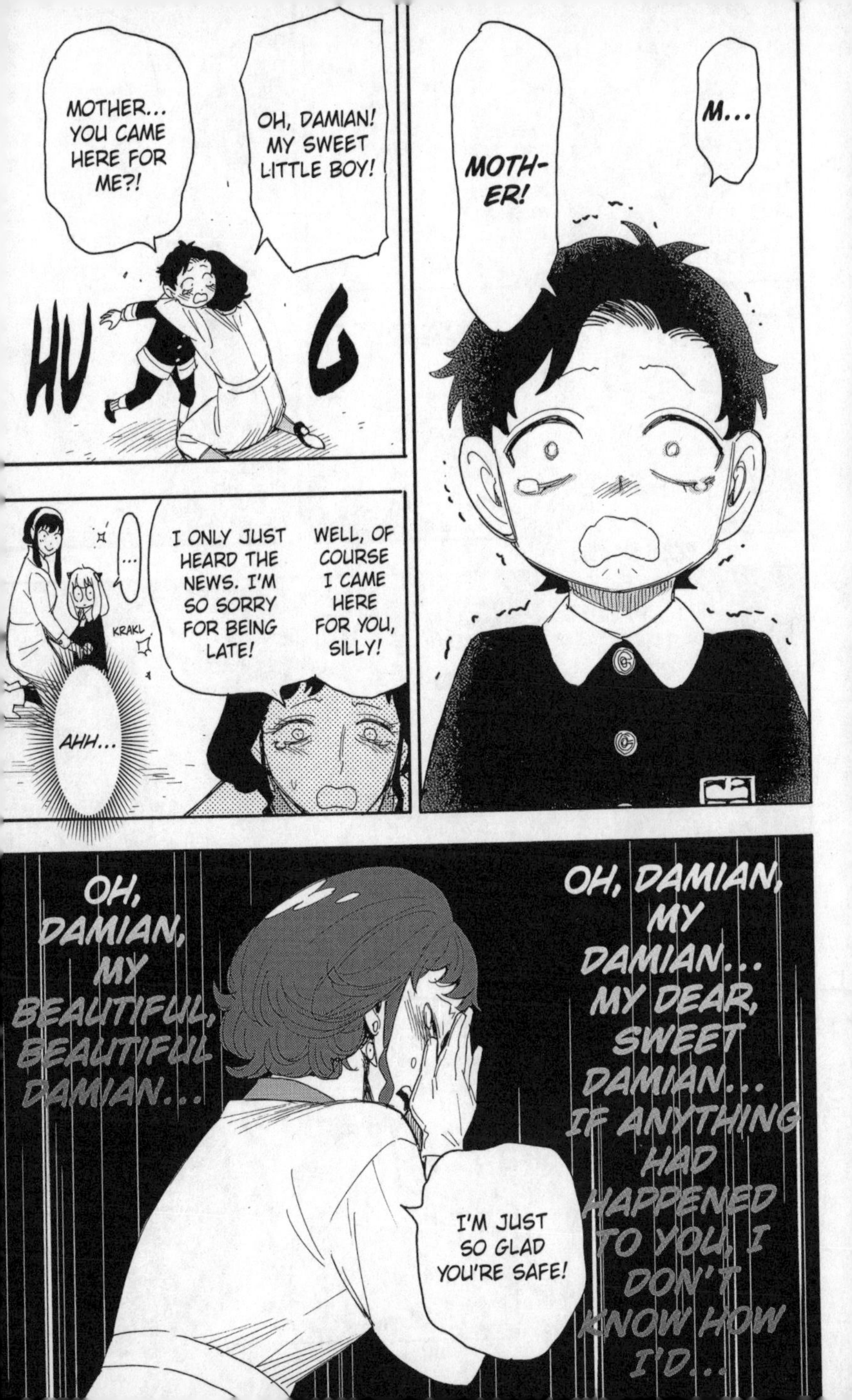
M...
MOTH-ER!
OH, DAMIAN! MY SWEET LITTLE BOY!
MOTHER... YOU CAME HERE FOR ME?!
HUG
WELL, OF COURSE I CAME HERE FOR YOU, SILLY!
I ONLY JUST HEARD THE NEWS. I'M SO SORRY FOR BEING LATE!
...
KRAKL
AHH...
OH, DAMIAN, MY DAMIAN... MY DEAR, SWEET DAMIAN... IF ANYTHING HAD HAPPENED TO YOU, I DON'T KNOW HOW I'D...
I'M JUST SO GLAD YOU'RE SAFE!
OH, DAMIAN, MY BEAUTIFUL, BEAUTIFUL DAMIAN...

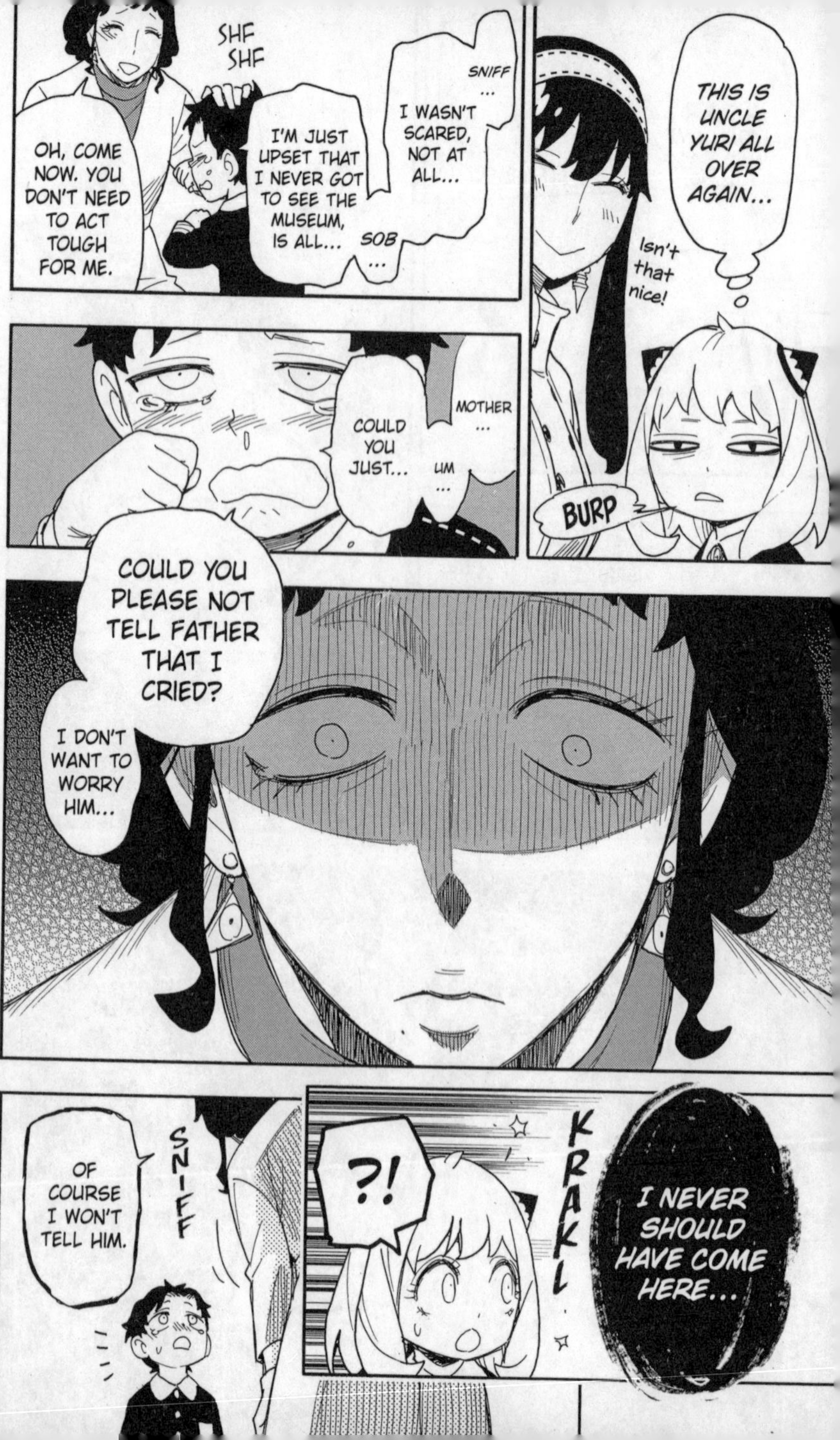
THIS IS UNCLE YURI ALL OVER AGAIN...
Isn't that nice!
BURP
SNIFF ...
I WASN'T SCARED, NOT AT ALL...
I'M JUST UPSET THAT I NEVER GOT TO SEE THE MUSEUM, IS ALL...
SOB ...
SHF SHF
OH, COME NOW. YOU DON'T NEED TO ACT TOUGH FOR ME.
MOTHER ...
UM ...
COULD YOU JUST...
COULD YOU PLEASE NOT TELL FATHER THAT I CRIED?
I DON'T WANT TO WORRY HIM...
I NEVER SHOULD HAVE COME HERE...
KRAKL
?!
SNIFF
OF COURSE I WON'T TELL HIM.

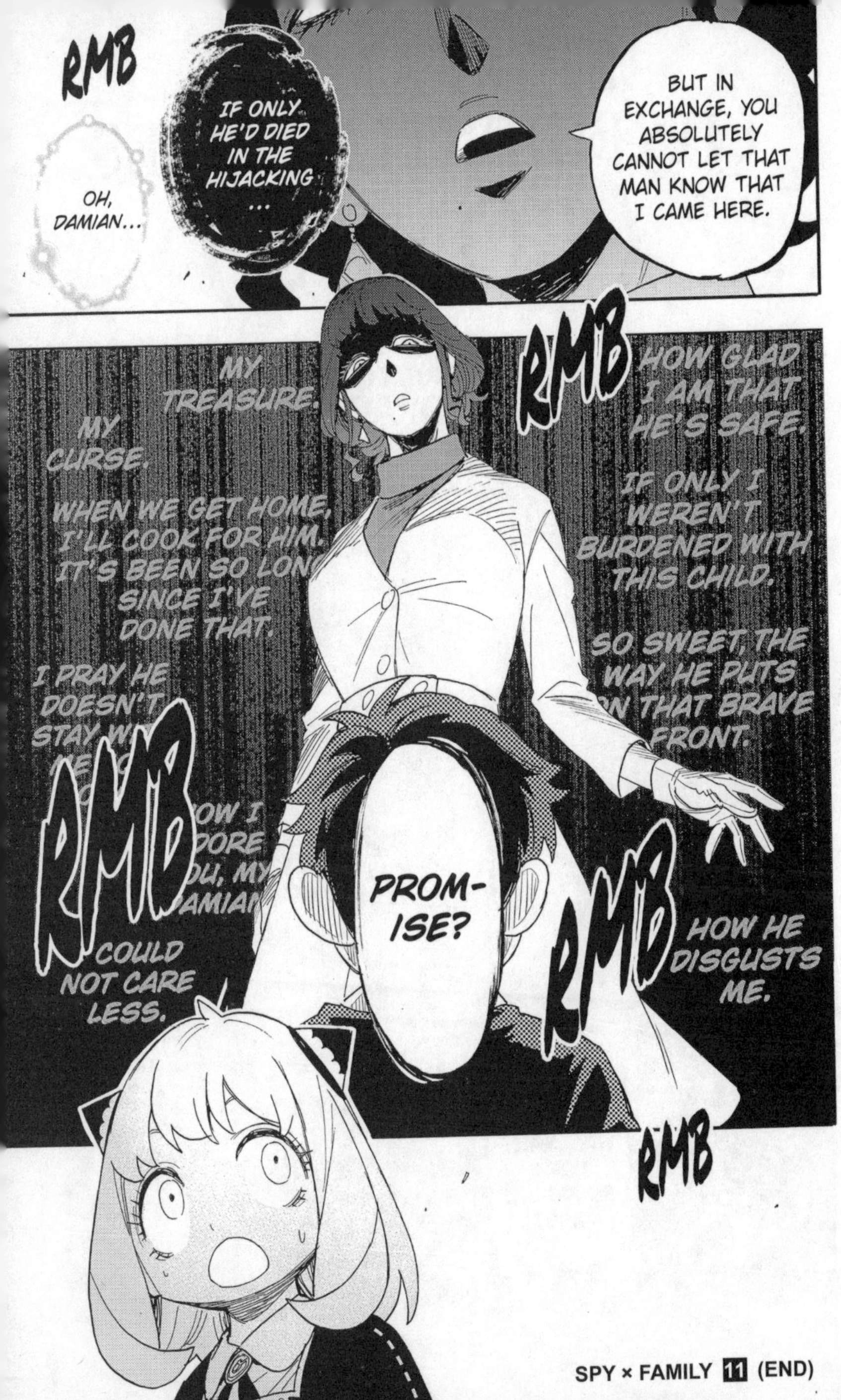
BUT IN EXCHANGE, YOU ABSOLUTELY CANNOT LET THAT MAN KNOW THAT I CAME HERE.
IF ONLY HE'D DIED IN THE HIJACKING...
RMB
OH, DAMIAN...
RMB
HOW GLAD I AM THAT HE'S SAFE.
MY TREASURE.
MY CURSE.
IF ONLY I WEREN'T BURDENED WITH THIS CHILD.
WHEN WE GET HOME, I'LL COOK FOR HIM. IT'S BEEN SO LONG SINCE I'VE DONE THAT.
SO SWEET, THE WAY HE PUTS ON THAT BRAVE FRONT.
RMB
PROM-ISE?
RMB
HOW HE DISGUSTS ME.
COULD NOT CARE LESS.
RMB

SPY × FAMILY 11 (END)

SPYxFAMILY CONFIDENTIAL FILES (BONUS)

TOP SECRET
EYES ONLY

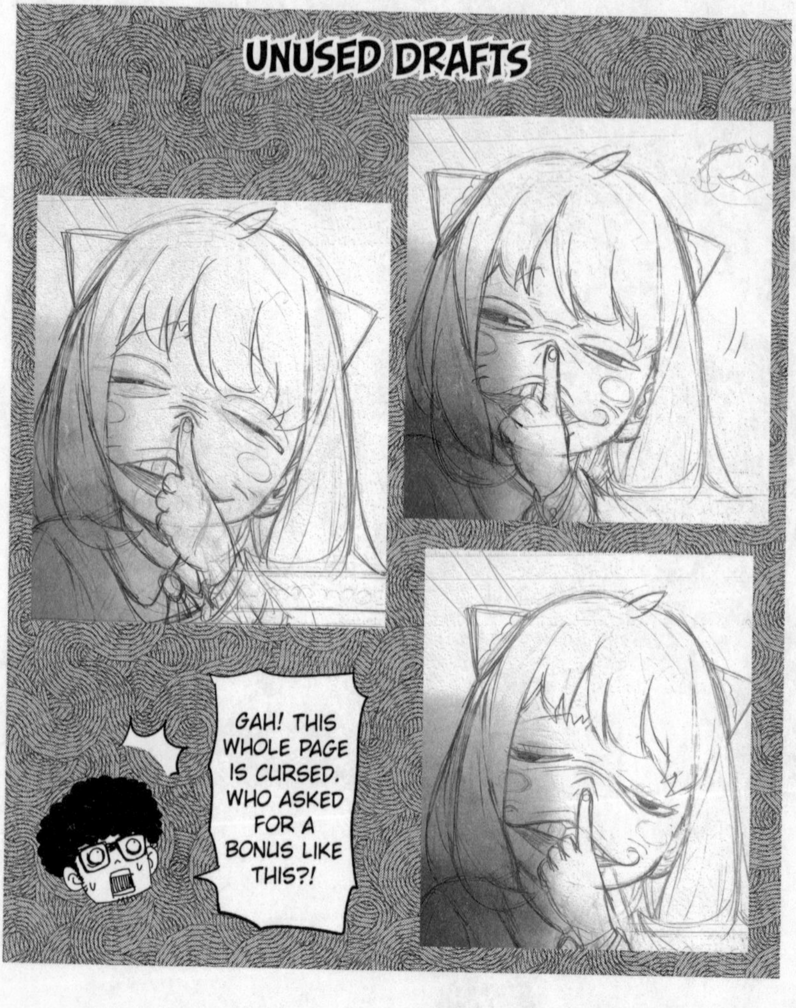
UNUSED DRAFTS
GAH! THIS WHOLE PAGE IS CURSED. WHO ASKED FOR A BONUS LIKE THIS?!

SPYxFAMILY VOL. 11

SPECIAL THANKS LIST

·CLASSIFIED·

ART ASSISTANCE	
SATOSHI KIMURA	KAZUKI NONAKA
MAFUYU KONISHI	YUICHI OZAKI
GRAPHIC NOVEL DESIGN	
HIDEAKI SHIMADA	ERI ARAKAWA
GRAPHIC NOVEL EDITOR	
KANAKO YANAGIDA	
MANAGING EDITOR	
SHIHEI LIN	

THE ROBOT VACUUM I MENTIONED IN VOLUME 9 STILL ISN'T OPERATIONAL. OUT OF IDLE CURIOSITY, MY STAFF TOOK IT OUT OF ITS BOX AND SET IT ON A TEST RUN, BUT IT HASN'T MOVED SINCE. IT JUST SITS THERE MOTIONLESS, GATHERING DUST. FROM TIME TO TIME, I KINDLY CLEAN IT OFF.

—TATSUYA ENDO

EYES ONLY READ & ~~DESTROY~~ EYES ONLY

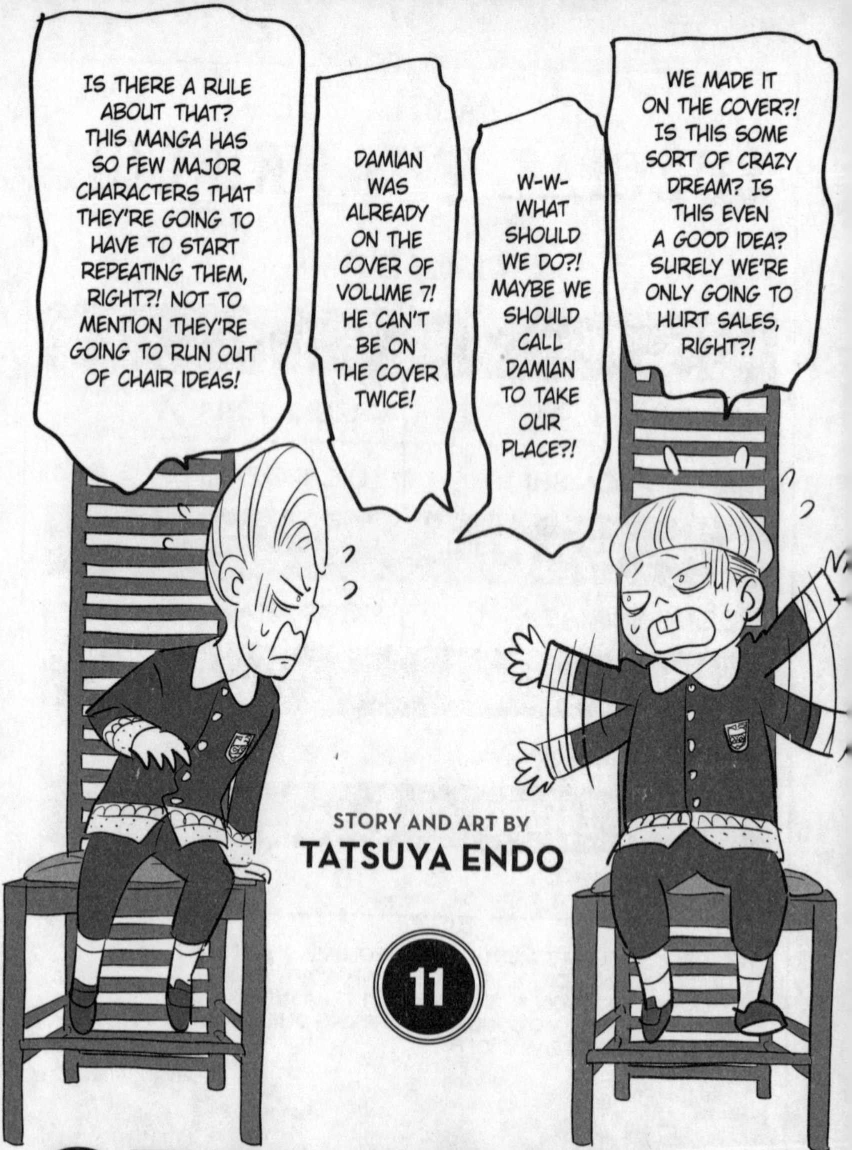
WE MADE IT ON THE COVER?! IS THIS SOME SORT OF CRAZY DREAM? IS THIS EVEN A GOOD IDEA? SURELY WE'RE ONLY GOING TO HURT SALES, RIGHT?!
W-W-WHAT SHOULD WE DO?! MAYBE WE SHOULD CALL DAMIAN TO TAKE OUR PLACE?!
DAMIAN WAS ALREADY ON THE COVER OF VOLUME 7! HE CAN'T BE ON THE COVER TWICE!
IS THERE A RULE ABOUT THAT? THIS MANGA HAS SO FEW MAJOR CHARACTERS THAT THEY'RE GOING TO HAVE TO START REPEATING THEM, RIGHT?! NOT TO MENTION THEY'RE GOING TO RUN OUT OF CHAIR IDEAS!

STORY AND ART BY
TATSUYA ENDO

11

SPY×FAMILY

FRANKY'S SECRET FILES

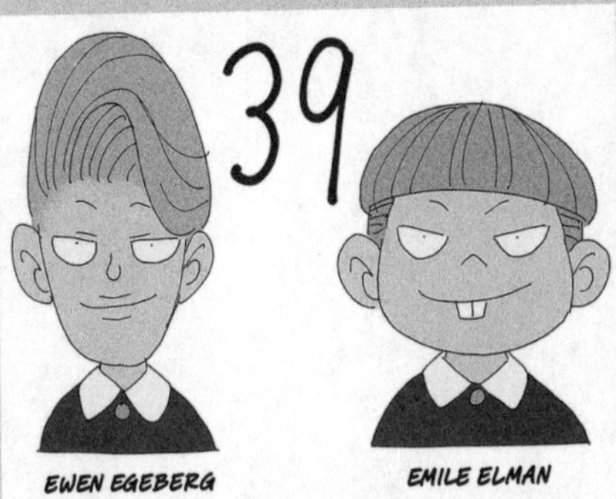
39
EWEN EGEBERG
EMILE ELMAN

This illustration was drawn for Twitter but was never actually posted. Mission 39 was the first new chapter of 2021, so it's believed Endo discarded the tweet so as not to "start the New Year with the likes of them."

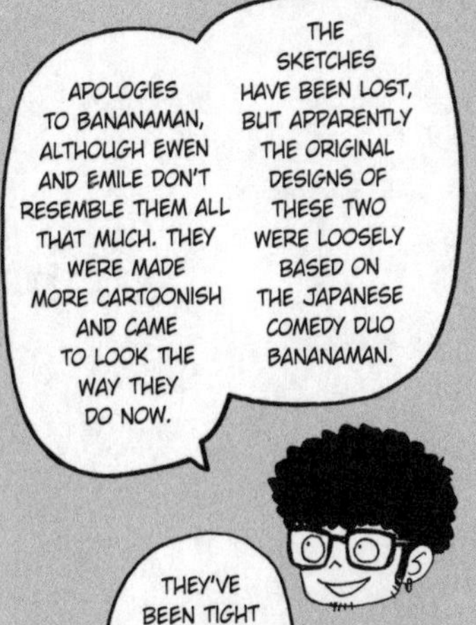
THE SKETCHES HAVE BEEN LOST, BUT APPARENTLY THE ORIGINAL DESIGNS OF THESE TWO WERE LOOSELY BASED ON THE JAPANESE COMEDY DUO BANANAMAN.
APOLOGIES TO BANANAMAN, ALTHOUGH EWEN AND EMILE DON'T RESEMBLE THEM ALL THAT MUCH. THEY WERE MADE MORE CARTOONISH AND CAME TO LOOK THE WAY THEY DO NOW.

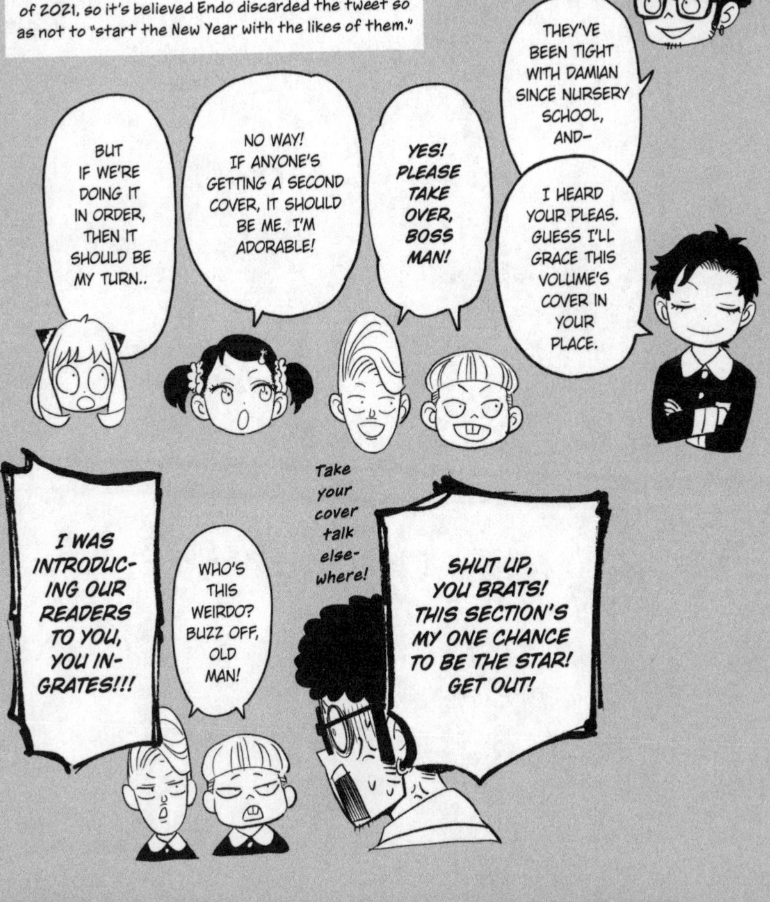
THEY'VE BEEN TIGHT WITH DAMIAN SINCE NURSERY SCHOOL, AND—
I HEARD YOUR PLEAS. GUESS I'LL GRACE THIS VOLUME'S COVER IN YOUR PLACE.
YES! PLEASE TAKE OVER, BOSS MAN!
NO WAY! IF ANYONE'S GETTING A SECOND COVER, IT SHOULD BE ME. I'M ADORABLE!
BUT IF WE'RE DOING IT IN ORDER, THEN IT SHOULD BE MY TURN..
SHUT UP, YOU BRATS! THIS SECTION'S MY ONE CHANCE TO BE THE STAR! GET OUT!
Take your cover talk else-where!
WHO'S THIS WEIRDO? BUZZ OFF, OLD MAN!
I WAS INTRODUC-ING OUR READERS TO YOU, YOU IN-GRATES!!!

All I do lately is go on walks. When I'm walking and I see a trendy cafe or boutique or something, I think, "Oh, how trendy," and then I walk on by.

In my next life, I want to be the sort of person who actually enters trendy businesses.

—TATSUYA ENDO

Tatsuya Endo was born in Ibaraki Prefecture, Japan, on July 23, 1980. He debuted as a manga artist with the one-shot "Seibu Yugi" (Western Game), which ran in the Spring 2000 issue of *Akamaru Jump*. He is the author of *Tista* and *Blade of the Moon Princess*, both available in North America from VIZ Media.

SPY x FAMILY 11

SHONEN JUMP Edition

STORY AND ART BY **TATSUYA ENDO**

Translation **CASEY LOE**
Touch-Up Art & Lettering **RINA MAPA**
Design **JIMMY PRESLER**
Editor **JOHN BAE**

First published in Japan in 2019 by SHUEISHA Inc., Tokyo.
English translation rights arranged by SHUEISHA Inc.

Printed in the U.S.A.

Published by VIZ Media, LLC
P.O. Box 77010
San Francisco, CA 94107

10 9 8 7 6 5 4 3 2 1
First printing, March 2024

RATED T+ OLDER TEEN ratings.viz.com

PARENTAL ADVISORY
SPY x FAMILY is rated T+ for Older Teen and is recommended for ages 16 and up. This volume contains realistic violence.

VIZ MEDIA
viz.com

SHONEN JUMP

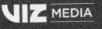

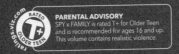

KILL SOME TIME WITH FORMER HIT MAN TARO SAKAMOTO!

Time has passed peacefully for Sakamoto since he left the underworld. He's running a neighborhood store with his lovely wife and child and has gotten a bit...out of shape. But one day a figure from his past pays him a visit with an offer he can't refuse: return to the assassin world or die!

SAKAMOTO DAYS

Story and Art by
Yuto Suzuki

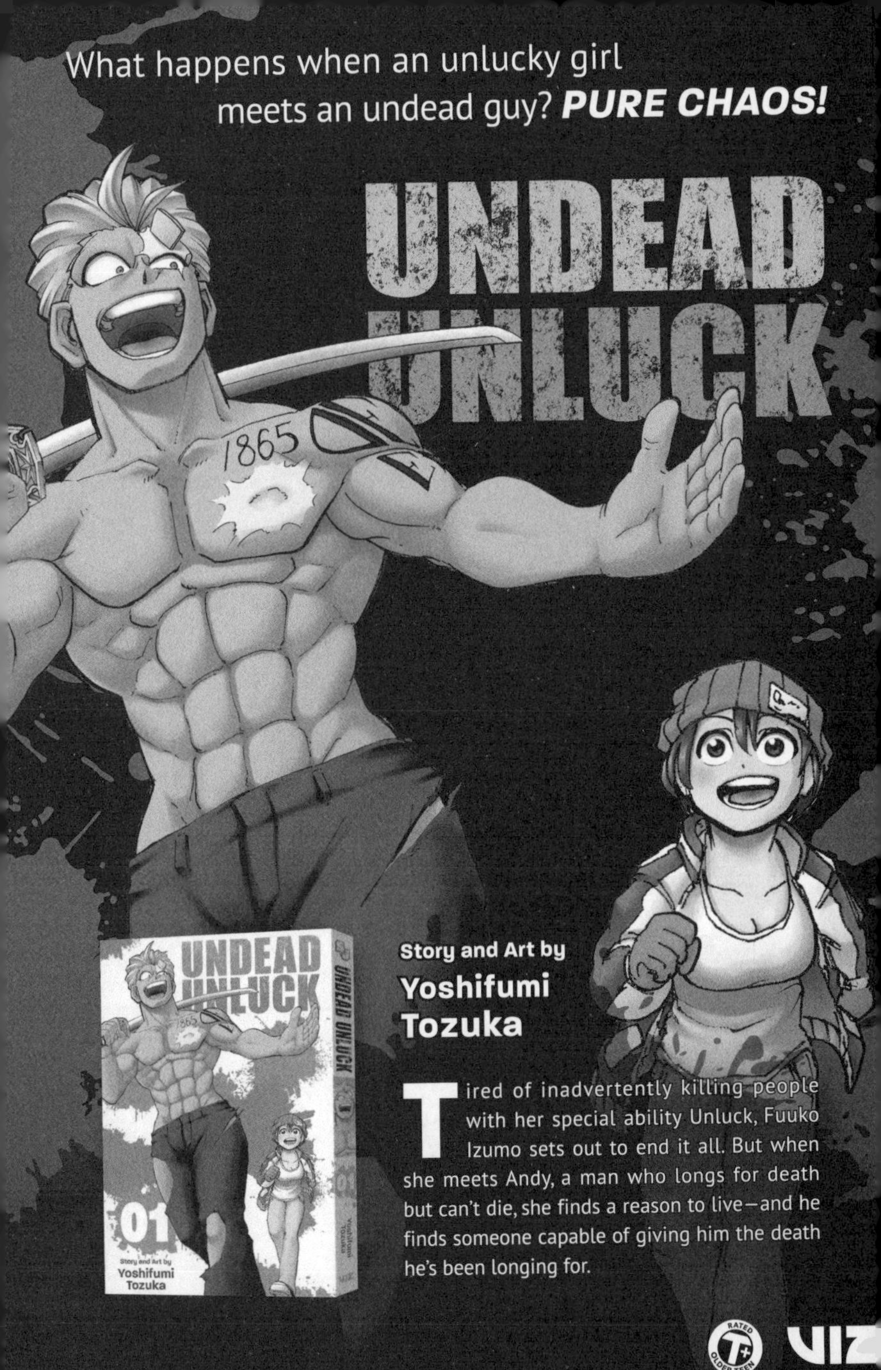
What happens when an unlucky girl meets an undead guy? PURE CHAOS!
UNDEAD UNLUCK
1865
UNDEAD UNLUCK
1865
01
Story and Art by Yoshifumi Tozuka
Story and Art by
Yoshifumi Tozuka
Tired of inadvertently killing people with her special ability Unluck, Fuuko Izumo sets out to end it all. But when she meets Andy, a man who longs for death but can't die, she finds a reason to live—and he finds someone capable of giving him the death he's been longing for.
RATED T+ OLDER TEEN
VIZ

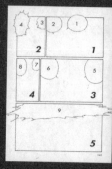

YOU'RE READING THE WRONG WAY!

SPY x FAMILY reads from right to left, starting in the upper-right corner. Japanese is read from right to left, meaning that action, sound effects, and word-balloon order are completely reversed from English order.